D0990396

FRONTIER AND REGION

Martin Ridge
(Photograph courtesy Henry E. Huntington Library
and Art Gallery, San Marino, California.)

FRONTIER AND REGION

Essays in Honor of Martin Ridge

Edited by
ROBERT C. RITCHIE AND
PAUL ANDREW HUTTON

The Huntington Library Press
San Marino

University of New Mexico Press
Albuquerque

Library of Congress Cataloging-in-Publication Data
Frontier and region : essays in honor of Martin Ridge / edited by
　　Robert C. Ritchie and Paul Andrew Hutton.
　　　　p.　　cm.
　　Includes bibliographical references and index.
　　ISBN 0-8263-1738-3 (cloth)
　　　1. West (U.S.)—History.　　2. West (U.S.)—Discovery and exploration.
　　3. West (U.S.)—Politics and government.　　4. Frontier and pioneer life—
　　West (U.S.)　5. West (U.S.)—Historiography.　　6. Frontier thesis. I. Ridge,
　　Martin.　　II. Ritchie, Robert C., 1938–　.　　III. Hutton, Paul Andrew,
　　1949–　.
　　F591.F884　　1997
　　978—dc21　　　　　　　　　　　　　　　　　　　　97-22538
　　　　　　　　　　　　　　　　　　　　　　　　　　　　　　CIP

CONTENTS

PREFACE   VII

Robert C. Ritchie

INTRODUCTION   IX

Paul Andrew Hutton

Part I. Locating the West

1. The "Finding" of the West   3
   Walter Nugent

2. A Promise of Rivers
   Thomas Jefferson and the Exploration of Western Waterways   27
   James P. Ronda

3. Diverging Trails
   Why the Midwest Is Not the West   43
   James H. Madison

Part II. The Political West

4. Type and Stereotype
   Frederic E. Lockley, Pioneer Journalist   57
   Charles E. Rankin

5. Federalism and the American West, 1900–1940   83
   Donald J. Pisani

6. Hetch Hetchy Phase II
   The Senate Debate   109
   Richard Lowitt

7. Parks for People
Lyndon Johnson and the National Park System   121
Melody Webb

Part III. The Popular West

8. "Sunrise in His Pocket"
The Crockett Almanacs and the Birth of an American Legend   141
Paul Andrew Hutton

9. Annie Oakley
Creating the Cowgirl   169
Glenda Riley

10. When Frederick Jackson Turner and Buffalo Bill Both Played
Chicago in 1893   201
Richard White

Part IV. The Historiographical West

11. More Shadows on the Brass
Herbert E. Bolton and the Fake Drake Plate   215
Albert L. Hurtado

12. Keeping the Faith
The Forgotten Generations of Literary Turnerians, 1920–1960   231
Howard R. Lamar

CONTRIBUTORS   251

INDEX   255

PREFACE

Martin Ridge joined the staff of the Huntington Library in 1977, fifty years after Frederick Jackson Turner walked through the front doors as the fledgling institution's first research associate. At the time of Martin's arrival, Ray Allen Billington, his old professor at Northwestern University, was the Huntington's senior research associate. This creative trio, representing three generations of historical scholarship, created a tradition of distinguished research, writing, and teaching to complement the Huntington's splendid collection of books, manuscripts, photographs, and ephemera relating to the American West.

Henry E. Huntington started acquiring western Americana in the last years of his prodigious collecting. After his death, research associates and staff continued to augment the library's western archives, accelerating those acquisitions as the Huntington's reputation in western studies blossomed. From 1945 to 1955 Robert Glass Cleland directed a vibrant southwestern-studies program, which assigned researchers to microfilm local newspapers and locate and acquire family papers for the Huntington. Today, the library staff continues to enrich and strengthen this extraordinary part of the Huntington's collections.

For nearly twenty years Martin has been an invigorating force in the life of the Huntington, serving as director of research and, on one occasion, as director of the institution. In both positions, he often facilitated the acquisition of some of the library's most illustrious collections. During morning and afternoon coffee breaks, daily lunches, and traditional walks around the gardens, Martin cheerfully helped scholars hammer out research questions and directed them toward fruitful western archival collections. Although officially retired, he continues to research at the Huntington, greet new scholars, and aid their work. Throughout his distinguished career as a teacher, editor, scholar, and administrator, Martin has published a steady stream of influential research, particularly on his most illustrious predecessor, Frederick Jackson Turner. His success in these areas has earned his election to the presidency of the Western History Association and of the Pacific Coast Branch of the American Historical Association.

On the occasion of Martin's retirement in 1992, it seemed appropriate to honor him by bringing together scholars who represent the vitality of the field to which he dedicated his career. With the Huntington offering its facilities, Paul Hutton graciously convened the scholars whose work appears in this volume. The diversity of their research is a tribute to frontier and western history and to Martin, who has played an extraordinary role in nurturing scholars and scholarship in frontier and western history.

ROBERT C. RITCHIE
Director of Research
The Huntington Library

INTRODUCTION

Collections of essays such as this one are often, by their very nature, somewhat problematical. How to bring a diverse group of scholars and topics together, no matter how skilled the authors and intriguing the subjects, is a daunting task for any editor. We feel, however, that this collection has melded nicely around the important issues of regional definition and identity that have become central to the lively and exciting debate that has so occupied the western history profession for much of the last decade.

Our authors approach this theme from a wide range of perspectives—exploration, conservation, politics, and the conscious construction of a western myth that proved vital to national as well as regional identity. These essays have no social, ideological, or historiographical axe to grind, but rather seek to reaffirm the vitality of traditional approaches to the history of the American West. While they may lack the somewhat contentious tone of much of the recent scholarly debate on the West, they nevertheless suggest several unexamined possibilities for research that clearly affirm the excitement generated by this lively field of study. Indeed, the genial tone of these essays is reflective of the emergence of the field out of a decade of debate that has matured, enlivened, and improved it immensely. The authors, coming from diverse positions within the scholarly community and from differing viewpoints on the nature of the field, are united by their commitment to Western studies and by their determination that the importance of the field is second to none.

The purpose of the original authorship of these essays was to honor Martin Ridge upon his retirement from the position of Director of Research at the Huntington Library, by dealing with topics that had engaged him in his long career of teaching and writing about the West. That purpose molded the thematic content and dictated the tone of the collection. While Ridge had emerged in the 1980s as the most articulate and prominent defender of the Turner thesis against the scholarly assault of the "new western history," his defense had always been waged with a good-natured encouragement and clear admiration for his opponents in the debate. His was always a voice of unity and never of division. The appearance in this collection of a mixture of "new westers" alongside Turnerians, as well as some who never felt obliged to join the debate at all, speaks to the wide range of scholars who admire Ridge. The essays constitute a tribute not only to Ridge's career but also to the constructive role he has played in keeping this important debate civil, focused, and positive. As a result, Western history has emerged not only reinvigorated, but also more relevant, respected, and central to the study of American history than at any time in the last half century. Ridge's key role in this vital evolutionary development of the field of study he so loves was a fitting capstone to a remarkable scholarly career.

Martin Ridge was born in 1923 in Chicago, a city central to the story of the West as both place and process. His undergraduate career at Chicago State University was interrupted by a three-year stint in the U.S. Maritime Service. After graduating he entered Northwestern University and soon began to work closely with Ray Allen Billington with whom he would be identified throughout much of his academic career. He received his doctorate from Northwestern in 1951.

Ridge's dissertation, a biography of Populist leader Ignatius Donnelly, was published to considerable acclaim in 1962 and was reissued in 1991. By this time he was well into an eleven-year teaching position at San Diego State University, after having previously taught four years at Westminster College in Pennsylvania. He also served as a visiting professor at Northwestern and at UCLA, and as associate editor of *Southern California Quarterly* (1963–1964), before moving to Indiana University in 1966 as professor of history and editor of the *Journal of American History*. As editor of the *JAH* Ridge had a profound impact on the direction and stability of historical scholarship during one of the most tumultuous decades of the century. In 1977 he joined his mentor Billington at the Henry E. Huntington Library in San Marino, California, as Director of Research and Senior Research Associate, where he worked to make the Huntington a center for western studies. In 1981 he also was named a professor of history at the California Institute of Technology, assuming Rodman Paul's classes. He received numerous awards during his busy career, including ACLS, Newberry Library, Huntington Library, Hearst, and Guggenheim fellowships. He also served as juror for the Pulitzer Prize in both history and biography.

Despite his national reputation as editor of the *JAH*, Ridge is most closely identified with the fields of frontier and western history. He was a founding member of the Western History Association, served on most of its important committees and as its president in 1986–1987. By the late 1980s he had emerged as the leading and most articulate defender of the Turner thesis and of the proposition that American exceptionalism can best be explained by the frontier experience. He combined his strong defense of the works of Turner and Billington with a deep respect and warm encouragement to the younger scholars who emerged as leaders of the so-called "new western history." Indeed, Ridge's entire career has been marked by a deep commitment to younger people in the field and a celebration of their achievements. His service on a dozen journal editorial boards and as co-editor of both the highly successful *Histories of the American Frontier* and the *West in the Twentieth Century* series gave him unprecedented influence over the direction and content of scholarship in western history.

His most influential publication was undoubtedly the revision and updating of Billington's *Westward Expansion* (5th edition, 1982), the reigning textbook in the field for over forty years. He authored or edited sixteen other books, including *The American Adventure* (with Walker Wyman, 1964), *America's Frontier Story: A Documentary History* (with Billington, 1969), *The New Bilingualism* (1981), *Frederick Jackson Turner* (1986), *Westward Journeys* (1989), *Atlas of American Frontiers* (1992), and *Frederick Jackson Turner: Three Essays* (1993) as well as some forty essays.

Ridge's scholarship touched on a wide range of topics, while his editorial work with journals and university presses encouraged an even broader definition of what constituted both frontier and region in the study of the American West. The essays in this collection are reflective of his wide-ranging interests. Some are by scholars of Ridge's own generation, while others are by younger writers who have been encouraged and inspired by Ridge's example.

The deceptively simple, obvious question of just where the West is has long intrigued Ridge. There is no easy answer to this question, as the essays by Walter Nugent, James Ronda, and James Madison make clear in the first section of this book. Nugent, in an essay that served as the basis for his Ray Allen Billington lecture at the Huntington Library, discovers many "Wests," all existing splendidly in the eye of the beholder—be they Pasadena businessmen boosters, promoting their unique West, white auto tourists seeking their own vanishing frontier, or African-American and Asian-American laborers building a place for themselves in an often hostile but always promising region. Nugent discovers these many "Wests" to be always synonymous with America—be they "Paradise Found, or Paradise Lost."

The route to that elusive Paradise was, to Thomas Jefferson and many others before him and since, along rivers. James Ronda writes of how Jefferson's dream of rivers was frustrated by geography, but of how that search was nevertheless instrumental to the intellectual "discovery" of the West. The Jeffersonian dream of rivers to the West eventually came true, Ronda declares, through the skill and ingenuity of nineteenth-century railroad men and twentieth-century road builders, for the "western canvas proved to have outlines and boundaries not of water, but of steel and concrete."

James Madison seeks to explain what the West is not—for it is not the Midwest. Rejecting Turner's concept of process on sequential frontiers (although reluctantly admitting its usefulness for the nineteenth century), Madison argues for a clearer regional identification in historiography. The definition of West and Midwest, according to Madison, is a question as much of time and place as of region, for it was in the early twentieth century that the Midwest ceased to be the West, while at the same time the West began to develop a clearer geographic sense of regionalism. Madison's argument goes to the heart of much of the debate over whether the West should be defined as Turnerian process or as a distinct geographic region. The argument often comes down not only to a debate over place, but also to one over time. "Each region's history," he forcefully argues, "in its own special way suggests also the foolishness of docilely accepting a national history that ignores place, that tells history stories in terms of some abstract, geography-neutral process." In the new century ahead, as the West grows in population and political influence, this sense of place will become increasingly important both in a geographic and historic sense.

Western politics fascinated Martin Ridge, and his biography of Ignatius Donnelly remains a classic political biography. Turner and his followers used politics as proof positive of the impact of the frontier on liberal political thought. Turner's critics easily found numerous examples of just the opposite, attributing every sort of backward, anti-democratic, illiberal mind set to the frontier. As we near a new century, and as the political power of the regional West increases, this subject has dramatically increased in importance.

That politics were regarded by nineteenth-century journalists as the proper vehicle for change (which in those more innocent times always meant progress), is the theme of Charles Rankin's discerning essay. Frederic E. Lockley, Civil War veteran and vagabond frontier journalist, used his pen to effect change across the West, attempting to uplift every sort of "benighted" western soul, be they "savage" Indian, "heretical" Mormon, or "ignorant" Anglo farmer. Lockley, whose invaluable papers reside fittingly in the collections of the Huntington Library, is a classic example of a type of person that reminds us, as Rankin puts it, "of the complexity—rather than the simplicity—of the past."

The complexity of the federal role in the West during the first half of this century is the theme of Donald J. Pisani's provocative essay. Pisani challenges not only the old myth of western independence, but also the fixation of the "new western history" upon overwhelming federal power. The story, he contends, is—as one might suspect—more complex. With the Forest Service as a prime example, Pisani persuasively argues that regional elites held onto considerable power despite the trend toward centralization of federal power. In such areas as road building, taxation, and welfare a mania for individualism and states' rights marked the West despite a willingness to feed excessively at the federal pork barrel. Westerners, Pisani notes, have proven particularly adept at frustrating centralization, so that the federal government "grew up to be a weak, irresolute, but wealthy giant, capable of rewarding local interests but incapable of providing much leadership or direction."

The power of western elites is certainly evident in the Senate debate on the creation of the artificial lake in the Hetch Hetchy Valley of Yosemite National Park. Richard Lowitt, a preeminent historian of the political West, describes how the concerns of local elites, both San Franciscans in favor of Hetch Hetchy and California agricultural irrigators who opposed the loss of potential water to the urbanites, took clear precedence over the outrage expressed by national preservationists. Indeed, Lowitt makes clear that some senators believed preservationist opposition to be a smokescreen for monopolistic power companies who feared the cheaper hydroelectric power Hetch Hetchy might bring to California. Ironically, while San Francisco got the dam, Pacific Gas and Electric triumphed on the important power issue so that the Senate's first multipurpose law regarding water power had decidedly ambiguous results.

Melody Webb, former superintendent of the Lyndon B. Johnson National Historical Park, shows that while the conservationist may have lost on Hetch Hetchy their views triumphed during the presidency of Lyndon B. Johnson. The Texan, who viewed himself as a westerner and relished his Hill Country roots, made conservation a pivotal part of his Great Society. In five years he established forty-seven new areas encompassing fifteen million acres—more new park areas than any president in history. Even more importantly, Webb contends, Johnson's parks were often innovative in concept and management and many were near urban areas for "his primary goal was parks for people."

If politics helped to define the regional West, it was the so-called "mythical West" that has always shaped perceptions of the frontier in the popular imagination. This has likewise had a dramatic impact on national, and even interna-

tional, perceptions of American national character. The self-conscious creation
of this mythical West was contemporaneous with the actual events of the settlement of the regional West. Key figures in this artful construct also emerged as
frontier legends, as the essays on Davy Crockett, Annie Oakley, and Buffalo
Bill Cody in the section of this book on "The Popular West" make clear.

In the opening essay of this section I discuss the evolution of the Crockett
legend through the early almanacs that were such crucial components of his
fame. The pseudo-historicity of the early almanacs, published while Crockett
was still alive, vanished from the post–Alamo almanacs. In nearly fifty publications between 1836 and 1856 Crockett emerged as a comic superman who
enshrined the humor of the Old Southwest in print and defined an emerging
national character. Eventually these popular little publications became increasingly political, evolving into mouthpieces for Manifest Destiny and a
wildly racist and jingoistic nationalism. While the almanacs ensured a continuing notoriety for Crockett, the real man quickly vanished into a Herculean
buffoon that at once parodied and soon eclipsed James Fenimore Cooper's
romanticized Leatherstocking as the frontier ideal. These publications lost
their audience as the Civil War approached, but emerged again in the next
century as grist for the mills of folklorists such as Constance Rourke and
Richard Dorson, and for film makers such as Walt Disney and John Wayne.

Annie Oakley emerged as a frontier heroine long after the Crockett legend
had faded, but hers was a fame even more self-consciously a creation than
Crockett's. Glenda Riley, Oakley's biographer and herself a pioneer in the field
of western women's history, persuasively argues that it was Oakley and Buffalo
Bill Cody who created the modern image of the cowgirl, paving the way for the
female rodeo stars that followed. It was Oakley who also changed the crude
image of frontier women presented in the antebellum Crockett almanacs and
post–Civil War dime novels into a perfectly Victorian gentility that made the
cowgirl an attractive and admirable ideal. Oakley's ladylike image, Riley argues, convinced America and the world that "women could perform and
compete without losing their domestic virtues." In casting aside her skillet and
getting a gun, Annie Oakley engaged in a quiet subversion that created the
modern image of the cowgirl, forever altering the image of western women.

Buffalo Bill Cody not only provided the stage upon which Annie Oakley
created the cowgirl image, but it can be argued without much exaggeration
that he created the modern image of the so-called "Wild West." His influence
was not only on his own generation, but upon all those that were to follow. But
Cody's story of the West was, as Richard White contends in his innovative and
imaginative essay, in contradiction to another "master narrative" of the West as
told by the great historian Frederick Jackson Turner. Like millions of other

Americans, they both came to Chicago in 1893 for the Columbian Exposition and there they each presented their stories. Almost everyone who came to Chicago went to see Cody perform, while very few indeed viewed Turner's brief appearance—but both men created a powerful, if somewhat contradictory, narrative for the West. Turner, White notes, "summoned the frontier from the dim academic backcountry, but in popular American culture the frontier was already central." Playing off images popularized by Cody, Turner simply, and brilliantly, told "Americans about the *significance* of this familiar frontier." White sees the vital narratives of both Turner and Cody following "separate, but connected, strands of a single mythic cloth."

History and myth melded into one that summer of 1893 in Chicago, when Turner and Cody presented their frontier narratives. They gave America its story, and no one would look at the American past in the same way again. The final section of this book deals with how historians have dealt with that western legacy.

Herbert E. Bolton was certainly not a strict Turnerian, but he did embrace the concept of the frontier and shared a keen sense of historical romanticism about the West with both Turner and Cody. Bolton's heroic narrative, however, was applied to Spanish soldiers and missionaries. This sometimes led him into conflict with the Anglo elites of California, who more readily embraced Turner's westward moving frontiersman, and contributed to perhaps his greatest error—the authentication of the fake brass plate supposedly left in California by Francis Drake in 1579. Albert L. Hurtado, one of the leading scholars on the Spanish Borderlands, presents a remarkable story of the historian as detective. Like all good detective stories, this has a larger moral about the role of the historian in society, vividly displaying the potential for controversy that the West's unique mixture of race, ethnicity, and religion brings to historians of the field. The Drake plate became, according to Hurtado, "the holy grail—a venerable Anglo-American, Protestant, religious relic" that figured dramatically "in a struggle for California's cultural high ground." Hurtado insightfully shows us how the usually wise and skillful Bolton foundered, displaying just "how difficult a task it is to safely navigate the broken cultural terrain of the American West."

The pilot who first set the course for that difficult navigation was, of course, Frederick Jackson Turner. In the final essay of our collection Howard R. Lamar confronts that Turnerian legacy and brilliantly explains its continuing popularity. Using four important authors—Bernard DeVoto, Constance Rourke, Archibald MacLeish, and Stephen Vincent Benét—Lamar examines how they embraced Turner's ideas and incorporated them into their own writings. These writers, Lamar declares, "did not work so much in the shadow of the master as to use his ideas for their own purposes" and in turn influenced countless other writers and readers across the century.

Lamar sees Turner as "the first to offer a coherent, logical, and at the same time, eloquent explanation of American exceptionalism." Turner not only explained the rise of a distinctive American character but also glorified the average American by constructing "a democratic, classless, and therefore a non-Marxist version of the American experience." To Lamar, Turner sparked a flame that could never be extinguished, one that "sparked the imagination of thousands of writers, who in turn gave millions a sense of understanding about America's past."

One of the writers whose imagination was sparked by Turner is, of course, Martin Ridge. He, in turn, has inspired countless others with his scholarship, his editorial pen, his encouragement, his advice, his courtesy, and his friendship—not the least among which are numbered the editors and contributors to this anthology in his honor. It is but slight recognition of all he has been and all he has accomplished. The thriving field of western history remains his great legacy.

PAUL ANDREW HUTTON
Professor of History
University of New Mexico

PART I

LOCATING THE WEST

CHAPTER ONE

THE "FINDING" OF THE WEST

WALTER NUGENT

The theme of a recent Huntington art exhibit was "Paradise Found, Paradise Lost? Conflicting Visions of the American West." This essay is about "the finding of the West," and as the exhibit title owes something to Milton, my debt is to Theodore Roosevelt, author in 1889 of the four-volume *Winning of the West.*[1]

"Finding" is used here in two senses. The first is literal: by what route did you get there, and by what means? This is "finding" in the sense of geography and logistics. The second sense is psychological: did you find what you were expecting, did it match your perceptions, did you find a place or its people interesting because they more than met, or failed to meet, your expectations, or were they simply different? So, to ask how did you find the Huntington, is answerable in the first sense, by "I drove down California Boulevard and took a right on Allen"; but in the second sense, by "I found it beautiful as usual, the people cordial, the working conditions serendipitous." Thus, "finding," no matter by whom (and a great variety of people found the West), involves migration and the many decisions that accompany it; it involves perceptions, and mental surprises, and how one makes sense out of what the senses tell you, even unprecedented things. These processes have been taking place in North America since at least 1492, and for Europeans in California since Junípero Serra founded the mission at San Diego in 1769, and since some Indiana investors founded Pasadena in 1874.

But my West is not limited to Southern California or the Pacific Coast. It includes the western half of the United States, some of it to become farms and ranches, some of it mines, much of it cities, but all of it entered into by people of European, Asian, and African stock since the 1500s but in considerable numbers only since the 1870s. The settlement of the Great Plains is very much part of this story. People began moving in earnest into the short-grass country of low rainfall in the 1870s, and with few interruptions, they continued, until the area was saturated with people by about 1915. As early as 1920, optimism waned. The Dust Bowl followed; it hastened—but it did not initiate—the depopulation of the Great Plains that is still taking place.

The story of the advance of European-stock people, of many ethnicities, onto the Great Plains in the forty years from the 1870s to about 1915, and their retreat ever since, is a fascinating story of great hopes and dashed expectations. How people found the Great Plains—and later wished they had not—is the final chapter in the story of Frederick Jackson Turner's frontier, which stated more precisely was a frontier of white farm and ranch settlement. Upon that land, Lakota had displaced Crow and Pawnee, and whites had displaced Lakota, Cheyenne, and other tribes. But, in the end, the environment itself, most of all the vagaries of rainfall and the ongoing depletion of the aquifer beneath the land, forced the withdrawal of many of those white migrants or their descendants. Turner's party is over, and has been for some time.

All that is certainly part of western history; but I focus now on a simultaneous, but quite different, western history: how people found (as they viewed it) the more remote West, from the Rockies to the Pacific. For, in looking at the occupation by Europeans, Asians, and Africans of the entire western half of the country since the 1870s, it seems to me there were two stories happening: the conclusion of the old frontier-of-settlement process, and the beginning of a quite new kind of process, not industrial in the same way as took place in the Northeast and Great Lakes states, but certainly urban, and before long, metropolitan. By "metropolitan" I mean: the development of a complex and interconnected economy, with spectacular man-made solutions to the natural absence of water; a mixing of ethnicities and races more complex than in New York or Chicago, or anywhere in the East; and the emergence of a quite unprecedented kind of urbanism, also unlike anything in the East, or in Europe, that was plainly visible in Southern California by the 1920s and that has continued to expand. In embryo, however, we can find it prior to the introduction of the automobile (which accelerated but did not start it), in the Los Angeles real estate boom of the late 1880s and in the creation of Pasadena even earlier than that. When I contemplate Los Angeles in 1890, I sense the opening chapter of a history that has continued ever since. When I contemplate Kansas, Nebraska, and the Dakotas in 1890, I know from hindsight that their farm-settlement story is almost over.

CREATING PASADENA, 1873–1874

The new story can be traced to many places; certainly Pasadena is one of them. A group of Indianapolis investors, in 1873, had it in mind to create an "Indiana Colony" somewhere in California and sent one of their number, Daniel M. Berry, to select promising land—land not likely to grow the corn they were used to, but, as promised by Charles Nordhoff, land that could grow oranges. Berry's letters back to Indianapolis, which are in the Huntington Library, reveal that he started with a well-thought-out plan, conceived from afar, and that then, like so many others whose plans for America had been devised at a distance (beginning with Columbus), he had quickly to adapt to the realities he found.

Berry arrived in San Francisco in August 1873, no doubt via the new transcontinental railroad, and proceeded to San Diego by coastal steamer. He surveyed that area and then sailed back to harbor at San Pedro. "If this is a harbor," he wrote of it, "it is certainly the largest your correspondent ever enjoyed, as it extends from the bluffs at the mouth of the San Gabriel river back to Japan."[2] But if Berry was unimpressed with the maritime future of Los Angeles, he was smitten by its fruit-growing possibilities. In less than a month in the Southland he had forgotten about corn, and about the wheat, barley, and other grains he saw in abundance in the San Fernando Valley. Discovering a 2,800-acre tract just east of a "wooded canyon" below the mountains, which we know as the Arroyo Seco, he wrote, "The same time and labor devoted to fruit here that we give at home to business would make us happy and rich in a short time."[3] In his next letter he observed: "The aristocracy here work and raise fruit. . . . Raise little orange plants to sell, raise grapes the third year to sell, raise limes in two years to sell, but it will take about two years to conquer an income from unimproved land."[4]

By late October the shock waves from the Panic of 1873 had reached Indianapolis, destroying the shareholders' enthusiasm for real estate anywhere, but Berry in each succeeding letter importuned, implored, and demanded that the company send funds to buy the Arroyo Seco tract. The company sent out another emissary, the young banker Calvin Fletcher, who wrote back, "All I can say is, that the conditions surrounding agriculture and horticulture are so different from those in Ind[iana] that we are poor judges of what we have." He immediately paid up his shares, his doubts resolved.[5] Berry, by then four months on the ground, was creating the San Gabriel Orchard Grove Association, very soon renamed "Pasadena, an Indian name for the Key of the Valley."[6] Berry declared:

*Pasadena Business Brochure
(Photograph courtesy Henry E. Huntington
Library and Art Gallery, San Marino,
California.)*

*Pasadena Street Scene
(Photograph courtesy Henry E. Huntington Library and Art Gallery, San Marino, California.)*

California is a new unfinished country, and hasn't a Presbyterian church on every corner and a sidewalk and a sewing society in front of every house. All is new, romantic, rude, quaint, peculiar. The wants of the people are fewer than in a rigorous climate and of course they live with less attention to conveniences about home than in the East. But what of that? If one waits for Eastern improvements before coming[,] land will be so dear that few can buy it. So I am willing to take the country barefooted and wait for shoes and stockings.[7]

By spring 1874, Berry shrieked at Indianapolis "to let corn alone," buy thirty more acres of orange trees, subdivide, "and then sell off to others who have lots next to it."[8] Berry, Fletcher, and their associates had advanced from corn to oranges very quickly, and from oranges to real estate speculation and development even more quickly.

Also by then he and others had named and created Pasadena and were laying a water line and planting orange trees along Orange Grove Avenue. He was writing back to Indiana on a letterhead proclaiming himself and a partner the "Los Angeles Real Estate Agency." By 1875 the company had laid out streets, built forty homes, planted 150,000 grapevines and 100,000 fruit trees, and much else. The earliest historical sketch of Pasadena, by one of Berry's group, concluded:

> Knowest thou the land where the
> citron and olive is fairest of fruit
> And the voice of the meadowlark never is mute?
> It is Pasadena.

The activities of Berry and his associates were no longer at the midwestern rural pace, the pace of the traditional settlement frontier. This breathtaking pace, while not unique for its time—Chicagoans were moving fast, too—would, however, become the normal mode in this new, far West: they comprised a unique concoction of entrepreneurship, adaptation, and rapture at the climate and beauty of the place.

The same mixture still bewitched boosters more than half a century later, as demonstrated by the following excerpt from a 1926 essay entitled "The Bubble that Never Broke," which appeared in the magazine *Southern California Business*.

> I'm going to tell you about a bubble that *never* broke, about the most beautiful bubble in all the world. This bubble ... is called Los Angeles. ...

In the beginning . . . was the natural beauty of the broad mesas with the high-backed Sierras behind them. There was the silver surf of the Pacific to cool and refresh the crescent curves of the golden shore line. There were the rose-hued sunsets and, above all, the sun itself showering the earth and all that lived upon it with a billion rays of warmth and energy. There were dark-eyed senioritas [sic] with pulses that fluttered like doves as they flirted with the gay caballeros. The mellow-toned mission bells filled the yellow, moonlit nights with thoughts of peace and love. Here was the world's playground. . . . Here, in addition to that, was a perfect setting for an industrial center.[9]

RAILROAD TOURISM TO LOS ANGELES AND THE WEST

In those fifty years between the founding of Pasadena and the 1920s, with the help of the great promotional drives of the railroads, and then the automobile, several real estate booms exploded. By 1890 the Los Angeles Chamber of Commerce, the Southern Pacific, and other railroads were already in full voice about the possibilities of Southern California—for making money, for curing tuberculosis and other diseases, or simply for vacationing. In 1894 the Southern Pacific issued a pamphlet called *California for Health, Pleasure and Profit: Why You Should Go There.* It was aimed at "three great classes of persons":

FIRST: those who find pleasure in seeing the beautiful and majestic creations of Nature, and in observing the strange and picturesque pursuits of a people.

SECOND: those whose health might be improved by residence in a healthful and pleasant semi-tropical climate, reinforced by medicinal springs, hot and cold, of every variety.

THIRD: those who wish to better their material condition by engaging in new, delightful, easily learned and profitable pursuits, in which the hard conditions imposed by competition in the older industries are practically unknown.[10]

The Rock Island Railroad advertised in the *Ladies' Home Journal* in February 1903 that "a month in California will do you more good than all the medicine in Christendom," and in 1906 a similar ad listed nearly twenty resort hotels, from the Coronado in San Diego to the Palace in San Francisco, including three in Pasadena, the Green ("A sun-kissed jewel in Pasadena's crown"), the Raymond ("where every sense is gratified"), and the Maryland ("where Italy

and California join hands)." The next year, in 1907, the Santa Fe Railroad offered excursion tickets on the all-first-class California Limited for $110 round-
trip from Chicago. The ad claimed to tell "the *truth* about California":

[The San Francisco fire] affected only a small fraction of California territory—a mere speck on the map. . . . [Visit] the great resort hotels at Coronado, Pasadena, Redlands, Riverside, Santa Barbara and Monterey. . . .
The old missions . . . telling the fascinating story of Spanish conquest . . .
the ocean beaches . . . where one may take a surf plunge in January . . . the
orange groves and palms and rose-gardens . . . [and] the perfect climate.[11]

Such advertisements not only sold tickets, they reinforced the stereotypes held
by people who lived farther east.

But private individuals, writing their own observations and not as flacks for
the railroads, were scarcely less boosterish. In 1889 one Stanley Wood of Chicago published a travel guide, called *Over the Range to the Golden Gate*, which
extolled the virtues of just about every place from Colorado to the Pacific. Of
Los Angeles he wrote:

the fact that hundreds of those who were deemed hopeless invalids on
their arrival here are to-day enterprising, energetic and successful capital-
ists, merchants, manufacturers, farmers and orchardists, attesting the effects of this sun-kissed land and health-renewing climate on the human
system; and so long as there are any sufferers from the blizzards, cyclones
and other life-destroying elements east of the Rocky Mountains, just so
long will Southern California . . . continue to receive thousands annually
of the best citizens of the republic.[12]

A Philadelphian, J. R. Newton, toured the West in 1909 and wrote one of
the last travel books based on a rail excursion. Coming up from Los Angeles
toward the San Gabriels, he found the scenery to be "something wonderful to
me, who has never seen anything like it before." In Pasadena, he stayed at the
Hotel Green and took the cable car to Alpine Tavern, which pleased him. But
he was puzzled by the Gamble House, then under construction:

It is of very odd design. We met the builder and asked him what style of
architecture he called it, and his reply was that he did not know, it being a
little of most anything, and could be called Greene & Greene, who were
the architects. . . . He said the cost of construction would be over $60,000.
I would not like to pay that sum for it, as it does not look the money.[13]

The railroads ferried many people to California and elsewhere in the West through the 1920s and later. The one-dollar fare from Chicago in 1887, the side trips to Yellowstone and Yosemite, the Fred Harvey diners and restaurants, all promoted tourism among the well-to-do and, for some, permanent emigration. The travelers' accounts and diaries that have survived were generally produced by upper-middle-class or plainly wealthy people. Certainly there were many less affluent folk who came by rail to seek fortunes or start new lives; but the written accounts are, perhaps inevitably, by those who could afford to take several weeks' vacation in the winter, visit expositions in San Diego or San Francisco, stay at the Coronado or the Greene or the Del Monte, and amuse themselves with the sun, the scenery, and even the people.

CROSS-COUNTRY MOTORING, 1903–1930S

The earliest auto trips across the country were likewise undertaken by people who had resources. But they also had a spirit of adventure (or foolhardiness!). The first successful transcontinental voyage by car took place in 1903, according to Carey Bliss in his book, *Autos Across America.* It was a six–thousand–mile, sixty–three–day adventure from San Francisco to New York in a two–seater Winton.[14] By 1907 three hundred automobiles were registered in California, and over a thousand by 1911, when the citizenry voted $18 million for improved roads—all part of the "good roads" movement that resulted in new patches of pavement in many states of the Midwest and West.[15] A wealthy Philadelphia woman toured Northern California by car in 1914 and reported that redwoods were being cut in Humboldt County to clear the route for "the new and beautiful state highway," which became Route 101. Some hotels were fine, she wrote, but others didn't quite measure up. At the Palace in Ukiah, she saw "the beds we had occupied being made up next morning with our sheets not even taken off to be shaken, but an attempt made to smooth out the wrinkles."[16]

By then, a few transcontinental routes had been designated, though none were remotely close to completion. The two chief routes were the Lincoln Highway, from New York to San Francisco through Chicago and Omaha, and the National Old Trails Road, from Washington to Los Angeles via St. Louis and much of the Old Santa Fe Trail. Later, the Lincoln Highway would become, for long stretches, U.S. 20 or 30 or 40, and ultimately would be superseded by Interstate 80. The National Old Trails Road soon devolved, in its western stretches, into U.S. 66 and then the Interstates that superseded Route 66—from St. Louis, I–44, I–40, I–15, and I–10. Another and less traveled route, better known under its later name of U.S. 2, crossed "the roof" of the country, with a few interruptions, from Maine to the Columbia Valley.[17]

The Lincoln Highway was the brainchild of an Indianapolis promoter, who in 1912 dreamed up the coast-to-coast highway for eastern tourists to drive to the Panama–Pacific Exposition in San Francisco. The president of the Packard Motor Car Company, a backer of the highway, urged it be named after President Abraham Lincoln (instead of the unproductive marble monument then under discussion in Washington). State governors and civic leaders extolled it, at least when the route crossed their territory. By 1914 the route was a settled matter, and maps appeared with New York and San Francisco joined by a thick line that, in the words of its historian Drake Hokanson, "looked like the Appian Way" but in reality included "the hairpins of Donner Pass, the endless zigzags along the Platte River in Nebraska, the bottomless gumbo of Iowa, and the grades of the Alleghenies."[18]

The first four miles of paved road—sixteen feet wide or less and in three different states—opened in 1915, but paving was far from complete in 1920.[19] A much more important shove to a national system of good roads came in 1916 with the passage of the Federal Highway Act, marking a transfer of interstate highway building from private to public expertise and capital. Concrete, bricks, and asphalt covered thousands of acres through the 1920s, and by 1931 the Lincoln Highway—also known by then as U.S. 20 and 30 in the nation's highway grid—was improved everywhere, except for thirty miles in Nebraska and Wyoming, with all-weather hard surface from New York City nearly to Omaha and about half of the rest of the route to San Francisco.[20]

Before the mid-1930s a transcontinental auto trip, whether via the Lincoln Highway or what became U.S. 66 in 1926,[21] or via another route, was enough of an adventure to provoke many diaries and travel accounts. They mark the development of roads from impassable to primitive to adequate; they also reveal the reactions of easterners to the West.

On one of these earliest adventures, in 1909, the twenty-two-year-old Alice Huyler Ramsey led her two fortyish sisters-in-law and a girlhood friend in a Maxwell from New York to San Francisco. It took them forty-one days of steady work. They crossed the Mississippi, trepidatiously, on a bridge of wood planks, survived bottomless mud in Iowa, which cost them thirteen days, obtained permission from the Union Pacific to drive over a railroad trestle where the roadway was washed out near Rawlins, Wyoming, and crossed the Sierras on a sandy wagon road of numberless cliff edges and switchbacks. They arrived with their high spirits intact.

Where did they locate the edge of the West? They had decided before leaving that "the great Father of Waters was the logical division between the conservative, conventional East . . . and the wide-open spaces of the little-known West." But the "western feeling" kept growing more palpable. At Ogallala, Nebraska, "We were in a truly western atmosphere," meaning that the road was no longer too muddy, but too sandy, and they kept having to open and close fence gates since the "road was a mere trail . . . as it crossed the ranches and hills" where ranchers had fenced in the open range. Then again, at Rock Springs, Wyoming: "I saw on a neighboring rise a coyote yowling his blood-curdling cry. There was no doubt I was truly in the West." But the ultimate was trail's end, the Golden Gate.[22]

Effie Gladding's account of a 1914 trip around California is all seriousness and gee-whiz. The buildings donated by Randolph and Phoebe Hearst at the University of California in Berkeley were fine; Carmel, "where artists and writers consort," was "picturesque." She lamented the "poor ruins" of the Soledad and San Antonio missions, celebrated the "plans for happiness and prosperity" at the Atascadero Colony, and with wide eyes remarked that the census "shows that 80 percent of the Los Angeles people are from the State of Iowa." In a rare remark, at least among these accounts, about ordinary workers or ethnics, she repeated the tale of a lemon grower in Corona whose workers came from Sicily; he had advanced them hundreds of dollars over the past twenty years to bring over "kinsman after kinsman, and . . . never lost a dollar." At a meal stop between Bakersfield and Tulare, their hostess (from Wisconsin) told them—while her Japanese cook prepared supper—that as late as 1911, "there were only a few people living in tents in this region"; but now, Fresno, for example, was home to "several thousand Armenian and Greek workers."[23]

In 1915 Emily Post published an account of her car trip from New York to Los Angeles via Chicago, Omaha, and Santa Fe. The arbitress of good manners also had a sprightly time with Iowa mud and abandoned the Lincoln Highway, which she called "an imaginary line," in favor of others no worse. She successfully forded the Huerfano River near Raton Pass, after watching an Englishman who had been following them in a low-slung sportscar come to grief: "The Honorable Geoffrey plunged in—and, bang! she blew up! The water flooding his carburetor sucked into the hot cylinders and was changed so violently into steam that it blew off the cylinder heads!" Mrs. Post was more than just polite, but kindly and empathetic, making many intelligent observations on the Acoma Pueblo, the Navajos, and even on Pasadena:

[B]esides having many splendid hotels, [it] is a floral park of much beauty, a little too neat, perhaps, for real allure and possibly a little over-obviously rich. . . . Back of tropically verdant lawns are rows of homelike bungalows smothered in vines and . . . many important and beautiful places that entirely compensate for the few crude garish ones.[24]

Many of the westbound travelers on the Lincoln Highway kept their eyes open for the first signs of "the West." Some were satisfied with crossing the Mississippi, but the majority "felt Western" as they crossed the Missouri between Council Bluffs and Omaha and struck out across the Nebraska prairie as the Lincoln Highway followed, for a time, the route of the Overland Trail. One such person was Beatrice Larned Massey, who traveled with her engineer husband and another couple in a Packard twin-six touring car in the spring of 1919 from New York to San Francisco. They were no Okies; they stayed in hotels, traveled without camping gear but with their golf clubs and tennis rackets, and used them at country clubs along the way. Despite this *tourisme de luxe*, they thought it prudent to carry four spare tires, cables, towlines, extra spark plugs, a twelve-inch Stillson wrench, and other items for automobile first-aid. Upon crossing the Missouri, Mrs. Massey was on the *qui vive*—especially for cowboys. In Medora, North Dakota, she was disappointed with what she saw at the Rough Riders Hotel:

Like the buffalo, the picturesque cowboy is almost extinct. On the big cattle ranches we saw *near* cowboys—boys in their teens herding the cattle, and some ordinary, dirty-looking men on horses. There were half a dozen men eating noon dinner . . . [in] a tumble-down old building about as romantic as any old woodshed.[25]

But some days later she arrived at Yellowstone. A woman traveling with the Masseys "would not be happy unless she met 'a real cowboy, of the William S. Hart type, and a real Indian.'" And near Old Faithful, her dream came true:

The real article came by on horseback, leading two saddled horses. He was a tall, fine-looking chap, with all the proverbial trappings of an old-time cowboy, riding as if he were a part of his horse.

They then discovered that he "had charge of the saddle-horses and riding parties" for the Park.[26] William S. Hart and grooms for dudes were the expectation; real ranch workers did not fit.

Between Glendive and Miles City, Montana, they met would-be homesteaders, who were, however, moving out of Montana rather than into it. By 1919 the High Plains had suffered years of drought.

Poor Montana! [Massey cried.] Burned, scorched to ashes from four summers of drought, and no rain in six months! Everywhere people told us the same story. The rivers and streams were dry as bones. 'Don't stop here for water' was a familiar sign. We met hundreds of families driving out, in old 'prairie-schooners,' with all their household furniture and their cattle. . . . They had tried to raise crops, and were literally driven out. The children looked pinched and starved. The women and men were the color of leather, tanned by the scorching sun of the plains, the dust, and the dry, hot winds. They had lost everything. Their faces were pathos personified. It wrung your heart to see them.

Yet this vision did not unleash any gloomy musings about the end of the homesteaders' frontier, and a few miles later, between Miles City and Billings, Mrs. Massey was gratified to see "fertile ranches where the irrigation system had turned an arid waste of sand into fields of green crops" (actually sugar beets). Apparently, the Yellowstone River still flowed, despite the drought; irrigating beet growers did not need prairie schooners.

The Massey party continued to Yellowstone, finding

the roads in most places worthy of the name "highways"; but on the steepest grades, where the outside of the road shelves off into space, with a drop of hundreds of feet, there are no walls or fences, not even railings.

Idaho, they found, had miserable roads; Utah the best roads since the East; Nevada, terrible; but in California

the motorists' troubles are ended, for from [just west of Reno] to San Francisco the roads are smooth as marble, with no dust, and the signs read "Smile at Miles—Miles of Smiles"—our welcome to California, the beautiful land of sunshine and flowers, of which so much has been said in song and story and the half can never be told.[27]

Mrs. Massey concluded, "In *some* time to come—the Lincoln Highway will be a real transcontinental boulevard." Nonetheless, her "advice to timid motorists is, 'Go.' "[28] It had cost the Masseys, incidentally, $3 to $6 a night for a room with bath, gasoline was 21 to 40 cents a gallon, and they spent, in all, about $13 a day for two.

Five years later, in 1924, the painter and author James Montgomery Flagg, a dyed-in-the-wool New Yorker, took a car trip to San Francisco and back. Almost nothing escaped his withering, critical gaze. Put-downs and racial slurs against blacks and Indians illiberally sprinkle his account. Gallup, New Mexico, seemed to him "as pretty as a dead horseshoe crab on its back. . . . Met a Mr. Young . . . formerly an assistant district attorney in New York. . . . We took a mutual pleasure in our disgust of the present day New York, with its hordes of Russian Jews and other unpleasant aliens." Yet on the way back, his soul perhaps ennobled by his California experience, Flagg records that a young Jewish family helped him out of deep sand in Nevada:

> Seven cars on the return trip this Jew and his son pushed out of the sand with unfailing good nature and cheerfulness. They shamed me finally into throwing off my selfish stupor and getting out to help them. They were real sports.[29]

In Rock Springs, Wyoming, he slept in a bed that lived up to the town's name; passed a Standard Oil workers' camp at Rawlins that he described as "a sort of benevolent tyranny, as the employes [sic] are forced to lead a sanitary and uniform existence," and added, "Wonder why Jawn D. doesn't start something like that in Greenwich Village!"[30] His knowledge was sometimes insecure, as when he thought the Johnstown Flood had happened at Jamestown, New York. In so many ways he marked himself as the kind of traveling companion one dreads. Flagg found the West, and returned with his prejudices virtually intact.

Another and different kind of New Yorker, Frederic Van de Water, soon to become author of the classic debunking Custer biography *Glory-Hunter* (1934), drove from New York to San Francisco in 1926 with his wife and small son, taking thirty-seven days "in a disreputable Ford" and spending a total of $248. Only 10 percent of the roads were "uncompromisingly bad," punctures and blowouts happened only every five hundred miles, tourist camps cost only fifty cents a night for a camping space, a shower, use of a kitchen, and even (once) an electric washing machine. Tourist cabins, originating in Oregon and California, cost another 50 or 75 cents a night and were "comfortable and clean."[31]

The Van de Waters floundered through the mud of Iowa, the consensus choice for the state with the worst roads (perhaps another reason why so many Iowans emigrated to Los Angeles). But, wrote Van de Water, "Once across the Missouri, we felt we . . . left the East entirely behind us. . . ." "Nebraska carries the motor tourist out of the last of the East and into the beginning of the authentic West", because there they saw their first prairie dog village, their first magpie, their first jackrabbit, and other truly western fauna. Beginning in Nebraska, they encountered more and more California tourists, until at least half the cars we met on the roads of Wyoming and Idaho bore Golden State licenses. What impels Californians to leave their homes and go touring we have never been able to determine. Possibly it is a desire to prove by personal investigation the complete supremacy of their own commonwealth.[32]

Van de Water does not record meeting any live homesteaders, but he reflected near Casper, Wyoming, on their problems:

Times have changed, as times will. No bleaching skulls, no wrecks of prairie schooners lie beside the reincarnations of the old overland trails. Instead, the roadside is adorned with burst tubes, wornout tires and now and then the rusted remnants of a car which its apparently disgusted owners left in a ditch to perish.[33]

In Yellowstone, he wrote, "camps are overcrowded" (already a complaint in 1926!). Park Superintendent Horace Albright "wisely spends what part of his appropriation he can spare chiefly upon sanitation."[34] The Van de Waters were impressed constantly with the openness and generosity of western people. They had spent the previous summer in France and England, and drew this comparison:

[We] know a little of the common folk of France, the blithe and childishly pleasant people who are eager to help you and expect large tips. [We] have met the ordinary folk of England, who are coldly polite and secretly disdainful and expect large tips. [But] from the Atlantic to the Pacific, while on the road, we succeeded in tipping no one. We were Americans and, in that part of the nation that is still natively American [that is, outside New York], we learned that democracy is something besides a word to be used in preelection speeches.[35]

Van de Water was obviously not saturated with multiculturalism but, for the 1920s, looked at his world tolerantly, more so certainly than Flagg, or another traveler named Herbert Carolan, who described his drive from Chicago to California in the early 1930s. It's not clear whether he wrote what he believed, or wrote what he thought the hoped-for wealthy buyers of his guidebook believed.

Carolan began by saying that "travelers from the eastern seaboard often patronize the Panama steamers, and carry their automobiles with them—or may come by airplane or streamline rail trains direct." He urged readers to take a steamer from San Francisco to Seattle, and "take your automobile with you. . . . There are music and dancing, and colored attendants seemingly as numerous as the passengers—so available and willing are they to aid your pleasure and comfort." He referred often to "coloreds" and "darkies," and declared that Chinese were "the only humans available who could survive as laborers and tracklayers" on western railroads, for "white men could not bear the hardships." As for the road trip, conditions had improved greatly in just a few years, although Route 66 was not yet fully in place. "The desert still exists," he revealed, "but we may now readily travel through much of it."[36] With Flagg beside him, if only the world were just!

Another travel account of the early 1930s, by Edward D. Dunn, has nothing at all to say about the people encountered or communities passed through. Dunn and his party of six traveled from New York to Los Angeles by way of Kansas City and Santa Fe, then up to San Francisco, and back east via the Lincoln Highway. Dunn, and/or his readers, were not poverty-stricken either, and one begins to sense that by the 1930s, not only had coast-to-coast car trips become almost ordinary and unremarkable, but also that books like these were as much guidebooks for potential travelers as adventure stories for wistful stay-at-homes. It may be that Carolan and Dunn prefigured the Temple Fielding guides that wealthy Americans took with them to Europe in the 1950s and 1960s. Theirs were guides for tourists, not migrants as many nineteenth-century accounts had been; their guides were almost never analytical or philosophical about the West as a region or about its already diverse population; they failed to reflect on any practical problem except the condition of the roads and the tourist accommodations. Stereotypes were never shattered and seldom even shaken.

Dunn recommended the newly opened Holland Tunnel as the best way out of New York, and certified that the Greenbrier in White Sulphur Springs "gave us very fair rates," though he did not say what they were, as was his usual custom. (For example, Dunn reported that La Fonda in Santa Fe charged $2.50 per person and $1 for dinner; and a ranch near Prescott, where they stayed a month, charged $25 per week per person, room and board, and another $7 for horses.) Dunn warned that "the greatest care must be exercised in selecting one [a ranch] that will not take tubercular patients, as there are a great many sufferers from that malady in this region."[37] Richard Nixon's older brother Harold was one such patient. He was in and out of a resort for tuberculars near Prescott from 1928 to 1932, before his death the following year, just about the time and place that Dunn was writing about.[38]

By this time, 1932, roads were reasonably smooth. In one day Dunn and his group drove the 450 miles from the ranch just north of Prescott to Los Angeles, stopping at Riverside for "tea" and then "through miles and miles of unfenced orange groves that grew right to the sidewalk."[39] He warned his readers that "the Huntington Museum in Pasadena may be visited only by obtaining permission in advance by telephone." Two of his infrequent perceptions are worth noting, because they suggest how the West was changing, and had changed, both in reality and in perception. Dunn passed through Reno, which by then had legalized gambling and relatively easy divorce. To his eyes:

> Guns, knives, desperation are sensed everywhere. Here and there in the crowd are divorcés, looking on, with some amusement, but the general expression of visitors is serious and tense, and the average patron is not a tourist—but a curious, homeless, mysterious type of person that might have come from—or be on his way to—the Port of Missing Men.[40]

As for the West—where it was and what it meant—Dunn wrote:

> The West stops at the Colorado River. California is without any traces of the frontier days that are still found in the great area of the Rockies. Californians have been recruited from the entire country, and very largely from the Middle- and North-West.[41]

Some easterners with more extensive experience in the West did probe its meaning more deeply, although through the prism of their own backgrounds and positions. Such a man was Robert Livermore, a mining engineer from Boston. In the words of historian Gene Gressley, who edited his journal, Livermore was "of good stock, but . . . not 'old family,'" a 1903 graduate of M.I.T., after which he spent the better part of thirty years in Colorado mining.[42] That period included the years of Colorado's bitterest industrial conflict, and also the heyday of Colorado Springs as a resort; some were calling it "the Newport of the Rockies." Livermore participated in both.[43]

Livermore was an *echt* Yankee Republican, a part-time deputy sheriff who called the Western Federation of Miners "rednecks," and who held other attitudes not greatly different from another young mining engineer, Herbert Hoover, two decades his senior. But Livermore's perceptions are nonetheless more than simple prejudices. He first journeyed West when he was a college student in the late 1890s. In July 1899 he observed of Rock Springs, Wyoming,

> "[It] is a hopeless town of the regular railroad type, full of tramps and drummers, not to mention a large assortment of Chinamen, whom the population occasionally use for amusement by killing off a few.[44]

In September 1899, on the open range near Culbertson, Montana, Livermore wrote:

> I camped last night near a settlers cabin on the line of the Great Northern. After I had eaten supper one of the settlers came over and asked me up to the house. We spent a pleasant evening listening to [their] phonograph. It was a queer sensation. Hearing Sousa's latest . . . in a little log shack in Montana![45]

Livermore spent the next several years in the East and in northern Ontario, and was glad to return to New Mexico and Arizona in 1916. Now a veteran, with the unusual perspective of an Easterner making a second visit, he reflected on recent changes from the window of his Santa Fe train as it steamed westward:

> Morning showed me the old familiar wide plains of Kansas, and later, the real west [n.b.!] of New Mexico, with its piñon covered hills and adobe houses. . . . There is really quite a lot of local color left in the west, in fact it looks much as it must have since history began, for civilization makes slight inroads on such an enormous country. Of course it is civilized, and all the charm that it used to have for me when there were still cowpunchers of the old sort, and more or less of the real untamed life of range and forest, has gone.[46]

His next paragraph, about Jerome, is a snapshot of 1916 Arizona:

> The population is a polyglot affair, of about every nationality, with a large proportion of Mex[icans]. Everyone owns an automobile, and drives madly up and down the hilly street. . . . We saw some Indians, squaws on horseback, one with a papoose, who drew aside and turned their backs as we whizzed by. I never get used to the anachronism [sic] of motors and the primitive, like that. We also passed a very western looking individual, with rope, gun, and bed packed pack-horse, who reminded me of the days when I used to travel over Montana that way, but his type is so rare now as to be noticeable.

Riding up from Phoenix to the newly opened Theodore Roosevelt Dam on the Salt River, the first of the "big dams" of the early twentieth-century West, Livermore wrote:

The first part of the way was through the wonderful luxuriance of the irrigated country under the Roosevelt dam, over broad smooth roads, and then, crossing the big ditch, suddenly into the original untamed desert from which the fields, orange groves, and palms, were converted by the magic of water. I understand though, that all is not going as well as it seems, as the ground has become saturated, and drainage is necessary. Also the alkali is being brought to the top. However all looked wonderfully prosperous to the eye.[47]

Few future engineers entertained, or expressed, such misgivings.

By 1931 Livermore was in his mid-fifties. The Depression did not lift his spirits. Another visit to California led him to remark on its further decline. As many engineers (and the public) were marveling over the huge dam under construction on the Colorado, soon to become Boulder (or Hoover) Dam, he noted

the wonderful roads over recently trackless deserts, and the way that vampire of cities L-A. is sucking the life blood (water) from the surrounding country for 300 miles. In Arizona although the desert has the semblance of its old wildness the feeling of remoteness has all gone. . . . Roosevelt Dam as we approached it from below is impressive but alas the great 30 mile lake was nothing but a mud puddle. The copper camps of Globe and Miami were dull, suffering from the depression, and the rest of the trip was dust and more dust to Tucson.[48]

Livermore is interesting because he was an Easterner who gradually *became* a Westerner—and in doing so he was one of millions of his generation and the next who populated California and the West through migration. As such, he was very well informed compared to the tourists of railroad excursions and the early auto trips, who visited and then went home. Nevertheless, his perspective was that of a middle-class white professional.

HOW AFRICAN- AND ASIAN-AMERICANS FOUND THE WEST

There are other perspectives. William Goetzmann is at least partly correct in defining the West as "the West of the imagination"—but the question should be asked, whose imagination? Only a few non-white, non-Anglo voices can be recorded in this essay, but they provide an inkling of how people who were quite unlike Livermore, or the auto tourists, or the train trippers, or the Hoosier colonists, found the West—in either sense of that term.

African-Americans, before 1941 and the boom in war industries, were seldom to be found; the West was the least black of American regions. But there were some blacks, and in unexpected places. In 1899 a young black couple from Fort Smith, Arkansas, took a train trip to Seattle with their small son. They were captivated by "the open spaces across the state of Washington, the open land for homesteading." They got off at Moscow, Idaho, where they knew a black man who ran a restaurant. There they found an abandoned homestead and farmed for the rest of their lives, as did the son, Eugene Settle, whose oral history is in the Idaho State Historical Society archives. Eugene Settle declared that he had never experienced racial discrimination in restaurants or school, where he was the only black person. "I think I missed a lot of prejudice and discrimination," he said, and he believed this was because he had lived on a farm most of his life; his daughter, on the other hand, met plenty as a teacher in Berkeley. Settle observed, "The worst setback that I got ever in my life since I've been old enough to know anything, and that's when I had to go to a segregated unit" (as a soldier in World War I).[49]

Erma Hayman had a different experience. Her father was a black man from Missouri who went to Montana for his health and a job in the copper mines, then moved to Nampa, Idaho, where Erma was born. She said, "I'll tell you one thing that no one ever talks about, is this was the only part of town we could live in. . . . I have tried to buy property other places a long time ago . . . and when they found out I was Black, the first thing they'd say was that it was sold." Similarly with restaurants and pool halls: "It's really been segregated here. I mean, it's worse than the South for a while."[50]

Many black people came to the Northwest as railroad workers—in menial jobs, or as cooks, or as the higher-status but dead-end Pullman porters. They simply stayed, if they could. One young man from Kansas, Shelton Hill, was in college and needed a summer job (this was 1926). The Union Pacific would hire such fellows as waiters or cooks on the "tacit agreement," as he put it, that the railroad would take them back out of Oregon when the job ended. Hill managed to stay, getting his degree from the University of Oregon—but he was still confined to being a waiter or cook.[51] Hill later headed the Urban League in Portland.

Another future black leader there, Otto Rutherford—whose father and uncle were barbers from Columbia, South Carolina—remembered that "Oregon was a Klan state . . . just as prejudiced as South Carolina. . . . Up until 1926 no . . . Negro or no Oriental could buy property." When Paul Robeson or

Marian Anderson came to Portland, he recalled, "the Benson [Hotel] would take them, but it was under their conditions, you know, eat in your room, ride the freight elevator." But a sizable black community did emerge after World War II. And in 1951, to Otto Rutherford's delight, came the "first civil rights law, and bless his heart, Mark Hatfield, although he's a Republican and I'm something else, he sponsored that."[52]

For Asians, the West was, of course, East—just as for Indians, from the Kiowa–Comanche to the Modocs and the Makahs, it was, simply, "home." Whites must always remember that "West" is a direction that is relevant to European immigrants (including colonial English) and their descendants. Asians who arrived from the west between 1910 and 1940 very often spent some time, involuntarily, at Angel Island in San Francisco Bay. It was not just Ellis Island West—and Ellis Island was fearsome enough. Angel Island meant long detention and, frequently, deportation, at a much higher rate than Ellis Island ever saw.[53] A poem inscribed on one wall of the Chinese detention barracks reads in part:

> There are tens of thousands of poems composed on these walls
> They are all cries of complaint and sadness.
> The day I am rid of this prison and attain success,
> I must remember that this prison once existed.[54]

Those Chinese who made it through Angel Island quickly joined Japanese migrants in experiencing many forms of discrimination, including laws prohibiting Asians from owning land. As one scholar recently pointed out, the West Coast to the Japanese was less a land of promise than a land of savagery.[55]

Still they came, many at first as contract farm workers to Hawaii, and then a step farther to the mainland. Many intended to make money and return home, as so many Europeans did before 1914; but then they married or secured land and even began in some cases to hire more recently arrived Japanese.[56] The Issei found the West to be a place of obstacles. The bafflement and shock of the young Nisei of Los Angeles, when they were relocated in 1942, cry out from their letters to Los Angeles Supervisor John Anson Ford:

> Over four months have passed [wrote Fred Tanaya] since I left Los Angeles to come to Manzanar Relocation Center. Despite the fact that at first many of us went through much hardships in trying to adjust ourselves to the new way of life, the majority of us seem to have successfully passed the first stage. The morale of the people is much higher now compared to few months ago. The Japanese people as a whole, I believe,

will come out of this temporary exile in wonderful shape. I believe the majority of the alien Japanese and nearly all of the Niseis have already cast aside any bitterness or resentment they might have held at first.[57]

Even native sons could find the West a hard place.

TURNER, BILLINGTON, AND THE MEANING OF THE WEST

In July 1893, on a hot and sultry night in Chicago, Frederick Jackson Turner delivered his paper on the significance of the frontier in American history.[58] It launched frontier and western history as respectable fields of intellectual endeavor; and it also went far to codify the idea, the myth, of the West as the ultimate expression of American culture. For about the first third of the next hundred years, Turner's ideas reigned virtually unchallenged; in the last two-thirds of these hundred years he has taken his lumps. One criticism, with which I agree, has been that Turner formed his idea of the West from the time and place of his own youth—Portage and Madison, Wisconsin, the zone between dairyland and the Great North Woods of the fur-traders, only twenty years after white farmers and townspeople pushed into it. Even as he retired from Harvard in 1924,[59] Turner wrote another historian: "I love my Middle West. . . . I am still a Western man." A clue: Middle West and West were the same for him. Yet he ended his days at the Huntington Library in Pasadena. How did Turner find this newest, farthest West?

He was not unacquainted with it. He taught the summer sessions at Berkeley in 1904 and 1906; hiked through the Sierras in 1904; gave the commencement address at the University of Washington in 1913; had several file drawers of notes on the West; and in 1928 called it "a neglected region."[60] Yet he thought of the "frontier" principally as a farm-making place, not as a region of extractive industry or, more crucially, as the cutting edge of American urban-industrial life. Why then did he come here?

This historian of the common man behaved like millions of other men and women. As Ray Allen Billington explains in his biography, Turner retired early (at sixty-two) from Harvard and returned to Madison, which he had left in 1910, to rejoin his daughter and grandchildren and to finish his great book on sectionalism (which he never did finish). But Madison had changed; his pension was inadequate; he succumbed to invitations to lecture and write articles in order to relieve the financial pressure; that took him away from his book; and that, together with a couple of very cold winters and rainy summers, depressed him. A winter vacation to New Orleans, San Antonio, Tucson, and finally

Claremont changed his perspective, and when Max Farrand invited him to the Huntington Library as Senior Research Associate at a salary that relieved his financial problems, he came to Pasadena. In short, like so many others, he found in Southern California the promise of health, achievement (his book), and release from financial pressure, from gray and cold climate, and from depression.

Turner died only four-and-a-half years after he came to the Huntington. Billington, however, lived a hearty nineteen years after moving there from Northwestern, and like Turner, he did the work of a master historian literally to the day he died. In his last book, *Land of Savagery, Land of Promise*, he addressed himself to what Europeans thought of the American West—how they found it—and explained how extremely ambiguous it was to them. His own decision to move West, and how he found it, I leave to Billington's eventual biographer. Without doubt he understood it, in all its diversity and ambiguity. He also understood its importance; in his biography of Turner, he quoted Turner as declaring, in 1896, that "the real significance of Western history is that it is national history."[61] And that is true, however we define "West"; it is synecdoche for America. Explain the part, and you have explained the whole. To find the West is to find ourselves, for better or worse. It can be Paradise Found, or Paradise Lost.

NOTES

1. Theodore Roosevelt, by the way, did not think California was part of the West. He called it "West of the West." Some people still believe that, apparently because of the absence in much of California of cattle and sheep ranches, which they regard as essential to westernness. I (and many Californians) disagree.

2. Daniel M. Berry to "Doctor Dear" [Thomas B. Elliott], San Diego, 1 September 1873, in Elliott–Berry Mss., Huntington Library.

3. Berry to "Doctor Dear," Los Angeles, 18 September 1873.

4. Berry to "Sis Helen," Los Angeles, 23 September 1873.

5. Calvin Fletcher, Jr., to Dr. Elliott, Los Angeles, 31 December 1873.

6. T. B. Elliott, "Pasadena. History of the San Gabriel Orange Grove Association," ms. in Elliott–Berry Papers, probably 1875.

7. Berry to "Sister Helen," n.p., ca. 1 January 1874.

8. Berry to (Elliott?), n.p., 18 April 1874.

9. G. Allison Phelps, "The Bubble That Never Broke," *Southern California Business*, March 1926, 14.

10. Southern Pacific Railway Company, Passenger Department, *California for Health, Pleasure and Profit; Why You Should Go There* (San Francisco: Southern Pacific Railroad, [1894]), 3.

11. *Ladies' Home Journal*, February 1903, 41; February 1906, 42; January 1907, 69.

12. Stanley Wood, *Over the Range to the Golden Gate, a Complete Tourist's Guide to*

Colorado, New Mexico, Utah, Nevada, California, Oregon, Puget Sound and the Great North-West (Chicago: R. R. Donnelley & Sons, Publishers, 1889), 169.

13. J. R. Newton, *Jottings from a Shoemaker's Diary, February 13 to March 23, 1909* (n.p., n.d.), 22, 45.

14. Carey S. Bliss, *Autos Across America: A Bibliography of Transcontinental Automobile Travel: 1903–1940* (Austin and New Haven: Jenkins & Reese Companies, 1982), xxi, 1–3.

15. Don DeNevi and Thomas Moulin, *Motor Touring in Old California: Picturesque Rambling with Auto Enthusiasts* (Milbrae, CA: Celestial Arts, 1979), 9–12.

16. Mrs. John E. Baird, *A Traveler's Mail Bag, Descriptive of the Paradise of the Pacific and California. Letters from Mrs. John E. Baird, February to August, 1914* (Philadelphia: Privately Published, 1915), 100, 106.

17. Bliss, *Autos Across America*, xxiv–xxv.

18. Drake Hokanson, *The Lincoln Highway: Main Street across America* (Iowa City: University of Iowa Press, 1988), 17.

19. Ibid., chaps. 1 and 2; quote is from p. 17.

20. Ibid., 113.

21. Susan Croce Kelly and Quinta Scott, *Route 66: The Highway and Its People* (Norman: University of Oklahoma Press, 1988), 17.

22. Alice Huyler Ramsey, *Veil, Duster, and Tire Iron* (Covina, CA: Castle Press, 1961), 38, 39, 52–53, 66, 67, 71, 75–76.

23. Effie Price Gladding, *Across the Continent by the Lincoln Highway* (New York: Brentano's, 1915), 29, 39, 41, 44, 58, 74–75, 90, 91, 135–36, 169, 173, 183, 187.

24. Emily Post, *By Motor to the Golden Gate* (New York and London: D. Appleton and Company, 1916), 189–90.

25. Beatrice Larned Massey, *It Might Have Been Worse: A Motor Trip from Coast to Coast* (San Francisco: Harr Wagner Publishing Co., 1920), 73.

26. Ibid., 92–94.

27. Ibid., 98, 129.

28. Ibid., 143.

29. James Montgomery Flagg, *Boulevards All the Way—Maybe; Being an Artist's Truthful Impression of the U.S.A. from New York to California and Return, by Motor* (New York: George H. Doran Company, 1925), 186.

30. Ibid., 213–14, 223.

31. Frederic F. Van de Water, *The Family Flivvers to Frisco* (New York: D. Appleton and Company, 1927), 8, 12, 16, 49, 74, 233.

32. Ibid., 127, 136–37, 150.

33. Ibid., 173.

34. Ibid., 195–96.

35. Ibid., 242.

36. Herbert Carolan, *Motor Tales and Travels In and Out of California* (New York: G. P. Putnam's Sons, 1936), xiii, 20, 63, 68.

37. Edward D. Dunn, *Double-crossing America by Motor: Routes and Ranches of the West* (New York: G. P. Putnam's Sons, 1933), 16, 30, 118.

38. Roger Morris, *Richard Milhous Nixon: The Rise of an American Politician* (New York: Henry Holt and Company, 1990), 94–96, 145–47.

39. Dunn, 125.

40. Ibid., 160–61.

41. Ibid., 127.

42. Gene M. Gressley, ed., *Bostonians and Bullion: The Journal of Robert Livermore, 1892–1915* (Lincoln: University of Nebraska Press, 1968), xiii–xiv.

43. Gressley, xvii–xxvi. Some of the following is based also on my reading of the Livermore Papers in the Massachusetts Historical Society, Boston.

44. Robert Livermore Papers, 1890–1968, Massachusetts Historical Society; Box 1, Diaries: July 13, 1898.

45. Livermore Papers, Box 1, Diaries, September 3, 1899.

46. Livermore Papers, Box 2, Diaries, November 7, 1916.

47. Ibid., entry of November 7, 1916.

48. Ibid., Diary, last folder, January 3, 1931.

49. Idaho State Historical Society, Oral History 280A, Eugene Settle. Used with permission of the Latah County Historical Society.

50. Idaho State Historical Society, Oral History 563, Erma Hayman. Used with permission of the Idaho Oral History Center, Idaho State Historical Society.

51. Oregon Historical Society Oral Histories: E. Shelton Hill.

52. Oregon Historical Society Oral Histories: Otto Rutherford.

53. For a brief description, see "Saving Voices of the Other Ellis Island," *New York Times*, 11 November 1990.

54. "By one from Xiangshan," in Him Mark Lai, et al., *Island: Poetry and History of Chinese Immigrants on Angel Island, 1910–1940*, quoted in Roger Daniels, *Asian America: Chinese and Japanese in the United States since 1850* (Seattle: University of Washington Press, 1988), 93.

55. Yasuo Okada, "The Japanese Image of the American West," *Western Historical Quarterly* 19 (May 1988): 159.

56. Interview of Riichi Satow, in Issei Oral History Project, *Issei Christians: Selected Interviews from the Issei Oral History Project* (n.p.: Sierra Mission Area, Synod of the Pacific, United Presbyterian Church USA, 1977), 25–30; Interview of Henry Fujii, Idaho State Historical Society Oral History #37, 2–10.

57. Fred Tanaya (former chair of the Japanese-American Citizenship League of Los Angeles) to John Anson Ford, Manzanar Relocation Center, California, 15 September 1942, in John Anson Ford Papers, Huntington Library.

58. For the circumstances surrounding Turner's delivery of "The Significance of the Frontier in American History," see Ray Allen Billington, *Frederick Jackson Turner: Historian, Scholar, Teacher* (New York: Oxford University Press, 1973), 127–31; Walter Nugent, "Happy Birthday Western History," *Journal of the West* XX (July 1993):3–4.

59. Billington, *Turner*, 386.

60. Ibid., 239, 448–49, 456.

61. Ibid., 456.

CHAPTER TWO

A PROMISE OF RIVERS
Thomas Jefferson and the Exploration
of Western Waterways

JAMES P. RONDA

Sometime during the year 1800 Thomas Jefferson paused to take stock of his services to the young American republic. The memorandum list he drafted held the predictable: the Declaration of Independence, legislation concerning personal liberty, and experiments with useful plants and domestic animals. But at the head of the list Jefferson put something modern readers are sure to find disconcerting. Pride of place went to Jefferson's prolonged efforts at making the Rivanna River a navigable waterway.[1] While mountain tops and elevated views attracted the Virginian, it was rivers that fascinated him. Their promise—both as routes for expansion and ties to bind West to East—became the central metaphor for all Jefferson's western plans. To follow Jefferson's rivers is to trace the courses and currents of a republic bound for empire.

Rivers had long figured in the dreams and schemes of European explorers and their ambitious patrons. Schooled in images drawn from the early chapters of Genesis, Europeans understood rivers as both passages to wealth and as symbols of its presence. As the biblical writer proclaimed, "A river went out of Eden to water the garden."[2] Columbus and his contemporaries looked at American rivers and saw more than passageways. Rivers were signs, messages from the interior about the nature and meaning of the New World. Searching for the paradise of Eden on his third voyage in 1498, Columbus found great rivers flowing out to the sea. Marveling at the delta of the Orinoco—"so great and deep a river"—the navigator was sure it signaled paradise close at hand.[3] Other adventurers who came later were less convinced about the nearness of Eden. Because they imagined the continent a barrier on the way to the fabled Orient, rivers became the centerpiece in the endless search for the Northwest

Remington rendered this illustration for his "The Great Explorer" series, which was featured in Collier's *magazine. This historical scene appeared in the May 12, 1906 issue.*

Passage. Giovanni da Verrazano, Jacques Cartier, and a host of followers all sought rivers that would link Atlantic to Pacific waters. While the river passage to India remained at the heart of much North American exploration, strategies designed to probe the continent itself also paid attention to rivers. European empire builders, especially the French, quickly recognized the role of rivers like the St. Lawrence and the Mississippi in an expanding colonial domain. Cartier took pains to inform Francis I "of the richness of the great river [St. Lawrence], which flows through and waters the midst of these lands, which is without comparison the largest river that is known to have ever been seen."[4] French explorers, traders, soldiers, and missionaries all shaped their enterprises to the courses of such imperial rivers.[5]

In Anglo-America the tradition of rivers, Eden, and empire found a congenial home in Virginia. From its earliest beginnings, the colony nurtured dreams about waterways heading west to the sunset. Late in the year 1606, as final preparations were underway for the first English voyage to what became Jamestown, the noted geographer and imperial promoter Richard Hakluyt set down his thoughts on what London Company employees might find at America's edge. Hakluyt and other Elizabethan expansionists were of two minds about America. No matter how fascinated they were with the material and imperial rewards the continent promised, they could not shake free from the dream of a passage to the Pacific. It was that obsession with the Pacific—"the Other Sea"—that dominated Hakluyt's thinking about rivers. He suggested company agents locate their post on a navigable river. But no ordinary waterway would do. The geographer urged English explorers to "make Choise of that which bendeth most towards the Northwest for that way shall You soonest find the Other Sea."[6] Standing by themselves, those words could have led English adventurers to think they might find a river canal across the country. But Hakluyt's conception of continental river systems was far more sophisticated. Travelers bound up the great river—a river Hakluyt was certain they would find—were directed to learn if the stream's headwaters were in mountainous terrain. A source of that kind would surely complicate finding a path to the Pacific. But, explained the geographer, "if it be out of any Lake the passage to the Other Sea will be the more Easy." Prefiguring Jefferson's speculations about the symmetrical geography of North American landforms and rivers, Hakluyt insisted that "it was Like Enough that Out of the same Lake you shall find Some Spring which run the Contrary way toward the East India Sea."[7]

Hakluyt's vision of rivers running east and west from a common source became the geographic foundation for generations of Virginia explorers and adventurers. John Smith speculated about a passage to "the back sea" while paddling up the Chickahominy.[8] The Virginia river exploration tradition grew in the middle decades of the seventeenth century with the travels of Edward Bland, Abraham Wood, and John Lederer. Conjectural geography gave impetus to such journeys and reported on discoveries both real and imaginary. And in all of this rivers played a central role. When *A Perfect Description of Virginia* appeared in London in 1649, its anonymous author claimed that just beyond the mountains were "great rivers that run into a great sea." When colonial promoter Edward Williams published his *Virgo Triumphans*, illusion became unquestioned reality. "What opulency does China teeme with," asked Williams, "which shall not be made our owne by the Midwifry of this vital passage?"[9]

Virginia's dreams of western empire grew grander and more seductive in the eighteenth century, thanks in large part to struggles against the French and their native allies. The Ohio country south and west of the Great Lakes promised wealth as well as access to the continent's mightiest rivers. The Mississippi and the Missouri offered the prospect of a greater Virginia, one that might fulfill the hopes of Richard Hakluyt. James Maury, schoolmaster and sometime tutor to Thomas Jefferson, was one of those Virginians caught up in the wonder of countries beyond the Blue Ridge. In a series of letters written to relatives in England in the mid-1750s, he neatly summarized all the speculative talk rattling through Williamsburg taverns and plantation houses. "Whoever takes control of the Ohio and the Lakes," predicted Maury, "will become sole and absolute lord of America."[10] But Maury had more on his mind than one river and the Great Lakes. Hakluyt's conception of symmetrical continental geography, and especially the role of rivers, got expanded treatment at the schoolmaster's hands. Because these geographic images became the core of Jefferson's own conjectural geography about the West and its rivers, Maury's words command special attention:

> When it is considered how far the eastern branches of that immense river, Mississippi, extend eastward, and how near they come to the navigable, or rather canoeable parts of the rivers which empty themselves into the sea that washes our shores to the east, it seems highly probable that its western branches reach as far the other way, and make as near approaches to rivers which empty themselves into the ocean west of us, the Pacific Ocean, across which a short and easy communication, short in comparison with the present route thither, opens itself to the navigator from that shore of the continent unto the Eastern Indies.[11]

Two years after putting those conjectures on paper, Maury became tutor to the young Thomas Jefferson. The impressionable student might have heard his

teacher talk about riverways to the Pacific. There may have been asides revealing at least one abortive Virginia expedition up the Missouri to find the passage
to India. It is more likely that Jefferson learned lessons about the destiny of a
greater Virginia beyond the mountains. But these seeds would take a long time
to sprout and flower. Like most Virginians, Jefferson was primarily interested
in the Atlantic world. The Pacific and a distant West may have been promising
but it was a remote promise at best.

That Atlantic world had markets at its center, markets for the produce of
Virginia's farms and plantations. An expanding Virginia demanded an efficient
internal transportation system, one that could move heavy commodities over
long distances at low cost. Virginians of all ranks and orders were convinced
that a water system—one employing existing rivers and new canals—was the
answer. Whatever Jefferson's philosophical worries about the relationship between commerce, private vice, and public virtue, he fully embraced the market
system. As he once wrote to a European correspondent, "Our people have a
decided taste for navigation and commerce."[12] It was a taste not to be denied.

Before the American Revolution it was the Rivanna River that captured
Jefferson's attention. In 1771 he set in motion plans to make that river a navigable waterway. But the Rivanna could never be the kind of great river so deeply
fixed in the Virginia imagination. That distinction might only belong to the
Potomac, the Ohio, or the Mississippi. Throughout the crucial decade of the
1780s those rivers, especially the Potomac and the Mississippi, occupied much
of Jefferson's time and attention. For him and many of his Virginia contemporaries, the Potomac seemed to offer the greatest promise.

Early in 1784 Jefferson began to think carefully about ways Virginia might
benefit from a water transportation system centered on the Potomac. A navigable Potomac could tap the riches of the Ohio country, fulfilling the colonial
promise of a greater Virginia in the West. Sounding much like Richard Hakluyt and James Maury, Jefferson lectured James Madison on the fundamentals
of a river-based imperial geography. "The Ohio, and its branches which head
up against the Patomac affords the shortest water communication by 500 miles
of any which can ever be got between the Western waters and the Atlantic, and
of course promises us almost a monopoly of the Western and Indian trade."
Jefferson's abiding fear was that another state—perhaps Pennsylvania or New
York—might develop a waterway system ahead of Virginia. "If we do not push
this matter immediately," he predicted, rival states would "be beforehand with
us and get possession of the commerce."[13] Madison hardly needed Jefferson's
words to convince him. Quick to grasp the relationship between market access
and land values, Madison calculated that navigation on the James and Potomac
Rivers would "double the value of half the lands within the commonwealth,

will extend its commerce, link with its interests those of the Western States, and lessen the emigration of its Citizens, by enhancing the profitableness of situations which they now desert in search of better."[14]

While both Jefferson and Madison agreed that the Potomac project was essential for Virginia's economic and political well-being, neither wanted to direct so ambitious an enterprise. Jefferson hoped that George Washington would lend his organizational skills and considerable prestige to the venture. And Washington did believe the undertaking to be a worthy one. "I foresee," he observed, "such extensive political consequences depending on the navigation of these two rivers and communicating them by short and easy roads with the waters of the Western Territory."[15] Knowing Washington's interest, Jefferson moved quickly to propose him as the project's director. The father of the nation would become the father of Virginia's waterway empire. In mid-March 1784 Jefferson sent Washington what amounted to an unofficial state paper on the Potomac and Virginia's western future. Jefferson began by accepting the obvious—that "all the world is becoming commercial." Whatever the consequences of such a spirit, to deny the power of that impulse was to court political impotence and economic ruin. Markets and transportation networks, what Jefferson called "this modern source of wealth and power," needed to be turned to Virginia's benefit. In the 1780s Jefferson's geography of empire was bounded by three rivers—the Potomac, the Hudson, and the Mississippi. As he explained it to Washington, the Mississippi would always be the main channel for agricultural and timber products bound out of New Orleans. What remained was "a rivalship between the Hudson and the Patomac for the residue of the commerce of all the country Westward of Lake Erie, on the waters of the lakes, of the Ohio and upper parts of the Missisipi." Comparing milages and portages, Jefferson played fast and loose with figures to assert that the Potomac route was dramatically shorter and less demanding. In a flight of rhetorical fancy, he claimed that "Nature has declared in favour of the Patomac, and through that channel offers to pour into our lap the whole commerce of the Western world."[16]

For Jefferson, America always seemed to be Virginia writ large. What the Potomac might be for Virginia, the Mississippi could accomplish for the young republic. Empire, expansion, commerce, and union—all issues that embroiled Atlantic nations at the end of the eighteenth century—came together along the banks of the Mississippi. At the end of the American Revolution both Spain and the United States were uneasy allies, bound by a common enemy but deeply suspicious about each other's continental ambitions. As Spanish officials saw it, the United States was an aggressive neighbor bent on invading the lands of His Most Catholic Majesty. Viceroy Manuel Antonio Florez was convinced that the newly independent American states would soon spill over the Mississippi and "carry out the design of finding a safe port on the Pacific."[17] Spanish fears of an imperialist invasion were matched by American nightmares of subversion and encirclement.

Nowhere did that nightmare take on more fearsome proportions then in the settlements of Kentucky and Tennessee. Farmers and merchants employed the Mississippi as the principal means for getting their products to European and West Indian markets. Regional and perhaps even national economic growth depended on free navigation and the right of deposit at New Orleans. The Mississippi Question had a political aspect far more dangerous than its economic dimension. Some in Kentucky and Tennessee argued that if the Confederation government could not negotiate a satisfactory treaty with Spain, the western states should become part of the Spanish empire. The Spanish decision in 1784 to close the lower Mississippi to American traffic and the confused negotiations the next year between John Jay and Spanish ambassador Diego de Gardoqui deepened the crisis. John Brown, a prominent Kentucky politician, put the whole matter to Jefferson in a pointed note. "The ill-advised attempt to cede the navigation of that River has laid the foundation for the dismemberment of the American Empire by destroying the confidence of the people in the Western Country in the Justice of the Union and by inducing them to dispair of obtaining possession of the Right by means of any other exertions than their own."[18]

Even before becoming Secretary of State in 1790, Jefferson had expressed his views on the Mississippi Question. While the economic rewards that flowed through river channels were not to be slighted, Jefferson increasingly thought about rivers in political terms. Rivers might advance the cause of empire while linking backcountry outposts to distant centers of power. "I will venture to say," he wrote to Madison, "that the act which abandons the navigation of the Mississippi is an act of separation between the Eastern and Western country. It is a relinquishment of five parts of eight of the territory of the United States, an abandonment of the fairest subject for the paiment of our public debts, and the chaining those debts on our necks in perpetuum."[19]

Some months after taking his place in Washington's administration, Jefferson drafted a comprehensive policy document on the Mississippi Question. With war between Spain and England seemingly days or weeks away, the Secretary of State was certain that Spanish officials would be eager to meet with American negotiator William Carmichael. Jefferson's directions to Carmichael reveal just how deeply he had thought about rivers and their role in an American empire. He insisted that the United States had a right to navigation on the Mississippi by both treaty and Nature. Written law and the higher Law of

Nature validated that right. This was no abstract "right" to be defended in polite conversation. Jefferson was convinced that transit on the river was fundamental for the political survival of the American nation.[20]

In the two decades after Independence, Thomas Jefferson considered American rivers by means of private letters and public papers. But nowhere did those rivers get more systematic and even poetic treatment than in *Notes on the State of Virginia*. Written in 1780 as a response to a questionnaire from Francois Marbois, the *Notes* became an armchair exploration of Virginia. And because Virginia was always another way to say America, Jefferson indirectly took on the larger task of charting the destiny of the republic's rivers. Chapter 2 in *Notes* provides a detailed list of Virginia's rivers. Scanning that list some two hundred years after Jefferson composed it, two things strike the modern reader. First is the yardstick by which each river was judged. And Jefferson did not merely describe rivers; he judged them. The Enlightenment sensibility calculated nature not by measures of beauty and the picturesque. While Jefferson and his contemporaries were fully capable of appreciating Nature and the Beautiful, such concerns were quite secondary. What mattered, especially in the case of rivers, was the Useful. Nature's beauty was to be found in nature's utility. When Jefferson applied that standard to rivers, the unit of measure was navigability. Rivers were important and worthy of attention in proportion to their capacity to carry the burdens of commerce. Jefferson assumed that western rivers would have the same kinds of channels and water flows as eastern waterways. The second chapter of *Notes* amounts to an annotated list of rivers and the key annotation is always a comment on navigation. Rivers like the James and the Potomac got Jefferson's approval, while the Little Miami of the Ohio was dismissed with a curt "affords no navigation."[21] The focus on navigation reflected the practical concerns of tidewater tobacco planters. But Jefferson's navigation commentaries went well beyond tobacco and a plantation economy. By the 1780s he believed that rivers would be the primary avenues for expansion into the Ohio country and beyond. Empire would follow a water trail; commerce could be a national unifying force. *Notes on Virginia* proposes a river geography, an empire of watercourses.

In that imperial geography, two rivers dominate the landscape. Jefferson certainly recognized the Mississippi as "one of the principal channels of future commerce of the country westward of the Alleghaney."[22] But it was the Missouri and its westward course that increasingly captured his attention and imagination. "The Missouri is," so Jefferson wrote, "the principal river, contributing more to the common stream than does the Mississippi." Drawing on images that had been part of the Virginia geographic tradition since Hakluyt and Smith, Jefferson confidently put the Missouri at the center of a passage to the Pacific. He speculated that the Missouri's rapid current meant the river had its headwaters at a high elevation. From unnamed St. Louis merchant sources Jefferson was led to believe that the Missouri ran some two thousand miles inland to its remote mountain springs. Beyond the Missouri was the River of the West, the Ouragon, a river Jefferson would later know as the Columbia. He envisioned the Missouri as not only the gateway to the Pacific but as the prime access route into the Southwest. In the 1780s Spain loomed large as a powerful continental rival. Some maps showed the Missouri taking its great bend as a hairpin turn and then running straight toward Spanish New Mexico. Jefferson estimated that the distance from the mouth of the Ohio to Santa Fe was about one thousand miles, or forty travel days. More important, he thought that the Missouri was at some point fairly close to the elusive Rio Norte and its course toward Santa Fe. Jefferson's image of the Southwest was a tangle of rivers, cities, and mines. The geography of the Missouri and its connections may have been fuzzy in places, but the message was clear. The Missouri was the river route of empire, promising a way west and a way to link West to East.[23]

Notes on Virginia was as clear a statement on rivers and theoretical geography as Jefferson would make for the rest of the decade. Yet the ideas contained in those pages did not mean that he was ready or able to launch exploring parties into the West. In the 1780s Jefferson was still an Atlantic man with a European agenda. But a series of events—interest in the French Laperouse expedition to the Pacific, acquaintance with the eccentric adventurer John Ledyard, and growing concern about an Anglo-Canadian presence in the Pacific Northwest—prompted Jefferson to think again about the rivers of empire. Sometime in 1792 he met the French naturalist Andre Michaux. Michaux had spent some years in eastern North America, botanizing and establishing experimental gardens. By 1791 he seemed ready to return to France. For reasons that are now not clear, Michaux stayed in the United States and in 1792 brought the American Philosophical Society a fascinating proposal. The botanist wanted the Society to fund a transcontinental trek to the Pacific. What Michaux suggested—an expedition up the Missouri, across the Rockies, and on to the Pacific—was hardly a new exploration strategy. Similar schemes were the common talk in St. Louis and Montreal merchant houses. But in this case, Michaux's ideas fit neatly with Jefferson's own conception of western river systems. By early December 1792 Jefferson was fondly calling Michaux "our South-sea adventurer."[24]

In the first weeks of 1793 Jefferson became deeply involved in planning the Michaux expedition. As vice-president of the American Philosophical Society, he took the lead in raising funds for the journey. But his real contribution was not financial but intellectual. Jefferson's wide reading in exploration literature taught him that discovery was a carefully programmed inquiry, not an aimless hunt for ill-defined treasures. Armed with precise instructions, explorers went in search of places and things already defined. At the end of April 1793 Jefferson sent Michaux detailed directions for the proposed journey. After giving his explorer orders about recording various aspects of the western landscape and cultures, Jefferson turned his attention to the route. The theories and conjectures in *Notes on Virginia* now stood some chance of being tested. What Jefferson wrote summarized several generations of speculation. "As a channel of communication between these states and the Pacific ocean, the Missouri, so far as it extends, presents itself under circumstances of unquestioned preference." In Jefferson's mental geography the Missouri's headwaters were somehow connected to another river—probably the Great River of the West—bound for the Pacific. "It would seem," so he wrote to Michaux, "by the latest maps as if a river called Oregon interlocked with the Missouri."[25] Jefferson's river highway was now complete. It remained only for travelers to follow its course and mark its currents.

Despite Jefferson's best efforts, the Michaux expedition failed. Caught up in the western intrigues of Citizen Genet, the erstwhile "South-sea adventurer" abandoned Pacific ambitions and eventually left for France in 1796. As fortune had it, the 1790s proved to be a Canadian decade on the rivers of the West. It was the age of Alexander Mackenzie and David Thompson. Missouri and Columbia river passages edged away from Jefferson as the Mississippi and Spain demanded more attention.

It was not until the summer of 1802 that now–President Thomas Jefferson was pushed to think again about western waterways. Summers at Monticello were always a time to escape the oppressive heat and incessant political chatter of the Federal City. Nothing was a more welcome escape than reading, and Jefferson asked his New York bookseller to send along a copy of Alexander Mackenzie's recently published *Voyages from Montreal*. Jefferson also wanted a copy of Aaron Arrowsmith's newest map of North America, a map that promised to depict "all the new discoveries in the Interior Parts." Most of Mackenzie's book was a dreary recounting of his 1789 and 1792–93 expeditions. But it was his imperial prophecies at the end of the volume that captured Jefferson's attention. Here Mackenzie sketched out an impressive plan for British domination of the West. Rivers—especially the Columbia—were at the heart of that plan. Mackenzie made the role of the Columbia clear when he wrote the following: "But whatever course may be taken from the Atlantic, the Columbia is the line of communication from the Pacific Ocean, pointed out by nature, as it is the only navigable river in the whole extent of Vancouver's minute survey of that coast: its banks also form the first level country in all the Southern extent of continual coast from Cook's entry, and, consequently, the most Northern situation fit for colonization, and suitable to the residence of a civilized people."[26] Mackenzie's Columbia promised not only a fur trade empire but the beginnings of permanent Euro-American settlement. That was a challenge Jefferson could not afford to ignore.

By the fall of 1802 the president was busy fashioning what would become the Lewis and Clark expedition. Warned by Secretary of the Treasury Albert Gallatin that any plans for western exploration would meet stiff Federalist opposition, Jefferson sent Congress a confidential appropriation message. That message gave the president his first opportunity to describe a large-scale, river-based trade system, one aimed at defeating any Anglo-Canadian rival. Jefferson argued that Mackenzie's northern route to the Pacific would be hampered by demanding portages and harsh winter conditions. On the other hand, the Missouri ran through what he optimistically characterized as "a moderate climate." More important, the Missouri was part of an almost uninterrupted transcontinental waterway system. "According to the best accounts," Jefferson reported, the Missouri offered "a continued navigation from its sources and, possibly with a single portage, from the Western ocean, and finding to the Atlantic a choice of channels through the Illinois or Wabash, the Lakes and Hudson, through the Ohio and Susquehanna or Potomac or James rivers, and through the Tennessee and Savannah rivers."[27] This litany of rivers was more than a catalog of American waterways. It was Jefferson's way of subduing nature, making its courses and currents serve the purposes of a growing republic.

Soon after sending his thoughts on rivers and commercial empire to Congress, Jefferson received two letters that even more sharply focused his thinking about waterways and expansion. Albert Gallatin's interests and abilities went far beyond those usually required for a treasury official. Gallatin read widely in geography, ethnography, linguistics, and the natural sciences. In early April 1803, as Jefferson was beginning to flesh out details for an expedition to the Pacific, Gallatin wrote the president a remarkable letter—remarkable for its grasp of imperial geography and prophetic vision of an expanding nation. "The future destinies of the Missouri country are of vast importance to the United States, it being perhaps the only large tract of country, and certainly the first which lying out of the boundaries of the Union will be settled by the people of the U. States." The exploration of western rivers was a "grand object" going well beyond fur trade competition. As Gallatin saw it, American explorers were pushing up the Missouri "to ascertain whether from its extent and fertility that country is susceptible of a large population, in the same manner as the corresponding tract on the Ohio."[28]

Gallatin's vision of a settlement empire was given a larger context in a letter from naturalist Bernard Lacepede. His observations confirmed Jefferson's own conception of both western geography and the role of rivers in territorial expansion. "If your nation," wrote Lacepede, "could establish an easy communication route by river, canal and short portages, between New Yorck, for example, and the town which would be built at the mouth of the Columbia, what a route that would be for trade from Europe, from Asia, and from America, whose northern products would arrive at this route by the Great Lakes and the upper Mississippi, while the southern products of the New World would arrive there by the Lower Mississippi and by the Rio Norte of New Mexico, the source of which is near the 40th parallel." Like Jefferson, Lacepede linked water highways to issues well beyond the daily routines of profit and loss. Commerce was a civilizing force, a power that tamed avarice and directed it in useful channels. "What greater means," declared Lacepede, "to civilization than these new communication routes."[29]

By the time Jefferson began to write exploring instructions for Meriwether Lewis, he had thought long and hard about the meaning of rivers. The Missouri was the master river for American expansion. It was empire's plain path. Tributaries were important in relation to the main stem of the Missouri. Drafted toward the end of June 1803, instructions for Lewis summed up years of thinking about rivers and western geography. "The object of your mission," wrote Jefferson, "is to explore the Missouri river, and such principal stream of it, as, by it's course and communication with the waters of the Pacific ocean, whether the Columbia, Oregan, Colorado or any other river may offer the most direct and practicable water communication across the continent for the purposes of commerce."[30] The word "commerce" has often been interpreted in this context to mean the fur trade. It is clear that Jefferson meant much more than the trade in peltries. American farmers would not be willing to settle in the western lands unless there was some means to transport agricultural goods to market. Jefferson's West promised continued vitality to the republic and that vitality depended on the incentives of commerce and inexpensive water transportation. When Lewis suggested a side trip toward Santa Fe before the main journey up the Missouri, Jefferson sharply reminded the captain of his primary task. "The object of your mission is single, the direct water communication from sea to sea formed by the bed of the Missouri and perhaps the Oregon."[31]

While Lewis's mission was "single," Jefferson was not about to ignore other western rivers. Once the process of ratifying the Louisiana Purchase treaty was underway, the president began to create a large-scale plan for the exploration of western rivers. "I have proposed in conversation," he explained to Lewis, "that Congress shall appropriate 10 or 12000 D. for exploring the principal waters of the Mississippi and the Missouri. In that case I should send a party up the Red river to its head, then to cross over to the head of the Arcansa, and come down that. A 2d. party for the Pani and Padocua rivers, and a 3d. perhaps for the Moingona and St. Peters."[32] The Red and Arkansas rivers were especially important in light of simmering boundary disputes with Spain. In April 1804 Jefferson sent Thomas Freeman instructions for the exploration of those rivers. These directions were freely adapted from the ones drafted for Lewis a year earlier.[33]

Jefferson's expectations about western rivers were built not only on a faulty geography but on a set of fantasies about the West as a physical setting. Jefferson and his explorers envisioned a West cut through with rivers longer and deeper than any in the East. One French observer captured that sense of western grandness when he wrote that "each step one takes from East to West, the size of all objects increases ten-fold in volume."[34] Such enthusiasm was bound to collide with harsh reality, producing along the way both more fantasy and bitter disappointment. The Freeman–Custis Red River expedition of 1806 was stopped by inadequate planning, low water, and the presence of armed Spanish forces. Jefferson's cherished dream of a Missouri–Columbia passage across the continent died at Lemhi Pass in August 1805 when Lewis and Clark found not Pacific waters but the seemingly endless Bitterroot Mountains. Lewis wrote the obituary for the dream in September 1806 when the expedition returned to St. Louis. "We view this passage across the Continent as affording immence advantages for the fur trade, but fear that the advantages which it offers as a communication for the productions of the East Indies to the United States and thence to Europe will never be found equal on an extensive scale to that by way of the Cape of Good Hope."[35] Navigability—the measure of utility in Jefferson's river world—had led him astray in the West. Western rivers were not like those in the East. In coming years the greatest irony was that the nearly impassable Platte River proved the route for both wagons and rails.

Jefferson and his contemporaries often talked about rivers as "communications," passages that could spread wealth and knowledge. Writing in the 1790s, inventor and promoter Robert Fulton expressed the Enlightenment optimism that nourished such beliefs. "An easy communication," he explained, "brings remote parts into nearer alliance, combines the exertions of men, distributes their labours through a variety of channels, and spreads with greater regularity the blessings of life."[36] Jefferson expected western rivers to communicate many things. They might carry messages of expansion and parcels of profit. Perhaps more important in his scheme of empire, rivers would carry the message of union and nation. Rivers were to direct the course of empire and yet confine its turbulent currents between banks of reason and law. Jefferson imagined rivers enlarging his Empire for Liberty while at the same time imposing order and stability. Those expectations—often contradictory images of growth and order—came through when the president wrote William Dunbar in late May 1805. The task of explorers and their patrons was to "delineate with correctness the great arteries of this great country: those who come after us will extend the ramifications as they become acquainted with them, and fill up the canvas we begin."[37] For Jefferson, filling the canvas meant painting river outlines. Once the boundaries had been sketched, the western portrait could be finished. But the realities of western geography were not kind to Jefferson's river drawings. As his explorers learned, dreams of navigation proved illusory. The Platte, the Green, and the Snake were not like the Rivanna, the James, or the Potomac. As fortune had it, the promise of rivers came to fruition in other ways west. Waterways, so much a part of the Virginia tradition, were left behind as a westering nation turned to railways and highways. The western canvas proved to have outlines and boundaries not of water, but of steel and concrete. Expansion and unification—the promise of Jefferson's rivers—came to life on the lanes of the Interstate Highway System.

My thinking about American rivers has been both influenced and challenged by two superb books by John Seelye. *Prophetic Waters: The River in Early American Life and Literature* (New York: Oxford University Press, 1977) and *Beautiful Machine: Rivers and the Republican Plan, 1755–1825* (New York: Oxford University Press, 1991) are essential reading. Donald Worster, *Rivers of Empire: Water, Aridity, and the Growth of the American West* (New York: Pantheon Books, 1985) has given me a sense of the ways Jefferson's thoughts about rivers shaped later public policy decisions. My reading of Jefferson has been made sharper (I hope) thanks to Charles A. Miller, *Jefferson and Nature: An Interpretation* (Baltimore: Johns Hopkins University Press, 1988). All who write about American rivers work in the shadow of Samuel Langhorne Clemens. I gratefully acknowledge my debt to Mark Twain and *Life on the Mississippi*.

NOTES

1. Thomas Jefferson, "A Memorandum (Services to My Country)," in Merrill D. Peterson, ed., *Thomas Jefferson: Writings* (New York: Library of America, 1984), 702; "Project for Making the Rivanna River Navigable, 1771," in Julian Boyd, et al., eds., *The Papers of Thomas Jefferson*, 25 vols. to date (Princeton: Princeton University Press, 1950–   ), 1:87–88 (hereafter cited as *TJP*).

2. Genesis 2:10.

3. J. M. Cohen, trans., *The Four Voyages of Christopher Columbus* (Baltimore: Penguin Books, 1969), 222.

4. David B. Quinn, ed., *New American World: A Documentary History of North America to 1612*, 5 vols. (New York: Arno Press, 1979), 1:305.

5. Andrew Hill Clark, "The Conceptions of Empires of the St. Lawrence and the Mississippi," *American Review of Canadian Studies* 5 (1975): 4–27.

6. Richard Hakluyt, "Instructions given by way of advice," in Philip L. Barbour, ed., *The Jamestown Voyages under the First Charter 1606–1609,* 2 vols. (Cambridge: Hakluyt Society, 1969), 1:49.

7. Ibid., 1:51.

8. John Smith, "A True Relation," in Ibid., 1:186.

9. Quotations from *A Perfect Description of Virginia* and *Virgo Triumphans* are in William P. Cumming, et al., *The Exploration of North America, 1630–1776* (New York: G. P. Putnam, 1974), 82–83.

10. James Maury in Seelye, *Beautiful Machine,* 36.

11. Ibid., 38.

12. Jefferson to G. K. van Hogendorp, Paris, 13 October 1785, *TJP,* 8:633.

13. Jefferson to Madison, Annapolis, 20 February 1784, *TJP,* 6:548.

14. Madison to Jefferson, Richmond, 9 January 1785, *TJP,* 7:592.

15. Washington to Jefferson, Mt. Vernon, 25 February 1785, *TJP,* 8:4.

16. Jefferson to Washington, Annapolis, 15 March 1784, *TJP,* 7:26.

17. William R. Manning, "The Nootka Sound Controversy," *Annual Report of the American Historical Association for the Year 1904* (Washington, D.C.: Government Printing Office, 1905), 302.

18. John Brown to Jefferson, New York, 10 August 1788, *TJP,* 13:494. The larger context is skillfully laid out in Reginald Horsman, *The Diplomacy of the New Republic 1776–1815* (Arlington Heights: Harlan Davidson, 1985), ch. 1.

19. Jefferson to Madison, Paris, 30 January 1787, *TJP,* 11:93.

20. Jefferson, "Outline of Policy on the Mississippi Question, 2 August 1790," *TJP,* 17:113–16. See also Jefferson's "Report on Negotiations with Spain, 18 March 1792," *TJP,* 23:296–312.

21. Thomas Jefferson, *Notes on Virginia,* ed. William Peden (Chapel Hill: University of North Carolina Press, 1954), 13.

22. Ibid., 7.

23. Ibid., 8–9.

24. Jefferson to Benjamin Smith Barton, Philadelphia, 2 December 1792, *TJP,* 24:687.

25. Jefferson to Michaux, Philadelphia, 30 April 1793, in Donald Jackson, ed., *The Letters of the Lewis and Clark Expedition with Related Documents 1783–1854,* 2d ed., 2 vols. (Urbana: University of Illinois Press, 1978), 2:669–72.

26. W. Kaye Lamb, ed., *The Journals and Letters of Sir Alexander Mackenzie* (Cambridge: Hakluyt Society, 1970), 417.

27. Jefferson, "Confidential Message to Congress, 18 January 1803," in Jackson, *Letters of the Lewis and Clark Expedition,* 1:12–13.

28. Gallatin to Jefferson, Washington, 13 April 1803, ibid., 1:33.

29. Lacepede to Jefferson, 13 May 1803, ibid., 1:47.

30. Jefferson to Lewis, Washington, 20 June 1803, ibid., 1:62.

31. Jefferson to Lewis, Washington, 16 November 1803, ibid., 1:137.

32. Ibid.

33. Jefferson to Thomas Freeman, Monticello, 14 April 1804, in Dan L. Flores, ed., *Jefferson and Southwestern Exploration: The Freeman and Custis Accounts of the Red River Expedition of 1806* (Norman: University of Oklahoma Press, 1984), 320–25.

34. Louis Vilemont to Minister, Sedan, France, 6 June 1802, in A. P. Nasatir, ed., *Before Lewis and Clark: Documents Illustrating the History of the Missouri, 1785–1804*, 2 vols. (St. Louis: St. Louis Documents Foundation, 1952), 2:699.

35. Lewis to Jefferson, St. Louis, 23 September 1806, in Jackson, *Letters of the Lewis and Clark Expedition*, 1:321.

36. Robert Fulton, *A Treatise on the Improvement of Canal Navigation* (London, 1796) in Seelye, *Beautiful Machine*, 231.

37. Jefferson to Dunbar, Washington, 25 May 1805, in Jackson, *Letters of the Lewis and Clark Expedition*, 1:245.

CHAPTER THREE

DIVERGING TRAILS
Why the Midwest is Not the West

JAMES H. MADISON

The Midwest is a region that shares much history with the West yet in the end is a different place. It would be advantageous for midwestern historians to claim the two regions as one, to believe William Cronon's statement that the field of western history "ought to continue its longstanding hospitality to *mid*western history as a legitimate part of *western* history," for such a happy incorporation would solve some of the fundamental problems facing scholars interested in the Midwest.[1]

First, historians of the Midwest have no prominent scholarly regional association and no journal. We once had an association and a journal, the Mississippi Valley Historical Association and the *Mississippi Valley Historical Review*, but they were gobbled up by the nation and became in 1964–65 the Organization of American Historians and the *Journal of American History.* The importance of a journal such as the *Western Historical Quarterly* and the association that publishes it and organizes annual meetings cannot be overemphasized.[2] Without such apparatus there can be no field, no sense of scholarly community around a subject, no us/them, no impetus to think of a genre of scholarship.

Second, there exists no long list of university presses that seek to publish and promote midwestern history. Indiana University Press launched a series titled *Midwestern History and Culture* in 1987, a series that has been modestly successful. Other books appear sporadically from other presses, but not in the quantity or, perhaps, the overall quality of western regional publications.

Third, most midwestern historians do not aggressively identify themselves by that label. The current issue of the American Historical Association directory lists only one historian in all the Big Ten university history departments who includes midwest as a stated field of interest.[3] This is not to say that such creatures do not exist. They do, but most find it inappropriate to identify themselves as such, preferring to be seen as social historians, agricultural historians, environmental historians, or even state historians.

In the end, then, there is reason to ask if there is a midwestern region and a midwestern history. While scholars in western history luxuriate in the glories of debating the boundaries, content, and approach in their field, those who are interested in the Midwest struggle to claim that there is such a field.

All these problems could be solved if we agreed that the Midwest was part of the West. In some important ways such arguments could be made. One place to begin is with Turnerian notions of the frontier process, with a westward movement that created a distinctive people different from Europeans and alike as frontier settlers and as westerners, whether that West was Ohio, Wisconsin, Colorado, or California. Turner's argument for sequential frontiers, for repeated common experiences across the nation, is still intriguing in thinking about the nineteenth century but less so for understanding the twentieth.[4]

Or one could make the claim that the West and Midwest are really one and the same region because so many of the people who settled the West were from the Midwest and brought a particular midwestern culture with them to Oregon or to California. Pasadena, California, for example, had its beginning in 1873 as the Indiana Colony, a corporation of thirty-one midwesterners who purchased 4,000 acres of land and within a few years planted 10,000 orange trees, two schoolhouses, and a Methodist and Presbyterian church. From the outset, they prohibited the sale of alcoholic beverages and agreed to grow grapes for raisins and table use, not wine. The Pasadena Board of Trade boasted in 1888 that the community was composed of "people of the highest culture and intelligence." Other midwesterners joined the Hoosiers in Pasadena and elsewhere. Chain migrations from West Branch, Grinnell, and other communities made Southern California "the seacoast of Iowa," with Long Beach the capital. Expatriate Hawkeyes kept in touch through a published directory, entitled *Iowa People in Los Angeles County California* (1909), and through the Iowa picnics, where hundreds gathered to visit and to sing the Iowa corn song. The large numbers of Hawkeyes, Hoosiers, and other midwesterners in California and elsewhere in the West created numerous outposts of midwestern culture and arguments for continuity between the two regions.[5]

There are at least two problems with this Midwest origins argument. There is evidence that the life in Pasadena, Long Beach, and elsewhere was significantly different from the beginning, so that midwestern culture adapted and changed of necessity, though the degree to which this was a process of transplantation or of uprooting is still unclear. The Indiana colony members, for example, struggled mightily to understand the complexities of irrigation pipe and to accept the notion that water was a commodity that had to be paid for. The second problem is that midwesterners constituted only one element in a mixture of western peoples, and even though they may have been a numerical majority and dominant culture in some particular places, they did not set the dominant tone for the entire region.

In the end, then, arguments for incorporating midwestern history into western history are not fully convincing. We remain two distinct subfields, two distinct regions. Scholars in both fields could quickly generate a long list of specific historical differences: midwestern farm boys drove pigs to market, not cattle; midwestern pioneer hunters aimed their sights more frequently at squirrels and pigeons than at buffalo; ragged midwestern cornstalk militia would never be mistaken for dashing cavalry men; sex ratios were nearly balanced from the first white American settlements in Ohio; Methodist churches were far more important in Iowa than bordellos or saloons; drainage tiles were greater necessities than irrigation ditches; flood protection was usually more necessary than drought relief; the "belts" of the Midwest were of corn and wheat, not six-shooters and, more importantly, not the gun belts of the mid- and late-twentieth-century defense industries; Abraham Lincoln and Henry Ford rather than Billy the Kid and Henry Kaiser became the Midwest regional heroes offered to the nation.

Just scanning the pictures of western history textbooks reminds us of what is not part of the midwestern story: long wagon trains, heroic railroad bridges across canyons, hydraulic miners, Chinese workers, dead Indian women and children in the snow, huge dams, Ansel Adams photographs of Yosemite and of Japanese-American internment camps. Above all, midwesterners were always the more "ordinary" people, the "colorless many" who had few large speaking roles on history's stage rather than the "colorful few" who have played such large parts, on some sections, at least, of the western stage.[6]

Of course, history does not come in the neat divisions suggested by such dichotomies and neither do regions. Regional identities, histories, and geographies are far more complex. Walter Nugent has recently added to the debate of where the West begins or, from my perspective, where the Midwest ends, reminding us how fascinating and inconclusive such discussion can be. As some of Nugent's survey respondents indicated, these are issues not only of *where* we place lines on a map   at the Gateway Arch in St. Louis, on the 100th meridian, where the humidity is or is not oppressive, or where Wrangler-brand jeans predominate—but these are question also of *when*.[7] Time and place are intimately connected when we think about regions: they share a relationship particularly important for historians of the West and the Midwest.

Two time periods are especially important in identifying a distinctive Midwest, a region that is not the West, yet has relationships to it—the twentieth century's very early decades and its most recent.

The Midwest was created in the early twentieth century. It was then that the region ceased to be West and declared its separation from the West. It is likely that this creation of the Midwest was part of a discourse, a regional realignment, or dance, that included the creation of the West as a twentieth-century region.[8] Evidence for the creation of the Midwest in the first two decades of the century begins with the adoption of new regional labels, as geographer James R. Shortridge has shown. The region beyond the Appalachians had from the beginning been labelled either the West, the Northwest, or the Old Northwest, terms that persisted through the end of the nineteenth century. As the region changed and as the trans-Mississippi West developed, these old labels became less meaningful and more confusing. The rise of the West thus necessitated the creation of the label "Midwest." That happened in the years between 1900 and 1920 when the term itself came into wide use. Among the earliest popularizers was Frederick Jackson Turner, who published an essay in 1901 titled "The Middle West." Many of the region's most prominent writers and intellectuals—Edward A. Ross, Booth Tarkington, Meredith Nicholson—joined Turner in popularizing the term. Some confusion remained. As late as 1925 F. Scott Fitzgerald in *The Great Gatsby* used "middle-west" and "West" interchangeably to refer to Nick Carraway's Minnesota homeland. But by the 1920s the region was generally and widely identified by its new name.[9]

A new label was the outward sign of the creation of the Midwest, of this place becoming identified as a distinctive region. Three elements were central to this creation process, this ceasing to be West. The first was agriculture. The particular mixture of midwestern resource endowments of soil, terrain, climate, and water combined with a dominant culture firmly anchored in the family farm to give the region a distinctive agriculture. No other place in the nation, perhaps in the world, could claim such intensive and sophisticated agricultural productivity over such vast distance. Farming had been the base of midwestern life from the beginning. By the early twentieth century the farms were fat and prosperous, dripping with hogs and corn. These decades would become the midwestern farmers' golden era, a time to glory in the region's success at producing food for the nation and the world beyond.

The second factor that created the Midwest was industry, particularly concentrated heavy industry. U.S. Steel's Gary Works appeared overnight on the

Lake Michigan sand dunes to become the nation's showcase steel mill. Machine shops in Cincinnati and St. Louis gathered some of the world's most skilled workers. But above all there was the automobile industry, which firmly anchored itself in the Midwest in these early decades of the century. Not only in Detroit but in Akron, South Bend, and Kenosha the automobile industry lifted the region to industrial preeminence. Perhaps for the first time in world history an interior rather than coastal region became the industrial core of a powerful nation-state.

The third factor that created the Midwest was the widespread confidence that marked the region by the early decades of the century. Midwesterners became increasingly convinced that their region was *both* the industrial and agricultural heart of the nation. They built their material prosperity and regional pride on the firm foundations of "the immediately useful and practical," to use Lewis Atherton's words. They acquired a powerful sense of place from their success as hog butchers, toolmakers, stackers of wheat, and players with railroads, all proudly "laughing the stormy, husky, brawling laughter of Youth," as Carl Sandburg boasted.[10]

This pride of achievement and confidence included also a particularly strong sense of the past, or more accurately, the creation of a particular past—a shared, constructed memory that was best expressed in the icon of the pioneer. In the early decades of the twentieth century the pioneer became the cultural hero and symbol of the Midwest. Long after most pioneers were dead, their lives became the basis for heroic stories of ordinary people who settled the region in family units and built a civilization in the wilderness. While tellers of these stories sometimes celebrated individualism, they usually depicted pioneers as members of families and communities, not Marlboro men, but ordinary men and women of log cabins and schoolhouses, of grist mills and churches. The pioneer stories became the region's dominant tales, celebrated in monuments and markets, in school histories, in the creation of the nation's finest state historical societies and historical journals, and in the history departments at the nation's best state universities, including, most notably, the University of Wisconsin. The pioneer story was a story of success, of achievement, and it served as the means by which midwesterners (a modest, even shy people, as Garrison Keillor reminds us) celebrated their success. The most useful pioneer success stories were those that incorporated pioneer motifs into agricultural and industrial achievement, stories that helped midwesterners to reconcile a supposed pastoral origin with an increasingly urban-industrial future. No one represented this success story better than Henry Ford, the Michigan farm boy who built the Model T and created the pioneer village of Greenfield.[11]

With long rows of corn, auto assembly lines, and pioneers' success stories the

Midwest developed sufficient confidence to claim its place as heartland, the center not only geographically but now also in culture, politics, and all other matters of importance. The region was no longer on the edge or border, no longer dependent, no longer the "other." The Midwest became America—its towns became "Middletowns" of representative Americans, its literature, with Booth Tarkington, Sinclair Lewis, and many others, became American literature, its tastes in food, accents, and soap powder the nation's standard, its sons the nation's presidents. The region confidently embraced the nation and became the nation, with some help even from Frederick Jackson Turner and the Mississippi Valley Historical Association, founded in 1907. The old days of fearing, hating, or worshipping the East passed. The West remained attractive, of course, and midwesterners were still ready to migrate there or to adopt some of its culture, whether in the form of Hollywood cowboys and Indians or Mission-style architecture, but the region beyond the 100th meridian was clearly an immature and unproven place to midwesterners, not yet so immediately useful and practical, and not yet a success story. After all, folks in Peoria and Muncie could smugly read in their magazine advertisements that a consumer product might be priced slightly higher west of the Rockies. As Henry Loomis Nelson, an editor at *Harper's*, concluded in 1904, the Midwest "is not as western as it was; it is not eastern, and its people are grateful for both blessings, as they would call them."[12]

Much of the regional confidence that marked the first two decades of the century persisted into the 1950s[13] but not to the century's last decades. Blow after blow struck the Midwest in the 1970s and 1980s, hitting harder than elsewhere, it seemed to many midwesterners, and helping to create regional identities different from those of the early twentieth century and different from those of the West. In this bleaker era the regional dance gave to the Midwest partners who seemed likely to break heartland hearts or, at least, step on some toes.

The strongest blows hit the Midwest family farm. It was clear by the 1980s that even in the best place in the world to grown corn and hogs there were risks and failures. Tractorcades and Hollywood films depicting the courage and resilience of midwestern farmers could not hide the widespread fear that one of the region's fundamental marks of distinction and success was in peril. The family farm would surely survive in the Corn Belt—with significant government aid—but few midwestern farmers were prepared to make the confident claims of the early twentieth century.[14]

The second blow came in the seemingly sudden appearance of the rust belt. Confident that what was good for General Motors would always be good for the region and the nation, few midwesterners were prepared for the industrial shocks of the 1970s and 1980s. Factories stretching from Cleveland to Detroit, Chicago, and St. Louis no longer proudly spewed out smoke and mass-produced consumer goods. Above all, there was the decline of the auto industry, which left the Big Three fighting for survival and created the specter of one of their most visible leaders begging the federal and state governments for a bailout.[15]

These economic woes heightened regional sensibilities as Midwesterners became aware of seemingly greater possibilities and successes in the Sunbelt and the West, where prospects of lower wages, lower energy costs, lower taxes, and fewer worker unions lured Midwest businesses, jobs, and people. As early as 1930 Los Angeles was producing enough auto tires to make Akron's manufacturers uneasy. Perhaps most unsettling was the rise of the gun belt, the Cold War defense industries that were of major economic benefit to other parts of the nation, especially the West, but not to the Midwest. Military industrialists, as Ann Markusen notes, deliberately and "pointedly shunned the industrial heartland" after World War II.[16] By the end of the 1970s the West's defense and high-tech industries were pulling along an economic boom that seemed as secure as that produced two generations earlier by U.S. Steel's Gary Works and Ford's Model T.

Along with the growing perception of regional inequities deriving from defense industry spending came a general fear that the Midwest was paying the freight for the West's gravy train. Some midwesterners became suspicious that western claims of being a "plundered provence," particularly the cries of "victimization" by the federal government, were in fact smoke screens to cover the squeals of fat hogs at the public trough. The New Federalism of Californians Richard Nixon and Ronald Reagan clearly left the Midwest out in the cold: federal grants-in-aid brought far fewer tax dollars back to the region than they did to the West. As the Midwest's fears of regional economic decline grew in the 1970s and 1980s, its governors and federal representatives, for the first time in the region's history, organized to appeal loudly for federal aid—long after such was the norm in the West.[17]

And more midwesterners became unhappily aware by the 1970s that they had failed to pioneer on the frontiers of race relations and of environmental protection, that instead they had created some of the nation's most segregated neighborhoods and most polluted water and air.[18] The pioneer success stories of equality and of abundant natural resources were harder and harder to tell, yet lingered still in many heartland hearts.

As the Midwest seemed to age and to decline, then, the West seemed to rise, economically, politically, culturally. There were growing signs after World War II that the West, particularly California, could now claim status as America's most American region, certainly as the trendsetter and as the region with the most confident success stories to tell the nation.[19] The Beach Boys quickly dismissed Midwest farmer's daughters to sing to all of America about "California Girls," Johnny Carson told jokes about California freeways to Illinois farmers, and the heartland became flyover country, the vast nothingness between the Coasts.

There is doubtless insufficient perspective for historians to sort out the meaning of these trends. It is likely, however, that the Midwest's "decline" in the last two decades has been exaggerated. The early 1990s brought a relatively strong economic recovery across much of the Midwest, compared to other regions. The end of the Cold War held out hope for a shift in federal spending away from defense, a shift that promised relative benefits for the region most distant from the gun belt. Whatever the degree of decline, it is nearly certain that the crises of the 1970s and 1980s have helped create a greater regional identity and even some regional pride. With a sense of lagging behind, a sense of conflict and tension, there may come, as Richard Maxwell Brown argues, greater regional creativity and identification.[20] While there is nothing to rival the West or western history in this regard, there are in recent years more works of Midwest-located fiction and history, cookbooks, and even a glossy regional magazine entitled *Midwest Living*, all exploring and often celebrating what it means to be midwestern.[21] Some of this is little more than recycled pioneer stories, some of it crudely constructed with only a whistle-in-the-dark reality. Some appears to be more genuine, indicative of thoughtful attachment to a particular place.

Whatever the meaning of the Midwest as the century ends, it is not western. Indeed, looking at these two regions, from frontier settlement to the present, it is the differences rather than similarities that need exploration.

Yet there are some common questions. Both western and midwestern experiences suggest the dangers of success stories, perhaps even the dangers of overweening pride. Both regions now know failure. Each knows the struggle to find a way to tell its story in something other than themes of pioneer success.

Each region's history in its own special way suggests also the foolishness of docilely accepting a national history that ignores place, that tells history stories in terms of some abstract, geography-neutral process. People created and continue to create these two regions for reasons and in ways that deserve far more attention than they have received. It is especially pleasing that western historians have led our profession in recent years in reminding us of that truth. So, although midwesterners cannot fully be a part of this particular place called the West, they can perhaps ride western coattails toward gaining some little respect for the "flyover region" as distinctive place.

After all, the Midwest did give the West some of what makes it so interesting, including not only the community of Pasadena, once the Indiana Colony, but the persons of Frederick Jackson Turner and Martin Ridge, both mid-westerners, even if they left the Heartland to stroll after lunch in a western cactus garden.

NOTES

1. Walter Nugent, "Where is the American West? Report on a Survey," *Montana: The Magazine of Western History* 42 (Summer 1992), 13.

2. The *Western Historical Quarterly*, of course, is not closed to midwestern history, as its statement of policy and occasionally its pages attest. And there are some midwestern regional journals, notably *Old Northwest*, though none has yet come close to the *Western Historical Quarterly* or the *Journal of Southern History* in scholarly impact.

3. American Historical Association, *Directory of History Departments and Organizations in the United States and Canada, 1992 93* (Washington, DC, 1992).

4. William Cronon, George Miles, Jay Gitlin, "Becoming West: Toward a New Meaning for Western History," in William Cronon, George Miles, and Jay Gitlin, eds., *Under an Open Sky: Rethinking America's Western Past* (New York: W.W. Norton, 1992), 2–27.

5. *Pasadena: Its Climate, Homes, Resources, Etc., Etc.* (Pasadena, 1888), 16; James H. Madison, "Taking the Country Barefooted: The Indiana Colony in Southern California," *California History* 69 (Fall 1990): 236–49; Jon Gjerde, "The Seacoast of Iowa: Chain Migration from the Middle West to California, 1880–1939," unpublished paper in author's possession; Carey McWilliams, *Southern California Country: An Island on the Land* (New York: Duell, Sloan, and Pearce, 1946); Kevin Starr, *Inventing the Dream: California Through the Progressive Era* (New York: Oxford University Press, 1985); Kevin Starr, *Material Dreams: Southern California Through the 1920s* (New York: Oxford University Press, 1990).

6. Walter Nugent, "Frontiers and Empires in the Late Nineteenth Century," *Western Historical Quarterly* 20 (November 1989): 400–2; Patricia Nelson Limerick, *The Legacy of Conquest: The Unbroken Past of the American West* (New York: Norton, 1987); Richard White, "*It's Your Misfortune and None of My Own*": A History of the American West (Norman: University of Oklahoma Press, 1991); Patricia Nelson Limerick, Clyde A. Milner II, and Charles E. Rankin, eds., *Trails: Toward a New Western History* (Lawrence: University Press of Kansas, 1991).

7. Nugent, "Where Is the American West?," 3–23. See also Wilbur Zelinsky, *The Cultural Geography of the United States*, rev. ed. (Englewood Cliffs, NJ: Prentice Hall, 1992), 109–40.

8. Gerald D. Nash, *Creating the West: Historical Interpretations, 1890–1990* (Albuquerque: University of New Mexico Press, 1991), 101–58.

9. James R. Shortridge, *The Middle West: Its Meaning in American Culture* (Lawrence: University Press of Kansas, 1989), 13–26; Frederick Jackson Turner, "The Middle West," in Frederick Jackson Turner, *The Frontier in American History* (New York: Holt, Rinehart and Winston, 1920, 1962), 126–56. F. Scott Fitzgerald, *The Great Gatsby* (New York: Charles Scribner's Sons, 1925, 1992), 7, 184. Turner was a historian of the *Middle* West: "It was," he

claimed in a commencement address in 1910, "in the Middle West that society has formed on lines least like those of Europe." Turner, *The Frontier in American History*, 282. See also Martin Ridge, "The Life of an Idea: The Significance of Frederick Jackson Turner's Frontier Thesis," *Montana: The Magazine of Western History* 41 (Winter 1991), 2–13.

10. Lewis Atherton, *Main Street on the Middle Border* (Bloomington: Indiana University Press, 1954), 109; Carl Sandburg, *Complete Poems* (New York: Harcourt Brace & Co., 1950), 3–4.

11. John Bodnar, *Remaking America: Public Memory, Commemoration, and Patriotism in the Twentieth Century* (Princeton: University of Princeton Press, 1992), 120–23; Michael Kammen, *Mystic Cords of Memory: The Transformation of Tradition in American Culture* (New York: Knopf, 1991), Chapter 12; Andrew R. L. Cayton and Peter Onuf, *The Midwest and the Nation: Rethinking the History of an American Region* (Bloomington: Indiana University Press, 1990), 118–26. The pioneer icon received major attention in post office murals and in the paintings of Thomas Hart Benton and other regionalists of the 1930s. See Marlene Park and Gerald E. Markowitz, *Democratic Vistas: Post Offices and Public Art in the New Deal* (Philadelphia: Temple University Press, 1985); Erika Doss, *Benton, Pollock, and the Politics of Modernism: From Regionalism to Abstract Expressionism* (Chicago: University of Chicago Press, 1991), 100–19. For Ford, see David L. Lewis, *The Public Image of Henry Ford: An American Folk Hero and His Company* (Detroit: Wayne State University Press, 1976).

12. Quoted in Shortridge, *The Middle West*, 23. See also Ronald Weber, *The Midwestern Ascendancy in American Writing* (Bloomington: Indiana University Press, 1992), and, for a different reading, Joanne Jacobson, "The Idea of the Midwest," *Revue Francaise D'Etudes Americaines* 48–49 (April–July 1991): 235–45.

13. For illustrations see Graham Hutton, *Midwest at Noon* (Chicago: University of Chicago Press, 1946; reprint, DeKalb, Ill.: Northern Illinois University Press, 1990); The Editors of *Look, The Midwest* (Cambridge, Ma., 1947). For some of the context see Robert L. Dorman, *Revolt of the Provinces: The Regionalist Movement in America, 1920–1945* (Chapel Hill: University of North Carolina Press, 1993).

14. Mark Friedberger, *Farm Families & Change in Twentieth-Century America* (Lexington, Ky.: University Press of Kentucky, 1988); Mark Friedberger, "The Transformation of the Rural Midwest, 1945–1985: *Old Northwest* 16 (Spring 1992): 13–36.

15. Richard M. Bernard, *Snowbelt Cities: Metropolitan Politics in the Northeast and Midwest since World War II* (Bloomington: Indiana University Press, 1990); Richard D. Bingham and Randall W. Eberts, *Economic Restructuring of the American Midwest* (Boston: Kluwer Academic, 1990); Jon C. Teaford, *Cities of the Heartland: The Rise and Fall of the Industrial Midwest* (Bloomington: Indiana University Press, 1993), 211–52.

16. Ann Markusen, *Regions: The Economics and Politics of Territory* (Totowa, N.J.: Rowman & Littlefield, 1987), 106. See also Ann Markusen et al., *The Rise of the Gun Belt: The Military Remapping of Industrial America* (New York: Oxford University Press, 1991).

17. Peter K. Eisinger and William Gormley, eds., *The Midwest Response to the New Federalism* (Madison: University of Wisconsin Press, 1988), 9, 36. These kinds of concerns had long been present in the Midwest, but without the loud, organized focus. See, for example, Frederick Jackson Turner, "Sections and Nations," *Yale Review* 12 (October 1922): 19.

18. Philip V. Scarpino, *Great River: An Environmental History of the Upper Mississippi, 1890–1950* (Columbia, Mo: University of Missouri Press, 1985); Aldo Leopold, *A Sand County Almanac and Sketches Here and There* (New York: Oxford University Press, 1949); Andrew Hurley, "Challenging Corporate Polluters: Race, Class, and Environmental Politics in Gary, Indiana, since 1945," *Indiana Magazine of History* 88 (December 1992): 273–302; Teaford, *Cities in the Heartland*, 230–39; Charles S. Bullock, "Civil Rights in the Midwest," Eisinger and Gromley, eds., *Midwest Response to the New Federalism*, 163–86.

19. Richard White, *It's Your Misfortune and None of My Own*, 496–533.

20. Richard Maxwell Brown, "The New Regionalism in America, 1970–1981," in William G. Robbins, et al., *Regionalism and the Pacific Northwest* (Corvallis, Or: Oregon State University Press, 1983), 61, 71.

21. Examples of recent writing include Richard Rhodes, *The Inland Ground: An Evocation of the American Middle West* (Lawrence: University Press of Kansas, 1991); William Least Heat-Moon, *PrairyErth: (a deep map)* (Boston: Houghton Mifflin, 1991); Carol Bly, *Letters from the Country* (New York: Harper & Row, 1981); Michel Martone, ed., *A Place of Sense: Essays in Search of the Midwest* (Iowa City: University of Iowa Press for the Iowa Humanities Board, 1988). For historical literature see James H. Madison, ed., *Heartland: Comparative Histories of the Midwestern States* (Bloomington: Indiana University Press, 1988). For cooking see Marcia Adams, *Heartland: The Best of the Old and the New from Midwest Kitchens* (New York: Crown Publishing Group, 1992).

PART II

THE POLITICAL WEST

Fred Lockley during the Civil War
(Photograph courtesy Henry E. Huntington Library and Art Gallery, San Marino, California.)

CHAPTER FOUR

TYPE AND STEREOTYPE
Frederic E. Lockley, Pioneer Journalist

CHARLES E. RANKIN

Common portrayal of the late nineteenth-century western journalist is like the dual image of the American Indian as noble savage. It is Janus-faced. On the one hand the western journalist is a fearless, pistol-packing, typesetting crusader, a man who dares tilt with oppression, corruption, and meanness, a righter of wrongs. More often than not, he is a tramp printer rather than a polished editor, a man who knows his types better than his grammar but who recognizes the good cause and champions it to the end regardless of the consequences.[1]

To this brew of characterization, one need add only a dash of cynicism and a healthy dose of irreverence to have an eminently recognizable variation on theme: the scapegrace, a reckless Peter Pan who punctures pretension and exposes hypocrisy. Western humorists like John Phoenix (George Horatio Derby), Artemus Ward (Charles Farrar Browne), Mark Twain (Samuel Clemens), and (Edgar Wilson) Bill Nye identify easily with this role.

Remove the polish, of course, and puncturing pretensions becomes insult. Expose hypocrisy for personal gain, and the result is scandalmongering. No less a western historian than Earl Pomeroy believed both these latter attributes— insult and scandalmongering—contributed to what he called a "distinctively regional flavor." The effect of such antics by western editors Pomeroy likened to that of a drunkard reeling through the streets. Like the drunkard, the western newspaperman is so blatantly distasteful he is not resented as immoral but rather is welcomed as a warning to others of what not to become.[2]

Serious journalists, who laid as much claim to the title "upright" as anyone, were equally disturbed by such an unbecoming identity. Straight-laced Wyoming editor J. H. Hayford, for example, advised Bill Nye to stop trying to be funny. "We advise Nye to rub the donkey off his coat of arms," Hayford wrote, and "endeavor to take rank among the respectable journalists." California editors were similarly outraged when taken in by Mark Twain's *Dutch Nick Massacre*, a trickster story about a down-on-his-luck mining investor who kills his family, slits his own throat ear to ear, and then rides into town to die within minutes in front of a prominent saloon, his wife's grisly scalp in hand. Other editors, who reprinted the story without disclaimer and without heeding numerous clues to its fabulous nature, charged Twain, then a Virginia City, Nevada, newspaper reporter, with subverting the profession and other, more undignified transgressions.[3]

In addition to the humorists, one should also include the swashbuckling hucksters who ranged the West from just after the Civil War to after the turn of the century. They were rough-cut men like Legh Freeman, former Virginian and galvanized Yankee, who, with his highly mobile *Frontier Index,* chased opportunity in the form of railroad construction camps, townsite booms, and mining strikes from Fort Kearney, Nebraska, to the Puget Sound, or they were polished knaves like F. G. Bonfils and Harry H. Tammen, buccaneer owners of the Denver *Post* who bilked Buffalo Bill Cody out of his Wild West show, among other things. The gallery is incomplete, of course, without such Indian wars campaigners as Henry Morton Stanley, John Finerty, and De B. Randolph Keim, and rogue adventurers like Richard Harding Davis. Real people all, but the tales of their exploits, often self-promoted, have contributed to a portrayal more colorful than accurate for what would have been the typical western journalist.[4]

In contrast to this racy, almost comic book-like character is the reverse side of the Janus face: small-town editors like J. H. Hayford or the publisher/editors of the West's emerging daily newspapers. Although they came somewhat after the pioneer era, perhaps the best-known examples of this type are William Allen White and Ed Howe—staid promoters of permanence and provincial identity who, as Robert Athearn put it, "manned the barricades of local pride."[5] Reflecting the values, attitudes, and wholesomeness—and just as often the bigotry—of America's small-town middle class, they championed community building, stability, and social uniformity, however diverse the actual makeup of their local populations. As Robert V. Hine has noted, the daily or weekly newspaper was a major industry in every town. Its reporting of gossip, recent arrivals, and various community events "generally created the illusion of a homogeneous society leisurely pursuing progress along a serene and confident path."[6] Or, as Mark Twain wrote in the Virginia City *Territorial Enterprise:*

Our duty is to keep the universe thoroughly posted concerning murders and street fights, and balls, and theaters, and pack-trains, and churches, and lectures, and schoolhouses, and city military affairs, and highway robberies, and Bible societies, and haywagons, and a thousand other things which it is in the province of local reporters to keep track of and magnify into undue importance for the instruction of the readers of this great daily newspaper.[7]

Less tongue-in-cheek, Lewis Atherton thought the reason for local journalism's fascination with mundane affairs was that people liked having their lives dignified by a newspaper report on their activities. It made them feel important.[8]

The two types represented in these caricatures are not wholly inaccurate nor are they new. They are pervasive, however, in popular culture as well as historical interpretations, and their heroism is rarely unsullied. Pragmatism, opportunism, or character flaws are forever undermining their virtuous idealism. One need only think of the journalist who willingly exchanges truth for myth by tearing up a reporter's carefully taken notes in *The Man Who Shot Liberty Valance,* saying, "This is the West sir. When legend becomes fact, print the legend." Or the other journalist in the story, Dutton Peabody, the town drunk whom Liberty Valance, portrayed by Lee Marvin, beats senseless in his own newspaper office for daring to fight evil with a pen. Or the unprincipled newspaper editor in John Ford's film version of Mari Sandoz's *Cheyenne Autumn* who seizes opportunity by switching sides. "Here it is," he bellows to his staff, sheaves of paper in hand.

Sun, Times, Chronicle. They're all saying the same thing we are. Bloodthirsty savages on the loose. Burning, killing, violating beautiful white women. It's not news anymore. From now on we're going to GRIEVE for the red man. We'll sell more papers that way.

Less flattering portrayals of journalists can be found in more recent films: the sycophant, chameleon-like dime novel writer in Clint Eastwood's *Unforgiven* who, other than Eastwood, is the only person to remain in the saloon at the end and live yet wets his pants at the point of a gun; or the insensitive newspaper editor portrayed in *The Grey Fox* who possesses, as the film's heroine declares, "the mentality of a grocery clerk."[9]

If such caricatures are larger-than-life—or lower-than-life—versions of reality, where lies the truth? Even cursory analysis would show that western journalism has no shortage of material on which to base an accurate history. First, of course, there are the newspapers themselves, and second, there are histories of individual newspapers, memoirs, autobiographies, and quasi-biographical articles on famous or notorious editor/publishers. Summary essays, book-length state and territorial histories, and a handful of studies that attempt regional perspective add to the fund, although most of these are more compilations of facts about newspapers than monographic historical treatments.[10] Of the few studies that attempt regional perspective, the tendency is more to focus inward on the important but routine business of publishing a newspaper than to look outward to the interconnections of newspapers with the communities they served.[11] Still fewer concentrate on any one editor with sustained emphasis.[13] In addition, numerous early state histories—so-called mug histories—treat the growth of newspapers topically, much as Hubert Howe Bancroft does in his histories of western states.[14] As often as not, mug histories were written by journalists. Thus, the treatment of newspapers, while often rewardingly detailed, is rarely conceptual and often flattering and uncritical.

A better way to get at the western journalist as a person would seem through personal papers, but such documents are remarkably uncommon. Awash in paper throughout their careers, pioneer journalists saved precious little of it for posterity. Itineracy among western journalists was legendary, but material on such men—and women, although most western journalists were men—is especially scarce. Rarely is there enough personal information to trace a western journalist across space and time and follow the full trajectory of his career. Rarer still are sources of ample quality and quantity to learn meaningfully of the private side of a journalist's life—the kind of material that reveals most clearly the hopes, dreams, and motivations, the thoughts behind the editorials, the roller coaster effect of professional enthusiasm and ennui.

The papers of Frederic E. Lockley, however, constitute an exception to these shortcomings. Historically, Frederic Lockley is all but unknown, yet in his time he was a prolific newspaperman. He wrote well and he wrote often, leaving a substantial newspaper record wherever he went, and he traveled much. Like many journalists of his day, he was self-educated and well-read, having become quite familiar with the classics of English history and literature. Born in 1824 the son of barely literate parents (his father was a London butcher and his mother made nails), Lockley immigrated to the United States amid the European upheavals of 1848. Between the time of his immigration and his enlistment in the Union Army in 1862, he threaded his way from New York to New Orleans, to Cleveland and Chicago, and back to New York in search of wage work and opportunity. Taking various jobs, he butchered beef in Cleveland, tended cattle boats down the Mississippi River to New Orleans, and kept books for a shoemaker in Chicago.[13]

Ultimately Lockley settled in New York City where he edited and proofread copy for *Frank Leslie's Illustrated Newspaper* and other book and magazine publishers. He wrote several editorials for Horace Greeley's New York *Tribune* and remembered meeting that hoary journalist twice but never gained regular newspaper work until after the Civil War. When the war came, Lockley was working as a door-to-door book salesman in upstate New York and Vermont. With the country locked in titanic struggle, selling books, as he said, proved "too suggestive of peddling figs in a hurricane." Having become a naturalized American citizen in 1859, he enlisted in the Union Army and served three years, two in the defense of Washington and another with General Ulysses S. Grant in the climactic Virginia campaigns of 1864 and 1865.[16]

After the war, Lockley headed west from New York to Cleveland, where he worked three years on local newspapers. In 1869, he led a group of land-seekers to Kansas at the bidding of the Kansas Pacific Railway, then settled in Leavenworth. Based in Leavenworth, he reported on affairs in Kansas and Indian Territory for such papers as the New York *World,* New York *Times,* and Chicago *Times,* as well as for a number of regional and national magazines. Most of his articles were signed with such pen names as "Okmulgee," "Indian," "Viator," or "Reno," and would be wholly unidentifiable today without corroboration from his private correspondence and memoirs. Eventually, Lockley followed the call of opportunity to various editorial capacities in Salt Lake City, Utah, Butte, Montana, Arkansas City, Kansas, and finally to Salem, Oregon. He died at age eighty-one at the home of a daughter in Missoula, Montana, in 1905.

Across the Atlantic, then across the continent, Lockley pursued adventure and opportunity. In countless words written for more than a dozen newspapers, he championed nineteenth-century notions of freedom and progress. His approach to newswriting was typical for the era. He mixed fact and opinion freely and thought editorial commentary superior to mere presentation of factual information. He saw politics as the best means for effecting social progress, and he embraced the idealistic, somewhat elitist belief in the press as educator and defender of the public interest. Typically also he subscribed to community boosterism, advocated temperance and ecumenical religious observance, and abhorred vice, crime, and violence. He was consistently indignant toward what he viewed as immorality and stridently opposed to corruption in any form. Like many Union veterans who went west after the war, Lockley was determined to impose northern values on a new land and subdue such renegades as Mormons, resistant Indian tribes, and corrupt politicians. Like a number of other journalists, he aspired to quality literary achievement. He may have lacked the talent for becoming an accomplished author anyway, but he fell short of the mark primarily because newspaper work simply used him up.[17]

Frederic Lockley's career is arguably significant for three reasons. First, unlike most western newspapermen, Lockley left a substantial historical record not only in identifiable professional writing but also in personal material. A faithful husband he was a devoted correspondent to his wife Elizabeth.[17] He wrote to her faithfully while a soldier in the Civil War and after the war, especially whenever he traveled or took work in a new place and left Elizabeth behind temporarily, he penned frequent and detailed letters to her. His work is thus punctuated by flurries of private correspondence, much of it coming at transition points in his career. These letters stand as the most honest expression of his feelings and provide a means for contrasting what he wrote privately with what he crafted for public dissemination. Comparison reveals a remarkable consistency and underscores the reputation he gained among his contemporaries for honesty and pluck. He could have used his private letters as newspaper reports, and indeed instructed Elizabeth to pass them on to local editors for publication on a few occasions.

Second, Lockley's career is significant for what it says about journalistic influence. Like many who pursued journalism in the West, Lockley wrote fervently, and like at least a few he believed what he wrote. Because he traveled widely and witnessed many of the wrenching changes that transformed the West following the Civil War, he was in a position to comment on a variety of historically significant issues, most connected with federal policy in one form or another toward Indians, Mormons, western railroads, settlement and the promise of western agriculture, and monetary policies. Lockley argued vociferously and with intellectual intensity, usually along pro-Republican political lines but not always. His views, while cogent and sometimes farsighted, rarely won out, however, at least with any immediacy. As a result, Lockley's career serves as a window on the relative power of newspaper journalism to effect change.[18]

Third, Lockley's experiences help to explode stereotypes and look beyond the one-dimensional labels commonly attached to pioneer newspapermen. His is something apart from the portraits derived either from the careers of successful newspaper owners or from the colorful or violent characters of legend. Although he was itinerant and knew how to set type, Lockley was not on the one hand a tramp printer who commanded only the level of respect accorded an artisan. Nor, on the other hand, was he a successful newspaper proprietor, although he tried newspaper ownership at least three times. Instead, he worked as a reporter or in editorial capacities. Together, the various components of his career, which are not often accessible to historical study, elaborate on the story of what being a newspaperman in the Old West was really like. With Lockley we are afforded an opportunity to learn of a man who lived a life very much like what the majority of western journalists and editors probably lived—someone able to comment on the issues, events, and leading figures of his time but who otherwise led a peaceful, rather nondescript life and who, by providing his communities with contemporary news and commentary, helped forge the quiet, often subtle particulars of the revolution we have come to know as western settlement. The influence of such a man, both to create stability and to effect what he perceived as progress, was not measurable like a sea change but rather like the slow accumulation of limestone deposits in a watery cave or the almost imperceptible erosion of water on rock.

When Frederic Lockley mustered out of the Union Army in June 1865, he looked immediately to the West for opportunity. Leaving his family in Albany, New York, he bought a train ticket for Chicago but stopped off in Cleveland first, where he quickly found work as a night editor. He wrote to Elizabeth optimistically, "I like Cleveland much," adding in another letter, "I calculate to make this city my resting place for the remainder of my days."[19] Abandoning the rented house in Albany they had lived in through the war, Elizabeth and Frederic's three daughters by a first marriage made what would be the first of a number of moves, this one to Cleveland, where they would establish a home and add to their family with birth of a daughter two years later.

After three years of newspaper work in Cleveland, however, Lockley had grown restless and dissatisfied. Long hours and low pay combined with a lack of job security to make him resentful. His employer, he said, was "harsh and exacting." Although his job was "employment I had been striving after half my life," he wrote in later years, "I recall how restive I grew . . . and how I hankered after [being] 'my own master.'"[20] As he and two co-workers sat around the tobacco-stained office stove, as he said, "in the wearisome wee' sma' hours, when 30' was on the telegraph," Frederic suggested they start a paper of their own—an inexpensive evening daily for Cleveland's working class. "Working men are agitating for a change in our social and political affairs," Lockley wrote, "and an organ started in their interest" might succeed. Pooling meager resources, Lockley and his partners assembled $4,000 in capitalization and issued the Cleveland *Evening News* in April 1868.[21]

Problems beset them from the start. They underestimated subscriptions and overestimated the capacity of their press. Advertising sales lagged for want of an "outside rustler." Papers went undelivered or were deposited at wrong addresses. Printing was poor. They had not planned well and were undercapitalized from the outset. None of the three partners was a good businessman, and Lockley lacked the confidence to become one. "I had an exaggerated idea of the importance of the editorial columns," he later admitted. "It is a saying in the trade that you may have an editor with the force and eloquence of a Paul, yet his labors will not avail without good business management." The paper struggled for two or three months, then Lockley and his partners sold it to their former employer and went back to work in their old jobs. "And this," Lockley observed, "was the inglorious result of our ambitious attempt at self-emancipation."[22]

Lockley saw founding a new paper as a means to effect change not only for himself but for Cleveland's working class, with whom he identified. Even before emigrating to the United States, he had developed strong views on economic theory and appropriate public policy. All his life he would advocate the interests of the working man, not from the perspective of union solidarity as became fashionable at the end of the century but rather in the cooperative form advocated by Horace Greeley and other followers of Fourierism at mid-century. Economics, he believed, was a matter of morality and could be argued like a philosophical proposition. Distrustful of unrestrained competition, he held monopolistic capitalism in contempt. Yet his sincere concern for the welfare of the workingman mixed with an elitist noblesse oblige born of his sense of intellectual superiority. All his life he hoped to become editor of an influential paper. Few other forums could afford him so democratic a podium from which he could expound on larger moral and philosophical questions.

Such was Lockley's hope for the Cleveland *Evening News.* With luck and better financial backing, Lockley and his partners might have learned from their mistakes and made a go of it. His sense of possibility was sound. There was room in Cleveland for an inexpensive evening daily devoted to work-ingmen's interests, an opening exploited by none other than Edward Willis Scripps ten years later when Scripps founded the *Penny Press* with $10,000 capitalization, thereby launching the Scripps newspaper empire. But for Lockley and his cohorts, three months and $4,000 had proven inadequate for achieving lasting success.[23]

Within a year, "possessed of a strong western fever," as he put it, Lockley headed west to conduct homesteaders to Kansas at the behest of the Denver Pacific Railway. In his pocket was a round trip ticket, but once arrived he wrote to Elizabeth as hopefully of Kansas as he had of Cleveland four years earlier. Although rough and undeveloped, Kansas, he urged, held huge potential and was improving rapidly. Would it "not be wise," he implored Elizabeth, "to be on the ground, to watch my opportunity[,] to take a stand so as to be born forward on the tide[?]"[24] He soon found work on one of several newspapers operating in the Missouri River town of Leavenworth, and left it to Elizabeth to break up housekeeping in Cleveland and convey their four children west to Kansas soon after.

Despite his initial optimism, Lockley's success in Kansas was as mixed as it had been in Cleveland. His income as a newspaperman in Leavenworth was meager, and, with birth of a son in 1871, his growing family now included five children. Consequently, in addition to his newspaper work, he wrote for a variety of magazines and solicited assignments from eastern and midwestern papers. His solicitations proved especially lucrative when he turned his attention southward to Indian Territory, where issues involving federal policy toward the so-called Five Civilized Tribes and such western tribes as the Cheyennes, Arapahos, Kiowas, and Comanches enticed editors of the New York *Times,* New York *World,* Chicago *Times,* and other papers to accept his reports.[25]

To Lockley, a correct Indian policy was as simple as it was difficult to effect. It should be fair to the Indians and observe treaty commitments, yet it should also prepare the tribes for eventual assimilation into the dominant society. He foresaw change as inescapable and hoped the tribes would prepare for it, yet he believed that white society should slow the inexorable juggernaut of settlement long enough for the Indians to adjust. Lockley visited Indian Territory at least four times. In his early visits, he championed the let-alone policy advocated by native leaders but eventually realized that however morally just, leaving the tribes alone was impossible. They would be invaded, probably sooner than later, and they must prepare for it.

On his fourth visit to Indian Territory, an extended tour among the five tribes in late 1872, Lockley sought to assess the Indians' progress toward becoming civilized in light of legislation then pending to combine the Indian Nations under a single territorial government. Providing exclusive reports to the Chicago *Times,* he attempted to address all the essential issues: the impact of two railroads then building across the territory; Native attitudes toward territorialization, allotment, and land in severalty; granting Indians American citizenship; the status of educational opportunities among the tribes; native observance of Christianity; the effectiveness of Indian legislatures; and lawlessness. His method was direct. He sought out what he termed "representative men," interviewed them, and plied them with questions he thought his white readers would ask if they were there.[26]

Lockley toured tribal capitals and railroad towns and assessed the condition of native orphanages, schools, churches, and newspapers. He traveled easily in Indian Territory, thanks largely to the assistance of Quaker Indian agents, then in charge of the tribes. Though indebted to the Quakers, Lockley noted to Elizabeth that his pessimistic views toward Indian capacity for rapid progress would offend the Quakers past reconciliation. "But this I cannot help," he wrote. "I came here to make a true report—and I must be governed by my convictions no matter who takes offense."[27]

Despite his pessimism, Lockley was capable of seeing—and reporting—from the Indians' viewpoint. To the Chicago *Times,* he wrote:

> I am not an advocate of the let-alone policy . . . but prejudice is an immense force to overcome. The Indian's previous dealings with the white man have not been of a nature to inspire any overwhelming feelings of confidence.[28]

He ascribed to the efficacy of the popular press and urged new perspectives on his white readers. "We are better acquainted with our red brothers now [that] we are brought into close neighborhood with them," he wrote in his final report to the Chicago *Times,* "and the mists which formerly enshrouded them in our imaginations, whether of romance or demonic attributes, are rapidly fading away." Public sentiment, he added, "demands that justice shall be done to the Indians, and sound statesmanship also dictates that whatever useful qualities lie latent in their natures shall be developed" and made available.[29]

To be sure, Lockley was a man of his times. Progress was inexorable and inevitable, and the tribes, he believed, simply must adapt to change or be overwhelmed. "These Indian nations trying to keep out the railroads, to preserve their tribal relations, to be exempt from molestation," he concluded, "are simply attempting the impossible. It is Mrs. Partington with her broom endeavoring to keep out the rising tide of the Atlantic."[30] The sooner the Indian peoples set about improving their attitudes toward progress, he believed, "the better for themselves. They can not be allowed to stand in the way of civilization, nor do their own interests demand it."[31]

Lockley had evinced even more pessimistic views toward the Kiowas earlier that summer. He came into brief but intimate contact with that tribe while reporting on a special peace commission sent among them in what would become southwestern Oklahoma. The council ground was located near an abandoned post called Fort Cobb, with the meeting itself held outdoors under a spreading oak tree. In attendance were a handful of Quaker Indian agents, interpreters, envoys from the Five Civilized Tribes, and hundreds of Kiowas, Comanches, and Apaches. Reporting for several eastern and midwestern newspapers, Lockley took copious notes while sitting in a folding chair. He was the only newspaperman in attendance, but more importantly, the council brought him into contact with a genuinely defiant tribe for the first time in his life and tested his humanitarian patience accordingly.

Through government treaties, the Kiowas had been confined to a reservation some sixty miles square. There, in time, Quaker agents hoped to turn them into peaceful farmers. Instead, the Kiowas and some of their Apache and

Comanche allies, used the reservation as a haven from which they might launch raids as far north as Kansas, west into Colorado and New Mexico, and south into Texas. In one recent raid, the Kiowas had attacked the Abel Lee family on their homestead in northwest Texas, killing the mother and father and a fourteen-year-old daughter outright in a bloody surprise attack and taking the three younger Abel children captive to hold for ransom. The council Lockley attended at old Fort Cobb was intended to negotiate an end to the raiding but instead became a vehicle primarily for securing return of the Lee children.[32]

Lockley observed that to have the care of such people as the Kiowas, as did Quaker Indian agents based out of Lawrence, Kansas, seemed "one of the most perplexing duties that can well be conceived." Indeed, "if the government would feed all who apply, and provide a country large enough for every vagrant to range over," the white race itself would make little progress. The solution seemed clear to Lockley. "To render the present Indian policy a success some method must be devised to set our red brothers to work."[33] But engaging Indians in "useful" activity, Lockley noted, was difficult. Work as whites defined it was alien to Indian nature, especially in the case of the Kiowas, a tribe accustomed to a raid-and-plunder style of life. The Kiowas probably would not raid any more that season, he wrote in late August, but "when the grass appears again the war fervor will burn in their veins, and they will be off on their forays 'by occult influence.'" And why shouldn't they? Such chiefs as White Horse, Big Bow, Son of the Sun, and Woman's Heart, "with a large share of their braggadocio warriors, can never be toned down to have their groceries doled out to them weekly, and receive lessons in agriculture from an agency farmer. It would be 'bad medicine.' Their untamed spirits would revolt at such humiliation, and their squaws would taunt them with their degradation."[34] Moreover, as commendable and deserving as was the Quakers' work, the Kiowas, with "their barbarous massacres of defenseless settlers in Texas and their daring raids on Government and private property," were outlaws and could no longer be endured. Still, it was cheaper to feed them than to fight them, and if promises of good behavior could be wrung from them perhaps their otherwise inevitable collision with the frontier military could be avoided. At any rate, "a due regard for humanity," Lockley wrote, "would dictate that one more effort should be put forth." This council would constitute that effort.[35]

Upon arriving at the council ground, Lockley found himself not only listening to the boasts and demands of a proud, defiant people, but rubbing elbows with them—literally. "The sensation is a curious one," he informed his readers, "to be elbowed at your meals by a crowd of savages whom you cannot talk to, and who, there is good reason to believe are meditating the removal of your scalp."[36] Indeed, they could talk matter-of-factly of their raids in Texas "with as complete self-possession as a merchant would talk of his late business operations."[37] Finding it all beyond forbearance, Lockley used Elizabeth as an outlet, writing more forthrightly than he otherwise did for the public prints of how he and the Quakers had welcomed White Horse, a particularly truculent Kiowa, "and his brother homicides" to camp with a hearty handshake. "I have been unable to restrain my disgust," he conceded.

> Twenty of their lousy chiefs are fed at our table, their intestinal organs being astonished with canned fruits, condensed milk, green vegetables and other delicacies. I cannot but feel that this hospitality extended to savages whose hands are red with the blood of our fellow citizens, and whose girdles are decorated with scalps torn from their heads, is somewhat fulsome. I want guarantees of future good behavior before welcoming them to my board.[38]

In this description, of course, Lockley betrays all the shortsightedness and bigotry toward racial difference characteristic of the age. Having just participated in a titanic civil war, he believed fervently in the imperatives of northern victory, which included molding a homogeneous nationalism. Determination to meld the West into the union of national interests left little room for tolerance of anomalous groups. Moreover, as a father of five children and a husband deeply in love with his wife, he could not dismiss images of the Lee family from his mind nor fully rationalize the feelings of outrage against brutality brought so close to home. To have done so might have made him more acceptable to late twentieth-century sensibilities, but it would have made him less human. And if anything, Lockley was human.

The council droned on for several days without tangible progress, and then broke up. The Kiowas, it seemed, would have to be taught a lesson. Still, the white man had certain responsibilities. "I admit that humanity should be consulted in dealing with these barbarians, as they have no moral law to guide them, and it is the duty of the strong to be not alone just, but merciful," Lockley wrote. "But does not my report of this fruitless peace mission show that these savages must be addressed through some other sense than their moral perceptions?" The peace commissioners had "talked Sunday school literature by the yard," but to no avail, and the blood of Kiowa victims "cries from the earth for revenge."[39] The council had been, as the Leavenworth *Commercial* headlined Lockley's summary report, "A Big Talk, A Big Eat, and nothing Accomplished."[40] The Kiowas had rejected the olive branch and chosen the sword. So be it. "Now let the government 'go for them,'" Lockley wrote. "Let troops enough be employed to make the work short, sharp, and decisive." Perhaps then, the Kiowas would admit to live "upon a smaller stretch of country than that inclosed [sic] between the Missouri and the Rio Grande."[41]

Lockley advocated progress, usefulness, Christian reform, and white cultural domination in all the definitions of those terms standard at the time. In short, he came down on the then politically correct side of every issue involving Native Americans. Although a western journalist, he was not an Indian-hater. Rather, he reflected the ambivalent views toward Indians held by most of white America. Unlike the stereotypical image of pioneer journalists, and perhaps unlike most real-life pioneer western editors, he advocated assimilationist policies in hopes they would benefit Indians and whites alike. Like the reformers who grew more vocal and influential a decade later, he had compassion for Indian peoples, and he hoped that racial accommodation might be achieved peacefully, although assuredly on the white man's terms. If it was necessary to punish resistant Indian tribes, as in the case of the Kiowas, that was an unfortunate necessity, but his hope remained that such a course would lead eventually to peace and assimilation.

However fair or discerning it proved to be, Lockley's work on Indian Territory became, like that of most journalists, as brief and fleeting as it was penetrating. In 1873, after four years in Kansas and less than two years of writing on the Indians, Lockley moved on to Utah. In Salt Lake City he found his greatest challenge, his greatest ambition, and perhaps his greatest failure. He would attack the Mormons relentlessly, driving the resolute faithful into ever stronger defenses and alienating others willing to compromise. As general of the Union armies during the Civil War, Ulysses S. Grant had demanded unconditional surrender and got it. Accommodation and compromise had not been part of the victory, and Lockley was determined they would not be in Mormon Utah. It proved a serious miscalculation.

With four other Kansas newspapermen, Lockley took control of the Salt Lake *Tribune* in summer 1873. Founded some years earlier by William S. Godbe and other Mormon schismatics in revolt against Brigham Young's non-intercourse economic policies, the *Tribune* had never made money. By mid-1873, the paper's financial situation was going from bad to worse, and Godbe, an otherwise successful Salt Lake City businessman and excommunicated Mormon, was willing to experiment with hiring newspaper experience from the outside.[42]

Lockley became chief editor of the *Tribune,* while his Kansas partners managed other facets of the paper, from business management, bookkeeping, and press and job shop to rustling advertising and circulation on the outside. As she had in Cleveland before moving to Leavenworth, Elizabeth remained behind for a few months before again packing up the children who now numbered five, and heading a thousand miles west to Utah. Not sorry to leave Leavenworth, meanwhile, Lockley embraced Salt Lake. "This city suits me," he wrote to Elizabeth shortly after arriving in mid-August. "We all think there is an excellent prospect before us," he added, "if the stud doesn't starve before the grass grows."[43]

Lockley and his associates from Kansas elected to follow a middle course, hoping to offend few and attract support from all quarters.[44] Lockley obliged by proceeding slowly at first, although he scarcely suppressed his true sentiments. To Lockley, Mormonism was mental slavery and despotism; a way of life that ran counter to the fundamental values he had fought for in the Civil War. Avoiding direct confrontation as best he could, he nevertheless wasted little time agitating for change. "A plurality of wives is unsuited to the spirit of the age," he wrote cautiously in an early editorial. "Elder [Parley] Pratt attaches great weight to the Bible as an authority [for polygamy], but he cannot hold up that sacred volume and resist the progress of the age." Southern slaveholders "thought they had just as sure a thing with the Bible," he added, but the Civil War had proven them wrong. "Retain polygamy, want of free schools, seclusion and opposition to progress, and has Mormonism any ghost of a chance to win the race?"[45]

Throughout his career, Lockley took a special interest in education, something he felt denied when young himself, and in Salt Lake City he took offense at Mormon reluctance to foster it. To Elizabeth, still in Leavenworth with the children, he wrote: "I am raising quite an excitement here about establishing free schools."[46] In his own mind, and that of his partners, the ultimate goal was clear: champion free thought and republican political institutions; become a voice for Gentiles and dissatisfied Mormons alike; and await the federal legislation needed to break the power of the church. "Their kingdom is passing from them," Frederic wrote of the Mormon leaders to Elizabeth. "We fully expect legislation in Congress this next session that will correct political evils and with that much done we are willing to let polygamy and revelation die out of inanition."[47]

An uneasy honeymoon between the church and the *Tribune's* new editor lasted until mid-September, then blew apart entirely with Lockley's expulsion from a Salt Lake City Council meeting. In exposing the close inter-working of public and private interests when a city councilman bungled the contract for a gas works, Lockley had gone too far. To the Mormons, the councilman's efforts constituted communitarianism, and the council's subsequent actions were intended to protect his good intentions from derision. To Lockley and Utah's growing Gentile population, the blunder was indicative of theocratic corruption and incompetence. The church hierarchy, well-represented on the city council, sought to silence the *Tribune's* impertinence by summarily upbraiding Lockley in open meeting. City Councilman Joseph F. Smith pronounced Lockley "a thief, a liar and an unknown person," and the council banished him from all future meetings.[48]

Excluding the *Tribune* reporter, of course, had an effect quite the opposite of what the city council had intended. "This gigantic infamy—this crushing despotism—this twin relic of barbarism," Lockley seethed in a letter to Elizabeth, "is doomed to destruction." With the titanic struggles of the Civil War fresh in his mind, he added: "The TRIBUNE has opened its batteries, and is now giving forth no uncertain sound." The state of society in Utah, he wrote in the *Tribune,* "is abnormal. It must be restored to health. . . . On one side are free speech, the solemn guarantees of the Constitution, advancement and Christian charity; on the other side, bigotry, fraud, rancor and delusion." The Mormons had made a mistake, he declared self-righteously to Elizabeth, "and I think I can be an instrument in hastening their doom."[49]

Lockley filled *Tribune* columns with vehement attacks on Mormon tyranny. News of Utah's blatant violation of the first amendment, one of the few things sacred to all newspaper journalists, swept east and west like a wave, depositing itself in the form of indignation in newspapers across the country. The *Tribune* happily displayed long columns of excerpts from what other papers said.[50]

Not since the Civil War had Lockley felt so justified in headlong pursuit of a cause, and he reveled in it. "These Mormon officials," he wrote to Elizabeth, "who are elected by the church and owe no accountability to the people are a terrible affliction. We are devoted to rooting them out."[51] He worked furiously, often fourteen and sixteen hours a day. Then, as he said, "too full of fight for repose," he would arise during the night to commit still more editorial ammunition to paper.[52] He worked to bring change to benighted Utah, but his real goal was to undermine Mormon exclusiveness and secure Gentile access to economic decision-making and political power. Enthusiastically pursuing what he perceived as destiny, he wrote to Elizabeth:

> People tell me [the *Tribune*] is the only voice that is raised for them—their only bulwark against injustice and oppression. This is an immense stimulus and I never felt such vigor before . . . I go savagely for the whole Mormon outfit—from the Prophet in his harem down to Jeter Clinton on the police bench.[53]

A few days later, he added, "I never enjoyed so much happiness."[54]

Plunging headlong into vigorous partisan journalism, Lockley, in addition

to free schools, championed all Christian faiths, boomed mineral development, and encouraged Gentile immigration to Utah to dilute Mormon political power. As he had in Indian Territory, Lockley saw himself as an agent for
Americanization of the West, an instrument by which exclusiveness might be
transformed into nationalism, and difference—whether racial, religious, social,
or cultural—obliterated by homogeneity. The driving force was to open all
alien lands to the vision, values, and purposes that had emerged triumphant
with Northern victory during the Civil War. He denounced polygamy and
called for strict enforcement of federal laws; he indicted the Mormon Church
for treason and corruption of the republican political system; and he agitated
constantly for change. As with Indian Territory, Utah needed to throw off
backwardness and ignorance and join the rest of the country in creating a more
perfect nation—for the good of the majority.

For seven years Lockley stormed the ramparts of Mormondom but with
little visible effect, and by 1880 he had grown tired of the fight. The Gentile
cause in Utah met with greater success in the 1880s as federal power and
coercion overwhelmed Mormon resistance and ultimately forced fundamental
changes. But Lockley was elsewhere by then and did not share in any sense of
victory. Rather, he had been a significant player in the test of wills during the
1870s, when the outcome was not at all foregone. When the time came, he was
happy to leave Utah behind. With knowing biblical allusion, he wrote to Elizabeth from Salt Lake City: "The knowledge that in a few short months I am
going to shake the dust of Mormonism off my sandals makes me the happiest
man the sun shines upon." Cashing in his share of the *Tribune* partnership, he
took his family to southeastern Washington and bought a farm.[55]

Lockley had poured himself into bringing what he saw as progress and
enlightenment to Utah. Whether he succeeded or failed is a matter of conjec-
ture. Gentile editors like Lockley undeniably contributed to mounting federal
resolve to break the political power of the Mormon Church and end polygamy.
In addition, *Tribune* financial records show that Lockley and his partners made
the paper an economic as well as a political power in the land. By 1880, the
paper was a substantial business property, its survival in the uncertain world of
western newspaper journalism relatively well secured. Yet the political and
social change Lockley had worked so hard to bring about largely escaped him,
as did most of the *Tribune's* greatness, which came later, and he could hardly
think his aspirations fulfilled.[56]

Despite their having settled comfortably into a rustic life and Elizabeth's
contentment there, Lockley remained on his farm in Walla Walla less than a
year. The call "to resume the pen redactorial," as he said, was too great.[57] He
became chief editor of the *Inter Mountain,* a newly established Republican

daily in Butte, Montana. Lockley and his family, who followed him yet again to another western newspaper opportunity, were in Butte for four years, during the city's heyday as a silver mining center. While there, he advocated community betterment through civic improvements, temperance, and anti-gambling laws, and he fostered support for schools and churches. Ultimately, he ran afoul of the paper's owners, however, some of whom were silver mining barons, by writing editorials supporting the gold standard. He was anti-silver because he perceived currency inflation as intellectual dishonesty, rewarding the few and bilking the many. Lee Mantle, a heavy investor in silver interests and the paper's chief owner, tried to dissuade him but to no avail. "He was a very scholarly gentleman," Mantle wrote of Lockley years later. "We could not induce him to write editorials favoring the free coinage of silver. He didn't believe in it and he insisted on writing what he did believe—hence the separation."[58] Lockley himself observed: "I found myself out of harmony with my surroundings."[59] His insistence on writing only what he believed was consistent with most everything he did as a journalist, but increasingly he perceived issues of public policy in moralistic terms, and sooner or later resolute moralism was bound to clash with popular consensus, the bedrock of community journalism.

It did just that in Lockley's next newspaper venture. From Butte, Lockley pursued opportunity to Arkansas City, a Kansas border town poised on the advent of the great Oklahoma land rushes. This time, family connections influenced his choice of destination. J. H. Sherburne, a successful trader to the Ponca Indians who had married one of Frederic's three older daughters, provided him with a $3,500 loan to purchase the Arkansas City *Traveler,* one of three local papers. Even today, Arkansas City touts itself as the "Gateway to the Cherokee Strip." For Frederic Lockley, however, the *Traveler* was gateway to yet another major disappointment.[60]

Chief editor of two major western newspapers, contributor to national and regional magazines, and correspondent to the New York *World,* New York *Times,* and Chicago *Times,* Lockley would now become sole proprietor of his own paper. At sixty-one years old his editorial abilities were well-honed, but he was unprepared for becoming a merchant of news in a small town with two other newspapers besides his own.[61] "I am going through a strange experience here," he wrote to Elizabeth in a letter that summarizes well his philosophy and his downfall in western newspapering.

[T]wice I have seriously thought I should have to give up. . . . During my long connection with journalism I have always prided myself that I was away from counting room influences. I felt myself in a humble way to be a public teacher; a sound and moral newspaper press I thought had much to do with our national life. Therefore I read and reflected and felt pride that no line I ever wrote was dictated by mercenary motives. When I took hold here I was aware that I was deficient in business qualifications; but I thought to win favor by putting a modicum of brains into the paper, and to enjoy a revenue that would support a man on the outside. In this sweet delusion I labored three months or more, reading my exchanges diligently, condensing news from all sources, and writing editorials with care and circumspection.

This kept me most of my time in my chair, and I now find that all this virtuous care was labor thrown away. People here do not support a paper because it contains good original matter; they want little local squibs telling who comes and goes and booming the town on all occasions; for any other matter the scissors are held in equal esteem with the pen. . . . Some will say a newspaper established fifteen years has gained a standing and a prestige that will carry it thro' the worst struggle. These people ought to come to Arkansas City and see how it is with the *Traveler*.[62]

The business side of journalism had always confounded Lockley, but he would muddle through, and he was well-equipped to compose "little local squibs" if he had to. Besides, Lockley was a fighter. Overcoming his initial despair, he remained at the *Traveler*. In his second year, however, he became aware of what he termed collusion between city officials and the town's saloon owners. His moral outrage spilled over into print and precipitated a war, not only between himself and his newspaper rivals, but between community factions as well. He succeeded in stirring a hornets' nest of class antagonisms and in the end frightened into silence those from whom he drew his support. As newspaper editors are sometimes wont to do, Lockley staked his reputation on turning the rascals out at the next election. The rascals stayed in office, however, and Lockley sold his interests not long after the ballots were counted, repaid his son-in-law, and moved with Elizabeth to Salem, Oregon, where he helped found the *Capital Journal* but soon retired.[63]

Some years later, at his son's urging, he wrote a lengthy reminiscence of his life and titled it "The Memoirs of an Unsuccessful Man." He was not wholly unsuccessful, of course. As an agent of change, Lockley could hardly expect the results of his labors to be immediate. Moreover, he did not stay in one place long enough to see the impact of his work take hold. But success or failure hardly holds the key to Lockley's historical significance. Rather, his experience as a western newspaperman is important for showing the mix and complexity of pursuing a professional career amid the rapid transformation of the nation, the western region, and the journalism profession in the late nineteenth century.[64]

If examining real lives like that of Frederic Lockley can expose oversimplified characterizations for what they are, so too can such lives help us avoid the temptation to erect new stereotypes. Just as journalists portrayed themselves as agents of civilization and all that was good with coming of the Anglo frontier to the trans-Mississippi West, few figures fit the role of agent of conquest as well as the frontier newspaperman. On the one hand, the frontier journalist, it has been said, created community identity, stability, permanency, law and order, and economic development by focusing public opinion on an agenda of issues that mattered to the community. His newspaper acted on behalf of "the people," established democratic values, served as a public forum for political argument, provided direction and vision to community growth and progress and in so doing, helped transform a supposed wilderness into a proud, upright society.[65]

On the other hand, the frontier journalist could easily be cast as the spokesman for all the false values and corrupt ethics Anglo society brought to the regional West. Capable of being a money-grubbing liar and hypocrite, he defended a morally bankrupt political system. His reckless, sometimes duplicitous intentions made his rhetoric and the value of the information he distributed questionable at best. At the very least, he encouraged values that led to environmental devastation, racism, and ethnic hatreds. What he advocated was not the choicest fruits of western culture but the material interests of the middle class. Often bigoted in his relations with groups distinguished by race, class, and gender, the pioneer newspaperman lacked real influence. He preached to the converted and mirrored, rather than led, the opinion of that part of the public with whom he identified.[66]

Somewhere between these two extremes, of course, lies the truth. From the knowing perspective of the late twentieth century, skewed as even it is by our own predilections, it would seem safest to say that the frontier journalist was all these things—at one time or another—and none of them all the time. Moreover, it seems unfair to withdraw completely our benefit of the doubt for such men as Frederic Lockley. Tracking his career as it arced across the late nineteenth-century West one discovers a complex individual whose concerns for his profession echo a number of modern-day questions—about ethics, objectivity, and passion for a cause; about the role of the individual in an increasingly integrated enterprise; and about what exactly constitutes success and failure. One also finds a journalist who was more interested in the intellectual challenge of his work than in the money he could make from it and who dared hold ideals above contrary community opinion. Both characteristics led him to frustration and disillusionment.

Within the limitations of his generation's intellectual constructs, which took as givens a sense of racial superiority, male domination in the public sectors of life, and thoroughgoing belief that all change represented progress along a linear path to the millennium, within these limitations, men like Frederic Lockley were nonetheless sincere in their inquiries, genuine in their sympathies, and honest in their resolve, however misguided they proved to be. Just like people in any given time and place, they had their own hopes, fears, dreams, flaws, and failures. They will never be consummate heroes in white hats, but they do command a degree of admiration. And they certainly merit understanding, for they remind us of the complexity—rather than the simplicity—of the past.

NOTES

1. See for example, Lucius Beebe, *Comstock Commotion; The Story of the Territorial Enterprise* (Stanford: Stanford University Press, 1954); Robert F. Karolevitz, *Newspapering in the Old West* (Seattle: Superior Publishing Company, 1965); James McEnteer, *Fighting Words: Independent Journalists in Texas* (Austin: University of Texas Press, 1992); John Myers Myers, *Print in a Wild Land* (Garden City, New York: Doubleday & Company, 1967); and JoAnn Schmitt, *Fighting Editors: The Story of Editors Who Faced Sixshooters with Pens and Won* (San Antonio: Naylor Company, 1958). Not all western journalists or newspaper editors were men, of course, as Sherilyn Cox Bennion demonstrated in *Equal to the Occasion; Women Editors of the Nineteenth-Century West* (Reno: University of Nevada Press, 1990), but among stereotypes of western journalists, women figure rarely if at all.

2. Earl Pomeroy, *The Pacific Slope* (New York: Alfred A. Knopf, 1965), 155.

3. T. A. Larson, "Laramie's Bill Nye," *Denver Westerners 1952 Brand Book* (Denver: Arthur Zeuch Printing, 1953), 41–42; Charles Neider, ed., *The Complete Humorous Sketches and Tales of Mark Twain* (Garden City, New York: Doubleday & Company, 1961), 718–20; Paul Fatout, *Mark Twain in Virginia City* (Bloomington: University of Indiana Press, 1964), 99–111.

4. On Legh Freeman, see Thomas H. Heuterman, *Moveable Type; Biography of Legh R. Freeman* (Ames: Iowa State University Press, 1979). The raciest and still best source on Frederick Gilmer Bonfils and Harry Heye Tammen, is Gene Fowler, *Timber Line; A Story of Bonfils and Tammen* (New York: Covici and Friede, 1933); but see also Bill Hosokawa, *Thunder in the Rockies; The Incredible Denver Post* (New York: William Morrow & Co., 1976), 15–166; and, in novel form, Lewis Graham *The Great I Am* (New York: Macaulay Company, 1933). On Henry Morton Stanley, John F. Finerty, and D. Be Randolph Keim in the West, see Oliver Knight, *Following the Indian Wars* (Norman: University of Oklahoma Press, 1960). On Finerty, see also Oliver Knight, "Introduction," in *War-Path and Bivouac*

(Norman: University of Oklahoma Press, 1961), vii-xvi. On Keim, see also Paul Andrew Hutton, "Foreword," in *Sheridan's Troopers on the Borders* (Lincoln: University of Nebraska Press, 1985), v-xvi. On Richard Harding Davis, see Fairfax M. Downey, *Richard Harding Davis: His Day* (New York: Scribner's Sons, 1933).

5. Robert G. Athearn, *The Coloradans* (Albuquerque: University of New Mexico Press, 1976), 169. On William Allen White, see *The Autobiography of William Allen White* (New York: Macmillan Company, 1946); and, most recently, Sally Foreman Griffith, *Home Town News; William Allen White & the Emporia Gazette* (Baltimore: The Johns Hopkins University Press, 1989). On Ed Howe, see Calder M. Pickett, *Ed Howe: Country Town Philosopher* (Lawrence: University Press of Kansas, 1968).

6. Robert V. Hine, *The American West; An Interpretive History*, 2d ed. (Boston: Little, Brown and Company, 1984), 270.

7. Karolevitz, *Newspapering in the Old West*, 1.

8. Lewis Atherton, *Main Street on the Middle Border* (Bloomington: Indiana University Press, 1984), 166.

9. *The Man Who Shot Liberty Valance* (Paramount, 1962); *Cheyenne Autumn* (Warner Bros., Inc., 1964); *Unforgiven* (Warner Bros., Inc., 1992); *The Grey Fox* (1988). Richard Slotkin has added a third category of caricature, at once an inversion and a depersonalization of the colorful rogue or staid, small-town businessman editor. To Slotkin, the New York newspaper publishers of the age symbolized American journalism. Such men, who wielded national influence through their papers' huge circulations, prestige, and domination of the wire services, were members of the industrial, monied elite, rather than representatives of the middle class. According to Slotkin, they pursued "corporatism" and "paternalistic coercion" to bring such unruly minorities as Indians, Southern blacks, and the urban working class into line with their paternalistic expectations. The editors and reporters who worked for such men, some of whom traveled west to cover the frontier, rather than likeable scamps, humorists, or Don Quixotes in printer's aprons, were unthinking pawns with little or no conscience, men who interpreted events through the same "cultural grid" as their employers. Rather than scions of democracy and free will, they were instruments of the persuasion necessary to enforce the deadly imperatives of what Alexis de Tocqueville described as the tyranny of the majority. Richard Slotkin, *The Fatal Environment* (New York: Atheneum, 1985). This argument ranges throughout the book, but see especially pp. 331–38.

10. The best territorial histories for the regional West are Porter A. Stratton, *The Territorial Press of New Mexico, 1834–1912* (Albuquerque: University of New Mexico Press, 1969); William H. Lyon, *The Pioneer Editor in Missouri, 1808–1860* (Columbia: University of Missouri Press, 1965); and William H. Lyon, *Those Old Yellow Dog Days; Frontier Journalism in Arizona, 1859–1912* (Tucson: Arizona Historical Society Press, 1994).

11. On newspapers as business enterprises, see Barbara Cloud, *The Business of Newspapers on the Western Frontier* (Reno: University of Nevada Press, 1992); and David Fridtjof Halaas, *Boom Town Newspapers; Journalism on the Rocky Mountain Mining Frontier, 1859–1881* (Albuquerque: University of New Mexico Press, 1981).

12. Heuterman, *Moveable Type* is an exception. Another exception would seem to be Walter Van Tilburg Clark, ed., *The Journals of Alf Doten* (3 vols., Reno: University of Nevada

Press, 1973), but for their bulk, Alf Doten's journals offer little introspection and social commentary.

13. See for example: Hubert Howe Bancroft, *History of Nevada, Colorado, and Wyoming* (San Francisco: Bancroft, 1890), 169–70, 305–8, 551, 527–32, 732, 735, 798–99; Hubert Howe Bancroft, *History of Utah* (San Francisco: Bancroft, 1890), 89, 92, 104, 115, 325–26, 715–19; Hubert Howe Bancroft, *History of Washington, Montana, and Idaho* (San Francisco: Bancroft, 1890), 377–80, 420–21, 438, 447, 471–72, 652–53, 678, 779.

14. Frederic E. Lockley Memoirs (hereafter FEL Memoirs), Frederic E. Lockley Collection, Huntington Library, San Marino, California (hereafter Lockley Papers). See also Charles E. Rankin, "Sweet Delusion: The Life and Times of Frederic E. Lockley, Western Journalist" (doctoral dissertation: University of New Mexico, Albuquerque, 1994).

15. FEL Memoirs, Box 1, ibid.

16. References on the transformation of American journalism in the nineteenth century are voluminous, but for an introduction, see Gerald J. Baldasty, *The Commercialization of News in the Nineteenth Century* (Madison: University of Wisconsin Press, 1992); Hazel Dicken-Garcia, *Journalistic Standards in Nineteenth-Century America* (Madison: University of Wisconsin Press, 1989); and Frank Luther Mott, *American Journalism,* 3d ed. (New York: Macmillan Company, 1962), 167–612.

17. Elizabeth Metcalf Lockley was born on May 29, 1843, the daughter of a tinware manufacturer. After her mother died when she was eight, she boarded around with relatives until going to live with her grandmother and an aunt in Schuylerville, New York, where Frederic Lockley met her while selling books. They were married on February 28, 1861, and had three children: Maud in 1868; Fred in 1871; and Daisy in 1875. Two later children died in infancy. Elizabeth Lockley died on October 25, 1929. Elizabeth was Frederic's second wife. His first wife, Agnes Jeannette Hill, whom he married in 1852, died on March 4, 1860. They had three children: Josephine in 1853; Louis in 1855; and Gertrude in 1857.

18. On whether newspapering as a frontier institution was an agent of social change or a defender of the status quo, see William H. Lyon, "The Significance of Newspapers on the Frontier," *Journal of the West,* 19 (April 1980), 3–13; and Oliver Knight, "The Frontier Newspaper as a Catalyst in Social Change," *Pacific Northwest Quarterly,* 58 (April 1967), 74–81. See also Robert L. Housman, "The End of Frontier Journalism in Montana," *Journalism Quarterly,* 12 (June 1935), 133–45; Pomeroy, *Pacific Slope,* 155–58.

19. Frederic Lockley to Elizabeth Lockley, August 24, September 3, 1865, Folder [6], Box 3, Lockley Papers.

20. FEL Memoirs, ibid.

21. Ibid. Frederic Lockley also wrote of the *Evening News* in "A Western Newspaper Enterprise," *Lippincott's,* 40 (April 1871), 389–99.

22. FEL Memoirs, ibid.; "A Western Newspaper Enterprise," 392, 394, 397–98.

23. E. W. Scripps founded the Cleveland *Penny Press* in November 1878, establishing the basis for the first modern newspaper chain. See Gilson Gardner, *Lusty Scripps: The Life of E. W. Scripps* (New York: Vangaurd Press, 1932), 66; Osman Castle Hooper, *History of Ohio Journalism, 1793–1933* (Columbus, Ohio: Spahr & Glenn Company, 1933), 105; Charles F.

Kennedy, *Fifty Years of Cleveland, 1875–1925* (Cleveland: Weidenthal Company, 1925), 19; Dennie Hall, "Edward Willis Scripps," in Joseph P. McKerns, *Biographical Dictionary of American Journalism* (Westport, Conn.: Greenwood Press, 1989), 634–36; *Dictionary of American Biography*, 16:517–18; Frank Luther Mott, *American Journalism*, 3d ed. (New York: Macmillan, 1962), 461–62, 551–54; and Archer H. Shaw, *The Plain Dealer: One Hundred Years in Cleveland* (New York: Alfred A. Knopf, 1942), 221–30.

24. Frederic Lockley to Elizabeth Lockley, September 12, 1869, Folder 15, Box 6, Lockley Papers.

25. The Five Civilized Tribes were the Cherokees, Creeks, Choctaw, Chickasaw, and Seminole.

26. Chicago *Times,* November 21, 1872.

27. Frederic Lockley to Elizabeth Lockley, November 7, 1872, Folder 17, Box 6, Lockley Papers.

28. Chicago *Times,* December 7, 1872.

29. Ibid., January 16, 1873.

30. Ibid., November 18, 1872.

31. Ibid., December 9, 1872.

32. On the Kiowas, see Mildred P. Mayhall, *The Kiowas,* 2nd ed. (Norman: University of Oklahoma Press, 1962); W. W. Newcomb, Jr., *The Indians of Texas: From Prehistoric to Modern Times* (Austin: University of Texas Press, 1961); Hugh D. Corwin, *The Kiowa Indians: Their History and Life Stories* (Lawton, Okla.: Hugh D. Corwin, 1958); and Wilbur Sturtevant Nye, *Bad Medicine & Good; Tales of the Kiowas* (Norman: University of Oklahoma Press, 1962). On the Abel Lee family episode, see W. S. Nye, *Carbine and Lance; The Story of Old Fort Sill* (Norman: University of Oklahoma Press, 1937), 153–54.

33. New York *World,* August 24, 1872.

34. Chicago *Times,* August 31, 1872.

35. New York *World,* August 17, 1872.

36. Ibid., August 29, 1872.

37. Chicago *Times,* August 27, 1872.

38. Frederic Lockley to Elizabeth Lockley, August 2, 1872, Folder 17, Box 6, Lockley Papers.

39. Chicago *Times,* August 29, 1872.

40. Leavenworth *Commercial,* August 27, 1872.

41. Chicago *Times,* August 29, 1872.

42. The other Kansans were George F. Prescott, A. N. Hamilton, William Taylor, and James R. Schupbach, all of Leavenworth. A sixth partner, George W. Reed, had been bookkeeper with the William S. Godbe owners and, when Godbe sold the *Tribune* to the Kansas newspapermen in November 1873, he stayed on and became a full partner. On the change of ownership see FEL Memoirs, Box 1, Lockley Papers; George F. Prescott to Frederic Lockley, July 26, 1873, MSS A809, Utah State Historical Society, Salt Lake City; George W. Reed Papers, Manuscript Collection 184, Marriott Special Collections, University of Utah (hereafter Reed Papers); J. Cecil Alter, *Early Utah Journalism* (Salt Lake City: Utah State

Historical Society, 1938), 354–55; O. N. Malmquist, *The First 100 Years; A History of the Salt Lake Tribune, 1871–1971* (Salt Lake City: Utah State Historical Society, 1971), 31–43; and Edward W. Tullidge, *History of Salt Lake City* (Salt Lake City: Star Printing Company, 1886), appendix, 13.

43. Frederic Lockley to Elizabeth Lockley, August 17, 31, 1873, Folder 18, Box 6, Lockley Papers.

44. FEL Memoirs, Box 1, Frederic Lockley to Elizabeth Lockley, September 14, October 26, 1873, Folder 18, Box 6, ibid.

45. Salt Lake *Tribune,* September 2, 1873.

46. Frederic Lockley to Elizabeth Lockley, September 4, 1873, Folder 18, Box 6, Lockley Papers.

47. Ibid., September 14, 28, 1873.

48. Salt Lake *Tribune,* September 10, 1873.

49. Frederic Lockley to Elizabeth Lockley, September 14, 1873, Folder 18, Box 6, Lockley Papers.

50. See, for example, Salt Lake *Tribune,* September 10, 13, 18, 23, October 3, and November 9, 15, 1873.

51. Frederic Lockley to Elizabeth Lockley, September 22, 1873, Folder 18, Box 6, Lockley Papers.

52. Ibid., October 19, 1873, FEL Memoirs, Box 1, ibid.

53. Frederic Lockley to Elizabeth Lockley, September 17, 1873, Folder 18, Box 6, ibid.

54. Ibid., September 22, 1873, ibid.

55. Ibid., April 28, 1880, Folder 20, Box 6, ibid.

56. See account books, Reed Papers.

57. Frederic Lockley to Fred Lockley, Jr., June 26, 1904, Folder 23, Box 6, Lockley Papers.

58. Interview of Lee Mantle in Butte *Daily Post,* January 4, 1913.

59. Frederic Lockley to Fred Lockley, Jr., March 6, 1903, Folder 23, Box 6, Lockley Papers.

60. Ibid.

61. Frederic Lockley had contributed to *Lippincott's, The Overland Monthly,* and *Kansas Magazine* in the 1870s. The other two Arkansas City papers were the *Democrat* and the *Republican.*

62. Frederic Lockley to Elizabeth Lockley, July 26, 1885, Folder 22, Box 6, Lockley Papers. See also, Frederic Lockley to Fred Lockley, Jr., August 30, 1902, March 6, July 29, 1903, Folder 23, Box 6, ibid.

63. The *Republican* merged with the *Traveler* in April 1887 following the city council election. R. C. Howard became editor-proprietor, and Lockley contributing editor. Lockley left the paper four months later.

64. Frederic Lockley to Fred Lockley, Jr., June 20, 1903, Folder 23, 1903, Lockley Papers.

65. Robert G. Athearn summarizes well the view of the pioneer editor as community builder in *The Coloradans,* 169–70.

66. Conquest is a term made familiar by Patricia Nelson Limerick in *Legacy of Conquest; The Unbroken Past of the American West* (New York: W. W. Norton & Company, 1987). For a

more sustained discussion of newspaper journalism, see Patricia Nelson Limerick, "Making the Most of Words: Verbal Activity and Western America," in *Under an Open Sky; Rethinking America's Western Past,* ed. William Cronon, George Miles, and Jay Gitlin (New York: W. W. Norton & Company), 178–80. See also William G. Robbins, "Some Perspectives On Law and Order In Frontier Newspapers," *Journal of the West,* 17 (January 1978), 53–62; and Slotkin, *Fatal Environment,* 168–76, 333–38, 466–76.

CHAPTER FIVE

FEDERALISM AND THE AMERICAN WEST, 1900–1940

DONALD J. PISANI

Western historians have long recognized the importance of the national government in the region's economic life,[1] but few have considered how the nature and structure of the American state have influenced the region's history. Donald Worster and Richard White are notable exceptions. "The West, more than any other American region," Worster maintains, "was built by state power, state expertise, state technology, and state bureaucracy." There, the marriage between government bureaucracy and private capital blurred the boundaries between public and private realms of power. The central government assumed new form as it "took firm charge of the western rivers, furnishing the capital and engineering expertise to lift the region to a higher plateau of development." The construction of dams and canals, and the allocation of water, contributed to the growth and proliferation of elites in and out of government. In Worster's provocative 1985 book, *Rivers of Empire*, state governments, water districts, and local water users all complement the water bureaucracy in Washington and collectively constitute what he calls "Leviathan." Government appears as a seamless web, as one unitary system in which power is highly concentrated but pervades every town and river valley. Westerners were defenseless against this juggernaut, "a big bruiser of a state" that ultimately served as an "agency for conquest," subverting democratic values and undermining the common good. In Worster's analysis, the parts matter far less than the whole: all institutions of government, local and national, were and are slaves to the imperatives of capitalism.[2]

In *"It's Your Misfortune and None of My Own,"* Richard White provides a strikingly original interpretation of government in the West. In the East,

83

White argues, "strong local communities and local economies preceded the creation of a national government and national economy, but the West is a child of a strong national government, and its economy can only be understood as a product of the larger national economy." "Federal power could expand so rapidly in the West," White adds, "because rival sources of political power in the [western] states, local communities, and political parties were so weak. Local communities and local politics inhibited the growth of administrative power in the East. But in the West existing local communities were Indian and Hispanic, and they were conquered peoples."[3]

The nineteenth-century West was united by more than its reliance on extractive industries. From the beginning, westerners depended on Washington for territorial governments, roads, railroads, and military protection—in the 1850s over 90 percent of the U.S. Army was stationed in western posts.[4] Therefore, the most "backward" part of the nation served as "the kindergarten of the modern American state." Government led rather than followed, and the West contributed to the growth of the civil service, army, and regulatory agencies (particularly in the realm of natural resources). The "basic bureaucracies of the nineteenth-century American state—the Bureau of Indian Affairs, the Land Office, the U.S. Geological Survey, and other Interior Department agencies— were primarily western bureaucracies." In the twentieth century, patronage gave way to professionalization and administrative centralization, and these institutions took on new life. Like Worster, White argues that private and public institutions were Siamese twins that grew up together.[5]

White's thesis reminds us that the federal government has been deeply involved in the life of the West since the beginning of Euro-American settlement—as an active partner in economic development. Nevertheless, neither Worster nor White carefully defines such slippery words as "centralization," "bureaucratization," and the "capitalist state," and both suggest that the flow of power in the twentieth century has been one way: toward Washington. State and local governments are almost invisible in their books.[6] Unquestionably, culture, markets, and many other aspects of American life have been "nationalized" during the last century, but within the United States power remains widely dispersed and highly resistant to absorption by the center. Congress and rivalries within and among the federal bureaucracies have *limited* national authority, and the states have played and continue to play just as important a role in the lives of westerners as the central government. Western historians need to look much more closely at how power is distributed within the American state. The expansion of federal and state power often went hand-in-hand. This essay looks at the impact of federalism on the West during the early decades of the twentieth century. It focuses on the U.S. Forest Service and the emergence of cooperative programs administered by the Department of Agriculture, programs that contributed to a dramatic expansion in the power and responsibilities of the western states.

"Federalism" is a hard word to define. It is at once a multitiered structural system, a division of powers, a bulwark of home rule and localism, and a political culture that assigns great power to the individual. The federal system was not created out of whole cloth. It owed as much to covenant theology (which emphasized the contractual nature of government), the structure of the British Empire, and the Articles of Confederation, as to the Constitution.[7] That document rested on the novel assumption that sovereignty ultimately resided with the people, not the state; hence it could be divided, or at least shared, between two levels of government. The resulting political system was not so much decentralized as non-centralized. In ordinary times, there was no way to concentrate power without violating both the spirit and letter of the Constitution.[8]

History counted for as much as the wisdom of the framers in explaining why American federalism flourished. Theda Skocpol, a political scientist, has observed that "the United States did *not* inherit a centralized bureaucratic state from preindustrial and predemocratic times," as did European nations. It lacked a landed aristocracy, a civil service, a military caste, an established state church, and an intelligentsia. Thus, there was no particular group born to lead. The absence of a well-defined "ruling class," and the sheer size of the nation, inhibited the growth of centralized power.[9]

Spared powerful neighbors, the United States avoided the chronic warfare that played such a large part in the emergence of the nation-state in Europe. Therefore, it did not need to raise large sums of money to support a military establishment, and it had little need for military castes or elites. The federal "system" was well suited to a very large nation in which inadequate transportation and communications contributed to the formation of many centers of power. Moreover, it protected liberty by keeping government close to the people; it allowed laws to be tailored to local needs (as with prohibition legislation prior to 1920); it made government more manageable—if not more efficient—by spreading the workload; it contributed to community spirit; it encouraged the formation of voluntary organizations devoted to influencing public policy; it increased the number of "pressure points" local interests could utilize to influence public policy; it maximized the chances for people to participate in government; it limited public criticism of the central government by transferring the resolution of many conflicts to the states; and it permitted each state to experiment in its statutes, taxation, and administrative structure.

American federalism was ideally suited to a nation with many different ethnic groups and religions. Of course, the system also had plenty of weaknesses. In dispersing power, it undermined responsibility and stymied planning. As Samuel Beer has noted, "It was not so much the slavery issue that disintegrated the nation; but the disintegrated condition of the nation, especially its political class, that made it impossible to cope with the slavery issue."[10]

It is tempting to argue, but hard to prove, that the central government's influence in the West increased dramatically during the Progressive Era. Richard White, like most western and environmental historians, thinks that a critical structural change occurred when policies to preserve and conserve the public domain began to take precedence over the older disposal policies. "Progressive Era natural resource agencies, including the Reclamation Bureau, Forest Service, and Park Service, eventually dwarfed the older bureaucracies that represented the initial federal presence in the West: the Bureau of Indian Affairs, the U.S. Geological Survey, and the General Land Office (which finally disappeared entirely)." These were bureaucracies "professionally staffed and centrally controlled." They were less responsive to local pressures and less democratic because "bureaucrats who made critical decisions on the use of public resources did so without any direct supervision by the people or their elected representatives." The commitment to manage western lands reflected the emergence of the "managerial state." Until the late nineteenth century, westerners "could treat the looming federal presence as temporary," but now "bureaucracies, national in origin and inspiration, often acted beyond western control." The central government "ceased to be a nursemaid to the future states and a prodigal distributor of resources to the country's citizens and corporations. Washington instead became a manager of western land, resources, and, inevitably, people." The significance is vast because these bureaucracies, and the alliances they formed with private business, came to define the modern American state.[11]

White does not define the characteristics of the bureaucratic state, but a few features are obvious. Modern government bureaucracies consist of professionally trained employees selected through a civil service or merit system—a process that supposedly reduces patronage and corruption, increases specialization, and insures staff continuity. These institutions classify positions and standardize salaries in the interests of efficiency, morale, and accountability. They centralize the purchasing of supplies and materials and streamline office procedures. They develop a sense of autonomy and *esprit de corps*—they are not simply the handmaidens of Congress or the President. They make judgments based on "the facts" rather than for the sake of political expediency. Given their

desire for independence, these agencies often publicize their activities to ma-
nipulate public opinion and develop a unique, dedicated "constituency."

Of course, these characteristics conform to textbook bureaucracies, not to
real institutions of government. To test White's hypothesis that national power
was centralized and concentrated during the early decades of the twentieth
century, we must look at the agencies themselves. Many historians, including
Samuel P. Hays, have argued that conservation policies contributed to bureaucratization and modernization. Therefore, it is useful to look at the U.S. Forest
Service as a case study.[12]

Of the new agencies created during the Progressive Era, none was more
important than the Forest Service. The national forests were created by politicians and foresters who assumed that state regulation of markets would prevent
the monopolization of natural resources by irresponsible corporations and
produce an adequate supply of reasonably priced timber. Just as the federal
government never got into the mining or oil business—except for the naval
reserves—it never seriously considered harvesting and marketing the products
of the national forests on its own. Nor, despite the efforts of Gifford Pinchot,
did the Forest Service expand the national police power to regulate cutting or
grazing on private land—particularly that land adjoining the national forests.[13]
In effect, Congress decided at the beginning of the Progressive Era that the
degree of national control over natural resources exercised by the central governments in Germany and Sweden was unacceptable in the United States.

Congress authorized the creation of forest reserves in 1891. Benjamin Harrison set aside 40,000,000 acres, William McKinley 7,000,000, and Theodore
Roosevelt about 148,000,000. Regulating the use of a land mass twice the size
of California, or about 10 percent of the total area of the United States, had
profound implications for the West and the reservations *initially* prompted
howls of protest from many westerners. Even before the transfer of administrative control over the forest reserves from Interior to Agriculture in 1905, Gifford
Pinchot had persuaded Congress to boost appropriations for his forestry office
in the Department of Agriculture from $29,000 in 1898 to $185,000 four years
later. During the same period, his staff grew from 11 to 179.[14]

The establishment of the Forest Service in 1905 represented a significant
administrative reform. By 1917, the number of its employees reached 3,544 and
its budget stood at $5,700,000.[15] The General Land Office, which supervised
the national forests before 1905, was virtually as ungovernable as the Interior
Department (known widely in the nineteenth century as "The Great Mis-
cellany"). The Land Office consisted of eight or nine relatively autonomous
divisions, but the Forest Service's hierarchical structure rationalized power and

accountability. After the firing of Pinchot in 1910, the Chief Forester was usually appointed from the upper ranks of career employees and served not at the pleasure of the President or Secretary of Agriculture, but until resignation, retirement, or death. The Chief, in turn, appointed his staff and the agency's other top officials. Thus, ostensibly, the bureau was insulated from many political pressures, and it took on a far different look than other bureaus in Agriculture.[16] The staff of the Forest Service was different, too. One historian has characterized the General Land Office's forest reserve field force as "old Indian scouts, rodeo artists, or Spanish–American War veterans who loved adventure and the wild lands; others were patronage appointees, a collection of saloon keepers, waiters, doctors, and blacksmiths."[17] The Forest Service, however, increasingly turned to the new forestry schools for its professional employees: Cornell, established in 1898; Yale in 1899; and Michigan in 1903.[18]

During the year following the transfer of the forest "reserves" from Interior to Agriculture in 1905, timber sales increased three times and revenue from the forests increased ten times—not from the lumber sales, but from modest fees for grazing permits that Pinchot introduced. Initially, the Forest Service spent this revenue as it saw fit, without authorization from Congress, just as the 1902 Reclamation Act provided the Reclamation Service with an independent source of income generated by the sale of public lands. Pinchot promised Congress that the forestry program would pay for itself, but these funds also rendered his agency largely impervious to congressional oversight.[19]

It did not take Congress long to reign in the Forest Service. The Service's special fund was abolished in 1908. Thereafter, the lawmakers reviewed the Forest Service budget every year. In the same year, the Service began to *decentralize*. Previously, all administrative work was handled in Washington, and officials in charge of the individual forests were rotated to Washington periodically for several months to maintain their organizational perspective and prevent them from falling under the spell of local interests. But in 1908 six administrative districts were created (a seventh was added in 1914), and district offices were established in Missoula, Denver, Albuquerque, Ogden, San Francisco, and Portland. Forest supervisors still watched over each of the 147 national forests that existed in 1920, but now they answered to the district supervisor, not directly to Washington. As the years passed, the districts assumed more and more responsibilities, from bookkeeping, to the distribution of supplies and materials, to the maintenance of forest experiment stations. The Forest Service had assumed many new functions and responsibilities, but spatially it was even more "decentralized" than the General Land Office.[20]

Decentralization continued after Henry Solon Graves succeeded Gifford Pinchot as Chief Forester in 1910. One career forester later recounted that the decade following 1910 was a low point for the Forest Service because the Ballinger–Pinchot controversy prompted Congress and the Department of Agriculture to place powerful new constraints on the agency. "Then we were punished," Inman F. Eldredge reflected years later, "and I mean in every possible way; the Department of Agriculture just went after our scalps. There were years when nobody got a promotion in the Forest Service."[21] A rider to the 1909 Appropriations Act—aimed directly at the promotional, self-congratulatory activities of the Forest Service and Reclamation Bureau—prohibited the use of federal funds to prepare or publish press releases, magazine articles, or similar publications. The Solicitor of the Agriculture Department assumed all the Forest Service's legal work in May 1910, and in the same year the agency's budget was changed from a lump-sum appropriation to separate allocations for each individual forest. No more than 10 percent of the total budget could be designated for "general expenses" or for "improvements" to be made at the discretion of the Secretary of Agriculture.[22]

What Pinchot, Graves, and other Forest Service employees quickly learned was that the political system had changed very little during the Progressive Era, and Pinchot was nothing if not a political realist. Westerners worried that federal conservation policies would rob them of their freedom as well as restrict access to resources. In 1905 no one knew how large Pinchot's Bureau might become or how many acres of western land it would ultimately "lock up." Therefore, Pinchot—recognizing the prejudice most Americans harbored towards entrenched bureaucracies—changed the name of his office from the Forestry Bureau to Forest Service and renamed the forest reserves national forests.

If Pinchot's agency was to survive, he had no choice but to woo powerful local interests, and he did so shamelessly. In 1903 the Public Lands Commission, of which Pinchot was a member, found that most stockmen who responded to a questionnaire favored "reasonable" grazing regulation, and their responses shaped Pinchot's permit policy. The General Land Office had not charged for permits, and the constitutionality of the fee system was hotly debated in the West. Since 30 percent of the West's sheep and 20 percent of its cattle used the national forests, grazing was considerably more important than private access to timber during the agency's early years of life. Use of the national forests dramatically increased after 1908, though Pinchot catered primarily to cattlemen. Between 1908 and 1917 permits to graze cattle, horses, and hogs increased by 57 percent and the number of cattle by 50 percent. (The number of sheep and goats grew by a scant 7 percent.) The Forest Service worked closely with stock associations, particularly local advisory boards, to determine the carrying capacity of the forests and other conditions of use.

Prior to World War I, pressure from livestock associations on Congress and the Department of Agriculture kept grazing fees so low that the revenue collected barely covered the cost of issuing permits. Fees were raised during the war, but they still lagged far behind the cost of leasing private pastureland, and the increase was contingent on the Forest Service lengthening permits from one to five years. During the 1920s, permits were stretched to ten years, but falling stock prices made the livestock industry even more resistant to higher fees. Grazing policies, inevitably, sought the middle ground between the objectives of the most extreme livestock owners and those of the Secretary of Agriculture. Sharp differences divided the various livestock associations, but it is fair to say that the Forest Service was "captured" by the industry.[23]

There were many other reasons that the Forest Service remained decentralized. Most field officers came from the West and to varying degrees sympathized with the needs and perspective of westerners. Moreover, they were never of one mind. For example, some thought that the Forest Service's basic mission was to grow and harvest trees; others that the Service should pay more attention to land-use planning. Interagency rivalries also contributed to the diffusion of power. The Secretary of Interior never accepted the loss of the forestry bureau, and he consistently opposed legislation to increase the Forest Service's responsibilities. The creation of Sequoia National Park in 1890 established the principle that parks could be established to preserve and protect trees. After 1916 this put the Forest and Park Services in direct competition, and the Secretary of the Interior feared that the Forest Service or Agriculture might take over the new National Park Service. Moreover, the Reclamation Bureau feared that the destruction of watershed cover would reduce the supply of water available to farmers on its irrigation projects and it frequently opposed Forest Service grazing policies. Later, during the 1930s, Agriculture's Soil Conservation Service (SCS) administered small tracts of forested public lands and promoted the cultivation of trees and shrubs on private land. Relations between the SCS and Forest Service were often frosty.[24]

The Forest Service also courted settlers. In 1906 it sponsored the Forest Homestead Act, which opened land within national forests suitable for farming. Between 1912 and 1920, 12,000,000 acres with agricultural potential were eliminated from the national forests, and over 1,100 homestead tracts were opened to settlement in 1916 alone. The Forest Service also provided large amounts of timber free or at cost to residents in or adjoining the forests, and it pacified western politicians and those who lived near the forests by providing substantial supplemental income in lieu of lost taxes: 25 percent of the gross receipts from timber sales were paid to the counties in which the forests were located to build schools and roads on private land, along with an additional 10 percent of proceeds to construct roads within the forests.[25]

In the years after 1910 the Forest Service was far more concerned with pleasing westerners that with increasing its autonomy. Whatever the dreams of Pinchot and other "centralizers," the Service's health hinged on its ability to reward, pacify, conciliate, and cooperate with westerners and their state governments. The Department of Agriculture pioneered in the use of grant-in-aid programs, part of a revolution in American government largely ignored by western historians. The most profound change in government during the Progressive Era was not the concentration of power in bureaucracies, but the revolution in taxation.

Federalism gave the nation many levels of taxation. During the Progressive Era, revenue from local real estate taxes declined, while the nation's liquid wealth—measured in stocks, bonds, notes, and other investments—increased. County property taxes peaked in the nineteenth century. They remained the major source of fiscal support for local government in the twentieth century, but by 1914 the states derived far more revenue from sales taxes. In 1902, 59 percent of all taxes collected within the states were imposed on real estate; by 1932 this shrank to about 20 percent of all levies. Washington could expand taxes more easily than any other level of government because it pooled the wealth of the entire nation. But since the costs of government increased faster at the state and local rather than federal levels, this raised the problem of "fiscal coordination"—how to transfer revenue from one level of government to another. "The growth of federal aid has occurred largely because it is much easier for Congress than state and local governments to raise revenue," political scientist David Berman has commented. "State and local taxes are less lucrative and less efficiently collected than the United States income tax and other federal taxes. State and local taxes are also far less flexible than the federal income tax in adapting to growth in the economy."[26]

The modest income tax Congress authorized in 1913 was a boon to agencies like the Forest Service. During the 1920s, it accounted for more than half of all federal tax revenues and produced unprecedented budget surpluses. Most of this money was used to reduce the debt left over from the war, but there was increasing pressure in Congress to distribute the "windfall" to the states. The percentage of federal subventions increased from 1 or 2 percent of total state revenue receipts before World War I, to an average of 7 or 8 percent during the 1920s, to 11 percent in 1932. Grant-in-aid expenditures increased from less than $3,000,000 in 1901 to $220,000,000 in 1931.[27]

The grant-in-aid originated in nineteenth-century transfers from the public domain to the states to promote such goals as the construction of turnpikes, canals, and railroads; the establishment of schools and colleges; the reclamation of desert land; and the cultivation of trees.[28] But since the arable public domain was gone by the beginning of World War I, and the most desirable land had disappeared decades earlier, monetary grants perpetuated the principle of federal aid to western economic development. The grant system that emerged in the second decade of this century had several features: the identification of common interests shared by many or all the states; the allotment of federal money on the basis of a formula, often the relationship of a state's population to the nation's; the allocation by each state of a sum equal to or greater than the federal appropriation; and the creation or expansion of state institutions to administer the programs.[29] Theoretically, these grants permitted the federal government to dictate policy in realms traditionally reserved to the states. But their basic goal was not to achieve federal control or even to impose federal standards. The grant-in-aid was designed to stimulate the state to assume new responsibilities. Although it simultaneously concentrated and dispersed power, the grant-in-aid did far more to strengthen the state governments than the national one.

The Department of Agriculture pioneered the grant-in-aid. The Smith–Lever Act (1914) established the Agricultural Extension Service to enlist scientific research in the cause of making rural life more attractive and farming more profitable. Federal allocations corresponded to the ratio of each state's rural population to the nation's rural populace. Extension agents were employees of the experiment stations, quasi-academic units attached to land grant colleges.[30]

More germane to the Forest Service, the Weeks Act (1911) and Clark–McNary Act (1924) encouraged federal–state protection of private watershed lands within the basins of navigable streams and the suppression of fires on public and private land. Designed to win political support for the Forest Service, they were alternatives to expanding direct federal regulatory power. The Weeks Act also laid the foundation for joint programs to eradicate insects and diseases that preyed on trees, to control floods, and to reduce soil erosion. The Clark–McNary Act provided for reforestation and federal–state tree nurseries as well as fire protection. The 1920s saw a rapid increase in cooperation, as the number of states participating in the Weeks and Clark–McNary programs increased from eleven, under the first Weeks Act allotment, to thirty-eight by the end of 1927. Federal expenditures increased from $37,000 to $710,000 during this period, but state and private expenditures rose from $220,000 to $3,450,000. The Forest Service set guidelines, but conditions from state to state varied too much for it to impose uniform standards. The Weeks and Clark–McNary laws stimulated states to create or expand forestry departments and enact new restrictions on logging and burning. In 1949 forty-four states appropriated $20,600,000 for fire prevention and control, over double the federal expenditure of $8,500,000. By 1950 sixteen states had forestry departments and another twenty-five assigned this function to bureaus within larger state agricultural or conservation agencies. Only seven states—all western—had no forestry program at all: Arizona, Kansas, Nebraska, Nevada, New Mexico, North Dakota, and Wyoming. By 1933 about half the forested land in the United States was under some form of organized protection, usually through the states, and the line between federal, state, and private policy was extremely blurry.[31]

The great failure of cooperative policy was in controlling lumber production in a glutted market. Production fell by 75 percent from 1925 to 1932, and at the beginning of the New Deal the prospect for expanding federal control over private forests seemed brighter than at any time in the twentieth century. Every scheme to increase federal regulatory power, however, was blocked in Congress. States' rights triumphed once again. Many practices remained beyond the control of the federal government, especially the tendency of timberland owners to flood the market in response to state tax policies that encouraged cutting prematurely to reduce property taxes—even in years of glut. For better or worse, the police power remained with the states.[32]

The success of the Weeks Act encouraged federal–state cooperation in a wide range of USDA activities outside forestry. In the West, highway construction was particularly important. In 1911 Congress rejected legislation to build a combined national highway and railway from sea to sea along the 35th parallel, with feeder lines to each state, and in the following year it spurned the National Highway Association's plan for a 51,000-mile continental highway system with three east–west and three north–south roads.[33] Despite the nationalizing and centralizing impulses unleashed by World War I, and despite the obvious need for a coordinated transportation system, Congress also turned down bills to create a National Highway Commission independent of the Department of Agriculture. Following the war, opposition to new bureaucracies reinforced demands for retrenchment and fears that an open-ended national program might bankrupt the central government. In 1921 Sam Rayburn, a member of the U.S. House of Representatives from Texas, complained during a debate over a national commission that he was "sick and tired of the federal government's everlasting sticking its hand into the affairs of my state. I am against any building up of more bureaucracies in Washington to reach out into the states and tell the people what they shall and what they shall not do."[34]

Before 1910—when motor vehicle taxes first became a source of revenue—almost all roads in the United States were constructed by counties, using local tax revenue. There was little expert supervision, and the roads were, understandably, poor and often impassable. The first national aid came in 1913, in an effort to expand rural mail delivery. Congress promised to spend $10,000 for every $20,000 appropriated by the states. State governors designated the roads to be built; the U.S. Department of Agriculture (USDA) passed judgment on the routes selected and built the highways. However, only Alabama, Iowa, and Oregon accepted the offer, and this experiment taught Congress several important lessons. The states were unwilling to contribute *directly* to a federal highway program; they demanded the right to locate roads and determine the type of construction; a definite apportionment formula was needed so that all states would be treated fairly; and construction would have to be under state rather than federal or local control. These discoveries shaped the federal highway legislation of 1916 and 1921.[35]

Under these laws, the states proposed the roads to be built, paid for construction, and received up to 50 percent of the cost from the Bureau of Public Roads in the USDA, which worked through twelve district offices. In the year following passage of the 1916 law, those states lacking highway departments established them, although often with insufficient funding and staff. One major weakness in the 1916 law was that it did not require direct state construction or supervision of highways, nor did it mandate state maintenance of completed roads. Consequently, the 1921 law required the states to supervise the construction of *all* federally aided work. Another weakness in the 1916 law was that it did not contemplate a coordinated system of roads. Therefore, the 1921 legislation confined federal aid to no more than 7 percent of a state's roads. The Bureau of Public Roads assigned a government engineer to work with each highway department, and most bureau policies were formulated in cooperation with state highway engineers and legislative committees. Between 1920 and 1932 federal grants-in-aid for highways more than doubled and state grants-in-aid to counties increased at an even faster rate. By the beginning of the New Deal, federal aid to highways exceeded all other aid programs combined; it had contributed to the construction of 206,000 miles of highways. That mileage, of course, soared during the 1930s with the institution of New Deal public works programs.[36]

The 1916 and 1921 laws were an exercise in accommodation, and they insured that there would be no centralized highway system. The legislation represented a strange alliance of local farm organizations, civic organizations, highway engineers, and commercial organizations. The farm groups opposed the construction of paved through roads, especially interstate roads that carried little or no traffic at a time when most long-distance freight moved by rail. They favored a program that placed primary emphasis on the construction of farm-to-market roads. They also feared any program administered outside the

Department of Agriculture because it might lead to the construction of more urban, and fewer rural, roads.[37] As historian Bruce Seely has shown, "the most basic feature of the national highway program was the sharing of power between the state and federal governments."[38] The Bureau of Public Roads (BPR) influenced state decisions not through intimidation, or by withholding federal funds, but by rendering the states dependent on federal expertise. Thomas MacDonald, head of the Bureau of Public Roads during the 1920s and 1930s, noted in a letter to U.S. Senator James E. Watson in 1922: "The Federal Highway Act recognizes the right of each State to pursue such administrative policies as it may care to follow, and this Department would certainly adopt no regulation which would force upon the consideration of any State plans or specifications which the State of its own volition was unwilling to consider." One of the rare conflicts between a state and the BPR came in 1925, when Montana withdrew from the federal program, claiming that federal standards raised the cost of construction. But the state's highway engineers opposed the decision, and Montana rejoined the program in 1926.[39]

Federal highway legislation was designed as much to increase state control over county road building as to encourage compliance with national standards. During the 1920s the states moved away from using property taxes to finance roads, and the federal program raised the question of how money raised at the state level from automobile registration fees, highway bond issues, and gasoline taxes would be spent. Taxes on gasoline constituted 3.4 percent of the state and local highway budgets in 1923, but nearly 44 percent by 1935.[40] The states shifted their aid to the largest roads, state authority over road building dramatically increased, and local autonomy shrank. Major roads were paved, and several reluctant states built a system of primary roads. The first outline of a national highway system began to emerge. Had federal aid been given directly to the counties, the results might have been very different. The point is that the structure of government in the United States dictated the shape of policy as much as the objective.

The 1921 law clearly discriminated in favor of the Midwest and against the Far West. It gave preference to farm and market roads, even though a much higher percentage of roads in the West were designed to carry through traffic.[41] State governments in the West exercised less authority over road building than state governments in the East; as of 1905 only California had initiated a highway construction program. Western states had less money to spend and larger areas to serve. Much of the region's land was untaxable, and much of the taxable land returned little income. Therefore, the West's counties demanded that the proceeds from motor vehicle taxes be distributed to them with no strings attached, as a form of revenue sharing. Since western counties were usually very large, and since a much greater percentage of western highways were through roads, it was far easier for counties to block or stall a state program there than in the East. The West needed special highway districts that followed major roads and spanned several counties, but the counties rejected that alternative. Instead, they lobbied Congress to permit federal expenditures to exceed 50 percent in states where most land was still part of the public domain. Since that effort failed, western legislatures were quick to impose taxes on gasoline so that they could take advantage of federal aid. Oregon, New Mexico, and Colorado took the lead in 1919.[42]

In many western states, including Nevada, North Dakota, and Utah, the new well-surfaced roads constituted a large percentage of the state's total highway mileage, and those roads would never have been built without the grant program. Despite the relative weakness of state governments in the West, the federal program served as an entering wedge in the persistent battle of state officials against the localism and parochialism so common to the region. For example, prior to 1916, Kansas had many unimproved but few through roads. The state highway office had been forced to approve roads proposed and subsequently constructed by the counties. Therefore, the Secretary of Agriculture ordered the state to set up a coordinated system, and in 1925 suspended federal payments until the state produced one. In effect, it mandated state construction and management of through roads, even though the counties continued to do most of the construction work. The experience of other western states, particularly Montana and Nebraska, was similar.[43]

Technology refused to stand still in the 1920s and 1930s, and by the latter decade long-haul trucking had appeared and more and faster automobiles increased the number of highway fatalities. Most roads built during the 1920s were rebuilt in succeeding decades to serve "high speed traffic," and demands for a national highway system increased. That system was authorized in 1944, but Congress did not appropriate the funds to build it until 1956.[44]

The 1920s and 1930s demonstrated the remarkable structural persistence of American government. At the depth of the Great Depression, many Americans assumed that the states were finished as functioning units. Critics of the old order charged that the nation needed planning, coordination, and leadership, not localism and home rule. If "centralization" is measured by the size of national expenditures, by the number of federal programs or employees, by the rate of expansion in services, or by the ratio of federal taxes to state and local taxes, then centralization clearly occurred during the 1930s. The federal government expanded the national police power as it related to labor, unemployment, social security, and a wide range of other activities. However, many of the new programs reflected the pork barrel more than fundamental systemic changes. Most state and local powers not only remained intact, but were strengthened by the Depression and New Deal. The New Deal might be characterized more appropriately as "democratic collectivism" rather than socialism or the triumph of the bureaucratic state.[45]

During the 1930s the federal government did not so much assume new powers as it moved into a vacuum. At the beginning of the Depression, the states suffered devastating budget cuts, and no states suffered more than those in the West. For example, higher education was cut by 53 percent in Wyoming and 34 percent in Washington. Property valuations declined by more than 14 percent in Washington state from 1930 to 1934, and by more than 50 percent in Arizona. Tax delinquencies were very high—nearly 38 percent in North Dakota. The real income of westerners declined faster than the national average, with the greatest declines in South Dakota, Arizona, and Idaho, followed by North Dakota, Montana, Kansas, Nebraska, Oklahoma, Utah, Oregon, and Washington. Put simply, the states were broke and many were on the brink of bankruptcy. They could not borrow because most were already perilously close to defaulting on their bonded debts. Revenue granted to the states by the federal government increased from $222,000,000 in 1932 to $667,000,000 in 1940. Federal subventions constituted about 3.4 percent of the federal budget in 1932. Three years later they had increased to about 30 percent of federal expenditures. "The states," as historian David M. Kennedy has remarked, "came begging for federal assistance; they did not have it roughly shoved down their throats."[46]

Some New Deal agencies were clearly federal, such as the SEC and FTC. Most, however, built on the cooperative model developed by the Department of Agriculture during the Progressive Era. The ICC regularly held joint hearings with state utility commissions. Insurance on bank deposits required close cooperation between the FDIC and state banking agencies. The National Resources Planning Board worked closely with state planning offices, and the TVA cooperated closely with the seven states it served. The CCC was essentially a cooperative program launched at a time when most states did not have the funds necessary to qualify it as a matching program. CCC troops replanted trees and sprayed forests to protect against insect damages, but their major responsibility was building roads, fighting fires (an extension of the 1924 Clark–McNary legislation), and improving state and local parks. More than 550 parks were developed or improved by CCC workers.[47]

Congress and local interests played a far greater role in shaping New Deal legislation than most historians have assumed, and few westerners showed an interest in the wholesale reform of American institutions or values. Relief came first, and the western states defied centralized authority and exercised wide discretion over the administration of federal policies and the allocation of federal money. In many states, those opposed to raising taxes put considerably greater pressure on state legislatures than those who lobbied for relief. Farm organizations, chambers of commerce, taxpayer leagues, and other groups insisted that the best way to ride out the Depression was the time-proven method of retrenchment and balanced budgets. An Oregon budget director claimed that the legislature that met in his state in 1933 was the worst in the state's history and consisted of "a lot of wild jackasses who believed that they heard the call of the people and were willing to destroy anything and everything so long as they could make a show of saving a nickel."

Most western states welcomed federal aid—though for patronage purposes as much as to provide relief. Although the proposition seems self-evident, we should never forget that the New Deal was both the creature of politics and the victim. A federal relief official noted that in the North Dakota of 1933, "no one save a Hoover Republican can get a [federal] job," and another federal agent reported that taking care of Republicans was a "positive mania" in Montana. In New Mexico the strongest support came from a coalition of liberal Democrats—few and far between in New Mexico—and Bronson Cutting's progressive Republicans. Moreover, throughout the West there were Democrats who were flatly opposed to the New Deal.[48] In the mid-1930s, the Colorado legislature was so slow to appropriate FERA matching funds that Harry Hopkins, head of the Federal Emergency Relief Association, cut off federal money. The western states were forced, kicking and screaming, to adopt regressive new taxes to provide the necessary matching funds. (The WPA was even harder to administer because it required no state appropriations.)[49]

Structural impediments within the federal system blocked the flow of power to Washington, and support for the New Deal in the West was often opportunistic and ephemeral. No part of the country benefited as much from the New Deal, but the region remained largely conservative. In Nebraska the AAA and relief payments allowed the state to survive the drought of the early 1930s, but when agricultural prosperity returned in the late-1930s Nebraska farmers abandoned the New Deal in droves (which contributed to George Norris's defeat in 1942 and a restoration of western Republicanism). The states had assumed new responsibilities for social welfare,[50] but the underlying values of westerners did not change. Individualism and states' rights remained strong despite federal aid.[51]

The New Deal expanded federal responsibilities and set a precedent for both the federal government and states to assume new responsibilities in the future, but we should remember that, in the words of historian Leonard Arrington,

New Deal expenditures were "appallingly low." Need may be a better measure of the impact of federal programs than dollars spent, but Arrington's sober appraisal of the New Deal is instructive: "If one adds all the New Deal loans and expenditures for the six-year period, they totaled less than $400 per United States resident. Divided by six, this means approximately $66 per person per year for all economic programs combined. Surely not a profligate undertaking!" In any case, two results of the New Deal have been virtually ignored by historians: the assumption of greater state control over wages and hours, highway construction, public health, and public utility regulation, and the transfer of relief responsibilities from the counties to state agencies. Political pressure from below, as well as from above, contributed to the creation of new state departments, such as public health. Aid to dependent children, old-age assistance, and a wide variety of other social welfare programs became the responsibility of the states. While more federal workers were hired during the 1930s than in the previous three decades of the twentieth century combined, in 1940 two thirds of all government employees still worked for states or counties.[52]

In 1949 the journalist Roscoe Drummond remarked that "in point of fact, our federal system no longer exists and has no more chance of being brought back into existence than an apple pie can be put back on the apple tree."[53] In the decades after World War II the federal government moved into areas previously reserved to the states, such as education, pollution abatement, and civil rights. But, as in the period from 1900 to 1940, appearances were deceptive; the states were very much alive. State appropriations for common schools and colleges soared, as did spending on highways, mental health, libraries, parks and recreation facilities, and in a host of other areas—some mandated by federal legislation. State revenues increased by 276 percent from 1948 to 1961, and per capita state expenditures increased by 242 percent. More important, the rate of growth of federal and state revenues during this period was about the same, even adjusted for federal grants-in-aid.[54] As one political scientist concluded at the end of the 1970s:

> Almost every major federal domestic program is designed to be implemented by state or local government. Even when federal money or standards shape a national program, it is state or local governments which locate and build highways, hire teachers and establish curriculum, set the levels of payment and eligibility criteria for most forms of public assistance, and negotiate the complex arrangements which are involved in programs such as urban renewal and model cities. . . . As a consequence of federal sensitivity to state and local interests and the decentralized imple-

mentation of federal programs, the overall impact of the growth of federal aid from $2.5 billion in 1950 to $53 billion in 1975 has been to enhance rather than undermine the capabilities of state and local government."[55]

Since the early 1930s, fiscal centralization had occurred at both the state and federal levels, even though the functions of government were widely shared. The revolution in taxation was complete by the 1950s. The national government collected less than 25 percent of all tax revenue at the beginning of the New Deal; by 1950 it took in about 75 percent of all tax proceeds. The remainder was divided equally between the states and localities. And by the middle of the century, 80 percent of the taxes collected by the central government were on income—as opposed to the tariff, liquor, and tobacco levies that had provided most of the national income half a century earlier. The structure of American government had not changed, but the era of dual federalism—clearly delineated realms of state and federal authority—had passed.[56]

Charles de Gaulle once complained that no one could possibly govern a country that produced 265 different kinds of cheeses, and certainly our system of government has produced as many competing institutions as France has cheeses.[57] Many forces shaped the decentralized American state, including ethnic pluralism, the absence of a well-defined aristocracy, and the American party system, but federalism deserves to be studied in its own right. The historian David Kennedy reminds us that "unlike Topsy, the federal government did not 'just grow,' without apparent reason or direction."

> Federal power has not expanded, as the British Empire was alleged to have done, in a prolonged fit of absent-mindedness, nor has it increased by some perverse process of nationalist usurpation. It is even arguable that federal power has grown exceptionally modestly in this country and that a modern Tocqueville would be just as impressed as his predecessor with the relatively small size of America's central governmental apparatus.

In fact, a case can be made that the prospect of centralizing control over business was greater in 1900 or 1910—when politicians at least considered using taxes to limit the size of business and debated various ways to control prices—than it is today.[58]

All institutions of government exhibit both centralizing and decentralizing tendencies, but in the United States the ethics of science, professionalism, and rational decision making have seldom triumphed for long over the centrifugal forces of localism. Linear views of the concentration of power often measure the power of a bureaucracy by its size and ignore the fact that government agencies rise and fall, come and go. The U.S. Geological Survey may have been larger in the twentieth century, but it reached the apex of its political power during the 1880s, when its director, John Wesley Powell, attempted to corner the market on government science. The General Land Office, the most visible symbol of national authority in the West during the late nineteenth century, rapidly shrank in size and influence after the last of the public domain passed into private hands in the first and second decades of this century. And today the Bureau of Reclamation is a pale shadow of the powerful institution it was in the 1940s, 1950s, and 1960s. The mere growth in size of the federal government is less important than where power is concentrated, and, except in wartime, it has been nearly impossible to concentrate power in the United States. This would be true even if the personalities of bureaucracies did not differ, and even if each bureaucracy did not have ambitions that often threatened rival bureaucracies.[59]

Similarly, although all three sectors of government have grown dramatically during the twentieth century, they have not grown at the same rate or at the same time. Local and state institutions rapidly expanded in size during the 1920s, when the number of federal employees actually declined from the war-inflated number, while Washington's power grew more rapidly during the 1930s and after. Some functions increase during wars and decrease during peacetime, others follow the reverse course. For example, the great building booms of around 1909 and 1925 pushed up the outlays of cities, but wars and the Great Depression reduced them. The prosperity of the Progressive Era encouraged the growth of regulatory agencies; the hard times of the 1930s stimulated relief and welfare agencies.

There are, of course, many institutions of government that historians have been slow to look at. Special jurisdictions—such as air pollution, drainage, mosquito abatement, and soil conservation districts—are created because local institutions are unresponsive, or because it is more efficient to focus on one issue or remove that issue from the political process. Such districts often provide greater autonomy and home rule than established institutions of local government. And, of course, sometimes they exist to subvert democratic rule.[60]

Frequently, special districts are established as alternatives to more centralized institutions. For example, California's irrigation districts have permitted farmers to build dams, canals, and ditches by taxing property within the district's urban areas along with rural farmland. These districts allowed local residents to capture the increase in land values that inevitably followed cultivation of the land, and they precluded state or national irrigation systems that might have limited water rights and created expensive and remote bureaucracies. In short, they preserved local autonomy and independence at the same time they captured outside capital (by permitting the sale of bonds retired through taxation). This institution became enormously popular and spread rapidly to other western states during the early decades of this century. Of course, the irrigation district is less flashy than the Bureau of Reclamation, which has received far greater historical attention. California contains a multitude of other special districts, including Southern California's gigantic Metropolitan Water District.[61]

Historians have also largely ignored the attempts to create regional authorities in the West. The interstate compact has received attention, notably from Norris Hundley.[62] In the West these were used to allocate water from interstate streams, but after World War II they became potential regional authorities.[63] Critics of the states argued that the state governments were artificial creations whose power had no relationship to the new problems government faced in the twentieth century, and that replacing them with governments covering river basins, or regions with common economic and social problems, made more sense. Beginning in 1937 the Tennessee Valley Authority spawned a number of plans to create regional authorities in the West. In 1945 Senator James Murray of Montana pushed for a Missouri River Authority and in 1949 President Harry Truman proposed a Columbia Valley Authority. However, proponents of these authorities were also often public power advocates and social planning was equated with socialism in the United States. Moreover, these authorities often represented an expansion of federal authority. Therefore, they made little headway in Congress—except among a handful of liberal members such as George Norris of Nebraska. Congress depended on the states, and the states were not about to commit institutional suicide.[64]

In conclusion, it is as easy to argue that the West contributed to a decentralization of power within the American state as the reverse. As the West's population grew in the twentieth century, the region exerted more and more power in Congress. Westerners gained seniority on key committees and found numerous ways to capture federal funds for defense-related industries, military bases, dams, and many other purposes. Time and again, they defeated attempts to direct their lives from Washington. The central government did not become Leviathan. Quite to the contrary, it grew up to be a weak, irresolute, but wealthy giant, capable of rewarding local interests but incapable of providing much leadership or direction. Powerful economic interests frequently attempted to capture the central government, but the objectives of these groups were so diverse and contradictory that the essential conservatism of westerners doubtless played a far larger role in shaping the federal government than "capitalism."

As the historian Michael E. McGerr recently noted, the organizational synthesis that has dominated twentieth-century U.S. history during the last few decades emphasizes homogeneity over diversity, the whole over the parts, and the "core" over the "periphery." It assumes that power can be traced to a few centers, and those centers until quite recently were located in Washington, D.C., and New York City. Yet, in McGerr's words, it is an "individualist sensibility, not the corporation or the bureaucracy, that distinguishes the United States from other industrial nations," and that sensibility is most evident in the American West.[65] Like it or not, such frontier values as mobility and freedom have served as powerful foils to the corporate state. Most western historians argue for western uniqueness. But what is unique about the West if it simply contributed to the centralization of power?

This essay makes no pretense at originality; it builds on arguments very familiar to political scientists, if not historians. It is not meant to discredit or to depreciate the work of scholars who look at the flow of political power from a different vantage point. It suggests, however, that historians of the American West need to be much more careful in their analysis of government. Simple models hide the past, or distort its lessons, rather than enlighten. The modern American state has done much to regiment and dehumanize people, but it has also reflected their wants, needs, frustrations, and deepest aspirations.

NOTES

1. See, for example, Richard Lowitt, *The New Deal and the West* (Bloomington: Indiana University Press, 1983), and Gerald Nash, *The American West Transformed: The Impact of the Second World War* (Bloomington: Indiana University Press, 1985).

2. Donald Worster, *Rivers of Empire: Water, Aridity & the Growth of the American West* (New York: Pantheon Books, 1985), 13, 51, 64, 131, 279.

3. Richard White, "*It's Your Misfortune and None of My Own*": *A History of the American West* (Norman: University of Oklahoma Press, 1991), 182, 58. See also White, " 'Far West. See also frontier': 'New Western History,' Textbooks, and the U.S. History," *Perspectives*, 30 (September 1992),11.

4. White, "*It's Your Misfortune and None of My Own,*"204.

5. White, "*It's Your Misfortune and None of My Own,*"58.

6. These institutions receive little more attention in the most balanced history of the twentieth-century West. Michael P. Malone and Richard W. Etulain, *The American West: A Twentieth-Century History* (Lincoln: University of Nebraska Press, 1989).

7. John M. Murrin, "1787: The Invention of American Federalism," in David E. Narrett and Joyce S. Goldberg, eds., *Essays on Liberty and Federalism: The Shaping of the U.S. Constitution* (College Station: Texas A&M Press, 1988), 20–47; Richard B. Morris, "Federalism: USA Style," in J. C. Boogman and G. N. van der Plaat, *Federalism: History and Current Significance of a Form of Government* (The Hague: Martinus Nijhoff, 1980), 79–96; Daniel J.

Elazar, "Our Thoroughly Federal Constitution," in Robert A. Goldwin and William A. Schambra, eds., *How Federal Is the Constitution?* (Washington, DC: American Enterprise Institute for Public Policy Research, 1987), 38–66; Martin Diamond, "The Ends of Federalism," *Publius* 3 (Fall 1973), 129–52; Diamond, "The Forgotten Doctrine of Enumerated Powers," *Publius* 6 (Fall 1976), 187–93.

8. Samuel H. Beer, "The Modernization of American Federalism," *Publius* 3 (Fall 1973), 49–95; Daniel Elazar, "Federalism vs. Decentralization: The Drift from Authenticity," *Publius* 6 (Fall 1976), 9–19.

9. Theda Skocpol, "Bringing the State Back In: Strategies of Analysis in Current Research," in Peter B. Evans, Dietrich Rueschemeyer, and Theda Skocpol, eds., *Bringing the State Back In* (New York: Cambridge University Press, 1985), 12; Seymour Martin Lipset, "American Exceptionalism Reaffirmed," in Byron E. Shafer, ed., *Is America Different? A New Look at American Exceptionalism* (Oxford: Clarendon Press, 1991), 3.

10. Beer, "The Modernization of American Federalism," 63. Also see Michael N. Danielson, et al., eds., *One Nation, So Many Governments* (Lexington, MA: D. C. Heath, 1977), 8; Harry N. Scheiber, "American Federalism and the Diffusion of Power: Historical and Contemporary Perspectives," *Toledo Law Review* 9 (Summer 1978): 635–36; George C. S. Benson, *The New Centralization: A Study of Intergovernmental Relationships in the United States* (New York: Farrar and Rinehart, 1941), 9–21; Arthur W. Macmahon, *Administering Federalism in a Democracy* (New York: Oxford University Press, 1972), 5–6.

11. White, *"It's Your Misfortune and None of My Own,"* 58, 391–92, 399, 401. Patricia Limerick makes a similar argument in her *The Legacy of Conquest: The Unbroken Past of the American West* (New York: W. W. Norton & Co., 1987). For example, she claims that "the Reclamation Act of 1902 put the national government in the center of the control and development of water, the West's key resource" (p. 87), and also maintains that "the Taylor Grazing Act of 1934 finally centralized the control of grazing on the public domain" (p. 156). Limerick notes: "When the other resources faltered or collapsed, federal support often turned out to be the crucial remaining prop to the economy. If anything, the twentieth century reinforced this 'frontier' characteristic; Progressive conservation and reclamation, New Deal public works, the World War II expansion of defense spending, and Great Society welfare only added to the general government's central role" (p. 138).

12. Samuel P. Hays, *Conservation and the Gospel of Efficiency: The Progressive Conservation Movement, 1890–1920* (Cambridge, MA: Harvard University Press, 1959).

13. Samuel Trask Dana, *Forest and Range Policy: Its Development in the United States* (New York: McGraw-Hill, 1956), 213, 235–36. Pinchot favored a comprehensive national grazing policy administered by the Forest Service or a new conservation agency under his leadership.

14. Dana, *Forest and Range Policy*, 119.

15. Richard H. Douai Boerker, *Our National Forests* (New York: Macmillan, 1920), 23.

16. Daniel R. Barney, *The Last Stand: Ralph Nader's Study Group Report on the National Forests* (New York: Grossman Publishers, 1974), 107–8.

17. Michael Frome, *The Forest Service* (Boulder, Co: Westview Press, 1984), 34. The differences between "old" and "new" resource agencies were not as great as many historians assume. For example, in 1900 the Interior Department began using competitive examina-

tions to select employees assigned to the forest reserves, and one prominent forester claims that "forestry as an art and a science did get recognition in Interior after the reserves were gone. In time, the quality of the forestry practiced on Interior holdings would rank high in professional circles. In education, competence, and ethical standards, the foresters in Interior would rank with the best in America." Henry Clepper, *Professional Forestry in the United States* (Baltimore: Johns Hopkins Press, 1971), 103, 105.

18. Dana, *Forest and Range Policy*, 203. Pinchot and others organized the Society of American Foresters in 1900; the first professional journal, *Forestry Quarterly*, appeared in 1902; and the first industry trade organization, the National Lumber Manufacturer's Association, was organized in December 1902—to stabilize prices, promote the adoption of uniform grades and sizes of lumber, and lobby for more equitable taxes on timberland. Not surprisingly, such organizations forged powerful alliances with federal agencies and congressional committees. Hence, three characteristics of professionalization—professional degree programs, national organizations, and specialized journals—contributed directly to the work of the Forest Service.

19. Darrell Hevenor Smith, *The Forest Service: Its History, Activities and Organization* (Washington, DC: The Brookings Institution, 1930), 34.

20. Smith, *The Forest Service*, 37; Dana, *Forest and Range Policy*, 151; Frome, *The Forest Service*, 34.

21. Clepper, *Professional Forestry in the United States*, 66–67. In his annual report for 1920, Chief W. B. Greeley noted that inadequate salaries had led to so many resignations that "complete demoralization" threatened the Forest Service (pp. 67–68).

22. Smith, *The Forest Service*, 39, 40, 44, 55; Harold K. Steen, *The U.S. Forest Service: A History* (Seattle: University of Washington Press, 1976), 86.

23. Steen, *The U.S. Forest Service:* 163–64, 166–67; Boerker, *Our National Forests*, 201–2; Smith, *The Forest Service*, 58–61; Dana, *Forest and Range Policy*, 229–31; Clepper, *Professional Forestry in the United States*, 69–73.

24. Luther Halsey Gulick, *American Forest Policy: A Study of Government Administration and Economic Control* (New York: Duell, Sloan and Pearce, 1951), 41–42, 59–61; Frome, *The Forest Service*, 27; Clepper, *Professional Forestry in the United States*, 59, 61–62, 117; Dana, *Forest and Range Policy*, 265; Donald J. Pisani, "Forests and Reclamation, 1891–1911," *Forest & Conservation History* 37 (April 1993): 68–79. Dana notes that in the late 1930s, "Owners of farms in which forests were distinctly a secondary crop were normally served by the Soil Conservation Service, while owners of farms in which forests were the major crop were served by the Forest Service. The distinction between 'farm forests' and 'forest farms' was, however, often difficult to draw." (p. 265).

25. Steen, *The U.S. Forest Service*, 85, 179; Paul Wallace Gates, *History of Public Land Law Development* (New York: Arno Press, 1979), 511–12; Boerker, *Our National Forests*, 195–96, 224–29.

26. A national sales tax was narrowly defeated in 1921. Since the federal government had preempted the income tax, the states turned to other taxes, particularly those on gasoline and sales. As property values fell during the 1930s, the sales tax became increasingly popular, particularly in rural areas. Although thirteen states enacted personal and corporate income

taxes between 1911 and 1921, in 1927 their combined yield was only 10 percent of all state and local revenue. In only four states—Delaware, Massachusetts, New York, and Wisconsin— did income taxes return more than 10 percent of all state revenue. Many states followed Florida's example. In 1924, in an attempt to attract wealthy residents, it enacted a constitutional amendment prohibiting income or inheritance taxes. Most legislators thought that other taxes were less painful. Morton Keller, *Regulating a New Economy: Public Policy and Economic Change in America, 1900–1933* (Cambridge, MA: Harvard University Press, 1990), 211, 221, 227; James T. Patterson, *The New Deal and the States: Federalism in Transition* (Princeton: Princeton University Press, 1969), 14–15; David R. Berman, *State and Local Politics* (Boston: Allyn and Bacon, 1981), 31.

27. Henry J. Bitterman, *State and Federal Grants-In-Aid* (New York: Mentzer, Bush, and Co., 1938), 126, 141, 146; Leonard D. White, *The States and the Nation* (Baton Rouge: LSU Press, 1953), 18; *Historical Statistics of the United States: Colonial Times to 1957* (Washington, DC: GPO, 1961), 712–13.

28. Morton Grodzins, *The American System: A New View of Government in the United States* (Chicago: Rand McNally & Co., 1966), 31, 33, 36.

29. Arthur W. Macmahon, *Administering Federalism in a Democracy* (New York: Oxford University Press, 1972), 74–76.

30. George C. S. Benson, *The New Centralization: A Study of Intergovernmental Relationships in the United States* (New York: Farrar and Rinehart, Inc., 1941), 100–101; Bitterman, *State and Federal Grants-in-Aid*, 370–86.

31. William G. Robbins, *American Forestry: A History of National, State & Private Cooperation* (Lincoln: University of Nebraska Press, 1985), 50–104; Steen, *The U.S. Forest Service*, 129–31, 173, 189–90, 193; Dana, *Forest and Range Policy*, 237; Gulick, *American Forest Policy*, 146; Clepper, *Professional Forestry in the United States*, 89. The state's right to dictate forest policies on private land was not upheld by the courts until 1949, and though New Deal U.S. Supreme Court rulings suggested that the high court would uphold a federal regulatory power under the commerce or general welfare clauses, the Forest Service was reluctant to follow this course.

32. Robbins, *American Forestry*, 134–37.

33. Keller, *Regulating a New Economy*, 71; Bruce E. Seely, *Building the American Highway System: Engineers as Policy Makers* (Philadelphia: Temple University Press, 1987), 38–39.

34. Seely, *Building the American Highway System*, 61–62, 67.

35. Bitterman, *State and Federal Grants-in-Aid*, 256.

36. Grodzins, *The American System*, 49.

37. Hal S. Barron, "And the Crooked Shall be Made Straight: Public Road Administration and the Decline of Localism in the Rural North, 1870–1930," *Journal of Social History* 26 (Fall 1992): 81–103.

38. Seely, *Building the American Highway System*, 68.

39. Seely, *Building the American Highway System*, 82, 122.

40. Bitterman, *State and Federal Grants-in-Aid*, 99. The number of registered automobiles more than tripled during the 1920s, and total state and local spending on roads increased five times.

41. Seely, *Building the American Highway System*, 58.

42. Mark H. Rose, *Interstate: Express Highway Politics, 1939–1989* (Knoxville: University of Tennessee Press, 1990), 4.

43. Bitterman, *State and Federal Grants-in-Aid*, 231, 254–76; Seely, *Building the American Highway System*, 63, 74; Leonard D. White, *Introduction to the Study of Public Administration* (New York: Macmillan, 1926), 91.

44. Seely, *Building the American Highway System*, 142.

45. David B. Walker, *Toward a Functioning Federalism* (Cambridge, MA: Winthrop Publishers, 1981), 86–87.

46. David M. Kennedy, "Federalism and the Force of History," in Robert A. Goldwin and William A. Schambra, eds., *How Federal is the Constitution?* (Washington, DC: American Enterprise Institute for Public Policy Research, 1987), 79; Leonard J. Arrington, "The Sagebrush Resurrection: New Deal Expenditures in the Western States, 1933–1939," *Pacific Historical Review* 52 (February 1983): 3; Bittermann, *State and Federal Grants-in-Aid*, 37–38; *Historical Statistics of the United States: Colonial Times to 1957* (Washington, DC: Government Printing Office, 1961), 727.

47. Robbins, *American Forestry*, 144, 147, 148; Grodzins, *The American System*, 138.

48. Patterson, *The New Deal and the States*, 82, 173, 180.

49. Patterson, *The New Deal and the States*, 64, 66, 69–71. On the New Deal in the West also see Lowitt, *The New Deal and the West*; the essays on the New Deal in Oklahoma, Wyoming, Montana, Colorado, New Mexico and Oregon in John Braeman, Robert H. Bremner, and David Brody, eds., *The New Deal: The State and Local Levels* (Columbus: Ohio State University Press, 1975), 166–375; Michael P. Malone and Richard W. Etulain, *The American West: A Twentieth-Century History* (Lincoln: University of Nebraska Press, 1989), 94–106; Barry Karl, *The Uneasy State: The United States from 1915 to 1945* (Chicago: University of Chicago Press, 1983), 139–42; Walker, *Toward a Functioning Federalism*, 74.

50. Nevada, Colorado, Idaho, California, Wyoming, and Montana enacted old age pensions even before 1933. However, in most states recipients had to be at least seventy and have lived within the state for at least fifteen years. The pensions were very small—the highest annual award was $390—and most of the systems were optional, leaving administration to the counties. See Patterson, *The New Deal and the States*, 12.

51. Anthony J. Badger, "The New Deal and the Localities," in Rhodri Jeffreys-Jones and Bruce Collins, eds., *The Growth of Federal Power in American History* (Dekalb: Northern Illinois University Press, 1983), 102–15.

52. Leonard J. Arrington, "The Sagebrush Resurrection: New Deal Expenditures in the Western States, 1933–1939," *Pacific Historical Review* 52 (February 1983): 15; Benson, *The New Centralization*, 107–15; Solomon Fabricant, *The Trend of Government Activity in the United States Since 1900* (New York: National Bureau of Economic Research, Inc., 1952), 28.

53. White, *The States and the Nation*, 2.

54. Daniel Elazar, *American Federalism: A View from the States* (New York: Thomas Y. Crowell, 1966), 199–201.

55. Michael N. Danielson, et al., eds., *One Nation, So Many Governments* (Lexington, MA: D. C. Heath, 1977), 6.

56. Arthur W. Macmahon, *Administering Federalism in a Democracy* (New York: Oxford University Press, 1972), 65–67.

57. Theodore J. Lowi, "Why is There No Socialism in the United States? A Federal Analysis," in Robert T. Golembiewski and Aaron Wildavsky, eds., *The Costs of Federalism* (New Brunswick, NJ: Transaction Books, 1984), 45.

58. Kennedy, "Federalism and the Force of History," 68.

59. Fabricant, *The Trend of Government Activity* 82–83.

60. John C. Bollens, *Special District Governments in the United States* (Berkeley: University of California Press, 1957).

61. Donald J. Pisani, *From the Family Farm to Agribusiness: The Irrigation Crusade in California and the West, 1850–1931* (Berkeley: University of California Press, 1984); Pisani, "The Irrigation District and the Federal Relationship: Neglected Aspects of Water History in the Twentieth Century," in Gerald Nash and Richard Etulain, eds., *Historians of the Twentieth Century West* (Albuquerque: University of New Mexico Press, 1989), 257–92.

62. See, for example, Norris Hundley, *Water and the West: The Colorado River Compact and the Politics of Water in the American West* (Berkeley: University of California Press, 1975). Also see Frederick L. Zimmermann and Mitchell Wendell, *The Interstate Compact Since 1925* (Washington, DC: Council of State Governments, 1951); Weldon V. Barton, *Interstate Compacts in the Political Process* (Chapel Hill: University of North Carolina Press, 1965); and Richard H. Leach and Redding S. Sugg, Jr., *The Administration of Interstate Compacts* (Baton Rouge: LSU Press, 1959).

63. White, *The States and the Nation*, 87, 90.

64. Marsha Derthick, *Between State and Nation: Regional Organizations of the United States* (Washington, DC: The Brookings Institution, 1974), 18–45; W. Brooke Graves, *American State Government* (Boston: D.C. Heath, 1946), 952–62.

65. Michael E. McGerr, "Is There a Twentieth-Century West?" in William Cronon, George Miles, and Jay Gitlin, eds., *Under an Open Sky: Rethinking America's Western Past* (New York: W. W. Norton & Co., 1992), 254.

CHAPTER SIX

HETCH HETCHY PHASE II
The Senate Debate

RICHARD LOWITT

"Much ado about nothing" or at best "much ado about little," remarked Senator James A. Reed as the second session of the Sixty-third Congress convened. Members, by special consent, were devoting that first week to resolving the cantankerous issue of whether San Francisco could construct an artificial lake in the Hetch Hetchy Valley of Yosemite National Park. The Senate, meeting in day and night session, debated the issue, thereby stalling discussion of the Federal Reserve bill, the centerpiece of the New Freedom legislative program. The debate consumed more than 380 pages in the *Congressional Record.*

What was involved, Reed remarked, was "the disposition of about 2 square miles of land, located at a point remote from civilization, in the very heart of the Sierra Nevada Mountains, and possessing an intrinsic value of probably not to exceed four or five hundred dollars." Putting water on two square miles of a park containing over 1,100 square miles of territory engendered "profound debate" in the Senate, while the country was "thrown into a condition of hysteria"[1]

Yet these two square miles prompted a national controversy that culminated with the December Senate debate. The previous history of the controversy has been examined many times by scholars, participants, and others writing from a preservationist or conservationist perspective. It split the Sierra Club, and some suggested that it helped bring about the death of John Muir the following year. It need only be recounted here in broad outline.[2]

Since 1901 San Francisco had been seeking permission from the secretary of the interior to construct a dam in the beautiful Hetch Hetchy Valley. Four secretaries had responded, each in a different way. Ethan Allen Hitchcock twice turned down the request. After the San Francisco earthquake and fire, however, James R. Garfield favored the grant, but Richard A. Ballinger ordered the city to show cause why it should not be eliminated from the Garfield permit. And Walter Lowrie Fisher, before leaving office at the end of the Taft administration, threw the matter into the lap of Sixty-third Congress and the incoming Wilson administration. Previously, Ballinger had called for the appointment of a board of army engineers to report whether there were other available sources that would be adequate for San Francisco's water needs. Their report, published in May 1913, played a prominent role in the congressional debate. It suggested several other sources of water supply that were both practical and abundant. The matter was simply one of cost, but with the exception of the Sacramento River, no thorough investigation had been made of sources other than Hetch Hetchy. Nevertheless, the board estimated that a maximum difference of cost between Hetch Hetchy and the next feasible available source of water supply would be $20,000,000, or 25 percent more than the original estimated cost.[3]

On September 3, 1913, after extended hearings and debate, the House approved the Hetch Hetchy measure (H.R. 7207) by a vote of 183 to 43, with 9 members answering "present." Not voting were 194 members. Meanwhile, the Senate continued to debate the measure until October 7, when Senator Key Pittman requested and won unanimous consent for the Senate to reconsider the measure, as unfinished business, during the second session. It was agreed that the measure would be taken up on opening day, Monday, December 1, 1913, and would be disposed of no later than December 6, 1913.[4]

Thus, when the new session got underway Hetch Hetchy was the Senate's main focus, taking precedence over a banking measure calling for the creation of a federal reserve system. At the outset, several points can be mentioned, though they were not stressed in the debate. First, by the end of 1913 the Bay Area was the only major urban complex in the entire country that was unable to provide water for its people through a public agency. Second, the Spring Valley Water Company, whose reservoirs and sources of supply were situated in the adjoining Coast Range mountains, was having difficulty in properly supplying a large number of customers. In 1901 the City Engineer had investigated various possible new sources of supply. Out of fourteen sites considered feasible, the Tuolumne River, which flowed through the Hetch Hetchy Valley, was considered "superior in quantity, quality and accessibility to all the others." And it was in 1901 that the city had first applied for permits to impound the water at the Hetch Hetchy Valley and nearby Lake Eleanor, both within the boundaries of Yosemite National Park, and convey it the 165 miles due west to the Bay Area.[5]

The great fire following the earthquake in 1906 only exacerbated the situation, as some of the hoses and other equipment of the Spring Water Company could not meet the demands imposed by the catastrophe. Instances of faulty and otherwise antiquated and impaired facilities were also abundantly evident. In 1909 and 1910, besides agreeing to buy out the franchise of the water company, the people of San Francisco approved the issuance of bonds totaling $45,600,000 to acquire privately-held lands. It then exchanged some land it already owned within Yosemite for additional land on the valley floor. By combining these holdings with the Hetch Hetchy Valley land, the city could then ensure clear title to all the land it proposed to submerge.[6] Thus, even before the final congressional debate got underway, San Francisco, acting in good faith under the permit awarded by Secretary Garfield in 1908, had heavily committed itself to Hetch Hetchy. The result was that the alternate sources suggested by the Army Engineers and some members of Congress would have incurred a serious financial burden upon the city.

One final general observation can be made: the concerns of John Muir and the horde of preservationists endorsing his views received relatively short shrift in the Senate debate. This is not to say that the preservationist position was not given attention, but only to say that other issues received far more attention and consumed many more pages in the *Congressional Record*. Irrigation, an urban water supply, and the issue of public power were central to the debate. Opponents of the measure (H.R. 7207) used arguments or submitted material that at times was incongruous. For example, some senators called for utilization of water for irrigation purposes; others insisted that damming Hetch Hetchy would deface nature.

Senator John D. Works spoke for the water users in the irrigation districts. The Army Engineers' Report (p. 35) stated: "There can be no question but that a large portion, if not all of the flow of the Tuolumne could be used for irrigation if stored." But before Works could develop this premise, he had to deal with the fact that the spokesmen and the congressman representing the Turlock and Modesto irrigation districts, the largest in the San Joaquin Valley, had both endorsed the measure during its journey through the House. Among the provisions in section 9 of the bill was one that recognized the prior water rights of these districts, [or as they might be enlarged to contain no more than 300,000 acres and to receive 2,350 second feet of the daily flow of the Tuolumne River whenever the amount could be beneficially used by these districts.] Moreover, the provision concluded, "The grantee shall never interfere with the rights." And among the conclusions of the Army Engineers was the following statement (p. 50): "The board further believes that there will be sufficient water if adequately stored and economically used to supply both the reasonable demand of the bay communities and the reasonable needs of the Turlock–Modesto Irrigation District for the remainder of this century."

Works argued that "ninety-nine percent" of the water users in the irrigation districts were not in accord with the provision in section 9. These interests claimed that they were betrayed by their spokesmen and by their representative, Denver S. Church.[7] Following this lead, Works claimed that thousands of acres in the Turlock–Modesto districts and throughout the San Joaquin Valley would be deprived of water, thereby sacrificing some of California's prime agricultural lands to the interest of San Francisco. He devoted the better part of both the day and evening session on December 2 and on into the next day to making the case of water users, actual and potential, throughout the San Joaquin Valley. Interspersed among his remarks were numerous telegrams, petitions, and other insertions supporting his views from water users insisting that the measure (H.R. 7207), the Raker bill, could not adequately provide for their needs.

If Hetch Hetchy water could be reserved for irrigation in the San Joaquin Valley, Works argued, San Francisco could secure its water from one of several sources discussed in the report of the Army Engineers. Endorsing Works's views were chiefly Republican colleagues from western states. Not included was the senior senator from California, George C. Perkins, who because of ill health never fully participated in the debate, although he inserted numerous items in the *Congressional Record* endorsing San Francisco's request for Hetch Hetchy water. Petitions from residents of San Francisco and other Bay Area communities noted that Congress had already granted Seattle, Portland, and Los Angeles water reserves. San Francisco's need for a present and future water supply was as great or greater.[8]

At the conclusion of his lengthy remarks, Works said that he "occupied the peculiar position of being the only representative from the State of California" who opposed the grant. Although he made his home in Los Angeles, Works insisted that his concern was for the best interests of all the people in California, and he bemoaned the fact that "some of the other representatives of the State have lacked the courage to stand up in the face of the appeals that are made to Congress in behalf of the city and defend the rights of the people."[9]

It was this very point—namely that "every Member of the House from the State of California endorsed it and voted for it" and that "after full hearings the House committee, without exception, reported it favorably" that enabled Colorado Senator Charles S. Thomas to reconsider his hesitations and to refute Works's reference in his opening remarks that the bill was an administration measure. Thomas was one of several Democratic senators who endorsed the proposal, arguing in the place of his Republican colleague George C. Perkins that the proposed grant to San Francisco was a valid one and that the price of water in the city was reputed to be larger than "in almost any other city in the country." Thomas's lengthy remarks were the first to endorse the measure.

While stating that urban domestic needs were superior to the agricultural interest in water, he mentioned that Senator Works's "own city took the waters of Owens River for its own needs, and every ranch man upon that river . . . was up in arms, declaring . . . with much truth—that it meant absolute destruction to the valley itself, making it practically uninhabitable." Any "great municipality" in need of an added water supply "can only acquire it," Thomas said, "by depriving other users of water of the right to it, which means controversy and litigation, perhaps bloodshed."

Securing water for a domestic supply, Thomas and other supporters of the Hetch Hetchy proposal argued, inevitably meant that the value of its use for agricultural purposes would be diminished. "San Francisco," Thomas said, "has been for 13 mortal years trying to get this source of supply—persistently, consistently, continuously. Are we to tell her now that she has other sources of supply nearly as good, or equally as good, and expect her to resort to them without encountering the same troubles, difficulties, and the same delay that has occurred in her pursuit of this one?"[10]

Several senators thought that was exactly what San Francisco should be told. The McCloud, Mokelumne, and Eel Rivers, Asle J. Gronna, Miles Poindexter, and others suggested, provided suitable alternatives.[11] Those who supported other sources, those seeking Hetch Hetchy water for irrigation purposes, owners of land that could be irrigated by water from another river, owners of possible power sites, and nature lovers not wishing to destroy the integrity of a national park generated a flood of mail that poured into Senate offices from every region of the country, calling for the defeat of the Raker bill. Most of the nation's prestigious periodicals and newspapers, chiefly endorsing the position of John Muir, Richard Underwood Johnson, and other prominent nature lovers, were united in opposition. Scientists, naturalists, mountain climbers, travelers, and others, by letters and telegrams, in newspaper and magazine articles, and in person, voiced their opposition. However, such was not the case in California, where the reverse was true. In California mayors, chambers of commerce, boards of trade, and businessmen were in accord in approving the Hetch Hetchy bill. Senator Perkins inserted in the *Congressional Record* five pages of endorsements of prominent citizens of California and editors of leading California newspapers, all urging its passage. They were joined by other distinguished citizens in supporting the bill.[12]

While most senators participating in the debate were from the West, on occasion other senators involved themselves. One was Frank Brandegee of

Connecticut, who suggested that a dam at Hetch Hetchy could be "a place of beauty, accessible and delightful" adding to the attractiveness of the park by providing a beautiful lake "interspersed with forest and wild scenery." The artistic and esoteric concerns of nature lovers would not be seriously impaired, while the urgent needs of a growing metropolitan area "for the necessities of life" would be satisfied. Democrat Marcus Smith of Arizona reinforced Brandegee's views, arguing that very few of the protesters ever saw Hetch Hetchy or knew "that it was five years after San Francisco secured its rights before Hetch Hetchy was added, by Executive order, to the Yosemite National Park." While a clear lake covering the "sunburnt bottom of Hetch Hetchy . . . would largely add to the beauty of the surroundings," Smith said, "that question becomes insignificant in the face of man's necessities."[13]

Members on either side of the issue usually found time to refer to the *Report of the Advisory Board of Army Engineers*. But opponents of the measure did so with greater frequency, to impress upon their colleagues the fact that other satisfactory sources were available to meet San Francisco's needs. The major portion of the 146-page report was devoted to examining these additional sources. Many of these pages were included as part of senators' remarks. Asle J. Gronna, more so than any other senator, inserted mounds of such material during the time he held the floor on December 5. At the conclusion of his remarks, George Norris asked his colleague whether San Francisco, if not allowed to dam the Hetch Hetchy, should be able to recover from the federal government "or from some other source" the funds already expended "in purchasing the land within that valley and the water rights that she was compelled to purchase under the orders of the officials of the United States." Gronna agreed that "it would be only justice to do that." But the matter was never considered by those opposed to the measure, and both senators concluded that the government could not meet the city's expenses.[14]

William Borah raised a technical, if not a legal, argument for opposing the grant. Expressing concern about the vast acreage dispersed by the government in the past half century, Borah focused on the terms that California had insisted upon in receding Yosemite National Park in March 1905—namely, that the park "shall be set aside and held for all time by the United States of America for public use, resort, and recreation." Now, a few years after "one of the most remarkable scenic displays in the world" had been set aside for "all the people of the United States," Congress was preparing to do otherwise. And in doing so, it would "enable the grantee to step in and become a dictator as to the commercial destiny" of a vast region. It was this feature that halted Borah in his "investigation as to the granting of any right of way at all." The grant would not only dismember the park, it would give a "monopolistic advantage," worth from $50 to $100 million, which Congress "ought not to consider." Borah developed his argument through a painstaking analysis of the bill, concluding that the grant placed San Francisco in a position "where, as a proprietor and owner she can sell and dispose of this water and light to the other bay cities or to the people of the San Joaquin Valley." It would not be wise to grant such a monopoly "even to a municipal corporation" that would "deal and traffic with the surrounding communities in regard to the water and light."[15]

Possibly recognizing that his technical and legal argument about a monopoly grant would not gain a favorable response, Borah devoted the remainder of the afternoon and some of the evening session on December 5 to evaluating other sources of water for San Francisco, endorsing the arguments of those opposed to the grant and critiquing those favorable to it. While the remainder of the debate, with one exception, largely followed the themes already discussed, on December 6, when the Senate would have to vote on the Raker bill, and when final remarks were in order, George W. Norris, who was ill at the time, developed a premise barely touched upon in the extended debate. This argument merits some attention because it exhibited for the first time a point of view that highlighted the Senator's entire career.

At the outset, Norris launched into a discussion of the Hetch Hetchy valley to challenge the arguments of the nature lovers. The valley in winter was filled with snow, possibly up to 40 feet. In the spring, owing to the narrow opening, the rushing flood of water could not all get out, thereby leaving the floor of the valley, irregular meadowland with some timber on it "but nothing of any value", covered with water. When these waters finally got out of the narrow opening, the floor of the valley became a marsh. As the summer advanced, it became "a place where it is absolutely impossible for men to stay on account of the millions and millions of mosquitoes that infest it." As the marsh dried up and the mosquitoes disappeared, the heat became almost unbearable, owing to the reflection of the sun from the huge granite cliffs. With only a small opening to the valley, there was "practically no circulation of air." Later in the season, when the heat was not so intense, the atmosphere became comfortable and the valley became a truly beautiful place, accessible only for a "very short time." Moreover, "practically all" of the land to be flooded was owned in fee simple by San Francisco. The city was compelled to buy it "to protect her water rights in this stream by the orders of the officials of the United States Government." The Senator also noted "that there has never been in that valley a vehicle." And as far as Norris knew, "the eyes of no woman or child ever beheld it." Indeed, aside from public officials, there had not been "an average of five persons a year who have gone in there to see it," except for one year. Federal funds could have changed virtually every condition Norris mentioned. Roads could have been built; the floor of the valley modified so that no water could stand there to eliminate the mosquitoes. But no work and no amount of money could do away "with the intolerable heat that will come from the reflection upon those giant walls."

What Norris wished to develop was a point specifically alluded to in passing by Harry Lane, namely, that there was something besides water in the proposal; "he thought there was a power proposition in it." For Norris there was a power proposition involved, and it was one of the reasons that led him to support the bill. It would "utilize one of the sources of nature to develop power," and such utilization, he said, "will not interfere in any way with the use of water or with anyone's right on the stream."

At the insistence of Representative William Kent, when the bill was discussed in the House, a provision, section 6, was added, prohibiting San Francisco "from ever selling or letting to any corporation or individual, except a municipality or a municipal water district or irrigation district" either water or electricity emanating from the dam to be constructed at Hetch Hetchy. Any "attempt to so sell, assign, transfer, or convey water or electricity in violation of this prohibition would revert the grant to the Government of the United States." If this section were not part of the bill, Norris believed the campaign against it would have been considerably reduced. He developed this point by delineating the massive letter-writing effort of the Sierra Blue Lakes and Water Power Company in opposition to the grant. And he went so far as to label one of his colleagues, Reed Smoot, who had received over five thousand letters, the focus of "the mighty cohorts of opposition."[16] All of this opposition existed because power from Hetch Hetchy would come into competition "with the various water-power companies of California," he added, and "there are lots of them there."

Harnessing the power available at Hetch Hetchy and putting it to public use in competition with power companies and corporations that currently enjoyed "almost a monopoly not only in San Francisco but throughout the greater portion of California" could only benefit consumers and challenge the private companies. Norris focused his attention on the Pacific Gas & Electric Company (PG&E) and its subsidiary and related companies, including the Blue Lakes Company, which he had mentioned in launching his discussion. PG&E owned "practically all of the hydro electric power of the State of California"; enactment of the Raker bill would mean competition with a corporation that, along with its subsidiaries, covered the north central portion of California serving more than two hundred communities. Norris commented extensively on the tentacles of PG&E influence throughout the region, developing a technique he utilized later in challenging what he and others would soon call "the power trust."

"Power corporations and other kinds of monopolistic corporation never come out in the open when they fight a proposition," Norris argued. He suggested that "they go around behind and, perhaps, get some nature lovers who are particularly honest to fight their battles." While Norris never claimed a conspiracy on the part of the PG&E, he did say that such fights were "always made under the name of somebody else and under the guise of being the fight of honest people and of honorable men." Virtually every argument he later made in support of public power and in opposition to private utility corporations, Norris utilized in his lengthy remarks. Enactment of the bill would mean "cheaper power, cheaper light, cheaper heat, cheaper transportation and an abundance of cheap water." Approval would also be "the very highest possible act of conservation." To Norris, conservation obviously did not involve locking up natural resources; neither did it mean "dealing out those resources to private capital for gain." It did mean, in this instance, developing cheap power and selling it at cost.[17]

His stress on section 6 pointed to the fact that the Hetch Hetchy proposition was the first multipurpose bill extensively debated in the U.S. Senate. Though Senator Miles Poindexter challenged his remarks about the number of women who visited the valley and his view of its bleakness for all but a few months of the year, no Senator challenged or debated the main thrust of his argument that hydroelectric power was a central issue.[18]

After lengthy amendments by Senators Clarence Clark and Porter McCumber, along with several minor ones, were rejected, the bill was ordered to a third reading, after which Poindexter asked for the yeas and nays. The measure carried 43 to 25, with 27 members not voting.[19] Thereupon, after six days and nights of almost continuous debate, at 12 o'clock midnight, the Senate resolved the fate of Hetch Hetchy in favor of San Francisco. On December 19 the secretary read a message from the president, who signed the bill "because it seemed to serve the pressing public needs of the region concerned better than they could be served in any other way, and yet did not impair the usefulness or materially detract from the beauty of the public domain."[20]

Reviewing the vote, several points can be made. First, the Democrats did not caucus to require all Democratic senators to support the bill. To be sure, most senators supporting the measure were Democrats, but Harry Lane, John W. Kern, and Morris Sheppard were among Democrats in opposition. Progressive Republicans were chiefly in opposition, but Norris played a key role in supporting the measure. Connecticut's old-guard senators (Brandegee and

George P. McLean), along with Henry Lippitt, Republican from Rhode Island, also voted yea. And members of both parties, more Republicans than Democrats, did not bother to vote.

Further, the Senate debates validate Alfred Runte's premise that national parks preserved only scenery. Anything in the area that others considered of potential material value was either not included or, as in the case of Hetch Hetchy, was quickly extricated from the park. And Norris Hundley's thesis of urban imperialism pertaining to water in California is assuredly validated by the Senate debates.

Finally, what could be considered Phase III, Hetch Hetchy and Municipal Power has yet to be carefully examined, although Judson King and Norris delineated its dimensions.[21] The Hetch Hetchy Dam was completed in June 1923, but San Francisco had not yet provided for road and trail construction to the reservoir, as called for in the Raker Act. Formal demand was made on the city by the secretary of the interior in July 1927 to fulfill these obligations to little avail. During the New Deal a road to the dam was completed. M. M. O'Shaughnessy, the city engineer of San Francisco, after whom the dam was formally named, died in 1934, several months before water from Hetch Hetchy, on October 30, 1934, was turned into the city's reservoirs. It had taken twenty years to build the dam and the conduits that extended 155 miles from the dam to the reservoirs, at a cost, according to Harold Ickes, of "pretty close to $1 billion."[22]

But the dream of William Kent, written into section 6 of the law, calling for San Francisco to develop power from these waters to be sold directly to the people, was never realized. Section 6 also said "the grantee is prohibited from ever selling or letting power to any (private) corporation or individual," at the risk of having the grant revert to the federal government. But San Francisco, instead of selling the power produced under the grant, delivered it to PG&E under a contract for a fixed compensation. The utility, in turn, sold it to consumers in the city and throughout the Bay Area, at rates fixed by the California Public Utilities Commission. At Secretary of the Interior Ickes's instigation, in 1935 an injunction was issued commanding the City and County of San Francisco to cease disposing of its electric power in this way. And in a case decided on April 22, 1940 Hugo Black, speaking for the majority (with only James Clark McReynolds in opposition), upheld the injunction.[23] However, to this day it has never been enforced.

In addition, it can be noted that every point of view expressed in the Hetch Hetchy debate from the preservationists' concern, to the call of irrigation farmers for more water, to the water needs of a major municipality, and to the struggle against a powerful monopoly, fits into an integral aspect of the Progressive movement. The tragedy is that everybody lost except Pacific Gas & Electric. The first significant multipurpose law with regard to water power yielded results that could not have satisfied any of the participants in the December debate in 1913 at the outset of the second session of the Sixty-third Congress.

NOTES

1. *Congressional Record,* 63rd Cong., 2d sess., 6 December 1913, p. 362. Hereafter, citations will be registered as CR followed by a page reference.

2. For volumes examining the controversy see Holway Jones, *John Muir and the Sierra Club* (San Francisco: Sierra Club, 1965); Alfred Runte, *Yosemite: The Embattled Wilderness* (Lincoln: University of Nebraska Press, 1990); Norris Hundley, Jr. *The Great Thirst* (Berkeley and Los Angeles: University of California Press, 1992); Michael P. Cohen, *The Pathless Way: John Muir and American Wilderness* (Madison: University of Wisconsin Press, 1984); William Frederick Bade, *The Life and Letters of John Muir,* vol. 2 (Boston: Houghton Mifflin Company, 1924); Robert Underwood Johnson, *Remembered Yesterdays* (Boston: Little, Brown, and Company, 1923); Samuel P. Hays, *Conservation and the Gospel of Efficiency* (Cambridge: Harvard University Press, 1959); Elmo Richardson, *The Politics of Conservation: Crusades and Controversies, 1897–1913* (Berkeley and Los Angeles: University of California Press, 1962); Elmo Richardson, "The Struggle for the Valley: California's Hetch Hetchy Controversy, 1905–1913," *California Historical Society Quarterly* 38 (September 1959): 249–58; Robert Shankland, *Steve Mather of The National Parks* (New York: Alfred A. Knopf, 1950); Roderick Nash, *Wilderness and the American Mind* (New Haven: Yale University Press, 1967); Judson King, *The Conservation Fight* (Washington, DC: Public Affairs Press, 1959); John Ise, *Our National Park Policy: A Critical History* (Baltimore: Johns Hopkins University Press, 1961); George W. Norris, *Fighting Liberal* (New York: Macmillan, 1945).

3. 63rd Cong., 1st sess., House Document No. 54, Hetch Hetchy Valley: Report of Advisory Board of Army Engineers, pp. 50–51. The other sources involved utilization of the McCloud, Mokelumne, Eel, and Yuba Rivers, respectively, or in the case of the McCloud and Mokelumne Rivers, with other lakes and rivers. To effectively utilize the Sacramento River a filtration plant would have to be constructed to insure pure drinking water. The report made no mention of water rights and the amount of water that would be diverted for irrigation on any of the rivers and the effect of diversion on water quality.

4. CR, 7 October 1913, 5483–84.

5. "Brief of the City and County of San Francisco Before the Committee on Public Lands Committee of the United States Senate: H.R. 7207," passim and p. 5 for the quote. Copy available in the William Kent Papers, 309–III, 67–84, Yale University.

6. "Brief of The City and County of San Francisco," p. 6.

7. See CR, 4 December 1913, 198–99 for a discussion of the role of Denver Church.

8. See CR, 3 December 1913, 95–96 for petitions submitted by Senator Perkins. Works devoted his remarks on December 3 to delineating other sources from which San Francisco could secure water for domestic purposes. Key Pittman noted that all California munici-

palities, with one possible exception, unanimously endorsed the bill. See ibid., 6 December 1913, 368.

9. CR, 3 December 1913, 115.

10. See CR, 3 December 1913 for Thomas's remarks, beginning on p. 115. He spoke following John D. Works. His comments on the Owens Valley are on p. 125.

11. CR, 3 December 1913, 125–26; 4 December 1913, 197. Initially, the Board of Army Engineers cited thirteen possible sources of additional supply (see p. 83).

12. See CR, 3 December 1913, 138–39 for story about support in Southern California. See also CR, 5 December 1913, 236–40.

13. CR, 4 December 1913, 183; 5 December 1913, 273–74.

14. CR, 5 December 1913, 272–73.

15. CR, 5 December 1913, 286–87.

16. See CR, 6 December 1913, 343, where Norris cites the senator from Utah as the member leading and guiding the opposition in the Senate.

17. CR, 6 December 1913, 339–52. Norris held the floor longer than any other senator on this final day of debate.

18. See CR, 6 December 1913, 378 for Poindexter's remarks.

19. CR, 6 December 1913, 385–86.

20. CR, 19 December 1913, 1189.

21. King, *The Conservation Fight*; Chapter 5 is entitled "Hetch Hetchy and Municipal Power." See also Norris, *Fighting Liberal*; Chapter 18 is entitled "Hetch Hetchy."

22. Harold L. Ickes, *The Secret Diary of Harold L. Ickes: The First Thousand Days 1933–1936* (New York: Simon and Shuster, 1953), 214.

23. *United States v. City and County of San Francisco*, 310 U.S. 587.

CHAPTER SEVEN

PARKS FOR PEOPLE
Lyndon Johnson and the National Park System

MELODY WEBB

The horrors of the Vietnam War have shaped people's perception of Lyndon Johnson. Few remember the contributions of his Great Society. Many African-Americans worship John F. Kennedy for giving them their civil rights, and the elderly venerate Franklin D. Roosevelt for Medicare.[1] So it is with Johnson's conservation record. Those who do acknowledge the Sixties for the growth of the modern environmental movement acclaim Stewart Udall as the greatest Secretary of the Interior. Some may give grudging recognition to Lady Bird Johnson for her work towards "beautification." Only a few appreciate Lyndon Johnson's commitment to expanding the opportunities for more Americans to enjoy their national parks.[2]

Nonetheless, Johnson made national parks a pivotal part of his Great Society. Between 1963 and 1968 he established more new park areas than any president in history. In addition, he pioneered resourceful concepts in cooperative management, devised an imaginative means for purchasing park land, recognized the significance of ecosystem management, exported the national park idea abroad, expanded historic preservation into America's urban landscape, and provided recreational areas for the nation's largest cities.

Ironically, one of the most controversial presidents in the twentieth century wanted to be "most of all a peace President and to be a conservation President."[3] He took great pride in his conservation record and, at least thirteen times, cited his administration's achievements in his speeches.[4] He also reveled in news articles and letters praising his conservation record.[5] Although known

President Lyndon B. Johnson with Secretary of the Interior Stewart Udall, January 30, 1967. (Photograph courtesy LBJ Library, Austin, Texas.)

as an egotist, Johnson was unusually careful to share with Congress the credit for his conservation accomplishments.[6]

Because of his success with Congress, many environmental writers perceived Johnson as a pragmatic schemer, reaping political capital from a popular cause. They doubted his sincerity and commitment to conservation.[7]

But Johnson's genuine commitment sprang from an intimate, almost mystical, tie to the land. "When I come here [to the LBJ Ranch in Texas] and stay two or three days it's a breath of fresh air," he told journalist Stewart Alsop. "I go away ready to challenge the world. . . . [No other place] can do for me what this soil, this land, this water, this people, and what these hills, these surroundings can do. They represent memories of half a century and they provide the stimulation and inspiration that nothing else can provide."[8]

Johnson used those memories in his speeches and expressed his concern that future generations would not have the same opportunities unless land was set aside and preserved. He described how, as a child of five or six, he would cross the dusty field and walk along the banks of the Pedernales River to visit his grandfather. "And those hills, and those fields, and that river were the only world that I really had in those years," he told the delegates to the White House Conference on Natural Beauty in 1965. "So I did not know how much more beautiful it was than that of many other boys'."

"All my life I have drawn strength, and something more, from those Texas hills," he continued. "Sometimes, in the highest councils of the Nation, in this house, I sit back and I can almost feel that rough, unyielding, sticky clay soil between my toes, and it stirs memories that often give me comfort and sometimes give me a pretty firm purpose."

Then he lamented that not all the boys in America had the privilege to grow up in a wide and open country. "We can give them something," he insisted, "and we are going to. We can let each of them feel a little of what the first settlers must have felt, as they stood unbelieving before the endless majesty of our great land. Thus, they, too, will reach for the wonders of our future, reinforced by the treasured values of our past."[9]

When Johnson became president in November 1963, he inherited a number of pending conservation bills. Some had been stymied for years. President Kennedy had requested the Wilderness Bill and the Land and Water Conservation Bill as well as congressional authorization for four recreation areas—Sleeping Bear Dunes in Michigan, Indiana Dunes in Indiana, Fire Island in New York, Assateague Island in Maryland, and Ozark Riverways in Missouri. Stewart Udall, Secretary of the Interior under Kennedy and Johnson, gave the bills only a 50–50 chance of passing.[10] Despite all the other issues Johnson was juggling, he still wrote a letter to Congressman Wayne Aspinall, Chairman of the House Interior Committee, affirming his support for the Land and Water Conservation Fund Bill.[11]

During the next five months, leading up to his Great Society speech, Johnson and his staff worked with Congress on these seven priority bills. At the department and bureau level, capable and hard-working men—Stewart Udall and George Hartzog, Director of the National Park Service—delivered the operational requirements to make Johnson's wishes reality. Then his White House aides forwarded the bureau and department paperwork to him with their own summary, a recommendation for action, and a check-off box. Johnson provided direct guidance on all of these bills through these check-off boxes and additional scribbled instructions, such as telling them who to call, when to seek compromises, and other politically savvy advice. As a result of his personal attention and interest, he eventually signed six of the seven Kennedy initiatives into law.[12]

Only six months into his new administration, on May 22, 1964, President Johnson delivered his Great Society speech. The Great Society focused not only on cities and classrooms but on the countryside too. He believed the Great Society was a "place where man can renew contact with nature." But parks were overcrowded, seashores overburdened, and green fields and forests were disappearing. Thus, he urged Americans to act immediately to prevent an ugly America. "For once the battle is lost, once our natural splendor is destroyed, it can never be recaptured."[13]

Johnson did act with dispatch. In the next four years he established twelve task forces on the environment and called White House conferences on natural beauty. He also directed his attention to establishing Redwood National Park— the nation's most significant unprotected natural resource. "I have expressed my concern and determination to save our countrysides," he reminded Americans. "I know of no better place to begin than in this work of saving the majestic redwood forests of the American West."[14]

By September 17, 1964, President Johnson's energies had paid off. He had signed five major conservation bills. The Land and Water Conservation Fund Bill allocated money for land acquisition for the National Park System. The Wilderness Bill established a National Wilderness Preservation System of federal lands that would be maintained in a wilderness state—an "area where the earth and its community of life are untrammeled by man, where man himself is a visitor who does not remain." Canyonlands National Park was the first new national park to be established since 1956. Fire Island National Seashore promised recreational opportunities for the millions of people in New York City. Ozark Scenic Riverways gave Missouri its first national park area and was the stimulus for a new system of wild and scenic rivers. Moreover, to protect

America's cultural heritage, he had established eight national historic sites, including one international park.[15]

On September 17, 1964, at an inauspicious breakfast in Portland, Oregon, President Johnson launched his New Conservation program. He voiced concern for three changing forces—the growing population and its pressures on the nation's recreational resources, technology and its waste products as threats to the destruction of nature, and urbanization and its effect of cutting off people from nature. "Conservation must move from nature's wilderness to the manmade wilderness of our cities," he expounded. "This requires a new conservation. . . . Its concern is not with nature alone, but with the total relation between man and the world around him. Its object is not just man's welfare, but the dignity of his spirit." He vowed to press ahead—to develop new recreation areas near large population centers and inaugurate a national system of scenic riverways. "And I tell you now that this hope will always be among the closest to my heart," he concluded. "So let us not leave our task with the reproach of our children already ringing in our ears. Far, far too much is at stake. These are the resources on which our future rests."[16]

After his landslide election in 1964, Johnson believed that he had a mandate for his Great Society. Ironically, in 1965, for the first time, he attempted to use national park areas to further political rather than conservation goals. When the new Democratic congressman from Iowa introduced a bill to commemorate former President Herbert Hoover to the embarrassment of Iowa's Republican delegation, Johnson threw his support behind the legislation. Then, by planning a bipartisan signing ceremony at the White House, Johnson hoped to pull off a political victory. When former President Dwight Eisenhower preferred to attend a golf tournament and aides neglected to invite Richard Nixon and Barry Goldwater, Johnson's plan backfired.[17]

Despite Johnson's interest in national parks, he visited only one while president. On October 3, 1965, he signed an immigration bill at Liberty Island in New York Harbor. Although Secretary Udall repeatedly invited Johnson to national park areas, he preferred to gain political mileage through White House signing ceremonies and sought solace from nature at his Texas ranch. Instead, Mrs. Johnson went. She visited Big Bend, Grand Teton, Padre Island, and Redwoods and became a staunch supporter of national parks.[18]

As the summer of 1965 heated up, Johnson signed the Voting Rights legislation, sent American troops into combat in Vietnam, and approved Medicare. Then in August, Watts blew up. Once again his attention turned to the cities and their need for recreation. The passage of the enabling legislation for Delaware Water Gap National Recreation Area established a 72,000-acre national park halfway between New York and Philadelphia. Now, an additional 15 percent of the nation's population would live within 100 miles of a recreational area. These were city people surrounded by noise, decaying buildings, and despoiled landscapes. Johnson sincerely believed they yearned for beauty and hungered for the opportunity to find refreshment in nature. "I hope that I might find some small place in history," he said, "as a President who cared and a President who tried and a President who, in small measure, succeeded in preserving and in enriching the natural beauty of our land and thus making more beautiful the lives of all our people."[19] Three weeks later he signed Assateague Island National Seashore into law—the last undeveloped seashore between Massachusetts and North Carolina—preserving more "Eastern wilderness."

As the Vietnam War escalated and race riots erupted throughout the nation, Johnson focused more and more on parks for people. "The real challenge of conservation is just beginning," he pronounced. "Great national parks and great national seashores located in faraway, distant places do not satisfy the needs of the people who are a part of our urban civilization. The serenity of nature must be more than a once-a-year experience." He urged the preservation of more land around and in cities.[20]

By late summer, he was able to boast that "for the first time, America is winning the battle of conservation. Every year now, we are saving more land than we are losing." While urban development consumed a million acres, nearly two million acres had been set aside for conservation—land where it was the most accessible to the greatest number of people.[21]

Yet in addition to his emphasis on parks near population centers, Johnson put personal energy into the preservation of two large western parks—North Cascades in Washington and Redwoods in California. For the redwoods, he enlisted the support of Walter Reuther of the United Automobile Workers Union, philanthropist-conservationist Laurance Rockefeller, and environmental organizations. When lumber companies deliberately moved into the proposed park area and began cutting the giant trees, Johnson swung into action. He dictated to his aides, "Let's go full steam ahead—get Carl [Albert] & the speaker to help." Rather than follow Udall's advice and seek emergency legislation to suspend all tree cutting, Johnson made a personal appeal to the lumber companies, which agreed to restrict harvesting. Still, 1966 ended without a Redwood National Park.[22]

Meanwhile bureaucratic infighting stalled North Cascades National Park. The area proposed lay within a national forest, and Agricultural Secretary Orville Freeman resisted its transfer to the National Park Service. Disgusted with the squabbling, Johnson sent identical letters to Secretaries Udall and Freeman: "I believe it essential that you personally and jointly inspect the area as quickly as possible. . . . I wish this matter to be resolved promptly." To ensure resolution he sent along his personal representative from the Bureau of the Budget. Although Freeman continued to object, the Bureau of the Budget recommended the area as outstanding and fully warranting park designation.[23]

In addition to establishing national parks, on October 15, 1966, Johnson signed two major laws that affected their operation—the Endangered Species Act and the National Historic Preservation Act. One recognized the loss of particular species of wildlife, the other the loss of historic places, especially in cities. "Both of these [laws]," Johnson said at the signing ceremony, "will help us to preserve for our children the heritage of this great land we call America."[24]

Innovative management of national parks also became a hallmark of the Johnson years. The concept of natural resources management shifted from simple protection of individual features or species to the preservation of total environments and the interrelationships of resources, known as ecosystem management. Managers began to recognize the value of natural fire, endemic insects and diseases, predation, and the overall competition of plants and animals. Park rangers taught these rudiments to children in environmental education classes held in national parks. Recognizing that the federal government could not provide all the necessary parks and recreation areas for the people, Johnson encouraged cooperative ties with the states, other federal agencies, and even other countries. Third World countries especially sought assistance from the National Park Service in developing their own national parks.[25]

Johnson opened 1967 with a special message to Congress on protecting the nation's natural heritage. For the first time, he called for "Parks for America." He asked for four specific park areas—Redwoods, North Cascades, Potomac Valley Park, and Apostle Islands—and a system of scenic rivers and trails. Redwoods remained his number one priority, and he called it a "last chance" opportunity.[26] Unable to confront effectively the increasing protest against the bombing of North Vietnam, Johnson seemed to turn his extensive political talents to something he could affect—the Redwoods park proposal. Recognizing that the donation of California's two state parks were critical to the proposal, he asked Laurance Rockefeller to persuade the new Republican governor of California, Ronald Reagan, "to go along with this very urgent and meritorious proposal." Rockefeller accepted the challenge and kept the President informed of his progress during the year.[27]

As race riots raged in Newark and Johnson prepared to meet Soviet Premier Aleksei Kosygin in New Jersey, he took time to write Wayne Aspinall, Chairman of the House Interior Committee, on Redwood National Park. He told him that of all the park bills before the committee, "I consider favorable action on a Redwood National Park bill to be of first and highest priority." Aspinall responded that he would work as quickly as possible.[28] President Johnson did not get any of his priority parks in 1967—only two presidential sites, commemorating John Kennedy and Dwight Eisenhower.

Once again, on March 8, 1968, Johnson went before Congress to request a program almost identical to that he had requested in 1967. This time he did not stop with Congress. He addressed radio and television audiences with a similar message. He reminded them that he had built his New Conservation on the promise to bring parks closer to the people and urged all Americans to join in the crucial task of conserving America the beautiful.[29]

By June 1968, Johnson had stunned the nation with his declaration that he would not run again. Although he spent much of his considerable energy negotiating peace with North Vietnam, he pushed harder than ever to accomplish the goals of his New Conservation. "There is no legacy that I would rather leave, than a permanent program of real conservation for this Nation," he told an audience in Nashville, Tennessee, on June 25. He reminded them that he had already passed 138 conservation bills, or 2½ bills for every month of his presidency, but that he had 42 more awaiting congressional action.[30] To aid in conserving more land closer to the people, Congress enlarged the Land and Water Conservation Fund by adding revenue from outer continental shelf mineral leases. Now, land acquisition costs for parks and recreation areas were no longer stumbling blocks.[31]

Johnson's last summer in office reverberated with race riots, anti-war protests, and the assassinations of Martin Luther King and Robert Kennedy. Nonetheless, he consoled himself with a major conservation triumph—the passage of the Redwood National Park bill. He called it his greatest conservation achievement. "It is a great victory for every American in every State, because we have rescued a magnificent and a meaningful treasure from the chain saw," he rejoiced. "For once we have spared what is enduring and ennobling from a hungry and hasty and selfish act of destruction."[32] At the same time, he signed bills establishing North Cascade National Park, a Wild and Scenic Rivers System, and a National Trails System. Gratefully, he basked in the praise of his conservation record.[33]

After Richard Nixon's election in November 1968, Johnson began to wind down. In mid-December, Secretary Udall disrupted his melancholy with a startling suggestion—why not give the nation and future generations a Christmas present of 7.5 million acres of new national park land?[34] The Antiquities Act of 1906 gave presidents the power to establish national monuments through presidential proclamations without seeking legislation from Congress. Previous presidents had used the law freely to preserve areas of historical or scientific interest.[35] Udall suggested creation of three new national monuments—Gates of the Arctic in Alaska and Marble Canyon and Sonoran Desert in Arizona—and enlargement of four existing parks or monuments—Arches and Capitol Reef in Utah, and Katmai and Mount McKinley in Alaska. Intrigued, Johnson asked the Department of Justice to weigh the legality of the proposal. He also asked Udall and his presidential aides to clear the idea with congressional leaders.

Historically, Congress had opposed national monuments established by presidential proclamations. The process failed to address congressional concerns and constituency requirements. On more than one occasion, Congress had refused to recognize the monuments and balked at funding them. When Johnson received Udall's report on congressional "checks," he was not satisfied and wanted more thorough coverage.[36] Then he fell ill and was hospitalized for several days. He decided not to make a decision on the monuments until January, when Congress reconvened and he could confirm Udall's checks.

By January 9, Johnson was receiving several summary memos a day from his aide, De Vier Pierson. Although the Justice Department advised him that there was no legal objection to the action and the Bureau of the Budget supported the proposal, Pierson recommended against it. He believed the action contradicted Johnson's transition policy not to bind the next administration with last-minute actions. Nonetheless, Johnson himself met with the new Interior Secretary-designate, Walter Hickel of Alaska, and received his muted concurrence.[37]

On January 14 Pierson sent Johnson a detailed description of the monument proposal. Johnson marked "ok" by Marble Canyon in Arizona, Capitol Reef in Utah, and Arches in Utah. He scribbled "maybe" by the land extensions to Katmai and Mount McKinley in Alaska, and left untouched Alaska's Gates of the Arctic, with 3.5 million acres, and Arizona's Sonoran Desert, with 1 million acres. He also instructed his White House staff to make congressional checks "at once in depth."[38]

On January 17, with only three days left in the Johnson Administration, Udall summarized his contacts with Congress. He claimed that the Interior Committee chairman, Wayne Aspinall, respected the President's prerogatives but favored congressional authorization.[39] He also attached a draft press release that boasted of the Johnson Administration's tremendous contribution to the National Park System and provided historical perspective—other presidents had established Grand Canyon, Death Valley, and Petrified Forest through executive proclamation.[40]

Although Johnson remained interested, he was not comfortable with Udall's assessment of Congress. He asked Pierson to call Aspinall. When he did, Aspinall blew up: "I told the people from the Department of the Interior that if the President took this action that I would see that it never got a penny for the maintenance of these lands and that I'll introduce legislation to repeal the Antiquities Act."[41] When Pierson reported this to the President, he felt betrayed and terribly distressed. According to Aspinall, Johnson called him personally to sound him out, not once but twice.[42] Finally, Johnson postponed making a decision until he could study the case-by-case report.

Meanwhile, Udall believed time had run out. When told that the decision had been postponed again, he exploded: "I've just had it. He has everything that he needs to know from me on it. He can just do whatever he wants to do."[43] Still emotionally upset, he released the story that Johnson had signed the proclamations, creating 7.5 million acres of parkland.[44] Within minutes, Johnson caught the story from the Associated Press teletype. He called Udall and "raised hell" with him. As further punishment, he told him personally to retract the story.[45] Even though Udall had an appointment to meet with the President on Sunday, January 19, he refused to go and could not be reached by the White House.

Johnson, however, remained fascinated by the idea of a last-minute conservation pronouncement. "Believe it or not," Pierson related, "I spent about an hour in the President's bedroom Monday morning, the 20th of January, while the President was putting on his morning suit for the inaugural ceremonies, going over these cases one last time while he was deciding whether or not he would sign any or all of them."[46] After weeks of indecision, Johnson's last official act established Marble Canyon in Arizona and enlarged Arches, Capitol Reef, and Katmai, adding approximately 300,000 acres to the national park system. The White House press release on the new monuments acknowledged that he had reviewed proposals that would have added millions of more acres of national parkland, but he believed it would strain the Antiquities Act far beyond its intent, would be poor public policy, and would be opposed by members of Congress.[47]

Even without those millions of acres of parkland, Johnson's conservation record was outstanding. In five years he established or designated forty-seven new areas encompassing 15 million acres. Only two other presidents compare— Theodore Roosevelt had nineteen in eight years, Franklin Roosevelt had thirty-six in twelve years. In several ways, Johnson's contributions were more difficult to achieve. Most of his park areas were near population centers. Thus, land prices were high and opposing forces even more virulent.

Many of the areas required his personal intervention—to cajole Congress, to enlist powerful supporters, to force compromise. Despite the pressures of the war in Vietnam, anti-war protests, and race riots, Johnson still found time and energy to direct his staff in conservation matters and to promote an environmental consciousness to the nation at large. In addition, several of his national parks offered new dimensions to conservation, such as wild and scenic rivers, national trails, a cultural park devoted to the performing arts, an international park in Canada, and cooperative park ventures with states and other federal agencies. To purchase these expensive new parks, he developed the Land and Water Conservation Fund, whose funds came from the profits of oil reserves from the outer continental shelf. His administration also introduced new concepts in management, such as ecosystem management, wilderness preservation, environmental education, and historic preservation.

Fundamental to Johnson's conservation efforts was his belief that every person—even the poor and working class—should have the opportunity to enjoy national parks. To ensure that opportunity, he saved 4 million acres within a day's drive of the major cities of the United States. While he believed in the preservation of western parkland and wrestled with designating great national monuments in Alaska and Arizona, his primary goal was parks for people.

NOTES

1. As Superintendent, Lyndon B. Johnson National Historical Park (1989–1992), I personally witnessed visitors reacting with surprise to President's Johnson's accomplishments with such statements as, "I always thought it was Kennedy [or FDR]."

2. Martin V. Melosi, "Lyndon Johnson and Environmental Policy," in *The Johnson Years, Volume 2: Vietnam, the Environment, and Science*, ed. Robert A. Divine (Lawrence: University Press of Kansas, 1987); Lewis L. Gould, *Lady Bird and the Environment* (Lawrence: University Press of Kansas, 1988); Paul K. Conkin, *Big Daddy from the Pedernales: Lyndon Baines Johnson* (Boston: Twayne Publishers, 1986); Vaughn Davis Bornet, *The Presidency of Lyndon B. Johnson* (Lawrence: University Press of Kansas, 1983); James L. Sundiquist, *Politics and Policy: The Eisenhower, Kennedy, and Johnson Years* (Washington, DC: The Brookings Institution, 1968); and Barbara Laverne Leunes, "The Conservation Philosophy of Stewart L. Udall, 1961–1968," (Ph.D. diss., Texas A & M University, 1977). On the other hand, John P. Crevelli, "The Final Act of the Greatest Conservation President," *Prologue* (Winter 1980): 173–91, recognizes Johnson's sincerity but still believes that Udall "was the educator of both the president . . . and the nation."

3. Lyndon B. Johnson, "Remarks at Battery Park, Burlington, Vermont, August 20, 1966," *Public Papers of the Presidents of the United States: Lyndon B. Johnson, 1966,* [hereafter cited as *Public Papers*], Book II (Washington,DC: Government Printing Office, 1967), 866. Similar sentiment is expressed in his presidential memoirs, *The Vantage Point: Perspectives of the Presidency, 1963–1969* (New York: Holt, Rinehart and Winston, 1971), 336; and Johnson's "Remarks at the Signing of a Bill Establishing the Delaware Water Gap National Recreation Area, September 1, 1965," *Public Papers, 1965*, Book II (Washington, DC: Government Printing Office, 1966), 958–59.

4. Lyndon Johnson's "Remarks on Conservation at a Breakfast in Portland Saluting the Northwest-Southwest Power Transmission Intertie," 17 September 1964, *Public Papers,*

1963–64, Book II (Washington, DC: Government Printing Office, 1965), 1081–86; "Statement by the President Reviewing the Work of the 88th Congress," 3 October 1964, ibid., 1201–3; Johnson's "Remarks to the Delegates to the White House Conference on Natural Beauty," 25 May 1965, *Public Papers, 1965*, ibid., 576–81; Johnson's Speech at Battery Park, *Public Papers, 1966*, ibid., 864–69; Johnson's "Remarks to Members of the National Recreation and Park Association," 13 October 1966, ibid., 1173–78; Johnson's "Remarks at the Signing Ceremony for Seven Conservation Bills," 15 October 1966, ibid., 1186–87; Johnson's "Remarks on the Accomplishments of the 89th Congress," 15 October 1966, ibid., 1190–99; "Statement by the President Upon Signing Bill Establishing the Indiana Dunes National Lakeshore," 5 November 1966, ibid., 1331–32; Johnson's "Special Message to the Congress on Conservation: 'To Renew a Nation,'" 8 March 1968, *Public Papers, 1968–69*, Book I (Washington, DC: Government Printing Office, 1970), 355–70; Johnson's "Remarks at a Reception for the Members of the Citizens' Advisory Committee on Recreation and Natural Beauty," 29 March 1968, ibid., 458–61; Johnson's "Remarks at the Dedication of the J. Percy Priest Project, Nashville, Tennessee," 29 June 1968, ibid., 757–61; Johnson's "Remarks Upon Signing Four Bills Relating to Conservation and Outdoor Recreation," 2 October 1968, ibid., 1000–03; Johnson's "Remarks Upon Signing Bill To Establish the Biscayne National Monument," 18 October 1968, ibid., 1052–54; and Johnson's "Remarks at a White House Reception for the Members of the National Council on the Arts," 21 November 1968, ibid., 1149–50.

5. See the multitude of letters and news clippings in the LBJ Library; in particular letter, Walter Reuther [union leader] to President, 2 February 1966, GEN LE/NR 7, White House Central Files [hereafter cited WHCF], Box 145, LBJ Library, Austin, Texas; letter, Michael Frome [environmentalist] to President, 15 March 1966, EX LE/PA 3, Box 146, ibid.; letter, Melville Bell Grosvenor [National Geographic Chairman] to President, 16 October 1968, ibid.; and memo, De Vier Pierson [presidential aide] to President, 21 October 1968, GEN PA 2, Box 16, ibid., enclosing clippings from *New York Times* with headline, "Johnson is Praised as Conservationist." Pierson in this memo reports that the CBS special on parks "was locked up some time ago and we can't get the recent figures into it." Apparently, Johnson was not content with reporters citing his already outstanding conservation record; he wanted his latest achievement to be included.

6. Johnson's Conservation Speech at a Breakfast in Portland, *Public Papers, 1964*, 1083; Johnson's Review of the 88th Congress, ibid., 1201; Johnson's "Special Message to the Congress Proposing Measures To Preserve America's Natural Heritage," 23 February 1966, *Public Papers, 1966*, 196; Johnson's "Remarks at the Signing of the Cape Lookout National Seashore Bill," 10 March 1966, ibid., 300; Johnson's Speech at Battery Park, ibid., 866–67; Johnson's Speech to the National Recreation and Park Association, ibid., 1175; Johnson's Remarks at the Signing Ceremony for Seven Conservation Bills, ibid., 1187; Johnson's Review of the 89th Congress, ibid., 1190–93; Speech on Signing the Indiana Dunes National Lakeshore Bill, ibid., 1332; Johnson's "Special Message to the Congress: Protecting Our Natural Heritage, January 30, 1967," *Public Papers, 1967*, 93–101; "Statement by the President Upon Signing Bill Establishing the National Park Foundation, December 19, 1967," ibid., 1157; Johnson's Speech at the Dedication of the J. Percy Priest Project, *Public*

Papers, 1968, 759; Johnson's "Remarks Upon Signing Bill To Enlarge the Land and Water Conservation Fund, July 15, 1968," ibid., 808–9; Johnson's Speech Upon Signing Four Conservation Bills, ibid., 1000–2; and Johnson's Speech Upon Signing the Biscayne National Monument Bill, ibid., 1054.

7. Lynton K. Caldwell, *Environment: A Challenge for Modern Society* (Garden City, NY: Natural History Press, 1970), 54; Richard A. Cooley and Geoffrey Wandersforde-Smith eds., *Congress and the Environment* (Seattle: University of Washington Press, 1970), xiv; and Melosi, "Johnson and Environmental Policy," ibid.

8. Stewart Alsop, "Lyndon Johnson: How Does He Do It?" *The Saturday Evening Post,* 24 January 1959, 13–14; also quoted in Merle Miller, *Lyndon: An Oral Biography* (New York: G.P. Putnam's Sons, 1980), 406.

9. Johnson's Speech to the White House Conference on Natural Beauty, *Public Papers, 1965*, 580. His Conservation Speech in Portland, *Public Paper, 1964*, 1083, expressed a similar sentiment: "I grew upon the land. The life of my parents depended entirely upon the bounty of the soil. I devoted much of my public life to protecting for our children the great legacy of our natural abundance."

10. Letter, Stewart Udall to The President, 27 November 1963, EX LE/NR, WHCF, Box 142, LBJ Library.

11. Letter, President Johnson to Wayne Aspinall, 17 December 1963, EX LE/NR, WHCF, Box 142, LBJ Library. Interestingly enough, the Bureau of the Budget, not the Interior Department, drafted the letter for Johnson's signature.

12. Sleeping Bear Dunes National Lakeshore was the only Kennedy national park initiative that LBJ failed to pass. Memo, Mike Manatos to Bill Moyers, 3 March 1964, on the Wilderness Bill, congressional personalities, and presidential involvement, EX FG 145, WHCF, Box 203, LBJ Library; Memo, Lee C. White and Lawrence O'Brien to the President, 22 April 1964, on Sleeping Bear Dunes National Lakeshore, GEN LE/NR 7, Box 145, ibid. On this memo LBJ scribbled "Talk to Gordon." Follow-up memos show his staff did exactly that. Memo, Lee White to Udall, 16 June 1964, ibid., reporting that the President had spoken with Senator Hart of Michigan on accelerating action on Sleeping Bear Dunes. Memo, Larry O'Brien to the President, 18 June 1964, EX LE/NR, Box 142, LBJ Library, indicates that when the Wilderness Bill was reported out of the House Interior Committee, Johnson asked his staff to remind him to call and thank Aspinall. On June 29, the staff recorded that the President had made the call. In memo, Lee White to the President, 30 July 1964, GEN LE/NR 7, Box 145, ibid., White asked the President if he should call two key senators on the Indiana Dunes bill as requested by Senator Douglas; LBJ scrawled "OK" with his characteristic "L" below it.

13. Johnson's "Remarks at the University of Michigan, May 22, 1964," *Public Papers, 1964*, ibid., 705.

14. Johnson's "Remarks on the Proposed Redwoods National Park in Northern California, June 25, 1964," *Public Papers, 1964*, ibid., 817.

15. The eight historic sites included: Roosevelt Campobello International Park; Fort Bowie National Historic Site, Arizona; Saint Gaudens National Historic Site, New Hampshire; Allegheny Portage Railroad National Historic Site, Pennsylvania; Johnstown Flood

National Memorial, Pennsylvania; John Muir National Historic Site, California; Fort Scott Historic Area, Kansas; and Fort Larned National Historic Site, Kansas.

16. Johnson's Conservation Speech in Portland, *Public Papers, 1964*, ibid., 1084–85. Later, this speech was developed into "Presidential Policy Paper No. 3: Conservation of Natural Resources," 1 November 1964, ibid., 1565–68. He also included the New Conservation concepts in his "Special Message to the Congress on Conservation and Restoration of Natural Beauty," 8 February 1965, *Public Papers, 1965*, 155–65, and his Speech to the White House Conference on Natural Beauty, ibid., 576–81. On 11 November 1964 the Outside Task Force on Natural Resources, and on 18 November 1964, the Outside Task Force on the Preservation of Natural Beauty concurred with Johnson's concerns and recommended several of his remedies. See 1964 Outside Task Force on Natural Resources and 1964 Outside Task Force on the Preservation of Natural Beauty, Task Force Collection, Box 2, LBJ Library.

17. See White House Aides correspondence in GEN LE/NR 7, WHCF, Box 145, LBJ Library from 4 August to 24 August 1965. White House Aide Horace Busby's note to Bill Moyers on August 10, states that "the President cut Nixon off the list." Yet, on the same day Busby sent a note to Claude Desautels [another White House Aide] stating that the President wanted to invite Richard Nixon, but "I am certain he will not want to invite Barry Goldwater, but you might check directly with Bill Moyers." LBJ did send a personal telegram to Eisenhower on August 11, offering to send a helicopter to Gettysburg for him. Telegrams also went to Nixon and Goldwater on August 11, inviting them. The ceremony was held on August 12—short notice for any to attend. Nixon complained in a letter, which upon reading LBJ scribbled on the bottom, "Check this, Sorry—" Meanwhile, the *New York Herald Tribune* and the *New York Times* (13 August 1965) reported that "not a single one of the five living Republicans who have run for president showed up." Thus, it is uncertain whether LBJ or well-meaning aides miscalculated the political ramifications.

18. Transcript, Charles Boatner Oral History Interview, 17 December 1968, Tape 1, by Joe B. Frantz, p. 24, LBJ Library. Johnson's "Remarks at the Signing of the Immigration Bill, Liberty Island, New York," 3 October 1965, *Public Papers, 1965*, 1037. Mrs. Johnson later served six years on the Advisory Board on National Parks, Historic Sites, Buildings, and Monuments (see transcript, Wayne Aspinall Oral History Interview, 14 June 1974, by Joe B. Frantz, p. 15, LBJ Library).

19. Johnson's Speech at the Signing of the Delaware Water Gap National Recreation Area Bill, *Public Papers, 1965*, ibid., 958–59.

20. Johnson's Speech at the Signing of the Cape Lookout National Seashore Bill, *Public Papers, 1966*, ibid., 300–1. See also similar refrains in his "Annual Budget Message to Congress, Fiscal Year 1967," 24 January 1966, ibid., 59–60; his Speech to Congress on Preserving America's Natural Heritage, ibid., 195–203; his "Remarks Upon Signing Order Establishing the President's Council and the Citizens' Advisory Committee on Recreation and Natural Beauty," 4 May 1966, ibid., 480–81.

21. Johnson's Speech at Battery Park, ibid., 867. See also his Speech to the National Recreation and Park Association, ibid., 1175; his Speech at the Signing of Seven Conserva-

tion Bills, ibid., 1186–87; his Review of the 89th Congress, ibid., 1192; Johnson's Statement Upon Signing the Indiana Dunes National Lakeshore Bill, ibid., 1332.

22. Letter, Walter Reuther to President, 11 February 1966, GEN LE/NR 7, WHCF, Box 145, LBJ Library. Reuther's letter has LBJ's scribble: "To Udall to prepare reply." Letter, President Johnson to Walter Reuther, 17 February 1966, ibid.; memo, Udall to The President, 31 August 1966, EX LE/PA 3, ibid., has LBJ's scribble at the bottom: "Marvin get Henry and Mike to at *once* check out with appropriate Com Chr & Leadership"; memo, Wilson to The President, 1 September 1966, ibid. (LBJ's scribble is quoted in text); and "Administrative History of the National Park Service," one of the four volumes of the Department of the Interior, prepared in late 1968, LBJ Library.

23. 1966 Task Force on Resources and Recreation, Task Force Collection, Box 19, LBJ Library discusses the stalemate; memo, President Johnson to Freeman and Udall, 12 August 1966, GEN PA 2, WHCF, Box 16, LBJ Library. Memo, Freeman to The President, 15 August 1966, ibid. Memo, Freeman to the President 28 December 1966, ibid. Memo, Udall to the President, 28 December 1966, ibid. Memo, Philip Hughes [Bureau of Budget] to The President, 5 January 1967, ibid.

24. Johnson's "Remarks at the Signing of Seven Conservation Bills," 15 October 1966, ibid., 1187. For more on Endangered Species Act, see also Melosi, "Johnson and Environmental Policy," 133; and Lewis Regenstein, *The Politics of Extinction* (New York: Macmillan, 1975). For background on the National Historic Preservation Act, see 1964 Task Force on Natural Beauty, Task Force Collection, Box 2, LBJ Library, and Special Committee on Historic Preservation, *With Heritage So Rich* (New York: Random House, 1966), which has a foreword by Mrs. Lyndon B. Johnson. Johnson first called for a law protecting private historic properties in his "Special Message to Congress on Conservation and Restoration of Natural Beauty," 8 February 1965, ibid., 54.

25. For description of these programs see "Administrative History of the National Park Service," LBJ Library.

26. Johnson's Message to Congress on Protecting Our Natural Heritage, *Public Papers, 1967*, ibid., 101–2. Later that year his 1967 Task Force on Quality of the Environment pushed an identical program (not surprising, since Udall wrote the report without Task Force meetings or even Task Force review of the final report), pp. 35–37, Task Force Collection, Box 24, LBJ Library.

27. Memo, Hughes to the President, 17 February 1967, EX LE/PA 3, WHCF, LBJ Library; letter, Johnson to Rockefeller, 24 February 24, 1967, ibid.; letter, Rockefeller to Johnson, 7 March 1967, ibid.; letter, Rockefeller to Johnson, 16 April 1967, ibid.

28. Memo, Hughes to The President, 30 June 1967, EX LE/PA 3, WHCF, Box 146, LBJ Library; letter, Johnson to Aspinall, 10 July 1967, ibid.; and letter, Aspinall to the President, 12 July 1967, ibid. See also, transcript, Wayne Aspinall Oral History Interview, 14 June 1967, by Joe B. Frantz, pp. 10–12.

29. "To Renew a Nation," 8 March 1968, ibid., 355–70; and President's "Conservation Message," 9 March 1968. He gave a similar speech to the "Citizens' Advisory Committee on Recreation and Natural Beauty" on 29 March 1968, ibid., 458–61; and sent a "Letter to the

President of the Senate and to the Speaker of the House Urging the Addition of New Areas
to the Nation's Wilderness System," 29 March 1968, *Public Papers, 1968*, 461–62.

30. "Dedication of the J. Percy Priest Project," 29 June 1968, *Public Papers, 1968*, 759.

31. "Remarks on Signing Bill to Enlarge the Land and Water Conservation Fund," 15 July
1968, ibid., 808.

32. "Remarks Upon Signing Four Conservation Bills," 2 October 1968, ibid., 1001.

33. See news clippings in EX LE/NR, Box 142, and GEN PA 2, Box 16, WHCF, LBJ
Library. See also congratulatory letters in EX LE/PA 3, Box 146, ibid., especially Melville
Bell Grosvenor of National Geographic Society, 16 October 1968: "Your patience, understanding with lack of rancor, and your firm leadership in these trying times are indeed in a
class with President Lincoln."

34. Udall initially suggested (on 26 July 1968) using the Antiquities Act of 1906. He was
allowed to work up specific proposals, which he presented to the President on 5 December
1968. See "Udall: National Monuments," Office of the President File, Box 12, LBJ Library
for complete file.

35. Under the authority of the Antiquities Act, Theodore Roosevelt established one
national monument. Woodrow Wilson issued seven proclamations that established new
national monuments or enlarged existing ones. Herbert Hoover created six new monuments totaling more than two million acres in the last weeks of his term. Franklin Roosevelt
added twenty-seven national monuments. Harry Truman signed eight proclamations and
Dwight Eisenhower two. Although the law stipulates that the monument should be as small
as needed to protect the values, previous presidents established such large areas as Grand
Canyon, Petrified Forest, Glacier Bay, Death Valley, and Grand Teton.

36. On De Vier Pierson's memo of 17 December 1968, Johnson scribbled "Call me." See
Office of the President File, Box 12, LBJ Library. This was followed on 19 December 1968 by
another, more detailed report from Udall. See "Udall: National Monuments," ibid.

37. Transcript, De Vier Pierson Oral History Interview, 19 March 1969, by Dorthy Pierce
McSweeny, pp. 17–18.

38. Johnson's scribbled instructions are on Pierson's memo to him of 14 January 1969, 6:35
pm, in "Udall: National Monuments."

39. Memo, Udall to the President, 17 January 1969, ibid.

40. Memo, Pierson to the President, 17 January 1969, ibid. See also, press release in EX
FG 145, WHCF, Box 206, LBJ Library.

41. Transcript, Pierson Oral History, 19 March 1969, pp. 17–18.

42. Transcript, Wayne Aspinall Oral History Interview, 14 June 1974, by Joe Frantz,
pp. 27–28.

43. Quotation comes from Pierson Transcript, p. 20; but Udall's transcript, p. 16, is
similar: "I've made my last arguments on the parks. You can do what you damned please.
I'm through."

44. It is unclear why Udall released an erroneous press release. Udall's transcript, 13,
implies that he released the press release to newspapers with Monday deadlines with instructions for them to hold the story. He blames one of them for leaking the story. Boatner's
transcript, 12–13, states that Udall gave him precise orders to release the story. He believed

that Udall was trying to force Johnson into signing the proclamations. Aspinall's transcript, 29, speculates that Udall wanted to "leave a little more record of some kind," but suddenly the governmental process was just too slow.

45. See Transcript, Stewart Udall Oral History Interview, 31 October 1969, by Joe Frantz, p. 13, LBJ Library; Pierson transcript, 20; transcript, Charles Boatner, 2 June 1976, by Michael L. Gillette, 11–15, LBJ Library.

46. Pierson transcript, 20–21.

47. "Statement by the President Upon Signing Five Proclamations Adding Lands to the National Park System," 20 January 1969, *Public Papers, 1968–69*, 1369.

PART III

THE POPULAR WEST

CHAPTER EIGHT

"SUNRISE IN HIS POCKET"
The Crockett Almanacs and the Birth of an American Legend

PAUL ANDREW HUTTON

The greatest impetus to the growth of the Crockett legend came from the Crockett almanacs. The pronounced success of the comic almanacs for 1835 and 1836 led their Boston creator, Charles Ellms, to continue them, even though their alleged author was now dead. The fiction of the Nashville imprint also continued, even though the almanacs remained eastern creations. They now expanded upon the writings of Crockett himself, as well as James S. French, James Kirke Paulding, Richard Penn Smith, and other popularizers, to create a tall-tale trickster with the strength of Hercules, the valor of Lancelot, the veracity of Baron Münchausen, and the wit of Brer Rabbit. This comic superman insured Crockett a rare immortality, enshrined the humor of the Old Southwest in print, provided an eventually triumphant rival to the romantic, class-conscious frontier hero of James Fenimore Cooper, and further defined the emerging national character.

At least forty-five almanacs were published by various firms before the series ended with the almanac for 1856. All of these publications seem to have originated in either Philadelphia, New York, or Boston, although the publisher sometimes supplied almanacs to local printers, who put their own imprint on them. The first seven of these almanacs bore the Nashville imprint, a calculated pretense by their eastern publisher to cater to the national interest in all things western. They shared a uniformity in format, style, content, and illustration that clearly separated them from those that came after 1841. These almanacs also departed from other comic almanacs of the period in their emphasis on one character—Crockett—and in their relation of hunting stories and sketches of frontier manners and mores. The Nashville almanacs also avoided the political partisanship and jingoistic rantings of the Crockett almanacs yet to come.[1]

The publisher's first problem was to deal with the death of Crockett. In a preface to *Davy Crockett's 1837 Almanack of Wild Sports in the West, Life in the Backwoods, & Sketches of Texas*, the Colonel assured his loyal readers that his westward travels would not interrupt the publication of the popular almanacs. Although he was off to Texas—where "land is so rich, if you plant a crowbar at night it will sprout tenpenny nails before morning"—he had thoughtfully prepared his 1837 almanac in advance. (That line was also prepared well in advance, since it was lifted from Paulding's play.) He ended with a flourish: "Reader, 'good bye,' I'll 'go where glory waits me, and I'll go through the Mexicans like a dose of salts.'"[2]

The publishers added that the Colonel had prepared enough material in advance to assure the publication of at least six more almanacs. Not missing a trick, the publisher also assured readers that profits from the almanacs would go to benefit the Colonel's widow and children.

The 1837 almanac's cover depicted Crockett in hunting garb and for the first time wearing a furskin cap, in this case a wildcat skin. That cover drawing is almost an exact copy of an engraving of the actor James Hackett portraying Nimrod Wildfire that was used to promote *The Lion in the West*.[3] It is altogether fitting, of course, that a true portrait of the real Crockett did not grace this almanac, for the reality of his life was quickly becoming irrelevant. Rather, we have the crude but vigorous almanac artist copying the image of an actor in a play loosely based on Crockett's character. Thus did legend, even at this early date, completely overwhelm reality.

Along with the usual astronomical calculations, the 1837 almanac contained a full complement of tall hunting stories. The best of them had the Colonel chased home by a huge black bear only to be saved by the quick work of Mrs. Crockett. But let Davy tell the story:

> I ran for home, hollering with all my might. Luckily a neighbor was at the house, who hearing my music, ran out with my big dog Rough, and wife. I had become almost exhausted. But old Rough seized him by the hind-quarter, so that his pace was slackened; the man now reached the spot, and gave him a blow over the head with his axe. My wife, although she could but just use her left hand as it was hardly healed, as she had lost her thumb and fore finger. They were bit off by a catfish as she attempted to skin one alive. But she caught up a hickory rail, and as the bear rushed at her with his mouth wide open she ran it down his throat. He corfed as if he had swallowed something the wrong end first. His attention was now

taken from me, and although completely broken winded, I turned and jumped on to the varmint's back, when I reached his vitals with my big butcher; and after a most desperate contest, in which we were all more or less bitten and my wife had her gown torn nearly off her, we succeeded in killing him. He was a real fat one and weighed six hundred lbs.[4]

Crockett's famous brag finds its way into the 1837 almanac as well, this time as a speech he supposedly gave in Congress. A primitive version of this speech was first penned by James Kirke Paulding in his 1817 *Letters from the South* as part of his story of a fight between a boatman and a wagoneer. He adapted it into two of the most humorous scenes in *The Lion of the West*. James S. French then borrowed Wildfire's brag, further refining it a bit and attributing it to Crockett in two incidents in Chapters 11 and 13 of *Sketches and Eccentricities*.[5] In the twentieth century a version of the brag was used by Walt Disney for Crockett's maiden speech in Congress in an episode of the 1955–56 television trilogy. It has a raw, racist character in the 1837 almanac not matched in other versions:

Mr. Speaker. Who-Who-Whoop-Bow-Wow-Wow-Yough. I say, Mr. Speaker; I've has a speech in soak this six months, and it has swelled me like a drowned horse; if I don't deliver it I shall burst and smash the windows. The gentleman from Massachusetts (Mr. Everett) talks of summing up the merits of the question, but I'll sum up my own. In one word I'm a screamer, and have got the roughest racking horse, the prettiest sister, the surest rifle, and the ugliest dog in the district. I'm a leetle the savagest crittur you ever *did* see. My father can whip any man in Kentucky, and I can lick my father. I can outspeak any man on this floor, and give him two hours start. I can run faster, dive deeper, stay longer under, and come out drier than any *chap* this side of big *Swamp*. I can outlook a panther and outstare a flash of lightning: tote a steamboat on my back and play at rough and tumble with a lion, and an occasional kick from a *Zebra*. To sum up all in one word *I'm a horse*. Goliah was a pretty hard colt but I could choke him. I can take the ragg off—frighten the old folks—astonish the natives—and beat the Dutch all to smash—make nothing of sleeping under a blanket of snow—and don't mind being frozen more than a rotten apple. Congress allows *lemonade* to the members and as it charged under the head of *Stationery*—I move also that *Whiskey* be allowed under the item of *fuel*. For *bitters* I can suck away at a noggin of aquafortis, sweetened with brimstone, stirred with a lightning rod, and skimmed with a hurricane. I've soaked my head and shoulders in Salt

River, so much that I'm always corned. I can walk like an ox; run like a
fox, swim like an eel, yell like an Indian, fight like a devil, and spout like
an earthquake, make love like a mad bull, and swallow a nigger whole
without choking if you butter his head and pin his ears back.[6]

Mixed in with tales of daring escapes from wild beasts, descriptions of
animals, and dialect humor, of which the real Crockett was a master, were such
stories as the Colonel's "Tongariferous Fight with an Alligator" and "Colonel
Crockett's Account of his swimming the Mississippi," in which he is attacked
by a bear, a wolf, and an "amphibious river calf." The almanac ends with an
account of the siege of the Alamo and the death of Crockett:

Col. Crockett's body was found in an angle of two buildings with his big
dagger in his hands, and around him were lying seventeen dead Mexicans, eleven of whom had come by their deaths by his dagger, and the
others by his rifle and four pistols, which laid beside him. In the dark he
had a decided advantage over them, as they could not get behind him,
and he stabbed them as they passed by in the charge. He had received two
musket balls in his body, both of which were mortal. A smile of scorn
played on his features.[7]

Such historical "facts" rarely again intruded into the almanacs, although the
1838 number again made brief mention of the Alamo. (The New York firm of
Turner and Fisher also published an 1837 almanac entitled *Crockett's Texas
Oldmanick. "Crockett goes a-head, though dead." Millions for Texas! But not a cent
for taxes!!! With comic engravings of all the principal events of Texas.*)[8] The
publishers of the 1838 almanac promised readers that plenty of fresh material
remained, for: "His posthumous papers contain a great number of Wild Frolics
and scrapes, together with adventurous exploits in the chase, both those in
which he was engaged himself, and others that come within his knowledge.
The engravings are mostly taken from his drawings, which are very spirited.
He drew on birch bark with a burnt stick."[9] Among the usual animal descriptions, hunting tales, and escapes from wild beasts, was a new emphasis on life
on the western rivers, including a brief biography of the "King of the Keelboat-
men," Mike Fink.

This fascination with life on the waters continued with a vengeance throughout the remainder of the Nashville almanacs, for in the 1839 edition stove-up
sailor Ben Harding was introduced as editor, publisher, and occasional narrator.
This Ben Harding (also called Hardin), unlike the Kentucky congressman
named Ben Harding (in reality based on the actual legislator Ben Hardin from

Bardstown, Kentucky) introduced in the 1836 almanac, is an old salt whose injured leg has forced him to give up seafaring. Having made a chance acquaintance of "Kurnel Krockett" he decided to devote himself to the continuation of his old friend's almanacs. Antagonism had marked their first meeting, as related in the 1839 almanac, and a passel of by now familiar tall brags passed between them in anticipation of a fracas until Ben learns just who he has chanced upon. He extends his hand, proclaiming, "Tell me for God's sake, old fogy, are you the feller that makes them allmynacks about cruising after panthers and snakes and swimming over the Mississippi?" Davy responds: "I'm a roarer at the bizness that you've mentioned, stranger. Going to Congress and making allmynacks is my trade." Ben is a big fan, so they put off fighting and commence to drinking and swapping tall tales. Ben gives as good as he takes, or as Davy put it, "He told such stories about what he had seed as made the gals dream o'nights for a fortnite arter he was gone."[10] Naturally, the almanacs began to carry these sea stories, uniting the tall-tale traditions of the seafaring Northeast with those of the Old Southwest. In this way, the publishers of the almanacs united the Northeast and the West in a popular-culture marriage of sorts that foreshadowed a more important economic and political union that was to emerge in dark days of civil strife yet to come.[11]

Ben Harding promised his readers wild times, and he delivered. He had taken possession of Crockett's papers and they held great promise for future almanacs:

Among the papers yet to print are the drollest yarns about wild scrapes, terrible fights with the wild varmints of the west, both two legged and four legged, and some with no legs at all, that ever was heered tell of. They are raal terrificashus. So much so that you must reed em through a pare of spektakles or they will make your eyes ake. It like to have broke the press down to print them, they are sich hard karakters. A little dog that swollered one of the leaves of the proof sheet was taken with Kollery morbuss, and his tung hung out haff a yard till he died in the cutest aggonny. You had best to hoop your ribs before you reed em or you will shake your bowels out a laffing.[12]

Davy's hunting stories now take on a more comic tone, as in the 1839 tale where he misses an elk at ten paces and is swooped up on its antlers for a ride—literally seizing his world by the horns. "I wish I may be shot," Davy confesses, "if the way he carried me through the prairie war not a caution to steamboats and rail roads. I never had such a ride in my life."[13] In the cover story of the 1840 almanac, Davy is frightened by a screech owl and then embarrassed at his reaction: "I spose awl the oaths I swore then, if they war straitened out, wood reech cleen acrost the Mississippi. It war the fust time that I had run from a cretur not so big as myself; and I felt stripid as a rainbow."[14] But Davy tended to triumph in the vast majority of his hunting tales, as in the "Tussel with a Bear" cover story of the 1841 almanac:

> I war going ahead like the devil on a gambler's trail, when, all at once, or I might say, all at twice, for it war done in double quick time, I felt sumthing ketch me around the middle, and it squeezed me like it war an old acquaintance. So I looked up and seed pretty quick it war no relation of mine. It was a great bear that war hugging me like a brother, and sticking as close to me as a turcle to his shell. . . . I begun to think that although there war to be won dinner made out between us, it war amazing uncertain which of us would be the dinner and which would be the eater.[15]

After a terrific battle Davy dispatches the beast with his "big butcher," but not before the bear's claws give the tale a patriotic finale: "When I cum to strip, arter the affair war over, the marks of the bear's claws war up and down on my hide to such a rate that I might have been hung out for an American flag. The stripes showed most beautiful."[16]

Usually, however, Davy made quick work of the forest creatures he encountered in the almanacs. These exaggerated tales, of course, simply expanded on the celebrated hunting skills of the real Crockett. The 1842 almanac contained a little story entitled "Sensible Varmint" that became one of the most famous Crockett hunting tales of all. As Davy related the story:

> Almost every body that knows the forest, understands parfectly well that Davy Crockett never loses powder and ball, havin' ben brought up to believe it a sin to throw away amminition, and that is the benefit of a vartuous eddikation. I war out in the forest one arternoon, and had jist got to a place called the Great Gap, when I seed a rakkoon setting all alone upon a tree. I clapped the breech of Brown Betty to my shoulder, and war jist a going to put a piece of lead between his shoulders, when he lifted one paw, and sez he, "Is your name Crockett?"
>
> Sez I, "You are rite for wonst, my name is Davy Crockett."
>
> "Then," sez he, "you needn't take no further trouble, for I may as well come down without another word." And the cretur walked rite down from the tree, for he considered himself shot.
>
> I stoops down and pats him on the head, and sez I, "I hope I may be

shot myself before I hurt a hair of your head, for I never had sich a compliment in my life."

"Seeing as how you say that," sez he, "I'll jist walk off for the present, not doubting your word a bit, d'ye see, but lest you should kinder happen to change your mind."[17]

This often repeated and particularly delightful story, which became closely identified with Crockett, provides a fine opportunity to trace the origin of a tall tale. The original story, as published in the October 13, 1832 number of *The Spirit of the Times*, did not have such a happy ending, but it also concerned the exploits of a real and celebrated hunter. Captain Martin Scott was a young army officer stationed at Fort Smith, Arkansas, in the years following the War of 1812 who was something of a legend in military circles for his remarkable marksmanship. Stationed with him at Fort Smith was Lieutenant Joseph Van Swearingen, equally celebrated as a poor marksman. In the 1832 newspaper story, entitled "Captain Scott's Coon Story," a hound trees a raccoon and calls on him to come down before the hunter arrives and shoots him. The coon asks who the hunter is and the dog is forced to admit that it is Van Swearingen. This news convulses the coon with laughter. Sure enough, the lieutenant reaches the tree and fires six times at the laughing coon without hitting his mark. The exasperated hunter departs, much to the chagrin of the humiliated dog. Another hunter then approaches and the coon asks the hound his name. When the hound gleefully responds Martin Scott the coon "cried in the anguish of despair, that he was a *gone coon*, rolled up the whites of his eyes, folded his paws on his breast, and tumbled out of the tree at the mercy of the dog."[18] The story was widely reprinted and often alluded to, most famously in Thomas B. Thorpe's classic 1841 tale "The Big Bear of Arkansas," in which the "creation bear" finally gives up "like Captain Scott's coon, to save his wind to grunt with in dying."[19] In time, however, Captain Scott's connection with the tale was lost as it became firmly identified with Crockett. This evolved tale is changed to also emphasize Crockett's sense of fair play, ending on a happy note. In such a way did Crockett become the archetype for all the frontiersmen of the Old Southwest.

Interestingly, the three men connected with this story all met violent deaths: Crockett at the Alamo in March 1836; Van Swearingen in combat with Seminoles at Okeechobee, Florida, in December 1837; and Scott in combat with Mexicans at the Battle of Molino del Rey, Mexico, in September 1847.[20] Perhaps that old coon got the last laugh after all.

While critters might well give the almanac Davy some problems, he usually quickly triumphed over his human adversaries. The 1840 almanac, however, told of the only time that the Colonel was ever bested at a shooting match. Davy had run across none other than Mike Fink himself, "a helliferocious fellow." They naturally took to their long rifles to see who was the best shot. An array of fantastic shots left the competition a draw until Mike spied Mrs. Fink, "a horrid handsome wife, that loved him the wickedest that ever you see," and picked her hair comb in half with a dandy shot. He called her to stand still so Davy could have a shot at the rest of the comb. But the colonel would have none of that: " 'No, no, Mike,' sez I, 'Davy Crockett's hand would be sure to shake, if his iron war pointed within a hundred mile of a shemale, and I give up beat, Mike, and as we've had our eye-openers-a-ready, we'll now take a flem cutter, by way of an anti-fogmatic, and then we'll disperse.' "[21]

Women, or "shemales" to use the Colonel's term, made up a goodly proportion of the colorful cast of characters populating the almanacs. Davy has an awful soft spot for the ladies, of course, perhaps best expressed in the 1849 almanac: "Well women are Margaret-nificent creeturs—tha're angels without feathers: the werry sugar maple jelly o' creation, an' whenever I see them scandalized, or insulted, then the volcano o' my galantry begins to rumble for overwhelmen eruption."[22] Such adoration of women begins, as with all men, with his dear old mother. She was a caution, at least as Davy described her in his 1845 almanac:

> Now I gin you a genuine portrait of my mammy, in her One-Hundredth and Forty-Eighth year, and an all-scream-glorious gal she is of her age. She can jump a seven rail fence backwards, dance a hole through a double oak floor, spin more wool than one of your steam mills, and smoke up a ton of Kentucky weed in a week. She can crack walnuts for her great grandchildren with her front teeth, and laugh a horse blind. She can cut down a gum tree ten feet around, and steer it across Salt River with her apron for a sail, and her left leg for a rudder.[23]

Such a woman naturally produced a remarkable progeny. Whatever they might set out to do they accomplished with a vengeance. In an age of fervent religious revivalism it was only natural to find Davy's sister, Comfort Crockett, embracing piety, although of a distinctly American type. She was, Davy recalled, "one of the go to meetin' gals' and one of the finest samples of Christianity, and womananity that I ever seed . . . and when she sung a psalm you'd a thought all the trees in creation war organ pipes, and a hurrycane blowing the bellows." She quite naturally devoted her life to saving others, both spiritually and physically, and became the guardian angel of travelers in the Rocky Mountains. On one notable occasion she rescued Frémont's lost party and guided them safely to California, and as a result "has worn out seven, out of her nine constitutions, used up four consumptions, and seven fever and agues in saving travellers from freezin, famine, wolves, and vultures."[24] This 1851 tale was about as close as the almanacs ever got to then current ideals of femininity.

Most of the women of the Crockett almanacs were absolute opposites of the feminine ideal, sharing with their male counterparts a rough and tumble character and a propensity to transform ugliness into a virtue. Davy naturally felt a great attraction for such gals. His first love was Florinda Fury of Gum Hollow. "Every winter she fatted up on bear's meat," he fondly recalled, "so that when she turned out in spring, she war bigger round than a whiskey barrel; and when I put my arms 'round the cretur, it war like hugging a bale of cotton." They were a true love match till Davy had a tussle with her brother— "and arter I had put one of his eyes in my pocket, she thought I didn't act like a friend to the family."[25]

Of course Davy, as he put it, "had a smart chance of sweethearts."[26] Katy Goodgrit was a great favorite of his "bekase when her spunk war up, she could grin a wildcat out of countenance, and make a streak of lightning back out."[27] Then there was Sal Fungus, "one of the most poundiferous gals in old Alligator Clearing," who died of a broken heart when Davy left for Texas. What a tragic loss that was, for Sal "could scalp an Injun, skin a bear, grin down hickory nuts, laugh the bark off a pine tree, swim stark up a cataract, gouge out alligator's eyes, dance a rock to pieces, sink a steamboat, blow out the moonlight, tar and feather a Puke [a Missourian], ride a painter bare-back, sing a wolf to sleep and scratch his hide off."[28]

None of these delicate denizens of the forest was more engaging than Lotty Ritchers, the "flower of Gum Swamp." She was perhaps the original sight for sore eyes: "She stood six foot in her shoes; but as she hadn't 'em on very often, she war not quite so high. She used to brag that she war a streak of litenin set up edgeways, and buttered with quicksilver. . . . It is told on her that she carried twenty eyes in her work bag, at one time, that she had picked out of the heads of certain gals of her acquaintance. She always made them into a string of beads, when she went to church, and wore 'em round her neck. She never pared her nales, and had holes cut in her shoes, so that her toe nales could have room to grow. She war a real beauty; but the young fellows war shy of her, bekase she never wood kort long befour she wanted to box with her bo, and her thumb nale war grate for pullin out eyes."[29]

Lotty, despite such virtues, could not hold a candle to Gum Swamp's most delectable beauty, Jerusha Stubbs, who had but one eye "but that was pritty enough for two," and allowed her to wake up in half the time. "Enermost all her teeth had rotted out," Davy recalled, "but then she had a pesky grate swallow, so that she could take down her vittles without chawing. I forgot to say how she had a hare lip, but then she had a long nose, which almost covered the place from sight."[30]

In courtship, as in hunting, Davy was almost always successful, but occasionally he met up with more than he could handle. In the 1839 almanac he recalled how "when I was a big boy that had just begun to go galling, I got astray in the woods one arternoon," and had to be rescued by a young woman. He was smitten by her charms—and why not: "She told me that her Sunday bonnet was a hornet's nest garnished with wolves' tails and eagles' feathers, and that she wore a bran new gown made of a whole bear's hide, the tail sarving for a train. She said she could drink of the branch without a cup, could shoot a wild goose flying, and wade the Mississippi without wetting her shift. She said she could not play on the piano nor sing like a nightingale, but she could outscream a catamount and jump over her own shadow; she had good strong horse sense and knew a woodchuck from a skunk." Davy promptly proposed, but she declined, declaring that she preferred to try bundling first. Davy thought this a capital idea. Along the path to her father's cabin she lost a garter, "but she soon made up for that by taking a rattling snake from his nest, and having knocked out his brains agin a stone, she wound him around her leg as brisk as a Yankee pedlar would tie up his budget." This made Davy all the more lovesick, but his ardor failed him upon reaching the cabin: "We went into a room where there was a bed, and by this time it was quite dark. She consented to haul off all but her under petticoat and so I thought I had a fine bargain. But I soon found my mistake. Her under petticoat was made of briar bushes woven together, and I could not come near her without getting stung most ridiculous. I would as soon have embraced a hedgehog. So I made an excuse to go out, and then I cut through the bushes like a pint of whiskey among forty men. I never went that way since."[31]

On another occasion Davy courted an educated lass who had just moved to Salt Creek. "She war very short in stature," he recalled, "but she war monstracious high in her notions, for she war always tarking about the moon and the stars, and all them kind o' things what you cant touch with a ten foot pole. When she lit down in our parts, thar war a great stir among the young fellers, for she war fairer in the cheeks than our gals, and bekase she had sich little feet, so it wouldn't take much leather to keep her in shoes." Such a prize required careful courting, but to Davy's surprise Miss Kitty Cookins declined his offer of a horn and seemed unimpressed by his brags. Instead she complained that "thar war no defined people in the clearing," and went on to speak of "litter-a-toor and novelties . . . and how she liked cun-gineral sperits, and Sally Tude and varture, and war going to cultivate bottiny and larn the use of yarbs." To

Davy's surprise she "read a little out of her book, and axed me if I was fond of poetness and duplicity. I telled her I didn't know about them kinds of varmints; but I liked a bear-steak, or a horn of mountain doo, and had drunk two sich fellers like her sweetheart onder in one evening."[32] Alas, this was another failure for Davy, this time because civilization was making inroads into his territory. He took note of this problem in the almanac for 1843:

> The gals about our plaice are gettin' wonderful perlite and perticklar. They used to have combs with iron teeth, and do up thar hare with wooden skewers; but now they must have pewter combs, and do up thar hare with spike nales. If they puts on a crocodile-skin shift, they must have the ruff side outwards, and thar bear-skin pettykotes must be combed as offen as wunst a month. I have heered in Kongress that Rome was ruined by luxuriousness and all that ar, and I'm afeered that old Kaintuck will be ruined by them ar gals that can't keep up the old ways of thar four-fathers.[33]

Such romantic adventures made Davy quite an expert on matters of the heart, so that he felt comfortable enough to give his readers a guide to frontier courtship in his 1841 almanac:

> If the reader is had any experience, he ought to know as there are more kinds o' courting than one. One kind are where you skin up to a gal and give her a buss rite off, and take her by storm, as it wur; and then there are one kind whar you have a sneaking regard, and side up to her as if you war thinking about something else all the time, till you git a fair chance to nab her, and then you come out in good arnest. Thar are one kind whar you ax the gal's parents, and jine the church, and ar as steddy as a steembote, till arter marriage, when you may do as you like, seeing as how the game is run down.[34]

He took these words to heart when courting his future wife, the redoubtable Sally Ann Thunder Ann Whirlwind, the grandest gal of all the almanacs and a true match for the Colonel. Davy had come to realize that it was time to settle down, for it was man's duty to "take a vartuous gal, and replenish the airth, especially in our parts o' the world, whar folks war pesky scarce, and the painters and bears war ennermost all the population, speckled with crocodiles and rattlesnakes." Sally Ann Thunder Ann Whirlwind came to Davy's attention when he caught sight of her "flog two bears, for eatin up her petticoat; an' every blow she hit 'em, war a Cupid's arrow goin' into my gizzard. So I put on my best raccoon skin cap and sallied out to see her."[35] He related his method of winning her heart:

> When I got within three miles of her house I began to scream, till you could see my voice a-goin' through the air like flashes of lightning on a thunder-bolt—it sounded most beautiful to her, for it went through the woods like a harrycane, and I warn't far behind it. When she heered it pretty nigh, she come out, and climbed up the biggest tree thar; and when she reached the top, she took off her barr skin petticoat, the one she died red with tiger's blood, the day her mother kicked the bucket; and then she tied it fast to a big limb, and waved it most splendiferous. I soon came up to her, and she made one jump down to meet me. I cotch'd her in my arms, and gin her such a hug that her tung stuck out half a foot, and then we kissed about half and hour, and arter that I popped the question. She 'greed to have me if I'd promise to have no babies; but she let me off from that agreement pesky quick arter we war tied together.[36]

And what babies they had. "I always had the praise o' raisin the tallest and fattest, and sassyest gals in all America," declared Davy. "They can out-run, out-jump, out-fight, and out-scream any crittur in creation; and for scratchin', thar's not a hungry painter, or a patent horse-rake can hold a claw to 'em." The oldest daughter "growed so etarnally tall that her head had got nearly out o' sight, when she got into an all-thunderin' fight with a thunder storm that stunted her growth." His middle daughter was once captured by Indians, who "determined to cook half of her and eat the other half alive" in revenge for the many lickings her pappy had given them. But she was rescued by a passel of panthers so "pleased with the gal's true grit" that they ran off the Indians and gnawed her loose from the stake. Davy's favorite was his youngest daughter, because, as he put it, she "takes arter me, and is of the regular earthquake natur. Her body's flint rock, her soul's lightnin, her fist is a thunderbolt, and her teeth can out-cut any steam-mill saw in creation. She is a perfect infant prodigy, being only six years old; she has the biggest foot and widest mouth in all the west, and when she grins, she is splendifferous; she shows most beautiful intarnals, and can scare a flock o' wolves to total terrifications."[37] This darling child showed the Crockett grit mighty early:

> Well, one day, my sweet little infant was walking in the woods, and amusing herself by picking up walnuts, and cracking them with her front grindstones, when suddenaciously she stumbled over an almitey great hungry he-barr. The critter seein' her fine red shoulders bare, sprung at

her as if determined to feast upon Crockett meat. He gin her a savag-
gerous hug, and was jist about biting a regular buss out on her cheek,
when the child, resentin' her insulted vartue, gin him a kick with her
south fist in his digestion that made him hug the arth instanterly. Jist as he
war a-comin' to her a second time, the little gal grinned sich a double
streak o' blue lightnin into his mouth that it cooked the critter to death as
quick as think, an she brought him home for dinner.[38]

The mother of such children, as might be expected, was a formidable female
indeed. On several occasions she was called upon to rescue her husband from
various denizens of the forest. The critters even dared to invade her home
where she simply dispatched them and plunked them right into her cooking
pot. Alligators were a particular problem for, as Davy remembered it, "the
infarnal critturs would get atop of our house, where the old bulls would have
such fights, for the females, that we could get no sleep at all. They not only
knocked off the chimney level with the house, but in their rampoosings they
broke the ridge pole of the house, and scratched off all the bark and shingles."[39]
Such animal ignorance of the sanctity of home and hearth forced Mrs. Crockett to rope one of the alligators and while her daughter rode upon its back
beating it with fireplace tongs she tossed a bucket of scalding suds down its
gullet and cut its throat with Davy's big butcher knife.

Mrs. Crockett was nothing if not patriotic, but, like Davy, her natural
feelings could get the best of her, as they did in an 1854 almanac tale:

> My wife, Mrs. Davy Crockett—whose maiden name war Sally Ann
> Thunder Ann Whirlwind—always had a nat'ral taste for Eagle's eggs: kase
> she war edicated to the idee that they give the blood the true sap o'
> freedom an' independence—made them that fed in 'em able to look the
> sun or lightenin' in the eye without winkin' or squintin'—an' likewise
> encouraged the growth o' that all daren disposition to stand no nonsense
> from man, woman, beast or Beelzebub, while they also hatched in the
> heart the spirit of fly-high-ativeness and go-ahead-ativeness.
>
> W-a-l-l, the first Easter mornin' arter the annexation of our State that
> we licked out o' Mexico, Sal war determined to du honor to the occasion
> by having a drink o' *Eagle egg nog* from the top o' one o' the tallest trees in
> the country, whar thar happened to be a nest of a kind of republic of
> eagles. So she took a bottle o' my blue lightnin', flogged a she Buffalo and
> milked her, and then walked up to the Eagles' nest to get the eggs to make
> her *nog*. But it happined that the hull Senate and House o' Representa-
> tives o' the eagle nation war then in session, and they met her with a

deputation of *bills* and claws, that quite turned her hair out o' comb; but the gal went into 'em bite, smite an' claw, an' made the feathers fly like a snow storm or a geese picken; but arter she had flogged the wings off of about a dozen of 'em, her foot slipped, and havin' to use her hand to keep from fallin', two fresh cock eagles flew right at her eyes, an' would a made a week's provision of her if I had'nt a walked, and shot 'em both through with the same bullet. Arter that I walked up the tree, and we both drank to our victory in *Eagle egg nog*![40]

Rarely, however, did Sally Ann Thunder Ann Whirlwind Crockett need rescuing by Davy or any other man. In fact it was she, and not the Colonel, who finally got the best of Mike Fink. Davy related how Mike—"the celebrated, an' self-created, an' never to be mated, Mississippi roarer, snaglifter, and flatboat skuller"—attempted to pull a prank on Mrs. Crockett:

I'll never forget the time he tried to scare my wife, Mrs. Sally Ann Thunder Ann Whirlwind Crockett. You see, the critter had tried all sorts of ways to scare her, but he had no more effect on her than droppin' feathers on a barn floor. At last he bet me a dozen wildcats that he would appear to her an' scare her teeth loose an' her toe nails out of joint.

So the varmint one night arter a big freshet took and crept into an old alligator's skin, and met Mrs. Crockett jist as she was taken an evening's walk. He spread open the mouth of the critter, an' made sich a holler howl that he nearly scared himself out of the skin. Mrs. Crockett didn't care any more for that, nor the alligator skin, than she would for a snuff of lightnin, but when Mike got a leetle too close, and put out his paws with the idea of an embrace, then I tell you what, her indignation rose a little bit higher than a Mississippi flood. She throwed a flash of eye-lightnin upon him that made it clear daylight for half an hour, but Mike thinkin' of the bet an' his fame for courage, wagged his tail an' walked still closer; Mrs. Crockett out with a little teethpick and with a single swing of it sent the hull head and neck flyin' fifty feet off, the blade just shavin' the top of Mike's head.

Then seein' what it war, she throwed down her teethpick, rolled up her sleeves, and battered poor Fink so that he fainted away in his alligator skin. And he war so all-scaren mad, when he come to, that he swore he had been chawed up and swallered by an alligator.[41]

Sally Ann Thunder Ann Whirlwind Crockett was indeed a perfect match for her celebrated husband, and more than a match for Mike Fink or any other

alligator-horse frontiersman. She, and the other fanciful females of the almanacs, represent both a commentary on eastern perceptions of the harsh domestic life of the frontier as well as a satire on then-prevalent conceptions of femininity. As literary creations they look back to the Amazons of antiquity and a
host of warrior queens and forward to future frontier heroines such as Calamity
Jane, Belle Starr, Annie Oakley, and their numerous dime novel imitators.[42]

Remarkable characters, both male and female, terrific battles with man and
beast, folk wisdom, and backwoods humor remained staples of the Crockett
almanacs throughout the 1840s. After 1841, however, a new political element
was added, as the almanacs increasingly became mouthpieces for westward
expansion and a wildly jingoistic nationalism. The first stirrings of this spirit of
"Manifest Destiny" began with Ben Harding's announcement in the 1841 almanac that Crockett was a prisoner in the Mexican mines. This followed
newspaper accounts of Crockett's captivity, but the almanacs continued with
the tale long after the newspaper stories were proven false.

The 1841 almanac printed a long letter from the Colonel on his imprison-
ment, escape, and recapture in Mexico. That old salt Ben Harding assured his
readers that "a depputashun of Kentucky chaps whose names is Oak Wing,
Brush Grinner, Steven Horn, Price Beef, and Mortal Brown, all tickler friends
of Crockett's, has cleared out for the mines, and expects to overhall the Kurnill,
and restore him to his individdle rites in old Kaintuck, for they has been
nobuddy fit to go to Kongress sot up for candy-dates cents he war grappled by
the cussed heathens in Texas." Harding promised that once "the Kurnill gets
back, we will hav a plenty of his adventurs and scrapes among the Spaniards."[43]

The almanacs delivered on that promise, especially after they were taken
over by the New York publishing firm of Turner and Fisher in 1843. These
almanacs retained the general look of the Nashville almanacs—in terms of trim
size, pagination, and paper stock—but content changed fairly dramatically.
The crude charm of the rough illustrations of the Nashville almanacs was now
replaced by professionally done etchings often signed by the artist. Politics, and
most especially the great question of national expansion, became common
topics of the almanacs.

Crockett, now very much alive, became a great exponent of the nation's
"Manifest Destiny"—that nebulous but God-given right to expand American
political and social institutions clear across the continent no matter who was in
the way. In the 1845 almanac Davy makes his position clear, declaring that "I go
for Texas and Oregon, clar up to the very gravel stone, for they both belong to
Uncle Sam's plantation." The almanac Davy was outraged at those who stood
in the way of expansion, identifying them as "all the Mixy Mexican Spanish
brown an' red niggars, an' the Malgamation party in Uncle Sam's lands, who go

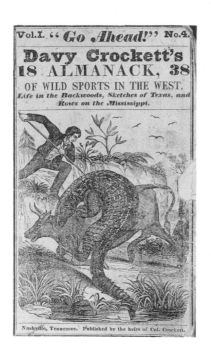

Covers for Davy Crockett's Almanac *between 1838 and 1847.*
(Photographs courtesy Henry E. Huntington Library and Art Gallery, San Marino, California,
and David Zucker Collection, Los Angeles.)

156

CROCKETT'S
HARRISON ALMANAC, 1841.

NEW-YORK:
ELTON, Publisher 104 Nassau-st.
and 290 Bowery.

Stereotyped by VINCENT L. DILL, 128 Fulton-street, New-York.

Improved Edition. **1842.** Containing Real Stories.

Boston.

Printed and published by S. N. Dickinson, and for sale by T. Groom & Co., Boston ; D. Felt & Co., Collins, Keese & Co., P. J. Huntington & Co., New York; Grigg & Elliot, and Thomas, Cowperthwait & Co., Philadelphia ; Cushing & Brothers, Baltimore; Oliver Steele, Albany.

DAVY CROCKETT'S
18 ALMANAC. **44**

LIFE AND MANNERS IN THE BACKWOODS: TERRIBLE BATTLES AND ADVENTURES OF BORDER LIFE: WITH ROWS, SPREES, AND SCRAPES IN THE WEST.

TURNER & FISHER, No. 74 CHATHAM STREET, NEW YORK

CALENDAR CALCULATIONS,
CORRECT FOR THE WHOLE UNITED STATES.

"I LEAVE THIS RULE FOR OTHERS WHEN I'M DEAD, BE ALWAYS SURE YOU'RE RIGHT, THEN GO A-HEAD."

DAVY CROCKETT'S
18 ALMANAC. **47**

Daring Adventures in the Back Woods; Wonderful Scenes in River Life; Manners of Warfare in the West; Feats on the Prairies, in Texas and Oregon.

TURNER & FISHER·
No. 74 CHATHAM STREET, NEW YORK,
No. 15 N. SIXTH STREET, PHILADELPHIA.

in for Annexation with the blackies," a viewpoint expressive of the increasingly vicious racism that marked the Turner and Fisher almanacs. After this swipe at New England abolitionists and the native inhabitants of the much-coveted land, Davy solves the problem by destroying the physical barrier between Texas and the United States—the Gulf of Mexico. "So, in order to remove this one little liquid obstacle out o' the way o' sich a great national wedding," declares Davy, "I've jist straddled across the neck o' this pond, like Captain Collossus straddling the Roads, an' commenced drinking it up instanter." He opens up his "flesh tunnel" and swallows up the Gulf, and then threatens that "if any human critter, Yankee, Texian of Mexican, dares to oppose instanter annexation, saw me up if I don't swallow them to. An arter that I'll jist mount my alligator, travel into the middle o' Mexico, lick all the tarnal Royalists out o' thar tarnal mustaches, strip Santa Anna of his powership, show him all naked in his villany and wooden-legged ambition . . . in spite o' old Spain an' all the monkeys called monarchs in creation."[44]

In the fantasy world of these jingoistic almanacs Davy emerges triumphant from the Alamo, although in *Ben Hardin's Crockett Almanac, Rows, Sprees, and Scrapes in the West*, published at Baltimore in 1842, the Colonel admits that "it war a tuff time in Tecksass then, but we stood up to our lick log til we licked the pesky Spanyards as clean as a barked hemlock." The same little volume has Crockett fighting with Houston at San Jacinto, where he had a "hellniferous time; and I thort I war a gone sucker, for the pettiferous Spanyards drawed up around me, and six on 'em drew a lead on me at wunst." Davy had to leap in amongst them and use his sharpened thumbnail to good effect.[45]

Davy returns to help the Texans ward off invaders in a story entitled "Colonel Crockett's Trip to Texas and Fight with the Mexicans" in *The Squatter's Almanac* for 1845, published in New York. Davy is outraged to hear that Santa Anna's troops have again invaded the independent Republic of Texas:

Considering Texas as one o' the stars that belonged to Uncle Sam's Striped Handkerchief, I swore, by the hem in Freedom's buckskin petticoat, that Santa Ann or any other tyrant should never wipe his nose with it; and hearin' that the etarnal Mexican Satan was about making another scheme to steal it and the little farm to boot, I recollected the all-bloody lickin' I gin him at Alamo, buckled on my old scythe which he knows is about equal to old death, and prepared to start off instanterly to carve the whiskered critter right up. So I jist sharpened my teeth on one o' my flyin' millstones, bolted up a little Yankee lightnin', an' bridled a he barr that I had larn't to outrun a thunderbolt, and put out like a high pressure hurrycane for Texas.[46]

The remarkable speed by which Davy's bear carried him to Texas "made the very hair o' creation stand straight up in double distilled wonder." Texas recognized her champion at once—"the very ground and trees knowed me the very moment I arrived, an' all seemed to shout, 'Etarnal Freedom, for Davy Crockett's come.'" Santa Anna was again caught napping as Davy laid into the Mexican army with his bone scythe—"an' if I didn't make Mexican heads fly about as thick as horsechestnuts in a hurrycane, then melt me into iron for steambilers. I fed five hundred flocks o' wolves on their meat, made a thousand quail traps o' their bones, wiped the sweat off with Uncle Sam's Striped Handkerchief, and come home to Kentuck as fresh as old Niagara."[47]

Note that the enemies of Crockett, and thus of American democracy and natural geographic expansion, are just as often identified as old world "Spanyards" as new world Mexicans. Not that Mexicans receive gentle handling in the racist almanacs, but the triumph of Crockett over decadent Europeans is considered all the sweeter by the almanac writers. It recalls Jackson and his western rifleman at New Orleans slaughtering England's finest and provides a ready example for a new generation to take up where the boys of '76 and 1815 left off.

Having done their best to keep the national thermometer rising with war fever, the almanac writers enthusiastically supported President Polk's request for a Declaration of War in May 1846. *Davy Crockett's Almanac* for 1847, published in New York late in 1846, presented the Colonel's opinion of the type of men fit to send to Congress. They were, quite naturally, men exactly like himself, "one that knows how to talk about Oregon, annex Texas, flog Mexico, swallow a Frenchman whole, and lick John Bull clean out of his breeches." This was followed by the Colonel's "Celebrated War Speech." With a nod to Tom Paine, Crockett began with "Fellow Citizens and Humans: These is times that come upon us like a whirlwind, and an airthqauke: they are come like a catamount on the full jump!" After a listing of grievances against the foe the Colonel concluded with a flourish, as well as a swipe at anti-war sentiment:

> Hosses, I am with you! and while the stars of Uncle Sam, and the stripes of his country wave triumphantly in the breeze, whar, whar, whar is the craven, low-lived, chicken-bred, toad-hoppin, red-mouthed, bristle-headed mother's son of ye who will not raise the beacon light of triumph, smouse the citadel of the aggressor, and squeeze ahead for liberty and Glory! Whoop! h-u-rah, hosses, come along—Crockett's with you—show us the enemy![48]

With the Mexican War won and the nation proudly stretching from sea to sea, the almanac writers turned to other current topics. None was a greater favorite than poking fun at recent immigrants to this new continental nation. The Irish quite naturally came in for the most licks. The real Crockett had always found the Irish a delightful curiosity, and the almanac Davy built on that legacy. "Thar's a difference between a Yankee and an Irisher," Davy noted, "a Yankee always thinks before he speaks, and an Irisher always speaks before he thinks. You have to hammer a Yankee to a red heat before he strikes, and you must hammer an Irish dead before he is cool. A Paddy is suspicious his own country is better than enny other, and a Yankee calkilates enny country is better than his own—but I expect I'm getting to philophererising and that's a waste of time."[49]

A true democratic spirit of insult animated the almanac writers, with no group spared. Blacks and Indians were treated with a particularly mean-spirited bigotry meant to appeal to the middling and working-class audience of the almanacs. This accurately and sadly reflected antebellum racial sensibilities. Such vicious humor remains particularly jarring to modern readers, despite its widespread acceptance in the years before the Civil War. These almanacs serve as clear artifacts of the prevailing racist popular culture of the time.

Yankees, usually represented by the sharp-dealing and woman-stealing peddler, were common fodder for almanac humor. These eastern characters were a frontier pestilence. "Of all the cursed Adam varmints in creation, keep me clear of a Yankee pedlar," declared Davy in the 1837 almanac. "They swarm the whole valley of the Mississippi, with their pewter watches and horn gun flints, peppermint drops and essences. Although the greatest chaps in creation for brag and sarce, they always play possum when there is danger, and skulk out the back door over the fence in no time. With their ribbons and dashy trash they are able to make love to the gals with every advantage over the real natives."[50]

Westerners were sometimes generically labeled Kentuckians, as Paulding had done with Nimrod Wildfire and as the almanacs often did with Crockett, but residence was more often made clear with an appropriate appellation. Suckers were from Illinois, Hoosiers from Indiana, Buckeyes from Ohio, Wolverines from Michigan, Mudheads from Tennessee, and Pukes from Missouri, and all were targets of Crockett almanac humor.

"The chaps from the Wolverine State are the all-greediest, ugliest, and sourest characters on all Uncle Sam's twenty-six farms," pronounced Davy. "They are, in thar natur, like their wolfish namesakes, always so etarnal hungry that they bite at the air, and hang their underlips, and show the harrow teeth of their mouths, as if they'd jump right into you, and swaller you hull, without salt. They are, in fact, half wolf, half man, and tother half saw mill."[51]

Wolverines were tame and civilized creatures compared to Suckers. "Of all human fish, big fish, and little fish, your regular Sucker is the etarnalist oddest fish I ever put my upper story lights upon," related Davy. "His whole life is a regular suck-in. Now I can swoller a Lake Superior o' lightnin water, meanin' whiskey, in a superior fashion—but when I do, it lasts me till I git dry agin; but a Sucker never takes time to git dry, for he hangs to a bottle like a buzzard to a hoss bone."[52]

Still, a Sucker was preferable to a Hoosier, who was, according to the Colonel, "a different class o' human natur altogether. They are half taller an' bristles, an' so all-sweaten fat and round, that when they go to bed they roll about like a cider barrel in a cellar . . . an' when they wake up, they have to fasten down their cheeks before they can open their eyes. A Hoosier can eat a hog, tail, fur and all, and in the fall of the year, the bristles come out on him so splen-differous thick that he has a regular nateral tippet about his throat, and a nateral hogskin cap on his head."[53]

The Pukes, however, were the most amazing of all the westerners. Pukes were, according to Davy, "the most all-sickenin' ugly critters that the wet Western land can breed an' turn out. Now I boast of being too ugly to get out of bed arter sunrise, myself, for fear I'd scare him back again, but then I ain't sickly ugly; the Puke is so etarnally so, that his own shadow always keeps behind him, for fear that his all-spewy lookin' face would make it throw itself up."[54]

Such sketches were reflective of the tension between localism and national-ism prevalent in the antebellum period, as well as being representative of a self-effacing brand of humor as common to the almanacs as it had been to the real Crockett. Like Crockett, the almanac writers were usually nationalists and while poking fun they also celebrated the uncouth manners and rough-edged mores, hard life and harder cider, common talk and commoner sense, tall tales and taller dreams, and independent and decidedly anti-establishment tone of the new America. The best of these stories embodied the still-living spirit of Davy Crockett.

That spirit took on a new cast in the later almanacs, as the stories about the Colonel became more fantastic. He evolved into an American Hercules, as comfortable diving for pearls in the South Pacific as he was hunting buffalo on the Great Plains, and as likely to be found battling cannibals in the Sandwich Islands as Indians in the Rocky Mountains. He was now more at home astride his pet bear than on a horse, although he might occasionally straddle a streak of lightening for speedier locomotion. That hardcore spirit of true democracy never left him though, as was evident when he almost got himself killed by refusing to bow to the Emperor of Haiti—"I merely said, 'I am Col. Davy Crockett, one of the sovereign people of Uncle Sam, that never kneels to any individual this side of sunshine.'"[55]

The Colonel now tended to make pets of critters rather than slay them, and soon collected quite a menagerie. This took some doing, for as Davy related it, "The snakes spit blue and red lightnin at me, the big bears growled all sorts o' low thunder, the wolves howled all sorts o' north-east hurrycanes, while the panthers an Mexican tigers screamed loud enough to set an edge on the teeth of a mill-saw." Davy quite naturally "licked the whole den of varmints so that they came and licked my hands in the most prostrate position—and they have formed my family circle ever since."[56]

He tamed a buffalo and taught it to sing a glorious bass in "Old Hundred" in nightly songfests without ever missing a note (and his horn also made an ideal tuning fork). A pet panther sang tenor while the Colonel's hyena provided the entire chorus, for he could outlaugh an earthquake. His beloved alligator Long Mississippi was not much for singing, but provided essential transportation over various bodies of water encountered by the Colonel, including a ride up Niagara Falls—"My pet an me shot up the rapids about as fast as a roughshod rockett, and landed on Uncle Sam's side, amid a salute of five hundred double barrelled rifles in honor of Colonel Crockett and his amphibious pet cataract navigator."[57]

The Colonel's favorite pet was quite naturally his bear Death Hug. "I larned it to smoke a pipe," recalled Davy, "and while it sot in one corner smoking, I sot in the other with my pipe. We couldn't talk to one another; but we would look, and I knowed by the shine of his eye what he wanted to say, though he didn't speak a word." They shared many a high adventure and the Colonel became so fond of Death Hug that he demanded equal treatment for him. When Death Hug was refused a berth on a Mississippi steamer the Colonel was outraged: "Taking this anti-republican refusal as an insult to my Congressional dignity, as well as to my well-bred pet Death Hug, Ben Hardin an me determined to revenge our insulted respectability on em by beatin thar double-breasted steamer down the river by an independent private conveyance, built on our own hook entirely." They cut down a hollow gum tree and with Davy and Ben manning the oars passed the steamboat in no time. Having disgraced the steamer altogether, Davy decided to launch his own ship, "to avoid all insults to my pet Bruin an myself, for I always have my bear with me for company." He hallowed out a ninety-foot alligator (no relative to Long Mississippi), seasoned it with snapping turtle tallow, hoisted in a 500-horsepower steam engine, and hammered down oak plank—"hoisted Uncle Sam's flag, took Death Hug for helmsman and have used it ever since as a steam packet up and down the Big Muddy." When Death Hug finally passed away the Colonel asked the local minister to give him a Christian burial but, as Davy related with disgust, "the skunk war so bigoted that he wouldn't do it, and I told him the barr war a better christian than he ever war."[58]

All his pets gathered under the Liberty Tree when the Colonel practiced his congressional oratory. They made a fine audience. "When I began my oration," declared Davy, "they opened their eyes and ears in the most teetotal attentive manner and showed a tarnal sight more respect than the members of Congress show one another during their speeches, and when I concluded by lifting my cap with twenty-six cheers for Uncle Sam and his states, with a little thrown in for Texas and Oregon, why choke me if those critters didn't follow with such a shout as set all the trees to shaking."[59]

The almanacs ensured a continued notoriety for Crockett long after his death, while at the same time creating a new Herculean Davy who accomplished deeds far beyond the capacity of any ordinary mortal. They invented a hard-edged hero for the mass popular audience that at first parodied but soon eclipsed Cooper's romanticized Leatherstocking as the frontier ideal. They enshrined the democratic humor of an expansive, rough-hewn, and bawdy people replete with local idioms, bizarre dialects, fantastic characters, cruel racism, eccentric wit, and clever tricks. The almanac Davy was part braggart, part trickster, part Herculean hero, part Münchausenean liar, and all American. He mirrored an emerging, still evolving, national character—celebrating its crudeness, its toughness, its daring, its egalitarianism, and, above all, its wit.

For twenty years the almanac Davy kept America laughing. But by the middle 1850s the nation was fast losing all sense of humor. The slavery question, and especially the issue of its expansion into the western territories whose conquest the almanacs had celebrated, tore at the fragile fabric of Union. The nationalism of the almanacs now found fewer adherents in the South, while Crockett looked a bit too southern to many in the North. Rustic tall tales from a seemingly distant past gave little solace to readers facing a dark future. Nobody was able to laugh at themselves anymore, except perhaps Abe Lincoln, and even he was constantly criticized for his jokes.

The year 1856 saw over two hundred people killed in fratricidal violence in Kansas over slavery. Dour-faced Democrat James Buchanan of Pennsylvania, who had been a congressman with Crockett, won the White House in a heated race with John C. Frémont, the frontier explorer-hero nominated by the new Republican Party. The election marked the end of the Whig Party. The year 1856 also marked the last appearance of a Crockett almanac.

It was then that perhaps the finest of all the tall tales appeared. It was in many ways the perfect metaphor for those dark days, for if ever a people were in need of a hero to save them it was America in 1856. (When that great President-hero finally emerged, he proved a master of Crockett's brand of rustic humor.) In the almanac story a Promethean Crockett saves the planet, bringing back warmth and light to the people:

One January morning it was so all-screwn-up cold that the forest trees war so stiff that they couldn't shake, and the very day-break froze fast as it war tryin' to dawn. The tinder-box in my cabin would no more ketch fire than a sunk raft at the bottom o' the sea. Seein' that daylight war so far behind time, I thought creation war in a fair way for freezin' fast.

"So," thinks I, "I must strike a lettle fire from my fingers, light my pipe, travel out a few leagues, and see about it."

Then I brought my knuckles together like two thunder clouds, but the sparks froze up afore I could begin to collect 'em—so out I walked, and endeavored to keep myself unfriz by goin' at a hop, step and jump gait, and whistlin' the tune of "fire in the mountains!" as I went along in three double quick time. Well, arter I had walked about twenty-five miles up the peak o' Daybreak Hill, I soon discovered what war the matter, The airth had actually friz fast in her axis, and couldn't turn round; the sun had got jammed between two cakes o' ice under the wheels, an' thar he had bin shinin' and workin' to get loose, till he friz fast in his cold sweat.

"C-r-e-a-t-i-o-n!" thought I, "this are the toughest sort o' suspension, and it musn't be endured—somethin' must be done, or human creation is done for."

It war then so antedeluvian and premature cold that my upper and lower teeth an' tongue war all collapsed together as tight as a friz oyster. I took a fresh twenty pound bear off o' my back that I'd picked up on the road, an' beat the animal agin the ice till the hot ile began to walk out on him at all sides. I then took an' held him over the airths's axes, and squeezed him till I thaw'd 'em loose, poured about a ton on it over the sun's face, give the airth's cog-wheel one kick backward, till I got the sun loose— whistled "Push along, keep movin'!" an' in about fifteen seconds the airth gin a grunt, and begun movin'—the sun walked up beautiful, salutin' me with sich a wind o' gratitude that it made me sneeze. I lit my pipe by the blaze o' his top-knot, shouldered my bear, an' walked home, introducin' the people to fresh daylight with a piece of sunrise in my pocket.[60]

NOTES

1. The Nashville almanacs for 1835–1838 have been reprinted in Franklin J. Meine, ed., *The Crockett Almanacks: Nashville Series, 1835–1838* (Chicago: The Caxton Club, 1955). It is a

lavish volume, now quite collectable, that uses all of the original illustrations but resets type for the stories. The 1839–1841 Nashville almanacs are reprinted in facsimile in Michael Lofaro, ed., *The Tall Tales of Davy Crockett: The Second Nashville Series of Crockett Almanacs 1839–1841* (Knoxville: University of Tennessee Press, 1987). The 1837 almanac, certainly one of the best, has been reprinted in an exact facsimile. See *Davy Crockett's Almanack, 1837: Reproduced in facsimile in the Huntington Library* (San Marino: Huntington Library and Art Gallery, 1971). Many of the best almanac stories, although unfortunately without any listing of original sources, are in Richard M. Dorson, ed., *Davy Crockett: American Comic Legend* (New York: Rockland Editions, 1939). Original Crockett almanacs are presently listed in rare book dealer catalogs for between $500 and $1,500 depending on condition and contents.

For discussions of the almanacs see Constance Rourke, *Davy Crockett* (New York: Harcourt, Brace, and Company, 1934) 247–58; Richard Boyd Hauck, *Crockett: A Bio-Bibliography* (Westport: Greenwood Press, 1982), 79–83; John Seelye, "A Well-Wrought Crockett: Or, How the Folklorists Passed through the Credibility Gap and Discovered Kentucky," in Lofaro, ed., *Davy Crockett,* 21–45; Michael A. Lofaro, "The Hidden 'Hero' of the Nashville Crockett Almanacs," in Lofaro, ed., *Davy Crockett,* 46–79; Catherine L. Albanese, "Savage, Sinner, and Saved: Davy Crockett, Camp Meetings, and the Wild Frontier," *American Quarterly* 33 (Winter 1981): 482–501; Catherine L. Albanese, "King Crockett: Nature and Civility on the American Frontier," *Proceedings of the American Antiquarian Society* 88 (part 2, 1979): 225–49; Creath S. Thorne, "The Crockett Almanacs: What Makes a Tall Tale Tall?" *Southern Folklore Quarterly* 44 (1980): 93–104; Joseph Leach, "Crockett's Almanacs and the Typical Texans," *Southwest Review* 35 (Spring 1950): 88–95; Richard M. Dorson, "Davy Crockett and the Heroic Age," *Southern Folklore Quarterly* 6 (June 1942): 95–102; Walter Blair, "Six Davy Crocketts," *Southwest Review* 25 (July 1940): 443–62; and Walter Blair and Hamlin Hill, *America's Humor: From Poor Richard to Doonesbury* (New York: Oxford University Press, 1978), 122–51. Also see Milton Drake, comp., *Almanacs of the United States,* 2 vols. (New York: Scarecrow Press, 1962).

2. James N. Tidwell, ed., *The Lion of the West: Retitled The Kentuckian, or A Trip to New York. A Farce in Two Acts by James Kirke Paulding. Revised by John Augustus Stone and William Bayle Bernard* (Stanford: Stanford University Press, 1954), 62; *Davy Crockett's 1837 Almanack, of Wild Sports in the West, Life in the Backwoods, and Sketches of Texas* (Nashville: Published by the heirs of Col. Crockett, 1836), 2–3.

3. Richard Boyd Hauck, "Making It All Up: Davy Crockett in the Theater," in Lofaro, ed., *Davy Crockett,* 102–10.

4. *Davy Crockett's 1837 Almanack,* 19.

5. James Kirke Paulding, *Letters from the South Written During an Excursion in the Summer of 1816* (New York: AMS Press, 1973), 89–92; Tidwell, ed., *Lion of the West,* 27, 54–55; [James S. Smith], *Sketches and Eccentricities of Col. David Crockett, of West Tennessee* (New York: J. + J. Harper, 1833), 144–45, 164.

6. *Davy Crockett's 1837 Almanack,* 40.

7. Ibid., 46.

8. Joseph Leach, *The Typical Texan: Biography of an American Myth* (Dallas: Southern Methodist University Press, 1952), 164.

9. Meine, ed., *Crockett Almanacks*, 116.

10. *The Crockett Almanac 1839. Containing the Adventures, Exploits, Sprees & Scrapes in the West, & Life and Manners in the Backwoods* (Nashville: Ben Harding, 1838), 22–23.

11. Seelye, "A Well-Wrought Crockett," 26–37.

12. *Crockett Almanac 1839*, 2.

13. Ibid., 25–26.

14. *The Crockett Almanac 1840. Containing Adventures, Exploits, Sprees & Scrapes in the West, & Life and Manners in the Backwoods* (Nashville: Ben Harding, 1840), 9–10.

15. *The Crockett Almanac 1841. Containing Adventures, Exploits, Sprees & Scrapes in the West, & Life and Manners in the Backwoods* (Nashville: Ben Harding, 1840), 9–10.

16. Ibid., 10.

17. Dorson, ed., *Davy Crockett*, 111–12.

18. Hauck, *Crockett*, 132.

19. T. B. Thorpe, *The Hive of the Bee-Hunter, a Repository of Sketches, Including Peculiar American Character, Scenery, and Rural Sketches* (New York: D. Appleton and Co., 1854), 92.

20. Francis B. Heitman, *Historical Register and Dictionary of the United States Army*, 2 vols. (Washington,DC: Government Printing Office, 1903), 869, 939.

21. *Crockett Almanac 1840*, 11.

22. *Crockett Almanac 1849* (Philadelphia: Turner & Fisher, 1848), 20.

23. *Davy Crockett's Almanac 1845* (Philadelphia: Turner & Fisher, 1844), 5.

24. *Crockett's Almanac 1851. Containing Life, Manner, and Adventures in the Backwoods, and Rows, Sprees and Scrapes on the Western Waters* (Philadelphia: Fisher & Brother, 1850), 24.

25. *Crockett's Almanac 1848* (Boston: James Fisher, 1847), 21.

26. Ibid.

27. Dorson, ed., *Davy Crockett*, 52.

28. Ibid., 55–56.

29. Ibid., 47–48.

30. *Crockett Almanac 1840*, 21, 28.

31. *Crockett Almanac 1839*, 14.

32. Dorson, ed., *Davy Crockett*, 153–55.

33. Michael A. Lofaro, "Riproarious Shemales: Legendary Women in the Tall Tale World of the Davy Crockett Almanacs," in Lofaro, ed., *Crockett at Two Hundred*, 126.

34. Dorson, ed., *Davy Crockett*, 153.

35. Ibid., 56.

36. Ibid.

37. *Davy Crockett's Almanac 1845*, 33.

38. Ibid.

39. *Davy Crockett's 1837 Almanack*, 8–10.

40. Lofaro, "Riproarious Shemales," 132.

41. *Crockett's Almanac 1851*, 16. This tale has been adapted into a modern children's book. See Caron Lee Cohen, *Sally Ann Thunder Ann Whirlwind Crockett* (New York: Greenwillow Books, 1985). Such adaptations, usually accompanied by delightful illustrations, have given a new lease on life to the almanac stories. For other examples of modern juvenile literature

based on the almanacs see Irwin Shapiro, *Yankee Thunder: The Legendary Life of Davy Crockett* (New York: Julian Messner Inc., 1944); William O. Steele, *Davy Crockett's Earthquake* (New York: Harcourt, Brace & World, 1956); Wyatt Blassingame, *How Davy Crockett Got a Bearskin Coat* (Pleasantville, NY: Reader's Digest Services, Inc., 1972); Robert Quackenbush, *Quit Pulling My Leg! A Story of Davy Crockett* (New York: Simon & Schuster, 1987); Walter Blair, *Davy Crockett: Legendary Frontier Hero* (Springfield, IL: Lincoln-Herndon Press, 1986); and Ariane Dewey, *The Narrow Escapes of Davy Crockett* (New York: Greenwillow Books, 1990).

42. An informative, comprehensive, and often humorous discussion of these tales is in Lofaro, "Riproarious Shemales," 114–52. For a provocative but often wrong-headed discussion see Carroll Smith-Rosenberg, "Davy Crockett as Trickster: Pornography, Liminality and Symbolic Inversion in Victorian America," in Carroll Smith-Rosenberg, ed., *Disorderly Conduct: Visions of Gender in Victorian America* (New York: Alfred A. Knopf, 1985), 90–108. The Carroll Smith-Rosenberg essay is highly regarded in academic and feminist circles and has led authors with little additional knowledge to reach surprising conclusions concerning Crockett. Julie Roy Jeffrey, in an acclaimed 1979 book on frontier women, totally confuses the almanac Davy with the real man, credits Davy with an extra wife, and condemns him soundly: "Avidly interested in proving his prowess to the world, Crockett viewed women as merely another prize in the race for reputation and notoriety. Not surprisingly, he had three wives, who, far from being shapers of values, were insignificant in the story of his life and certainly far less important than the other symbols of his vaunted achievements, pelts, votes, and fame. The vulgarity of the swaggerer annihilated woman's sphere, while his sexuality threatened woman's purity and innocence." Julie Roy Jeffrey, *Frontier Women: The Trans-Mississippi West 1840–1880* (New York: Hill and Wang, 1979), 19–20.

43. *Crockett Almanac 1841*, 2.

44. Dorson, ed., *Davy Crockett*, 157–58.

45. Leach, *Typical Texan*, 111–12.

46. Dorson, ed., *Davy Crockett*, 93.

47. Ibid., 93–94.

48. Ibid., 43–44. Also see Verne Bright, "Davy Crockett Legend and Tales in the Oregon Country," *Oregon Historical Quarterly* 51 (September 1950): 207–15.

49. *Crockett Almanac 1841*, 22.

50. *Davy Crockett's 1837 Almanack*, 17.

51. Dorson, ed., *Davy Crockett*, 125.

52. Ibid., 124.

53. Ibid., 123.

54. Ibid., 123.

55. Ibid., 98.

56. Ibid., 120.

57. Ibid., 12, 115, 118.

58. Ibid., 72–74, 158–59.

59. Rourke, *Davy Crockett*, 239–40.

60. Dorson, ed., *Davy Crockett*, 16–17.

CHAPTER NINE

ANNIE OAKLEY
Creating the Cowgirl

GLENDA RILEY

Whether found on a library shelf or a coffee table, most accounts of women in American rodeo identify Lucille Mulhall as the nation's first cowgirl. Some even claim that then–Vice President Theodore Roosevelt coined the word in 1900 for Mulhall alone.[1] But, in so doing, they overlook or demean the public impact and athletic skill of the women who performed in the early Wild West shows. In fact, neither the image of the cowgirl nor the concept originated with rodeo. As early as the mid-1880s, Annie Oakley of Buffalo Bill's Wild West was the first to create a picture of the cowgirl in the public mind and Cody the first to develop and expand the idea.

Without Annie Oakley's widespread influence, such early rodeo stars as Annie Shaffer of Arkansas and Lucille Mulhall of Oklahoma would have encountered far less acceptance by audiences and the media. These and other women who began to perform in circuses, Wild West shows, fairs, and rancher's conventions and expositions, and began to enter rodeos during the mid-1890s, had Annie to thank for establishing the model of an athletic woman who rode and shot in public. As a dedicated athlete who trained, dieted, competed, and set records, Annie demonstrated that women could develop physical prowess and engage in exhibitions and contests. As a result of Annie challenging what she called "prejudice" in the Wild West arena and on shooting and rodeo grounds, as well as actively campaigning for women as shooters, a wide variety of other cowgirls also found a place on the circuit.[2] But it was more than Annie's popularity and athletic skill that defined and popularized the cowgirl. As the first cowgirl, Oakley projected an image so feminine, ladylike, Victorian, and appealing that most people could see little harm in cowgirls. Unlike the rowdy women and girl "pards" making their debuts in such dime novels as George Brown's *The Tiger of Taos* or Joseph Badger's *The Barranca Wolf,* Annie fulfilled most of the era's expectations of true womanhood.[3] With her girl-like face, flowing hair, calf-length skirts, and demure behavior, Oakley made it not only acceptable, but attractive and admirable, for women to ride and shoot before audiences.[4] In the Wild West arena and at the rodeo grounds, viewers came to applaud women whose hands wielded not skillets or needles, but reins and rifles.

Of course, when Annie joined Buffalo Bill in 1885, she had no intention of opening what were then called "arenic" sports to women, nor of working with Buffalo Bill Cody in creating a widely recognized genre of western women called the cowgirl. Annie was an Ohio farm girl who had been shooting game since she was ten or so, and had later participated in an occasional shooting contest in southwestern Ohio. After defeating professional shooter Frank Butler in a match, then marrying him, Annie performed in vaudeville and the circus arena as part of the shooting team "Butler and Oakley." In 1885 Annie simply wanted a job away from the vaudeville stage and circus tent, a job that would pay reasonable wages and involve her in wholesome, family entertainment.[5]

In the meantime, William F. Cody had achieved a reputation as a hunter and scout in Nebraska, starred in western melodramas, and in 1884 organized his Wild West Exhibition. This extravaganza included several Native American women who usually rode on ponies led by their husbands in the opening parade and appeared in "The Battle of Summit Springs" or "Custer's Last Fight."[6] The following year, Cody hired Annie Oakley, who noted that she was the only Anglo woman in the troupe. "There was I," she later wrote, "facing the real Wild West, the first white woman to travel with what society might have considered an impossible outfit."[7]

But everyone treated Annie well and she quickly proved to Cody that she was an accomplished shooter. That first season Annie began her act by shooting clay pigeons sprung from a trap, then shot pigeons from two traps at a time, picked up her gun from the ground and shot after the trap was sprung, shot two pigeons in the same manner, and shot three glass balls thrown in the air in rapid succession, the first with her rifle held upside down upon her head, the second and third with a shotgun.[8]

To achieve these and other feats, Annie exercised every morning. She later recalled that she could "hold the strongest horse." Annie filled her afternoons with rehearsal, then "a rub of witch hazel and alcohol." Rolled in a blanket she lay down in a hammock to nap. "Then a 5 o'clock dinner," she added, "and I was ready for the night's performance."[9]

With the help of Frank, who now served as her manager and publicity agent, Annie also demonstrated that she was a sage performer who seemed content to let the Cody's Wild West and its fans deify her into the archetypal western woman. That initial season Annie skipped into the arena wearing a western-style blouse and calf-length, fringed skirt of a material resembling buckskin. She topped off her outfit with a western hat with an upturned brim accented by a silver star.[10]

In the meantime, Cody was treading unfamiliar terrain. He had few guidelines to follow regarding women's participation in his Wild West pageant. Historians of the day, notably Frederick Jackson Turner, virtually ignored women in their accounts of the American West. Moreover, even though popular writers, poets, and artists included women in their work, they tended to present them as victims. Consequently, popular culture was replete with women defeated by harsh climate, hard work, or the supposed "rape, pillage, and burn" mentality of Native Americans.[11]

But popular culture also occasionally supplied a glimpse of a strong western woman, such as Annie, who could handle a horse or a gun. Sometimes a story or a painting revealed one or two of the women who were really the earliest cowgirls, although no one called them by that name.[12] From Kansas to Montana and Wyoming to Texas, such women ran ranches and drove their cattle to market, or worked as partners with their husbands, performing a variety of jobs including wrangling cattle. In addition, during the 1880s women farmers and those who went west as "girl homesteaders" found favor with the media.[13]

Cody developed a similar pattern when representing western women in his Wild West. By 1886 and 1887, he had hired additional Anglo women, including several actresses who portrayed victims, screaming and fainting their way through such skits as the "Burning of the Settlers' Cabin" and the "Attack on the Deadwood Stage." But Cody's Wild West also continued to feature strong women, including in the 1886 program trick-riders Georgie Duffy of Wyoming and Dell Ferrel of Colorado, and sharp-shooter Lillian Smith, billed as "The California Girl."[14]

Cody was already in the process of inventing the cowboy, turning him from a rugged, often unsavory manual laborer who worked at a low-paid, dusty, seasonal job into a cultural hero.[15] He also began to develop cowgirls—strong female figures who women viewers could admire. Cody and his partner Nate Salsbury also hoped that the appearance of women in the arena would re-assure female viewers and calm their fears. Cody regularly reminded audiences that "ladies and children can attend my exhibition with Perfect Safety and Comfort."[16]

For eight of Annie's sixteen seasons with the Wild West, management placed her in the number-two spot on the bill, to help women relax during the frequent bursts of gunfire. Annie began shooting with a pistol, then accelerated the noise and excitement until she shot with a full charge in her rifle and shotgun. In the words of publicity agent "Arizona" John Burke, "Women and children see a harmless woman there, and they do not get worried."[17]

As Cody concocted the cowgirl, he tried to shape these women performers the way he hoped potential audiences wanted to see them. During the early 1890s the Wild West program advertised cowgirls and prairie girls, often meaning women riders who guided horses through complicated drills, performed bareback tricks, and rode broncos. They participated in one of the Wild West's most popular acts, the Virginia Reel on horseback, in which women and men rode as dance partners. During her early years with the Wild West, Annie Oakley sometimes performed in the Virginia Reel, but its real star soon emerged: Emma Lake Hickok, daughter of Agnes Lake, a circus owner married to Wild Bill Hickok before his fatal shooting in Deadwood.[18] These women riders often elicited near-rapture from many viewers. In 1887 one fan said of them, "All honour to the American frontier girls who ride so fearlessly!"[19] Due to their popularity, in 1888 women performers also staged the "Ladies' Race by American Frontier Girls."[20] In 1898 Cody's staff coined the graceful term "rancheras" to describe the women riders in the show. These women Cody billed as "a bevy of beautiful rancheras, genuine and famous frontier girls in feats of daring equestrianism." But as more women joined the Wild West shows, the term "rancheras" lost ground to the more descriptive one, "cowgirls."[21]

Even Annie Oakley's niece Fern came to think of her aunt as a cowgirl. She later wrote that as Annie rode into the arena, her long brown hair flying in the breeze, she "was typical of the Western cowgirl."[22] Fern would have been more accurate had she said that Annie was the foremost of Western cowgirls.

Annie continued to ride, including bucking-horses, but she gained her major fame as a highly skilled shooter.[23] Annie maintained her preeminence by continuing to train and perform like a top athlete. She and Frank continually tested and added new feats to Annie's Wild West act. In addition, Annie rode and sprinted daily. In 1894 one observer urged American woman to copy Oakley, especially by running to improve their health.[24]

As Oakley's legend grew during the 1890s, her example encouraged a growing number of young women to leave home and join the show circuit as riders and shooters. During the early years, like Annie, these were Anglo women, often from rather conventional backgrounds and from areas other than the western United States.[25] Shooter May Lillie, for example, grew up in Philadelphia and attended Smith College, while the "Texas Girl," Lillian Ward,

Annie Oakley, ca. 1902.
(Photograph courtesy Buffalo Bill
Historical Center, Cody, Wyoming.)

Annie Oakley Poster
Trick rider and expert shot,
Oakley appeared in Buffalo Bill's
Wild West for 16 years. (Photograph
courtesy Buffalo Bill Historical Center,
Cody, Wyoming.)

moved from Brooklyn to Texas for health reasons. Some accompanied husbands; May Lillie was the wife of Pawnee Bill, while Minnie Thompson formed a partnership with her husband to run Wild West shows and circuses.[26] Some joined Wild West shows for the money they could earn, and others for excitement. May Lillie once said that being a Wild West performer gave a woman far more enjoyment than "any pink tea or theater party or ballroom ever yielded."[27]

During the 1890s growing numbers of such women began to participate in local riding contests and rodeos. Two of the most well known during 1890s were bronc riders Annie Shaffer and Lulu Bell Parr. But the most famous was young Lucille Mulhall, who made her debut in 1897 at age thirteen, and by 1900 had proven herself a seasoned performer both in the arena and on the vaudeville stage.[28]

During the early 1900s many more young women followed. The pull of the circus and Wild West arenas on young men is widely recognized, but star-struck women fled their homes as well. The influence of Oakley and others like her on the nation's women was widespread and not to be underestimated. A representative case was Jane Meekin, who in 1911 left her family in Wisconsin to take her chances on the show circuit. She called herself "Little Jean" and fired two pearl-handled revolvers.[29]

But Annie's appeal to women extended beyond the Wild West arena; she also proved an adept competitor in shooting matches. Because she worked with the Wild West for only part of the year, signed on season-by-season, and had no health or retirement benefits, Annie also competed in a large number of shooting matches to supplement her earnings. No matter who she worked for, from vaudeville impresario Tony Pastor to Buffalo Bill Cody, Annie secured permission to shoot matches in between shows or during her time off. For instance, when the Wild West played in London in 1887, the elite Notting Hill Gun Club issued Oakley an invitation. The following year, a club in Newton, New Jersey, offered Annie 75 percent of the gate receipt to compete against English shooter William Graham. In 1889 she won a match that she later recalled with glee: "I won two fine prizes here and a full purse of money was sent to my New York bank." Besides winning purses, Annie also reaped returns from the side-bets Frank placed on her. In addition, she often set new shooting records, including smashing 943 out of 1,000 glass balls thrown into the air.[30]

In addition to the income and acclaim that matches brought, Annie also took great satisfaction in providing a role model for women shooters. Oakley, who maintained that she wanted a "fair chance" for women, worked hard and tried to establish a high standard in both her conduct and performance. As

early as 1886 Annie proved herself courageous and determined. While practic-
ing the day before a match against well-known shooter William Graham,
Annie injured her left hand. According to her, the doctor "used a 14-inch catgut
for five stitches," suspended her arm in a sling, and ordered her to avoid using
her hand for two weeks. The next day, Graham took one look at Oakley and
agreed to call off the match until his backer claimed they had won by default
and demanded the purse. Although Frank preferred to take the loss, Annie
picked up a gun with her right hand and began to shoot. She and Graham each
brought down ten birds. On the eleventh, Oakley only cut the tail feathers off,
so she whipped her left hand out of the sling onto the barrel to fire a second
shot, ripping three of her stitches open so that blood began to flow. Frank
dashed forward, called a halt to the proceedings, and told the audience they
could have Annie's percentage of the gate. Oakley recalled that she retired from
the field "amid cheers."[31]

Understandably, Oakley soon captured the hearts of numerous women. An
1892 letter from Sampson Morgan, editor of *The Horticulture Times*, described
how his daughter enjoyed Annie's shooting and tried to emulate her.[32] Then, in
1893 *The American Field* paid Annie the ultimate compliment: she could "successfully compete with any man." The article continued: "Many of her sex are
experts when firing at hearts, but I question if there is another woman in this
fair land who can pierce the heart aimed at four times out of five, especially if
they will keep twelve paces away from the object of their aim."[33]

In time, other women joined Oakley on the match circuit. In 1899 a Mrs.
M. F. Lindsley, who shot under the name of Wanda, competed with Annie in a
match in White Plains, New York. Lindsley fell behind Annie, who tied one of
the male shooters for first place. In 1901 four women competed in a New York
match. In subsequent years, women continued to join gun clubs and to enter
matches. In 1902 Anna Held, a popular actress and wife of Florenz Ziegfeld,
revealed her shooting abilities in a New York match. The following year, a Mrs.
S. S. Johnston of Minneapolis, was only one of the lady contestants in the
annual Grand American Handicap. At the Tenth Annual Grand American
Handicap held in Kansas City in 1902, three women shooters took part.[34]

Thus did Annie Oakley establish herself in the annals of American sport.
The guns, medals, and other memorabilia she and Frank collected at first filled
trunks, then entire rooms. Many who viewed Annie and Frank's collection of
guns, medals, and gifts ranked it as the finest in the United States and Europe.
Responding to requests, Annie and Frank created an exhibit of medals and
memorabilia that toured the world.[35]

Even Wild West programs emphasized Oakley's athletic ability. One, distributed in 1893, noted:

The first two years before the public she devoted to Rifle and Pistol Shooting, and there is very little in that line she has not accomplished. At Tiffin, Ohio, she once shot a ten-cent piece held between the thumb and forefinger of an attendant at a distance of 30 feet. In April, 1884, she attempted to beat the best record made at balls thrown in the air—the best record was 984 set by Dr. Ruth. Miss OAKLEY used a Stevens' 22 cal. rifle and broke 943. In February, 1885, she attempted the feat of shooting 5,000 balls in one day, loading the guns herself. In this feat she used three 16-gauge hammer guns; the balls were thrown from three traps 15 yards rise; out of the 5,000 shot at, she broke 4,722; on the second thousand she only missed 16, making the best 1,000 ball record, 984. Besides the thousands of exhibitions she has given in Europe and America, she has shot in over 50 matches and tournaments, winning forty-one prizes; her collection of medals and fire-arms, all of which have been won or presented to her, is considered one of the finest in the world.[36]

In addition to setting records in matches, Annie established a another precedent for sports-minded women by seizing every opportunity to go hunting. Frank and Annie often hunted in between Wild West performances. On one occasion, Annie, Frank, and shooting star Johnny Baker went hunting and bagged, in Annie's words, "a large hare brought down by Johnny Baker, and a small roebuck brought in by a briar-scratched Annie Oakley." Other times, they downed prairie chickens, rabbits, ducks, and grouse. And when Annie and Frank visited Ohio, they hunted. Irene Patterson Black, a descendant of Annie's, remembered that during Annie's visits the family could be assured of a tasty evening meal. When the women brought up the subject of supper, Annie went to the woods and brought down a quail or other small game.[37]

Annie and Frank also accepted numerous invitations to hunt. In 1887, for example, Annie and Frank spent two weeks roaming over English noble W. Crawford Clark's 5,000 acres, shooting partridges and game hens despite, according to Annie, "the latter being scarce and the mountain climbing hard." Rising at dawn to follow the pointers for twelve to fifteen hours and returning to "a hot bath, a delicious dinner," and "gathering around the open fire in easy chairs to talk over the day's sport and bygone days," all followed by a 9:30 bedtime, was Annie's kind of life.[38]

When in 1896 Annie and Frank hunted near Hot Springs, Arkansas, a member of the party wrote that Oakley killed quail as others hoisted their guns to their shoulders. He joked that because Annie shot so rapidly, he twice shot at one of her birds after she had already killed it. In that hunt, Annie killed sixteen more birds than any other hunter. The following fall, the Butlers hunted in Crowson, Tennessee, where one observer remarked that "Annie's shooting in the field excited a great deal of admiration from all who were fortunate enough to see" this "clever hunter." Tennessee hunter Joe Eakin, who held a record of six dozen quail in one day, said of her, "Miss Annie's so quick with her gun that if you want to get a shot at a bird you must shoot mighty quick or wait till she misses, and that may keep you waiting some time."[39]

That women followed Annie into shooting matches and the hunting field was indicated in a 1900 letter from N. J. Hotchkiss, editor of a Fox Lake, Wisconsin, newspaper. Hotchkiss wrote that after seeing Annie perform, his wife had taken up shooting "head over heels." She wants "to shoot blue rocks this summer against me," he added, and "I owe thanks to you for getting her interested."[40]

But Annie did more than provide a model for other women shooters. Oakley also gave women lessons in shooting, hunting, and camping. This began during Annie's first season in London, when a number of society ladies asked Annie to give them shooting lessons. Oakley later recalled that she held her first classes on gun-maker Charles Lancaster's hunting preserve. She charged each of her five pupils five dollars. This endeavor proved so successful that she placed an advertisement in the London newspapers announcing that she would give lessons in the use of pistols, rifles, and shotguns "to ladies only." When she returned to the United States, Oakley continued to give lessons and to extol the virtues of women shooters.[41]

Many people applauded Oakley's efforts. In 1891, for example, a Glasgow, Scotland, journalist observed that Annie "is only another living illustration of the fact that a woman, independent of her physique, can accomplish whatever she persistently and earnestly sets her mind to overtake."[42]

Gradually, Annie began to build on such support by actively campaigning for women as shooters. She argued that hunting and shooting provided fine sport and exercise, and that women could also use skill with weapons to thwart life-threatening attacks on them and their families.[43] In 1893 Oakley issued a comprehensive public statement regarding women shooters with the following disclaimer:

> I do not wish to be understood to mean by this that woman should sacrifice home and family duties entirely merely for outside pleasure but that, feeling how true it is that health goes a great way towards making home life happy, no opportunity should be lost by my sex of indulging in outdoor sports, pastimes, and recreations, which are at once healthy in their tone and results and womanly in their character."[44]

Once she had established her arguments, Oakley continued to repeat them. In an essay signed by "Gyp" and written around 1894, Annie queried why a woman should stay home while her husband went hunting; did she remain at home because the neighbors might criticize her for joining him in the field? According to Annie, if a woman's husband approved, then the woman should accompany him and "hang" the neighbors. Women would be healthier, Annie maintained, and more marriages might be happier as well.[45]

Several years later, in January 1897, *The New York Journal* offered an article headed "Without Shooting Herself, Taught by Annie Oakley." In her newspaper instructions, Annie insisted that nervousness constituted the principal detriment to women's shooting. Oakley assured all concerned that shooting "is one of the best kind of tonics for the nerves and for the mind." She recommended that would-be shooters begin with a 22-caliber, five-pound, 20-gauge or a six-pound, 12-gauge, hammerless shotgun. She also encouraged women to shoot at the traps and hunt alongside their husbands and sons, in spite of public opinion: "I don't like bloomers or bloomer women, but I think that sport and healthful exercise make women better, healthier and happier."[46] When, in March 1897, Oakley participated in the Sportsmen's Exposition in Madison Square Garden, she used her appearance as a forum to continue her campaign for women to learn shooting. And later that year, Annie warned women shooters to ignore the costumes advertised in fashion plates and newspapers. Anyone who wore them to shoot could not stoop, much less aim and fire. Instead, Oakley advised women to select any one of the "natty" skirts or the gaiters and knickerbocker suits worn for bicycling when they shot on a range or in the field.[47]

The following year, as the nation tottered on the brink of war with Spain, Annie sent a handwritten letter on April 5, 1898 to President William McKinley advocating women shooters. In case war erupted, Oakley was prepared "to place a Company of fifty lady sharpshooters" at his disposal. Oakley guaranteed that "every one of them will be an American and as they will furnish their own arms and ammunition will be little if any expense to the government." The President's personal secretary fired back an answer; he had forwarded her offer to the Secretary of War.[48]

Despite this brushoff, Oakley continued to encourage women to take up shooting and allied activities. By the end of the decade, she had succeeded in drawing attention to the benefits of outdoor exercise for women. In 1900 one supporter pointed to her as a splendid example of "what athletic exercises and out-door life is doing for the American girl of this generation."[49]

In 1901 Annie declared that "any woman who does not thoroughly enjoy tramping across the country on a clear, frosty morning with a good gun and a pair of dogs does not know how to enjoy life." In her view, "God intended woman to be outside as well as men, and they do not know what they are missing when they stay cooped up in the house with a novel," an activity she personally deplored.[50]

Many people supported Oakley's efforts. Also in 1901, Mrs. S.S. Johnson publicly revealed her experience with guns. Although her husband had urged her to take up shooting, she had done so with great hesitation. Then, when it came her turn to shoot among a crowd of men, she felt "quite shaky," but managed to perform acceptably. Eventually, she honed her skill and competed in matches with Annie Oakley herself. Then, in 1902, a male commentator also applauded Annie's efforts. Women had a "right," he argued, to share in shooting, for the "elevating sports of men are equally good for women."[51]

Encouraged by such remarks, Oakley stepped up her own endeavors and reemphasized her dual theme. In 1902, after retiring from the Wild West after a train accident, she increased her arguments on behalf of women shooters.[52] As the urban crime rate rose, Annie also argued that women should carry guns for self-defense. When in the streets, Annie urged during a 1904 visit to Cincinnati, a woman should not carry her revolver in her handbag, but should have it ready at all times by concealing it within the folds of a small lady's umbrella. Wearing a stylish, floor-length dress with full sleeves and a high collar, Annie posed for photographs showing women how to prepare themselves and their umbrellas to fend off thieves or "murderous attack." That same year she demonstrated from her Nutley, New Jersey, home how women could effectively handle firearms despite long, heavy skirts and full sleeves. One of the accompanying photographs showed her as a gentle, grandmotherly figure—a gray-haired lady in a dark dress with a full, ruffled, long-skirt—sitting by her bedside table loading a revolver to be placed in a night-stand drawer.[53]

Three years later, Annie mentioned that she had received hundreds of letters from women who wanted to emulate her and who asked for further advice. She said that such letters "pleased me very much," and urged women to develop their talents at traditionally male endeavors.[54] Her message was clear; women were to renounce timidity and passivity at once.

In addition to being a superb athlete committed to women's advancement in shooting, over the years Annie developed into a consummate entertainer. With Frank's help, by the 1890s and early 1900s Annie shaped an act and an image with universal appeal, yet one that reflected her and Frank's moral beliefs and values. Although Annie's and Frank's show business acumen dictated the inclusion of dramatic elements, their own personalities demanded a "clean" aura based upon solid family values. Neither tricks nor the inclusion of sex held any allure for Oakley and Butler. Consequently, they shaped a routine and a persona for Annie that suited waning Victorianism and offered something to please everyone in their audiences. By the mid-1890s Oakley's act skillfully blended six basic elements: guns, horses, heroes, villains, Victorianism, and the American West. These constituted the performance text—the message—that Annie and Frank conveyed to their viewers.[55]

The most obvious dimension of Annie's act and demeanor was exceptional skill with that western symbol—the gun. Employing guns as safe emblems of entertainment and sport, she performed a wide range of feats, including shooting an apple off a dog's head, shooting the ash off a cigarette Frank held in his teeth and a dime out of his fingers, shooting holes in playing cards, and bounding over a table then shooting two glass balls already in the air when she began to jump. She also pointed her rifle backward over her shoulder, sighted in a mirror, and hit targets behind her back.[56] During her lifetime Oakley owned hundreds of firearms and once estimated that they would line her tent "on all four sides if they were stacked as closely as I could stack them." Besides preferring Stevens model pistols, this five-foot, hundred-pound woman owned three Stevens .22 caliber sporting rifles, and sometime during the 1890s obtained one of her favorite rifles, a .32/20 Model 92 lever-action repeater. Among shotguns, early in her career Oakley favored a 16-gauge, hammer-type, especially the Parker Brothers models. Around 1890 she remarked that she preferred hammerless shotguns weighing about six pounds. Whether they weighed six pounds or as much as twelve, however, no one ever saw this diminutive woman have any difficulty hefting a rifle or shotgun to her shoulder; she could even shoot one-handed.[57]

As such a daring and accomplished shooter, Oakley provided a way for women to identify with the Wild West show and with the West. Instead of women watching men perform magic tricks with the assistance of a comely woman, or throw knives at objects in a woman's hand or on her head, they could instead admire a woman, Annie Oakley, shoot things out of men's hands and utilize men in other ways as assistants in her act. In addition, Oakley's presence in the Wild West reassured women viewers that women not only existed in the West, but contributed a good deal to western development.

In addition to her handling of guns, Annie's skill with horses assumed legendary proportions. She became a female cowboy who, being brave, strong, and clever, could easily handle the mainstay of western life, the horse. In 1887, for example, she trained a horse named Gypsy to follow her everywhere, including up flights of stairs and into a freight elevator. About the same time, when Annie drew a "small, sleepy-looking buckskin" as her mount in a horse race, she turned it into a "wide-awake little horse" that went on to win every

race it ran.[58] Often, the favorable reviews that usually followed her performances called Oakley a superb equestrienne.[59]

In 1898 Annie again charmed the public with her ability and her obvious
love of horses. Just one week after she bought a high-strung, dark bay named
Prince, Annie and Prince entertained female visitors to Stirrat's stables in New
York City. Annie simply gave Prince a word and a nudge; he kneeled and
bowed to the ladies, shook hands, and performed other tricks. Then Annie
tightened the reins to convince the fractious horse to draw up his left forefoot
and drop to one knee in a salute.[60]

The third characteristic of Annie Oakley—heroes—is more complicated. In
numerous ways, Annie herself played the hero on and off stage. For instance,
like a good westerner, she always acted in a clean-cut, outdoor, athletic way.
She not only rode well, but performed cartwheels and sprinted.[61]

Annie likewise proved reliable and tough. She frequently pushed herself to
work under adverse conditions, including her own poor health, inclement
weather, or accidents. When a portion of a grandstand collapsed in 1891 during
a performance in Nottingham, England, five hundred people plunged to the
ground during Annie's performance. Yet she continued her shooting and,
according to one witness, "finished her work without a single miss, under the
circumstances and excitement displaying remarkable nerve for a lady."[62]

Annie also maintained scrupulous honesty. Unlike other performers who
relied upon an accomplice to shatter targets by means of wires or other devices,
Oakley never used the many tricks or illusions so popular during the 1890s. In
one, an eight-inch-wide metal funnel painted to match the target surrounded
the usual one-inch bull's eye; this device caught any bullet within reasonable
range and funneled it into the bull's eye. In the cigar-ash trick a shooter need
not come anywhere near the target; the smoker simply pulled a wire in the
cigar's center and the ash dropped off at the appropriate moment. Although
temptations to employ such artifices or cut corners must have existed, Annie
and Frank strove to keep her act honest. In 1896 New York City's *Sunday
Mercury* ranked Annie among the "bona fide" shooters of the world, those
"who do what they claim".[63]

But Annie and Frank also realized that a truly admirable hero had a foible or
two. To increase her appeal, they allowed her to reveal the odd traits and
eccentricities of any good hero. When she missed a shot, she stamped her foot
on the ground and pouted in full view of the audience. When she hit her mark,
she gave a satisfied little kick. At the end of her act, she blew kisses to the crowd
and gave a distinctive jump-kick as she exited.[64]

Unlike Oakley's heroism, the fourth component of her act—the presence of
villainy—lay latent and implied. For instance, although Annie did not use her

guns as instruments of violence, except perhaps when shooting live pigeons, an element of potential violence always existed. She could easily shoot anyone who threatened her family, friends, or herself. In addition, she obviously possessed power. Frequent explosions of gunfire, smoke, and glass shards drifting from above convinced audiences that Annie was in control.

Oakley's consumption of ammunition was in itself intimidating. In 1899 Frank estimated that Annie had fired 48,000 shots during the past season at a cost of $300 a week. In a pamphlet issued during the late 1890s, titled *Annie Oakley: A Brief Sketch of Her Career and Notes on Shooting*, Annie estimated that "the various shells, primers, wads and metallic cartridges" she had used would supply an army. She feared that the amount of ammunition she had consumed during her career would "appall most persons."[65] Clearly, Annie could vanquish any villain who dared approach her.

The fifth factor—Victorianism—made Annie acceptable and appealing to everyone in her audience, young or old, male or female, old-fashioned or modern. Throughout her career, Annie refused to wear trousers or other masculine attire. Instead, she donned skirted outfits of fine broadcloth or tan gabardine that resembled buckskin, but were lighter and easier to maintain. During the summer, she switched to costumes of washable material, usually in blues or tans. When clothing styles relaxed among some women, especially arena "cowgirls," Annie maintained her formal, ladylike look. While other women adopted bloomer outfits, split skirts, and even trousers, Annie wore skirts.[66]

Annie demonstrated Victorian modesty in other ways as well. She adhered to prevailing standards of female decorum by refusing to ride a horse astride. In keeping with her ladylike beliefs, she declared riding astride a "horrid idea." Instead, she performed horseback tricks from a side-saddle, a contraption with a flat seat, upon which the rider sat sideways, and a thick, leather-covered hook, which the rider used to anchor herself by her leg to the horse's back. Using this device and wearing full, ankle-length skirts, in exhibitions Annie Oakley lay back against her horse while traveling at a gallop. With her skirt draped gracefully over her legs, she pointed her rifle in the air and almost always hit her target. Or she might sit upright, shooting while her mount jumped a fence.[67]

In the arena, Oakley refrained from shooting while riding, perhaps to avoid competing with Cody, but she would retrieve a handkerchief or her hat from the ground by dangling off the side of her horse from the side-saddle, or by draping herself across the horse's back and reaching down the other side. Using the side-saddle to her advantage, she created the illusion, whatever her mount's speed and gait, that she floated on the horse's back.

Annie's personal behavior also reflected Victorian standards; it assured women that, although independent and perhaps employed, they could still be domestic. She furnished her tent/dressing room with a Brussels carpet, a rocking chair, and a parlor table. Between appearances, Annie sat in the chair, her guns lining the walls, and did fancy embroidery. After shows, Annie often entertained guests with punch, tea, cakes, and ices.[68]

Annie also indicated that women could show dependence upon men. She always worked with male assistants; she even chose male dogs for her act. Of course, she depended primarily upon Frank, who supported and encouraged her. He also arranged gun licenses, issued press notices and photos, penned articles under the pseudonym "A Wandering American," wrote letters under his own name, handled correspondence and contracts, arranged to get arms and ammunition through customs, and served as their financial manager. In 1902 Annie told a reporter, "I owe whatever I have" to Frank's "careful management."[69]

In addition to demonstrating her dependence upon Frank, Annie projected a Victorian-style family impression. Annie assuaged fears concerning the changing American family and underwrote traditional values by regularly including Frank and their current dog in her act. As her family, Frank and the dog helped establish a domestic aura and sent a message of family unity. When Annie shot a coin out of Frank's finger or an apple off a dog's head, she illustrated the trust that should exist between family members.

The sixth factor—the American West—was especially important because it united the other five into a coherent package. Guns, horses, heroes, villains, and Victorianism appeared in everything from circuses to melodramas, but in the arena the West unified them and gave them a twist that other shows and exhibitions lacked. Annie especially incorporated the western motif by wearing a cowboy-style hat and dresses that, as one viewer observed, "reminded one very forcibly of the wild West." Oakley also used western tack and western-style guns, often ornamented with tooled silver.[70]

In addition, Annie and Frank made much of Chief Sitting Bull christening her "Watanya Cecilla," or "Little Sure Shot," then adopting Annie in St. Paul, Minnesota, in 1884. Just two weeks later, Frank placed an advertisement in the *New York Clipper* announcing that "the premier shots, Butler and Oakley" had made friends with the most fearsome Indian chief of all. Frank added that Sitting Bull had given them, along with other gifts, the pair of moccasins he had worn at the Little Big Horn. Although Annie had sympathy for Sitting Bull and his people, who, in her view, "had been driven from their God-given inheritance and were living on broken promises," she allowed the story of her adoption by Sitting Bull to be exploited in Wild West publicity.[71] When Annie and Sitting Bull reunited in 1885 after John Burke escorted Sitting Bull from Standing Rock to tour with the Wild West, their subsequent season together further marked Annie as a western woman, in spirit if not in truth.

Over the years, several other vehicles further emphasized Annie's western cowgirl dimension. In 1887, for example, Buffalo Bill Cody started selling booklets to Wild West audiences. Hawkers carried stacks of them through the crowds, selling booklets by the hundreds. An early booklet concerning Annie appeared in London in 1887. Titled *The Rifle Queen*, it ran sixty-four pages and sold for the bargain price of two cents. *The Rifle Queen* described Oakley's supposed childhood in Kansas (rather than Ohio), including her trapping wolves, foiling train robbers, riding out a blizzard, shooting a bear, and defeating a desperado. Many readers took it as the truth, as did many journalists who then reported Oakley's fictional exploits as fact.[72]

Later in the 1890s Annie also appeared in at least one motion picture. This came about as a result of Buffalo Bill Cody's close connection with Thomas Alva Edison, who designed the Wild West's 600-horsepower electrical plant. When Edison invented his battery-powered kinetescope moving picture machine, he naturally turned to Cody and such performers as Oakley as subjects. In Fall 1894 Cody and fifteen colorfully dressed Indians, and later Annie, went to Edison's "studio" in East Orange, New Jersey, to act before Edison's invention. Edison soon discovered that his rudimentary camera could reproduce Oakley's shots, the smoke from her rifle, and the splintering of glass balls.[73] Edison showed these early films in nickel-in-the-slot machines, called peepshow machines and later dubbed nickelodeons. People who had never seen Annie in one of her many live appearances could now view her at last, courtesy of Edison's invention.

Moreover, Annie frequently played a cowgirl on the stage. Because Annie and Frank had to earn an income during the Wild West's off-season—the late fall, winter, and early spring months—they sometimes tried to capitalize on her cowgirl image by taking it on the theater circuit, much as Cody himself had starred in western melodramas during the 1870s and 1880s.

Oakley first took to the boards in 1888 when she opened in *Deadwood Dick, or the Sunbeam of the Sierras* in Philadelphia on Christmas eve to less than enthusiastic reviews. Bombastic and unreasonable were among the terms applied to the show's plot. Other kinder critics lauded Annie's dramatic ability and predicted a brilliant future for her or heaped high praise on the troupe, who played the roles of "denizens of that far region," the American West, with realism and deftness. *Deadwood Dick* closed at the end of January 1889, however, after the show's manager decamped with the receipts.[74]

Obviously, Annie and Frank recognized the appeal of western themes. They simply needed to discover a workable formula for putting her western persona on the road and keeping it there. During the fall of 1894 Annie and Frank tried again with a play titled *Miss Rora*. Publicity described *Miss Rora* as a drama illustrating "life on the frontier"; Annie played the role of a "wild, wayward Western girl." On stage, Annie wore what one viewer termed "picturesque North American attire," shot at glass balls and a variety of other targets, and rode her horse Gypsy, even though the horse's hoofs sometimes broke through the stage floor.[75]

Reviewers generally liked *Miss Rora* and judged Annie a good actress and a marvelous shooter. After the Christmas holidays, Annie and Frank took *Miss Rora* to England, where it did well throughout the winter and spring of 1895, generally playing to full houses. *Miss Rora* traveled through Great Britain for ten weeks, but because of the depression that prevailed there as well as in the United States, the company only made expenses. Annie ended her English tour at the Alhambra Theater, where she performed between acts of the ballet *Ali Baba*, while stagehands moved the heavy, unwieldy scenery.[76]

Given the outcome of *Deadwood Dick* and *Miss Rora*, Annie understandably limited her stage appearances to vaudeville and refrained from acting in another western drama until November 1902. She then opened in *The Western Girl*, written by the prolific and popular Langdon McCormick. This time, publicity employed terms similar to those used by Buffalo Bill's Wild West. It described *Western Girl* as a portrayal of "the days of the Old West as never before attempted on the dramatic stage." Advertisements and posters also announced that the play would feature Annie's own horses, especially Little Bess, "A Rocky Mountain Pet." Much like Cody's Wild West, the stage properties would include "The Old Historic MAIL COACH Procured Especially for this GREAT PLAY," which was the old Leadville stagecoach. The spectacular scenery, painted on high-grade linen cloth, would reproduce the "days of the wild and wooly West."[77]

In the context of a melodramatic plot, the play featured Oakley shooting, riding, and defeating evil at every turn. She shot a liquor bottle out of her drunkard father's hand and caused him to forswear drinking; shot off the villain's hand just as he was about to plunge a dagger into the hero's back; won a prize at glass ball shooting in a barroom; and lassoed the villainess, who was about to murder the heroine's blind sister. In case all these elements did not suffice, the play also featured singing and yodeling specialties.[78]

Much to Annie's and Frank's satisfaction, *The Western Girl* generally played to full houses and received rave reviews. Apparently, no one questioned the authenticity of the play's representation of the Old West. When *The Western Girl* appeared in Atlantic City in late 1902, one reviewer applauded the play's re-creation of "the western hills in the days before the railroad brought civilization to the early pioneers, and bandits and outlaws had only the small check of scattered United States troops."[79] Neither did critics question Oakley's audacity at presenting herself as "the" western girl.

Soon, audiences packed theaters to see Oakley as the western girl, and often went wild with their applause, demanding as many as six curtain calls. The *Wilkes-Barre Record* put its finger on the appeal of *The Western Girl*, saying it was a "dashing, sparkling, not to say sensational, melodrama" that remained "clean and wholesome throughout."[80] But because of the cost of moving a large company and heavy sets every few days, the play proved less successful financially than critically and thus closed in March 1903. Still, despite its short run, *The Western Girl* added one more building block to the public's conception of Annie Oakley as a cowgirl.[81]

Thus, between 1885, when Annie joined Buffalo Bill's Wild West, and 1902, when she left Cody, Oakley developed a strong and clear cowgirl persona that leaned more toward the feminine than the masculine. During the late 1890s and early 1900s other cowgirls modeled themselves after Annie. During these years most Wild West and rodeo cowgirls still wore dresses or skirts and bodices, gloves, and hats with turned-up brims. During the late 1890s and early 1900s, Lucille Mulhall, who, like Annie, was five feet tall, also dressed girlishly and acted in a feminine manner. And, again like Annie, Mulhall attracted numerous fans, garnered favorable reviews, and received hundreds of gifts.[82]

Too, only a few of the early cowgirls rode their horses astride. Show programs explained that those cowgirls who adopted the "cross-seat" did so for safety and for freedom of movement. To offset criticism, Cody and others billed such riders as prairie beauties and natural flowers of the American West, while Wild West show programs regularly denied that cowgirls belonged to the class of "new women." Cowgirls, promoters maintained, simply represented lively, athletic, young women who wanted the opportunity to develop their skills.[83]

During the mid-to-late 1890s, however, many cowgirls, both in the Wild West arena and in rodeos, began to change their behavior and deviate widely from Oakley's model. Gradually, a likeness of cowgirls as tough women, unnaturally muscled, and hardened in sentiment, emerged alongside the feminine cowgirl. This shift occurred partly because many cowgirls adopted masculine styles of clothing. Although they at first wore divided skirts, these soon evolved into bloomer or trouser outfits bedecked with fur, feathers, beads, fringes, quill-work, and painted designs, set off by knee-high boots and Stetson hats.[84]

Moreover, in rodeo by the mid-1890s, women rode broncs, diving horses, and steers, as well as performing fancy roping and bulldogging.[85] These cowgirls rode astride, which most Americans still thought immodest as well as potentially harmful to women's reproductive systems. A special saddle with a padded seat, a heavy roll of padding across the front of the seat, and thick, stiff leather between the saddle and the stirrup appeared, but most photographs and posters from the era show cowgirls using men's lighter roping saddles.[86]

The changes in cowgirls were both noticeable and alarming to many Americans. The publicity produced by the growing number of Wild West shows inflicted a great deal of damage on the cowgirls' reputation, for it grew increasingly masculine in tone and even risqué. At least seventy-two troupes, and probably more than that, competed for audiences during this period. To draw attention, their advance agents plastered board fences, billboards, and the walls of buildings from barns to outhouses with publicity representing increasingly masculine-looking cowgirls. During the early 1900s, for example, Pawnee Bill billed his cowgirls as "Beautiful Daring Western Girls and Mexican Señoritas in a Contest of Equine Skill." But Tiger Bill's Wild West went further; it pictured women shooters in the attack on the settlers' cabin. These women not only wielded guns alongside men, they wore above-the-knee skirts, knee-high boots, and men's Stetson hats.[87]

Other shows followed the trend. Owners, managers, and publicity agents who realized that Wild West shows were losing ground to such other mediums as film and radio, had to use every attention-getter they could devise. As a result, Tompkins Real Wild West and Frontier Exhibition issued posters that showed a woman riding astride, attired in a split skirt, her whip raised in the air, while another woman hung from a cross-saddle to retrieve something from the ground. Both rode amidst men.[88]

The Buffalo Ranch Real Wild West's advertising also portrayed women riding with men and participating in equestrian football and camel races. In other publicity, it claimed that Cowboys, Cowgirls, Indians, and Mexicans constituted the four elements of the Old West. It even out-reached Buffalo Bill Cody and his Congress of Rough Riders by presenting a Congress of American Cowgirls. During the early 1900s, however, Cody added a group of "Western Girl Rough Riders" to his exhibition. These women rode in the Grand Review as part of the Rough Riders of the World, which included Indians, Cowboys, Cossacks, Mexicans, Scouts and Guides, Cavalry, and other soldiers.[89]

In 1910 a four-color lithograph circulated by the Buffalo Bill/Pawnee Bill

Film Company topped them all. The focal point of this poster for a film titled "The Life of Buffalo Bill" pictured a cowgirl riding astride, six-gun slung around her waist. Above her head she twirled a lariat, intent on roping a massive, steam-snorting bull.[90] Clearly, the cowgirl was no longer a lady.

When in the following year, 1911, Oakley returned to the Wild West arena by joining Vernon Seavers's Young Buffalo Show, she refused to follow this pattern. Although the term "cowgirl" was now widely used, Annie rejected its current connotations.[91] Instead, Annie continued to project the image that had worked so well for her in the past; she wore her usual conservative clothing and acted like a Victorian lady. She drew audiences and received favorable reviews despite, or perhaps because of, the dress and actions of her competitors. Oakley also continued to appeal to a number of other cowgirls who emulated her style. Some, like young Vera McGinnis, rode side-saddle, while others, like trick-rider Tad Lucas, made all her own costumes, feminine in style and excellent in quality. And Pearl Mason, who became the World Champion Bronc Rider in 1918, maintained that her behavior was always that of a "lady."[92]

Annie toured with the Young Buffalo Show until 1913, when she retired from what she called "the show business" for good. Since Oakley joined Cody's Wild West in 1885, times had changed radically for American women and she stood in the forefront of those changes. She had opened Wild West shows to strong women performers. As early as 1886, Cody and Salsbury added several women riders and shooters, besides Oakley, to the Wild West. Between then and 1900, more than a dozen women toured with this or other shows either part- or full-time.[93] In 1888 alone, the *New York Times* noted that Cody's Wild West included five female performers. After 1900, numerous others followed, constituting about 10 percent of an exhibition's cast.[94]

Oakley also helped open rodeo to women. Annie joined Buffalo Bill Cody's Wild West in 1885, the same year that the "first" cowgirl, Lucille Mulhall, was born. Annie had already captured public attention as a cowgirl by the time Mulhall began to learn to ride and rope on the Oklahoma plains during the early 1890s, and when Annie Shaffer, probably the first woman bronc rider, competed at Fort Smith, Arkansas, in 1896.[95] And by the time thirteen-year-old Lucille Mulhall made her 1899 debut in her father Zack's Wild West show in St. Louis, Annie's cowgirl image was known and loved throughout the United States as well as many European nations.[96]

Due to Oakley's influence, by the early 1900s cowgirls gained wide acceptance. In the rodeo arena, they did everything from riding bucking horses to competing with lariats. Many hoped to make it big in show business, just as Annie Oakley had done. Bertha Blancett of Wyoming, for example, performed in both rodeos and films; she worked with Bison Moving Picture Company doing such stunts as stopping her mount in the middle of a dead run. Then, during the 1910s Prairie Lillie Allen excelled at riding broncs, Mildred Douglas Chrisman executed daring jumps from the back of one relay horse to another, and Fox Hastings became one of the few women bull-doggers.[97] During the early 1920s Florence Hughes Randolph won acclaim by bronc riding, trick riding, and competing in Roman standing races. Randolph also competed in the World's Championship Rodeo in Madison Square Garden on ten occasions.[98] In 1926, as Annie's health waned, many Americans continued to think of her as the nation's first cowgirl. In May of that year, the Dayton *Daily News* featured Annie in its Sunday supplement. In it, Annie recalled her campaign on behalf of women shooters: "I had an ideal for my sex," she said. Moreover, the author of the piece described Annie as a Wild West star and as "The Western Girl," noting that she continued to set shooting records during her retirement years. But the accompanying photographs were the most poignant of all; older ones pictured Annie in western garb, while contemporary shots showed a withered lady with silver hair.[99]

When, later in 1926, Will Rogers commemorated Oakley's life and career in his syndicated column, Annie received thousands of letters from fans, amateur shooters, and riding enthusiasts who remembered her feats in the arena and on shooting-match grounds. One man claimed that he had seen Annie perform on seven different occasions. In his estimation, she had "shone in your art as no other woman ever did." A woman writer revealed that she too had seen Annie perform and had looked into Annie's eyes, trying to discover what made her the "chief attraction," despite being a woman.[100]

When Annie Oakley died on November 3, 1926, thousands of others who remembered and appreciated her mourned. But soon after her death, Oakley's reputation at the first cowgirl began to recede and fade. Rather than being remembered as an athlete, Annie lived on in the American mind as a show-business star and a lady. What might be termed the "Annie Get Your Gun" mentality soon prevailed, overshadowing Oakley's achievements and shooting.

The representation of Annie Oakley as a woman who got her man rather than her target began with Barbara Stanwyck's 1935 film, *Annie Oakly*. The film's promoters billed Stanwyck as "Queen of the Roaring 80s," and promised that *Annie Oakley*, which also starred Preston Foster as Frank Butler (called Toby in the film) and Melvyn Douglas as Buffalo Bill, would "thrill" viewers with a "drama of fighting men and red romance." Despite this turgid publicity, Stanwyck portrayed Oakley as spunky enough to gain approval from Annie's supporters.[101]

The plot of *Annie Oakley*, however, retold Annie's story in a way that suited the times. It focused upon Annie's shooting match with Frank and their subsequent love affair. Opposite to what Oakley had done in real life, Stanwyck's Annie threw her match with Toby (Frank). Because Stanwyck's Annie was infatuated with Toby, she then accepted a job with Buffalo Bill's Wild West. Naturally, Toby returned Annie's interest, even though she was not much of a lady. Stanwyck's Oakley wore short skirts, rode astride, revealed that she let Walker win the Cincinnati match, and continued to outshoot him. After a series of mishaps, including a separation and reunion, Annie fell into Toby's arms at the end of the film.[102]

Next followed a version of Annie's life written by a brother-and-sister team, Dorothy and Herbert Fields. Titled *Annie Get Your Gun*, the story was intended for production on the musical stage. The Fields's explained that they "dreamed" up the show for the "wonderful Merman," actress Ethel Merman. When producers Richard Rodgers and Oscar Hammerstein II agreed to produce their version of Annie's life, the Fields were delighted. On May 16, 1946, Ethel Merman opened as Annie at the Imperial Theater in New York City wearing a fringed and sequined suit with hat, gloves, and boots to match. This rendition also featured Annie's supposed loss of the shooting match to Frank, a falsehood later repeated in numerous revivals of *Annie Get Your Gun*.[103]

In 1950 Hollywood tackled Annie's story again; Betty Hutton and Howard Keel starred in the MGM version of *Annie Get Your Gun*. Billed as "The Biggest Musical Under the Sun in Technicolor," *Annie Get Your Gun* dressed Annie in 1950s fashions. Hutton sported an outfit composed of a short, tight-fitting jacket and a slim, knee-length skirt, both generously decorated with gold braid. And in the ballroom scene, Hutton showed an abundance of decolleté above the bodice of a low-cut ball-gown decorated with medals. Moreover, according to this version of Annie's story, Frank quit the Wild West in a pout because Annie outperformed him. When Annie ran into Frank again at one of Cody's balls, she and Frank decided to shoot it out for champion. Annie took Sitting Bull's advice to lose the match. Hutton thus once again reinforced the message that a woman must never defeat a man—and that a true man could never accept nor love a woman who did so.[104]

A critic in Nutley, New Jersey, where Annie and Frank had owned a home between 1892 and 1904, protested that Hollywood had "wronged our Annie in Technicolor fantasy." He added that the latest film version of Annie "wore dresses up to her knees and sang like Betty Hutton." In addition, Annie's long auburn hair had turned blond and curly. Those "varmints out in Hollywood" had given a "torchy" side to Annie Oakley, even though her Nutley friends remembered her as a "distinguished lady."[105]

Despite such protests, however, Annie Oakley's athletic ability and shooting records were soon forgotten. Rather, Annie Oakley became Barbara Stanwyck, Ethel Merman, and Betty Hutton rolled into one.[106]

An additional factor that caused people to forget Annie's accomplishments and influence as a cowgirl was the gradual decline of women's participation in rodeo beginning during the 1930s. During the 1920s and early 1930s, rodeos were contests in which women paid entry fees and hoped to walk away with some of the prize money. Rodeos featured three women's events: trick riding, a relay race (at grounds that had tracks), and bronc riding.[107] Of the three, trick riding drew the most competitors. In this event, enlarging on Oakley, who had ridden standing on a horse's back and hanging from its side, women performed stands, vaults, drags, and other stunts for numerical scores.

But by the mid-1930s, this event began to disappear, largely because the effects of the Great Depression reduced the number of horses that rodeo companies could maintain for their contestants and cut the prize monies offered. As a consequence, most rodeos dropped the event but hired women trick-riders on a contract basis as entertainers. Although a few women accepted these contract jobs, the small salaries that they now received offered slight motivation to perform difficult tricks and to develop new ones.[108]

Relay races underwent a similar rise and fall. At least partly because Oakley had achieved fame not only as a shooter, but as one of the most skilled women riders and racers of the day, other women riders also sought the spotlight and enlarged upon Annie's riding feats. In rodeo relay races, each woman contestant had three horses assigned to her. She would circle the track on the first horse, shift to the second for another round, and ride the third horse in the final go-around, often jumping from horse to horse. Again, the Depression increased the expense of maintaining the necessary horses as well as cut into the purses offered, thus causing the number of women racers to decline during the 1930s and early 1940s.[109]

Eventually, bronc riding also disappeared. Due in part to Annie's riding broncs in the Wild West, many people had come to accept the idea of women riding broncs. As early as 1910 at the Jefferson County Fair held at Denver's Stockyards Stadium, women riders had joined the men in forming the Broncho Buster's Union and asking five dollars a day for wild-horse riders. But, by the mid-1930s, rodeos all over the country were cutting back the women's bronc-riding event. Women's bronc riding faltered along for a few more years, only drawing fifteen to twenty women riders at any one time. Then, beginning in 1941, World War II demanded so many horses that rodeo owners had trouble keeping enough horses for both men and women riders. That year was the last that the Madison Square Garden Rodeo included a woman's bronc-riding event. Within a few years, the event disappeared entirely.[110]

Today, women in rodeo compete in seven events: the barrel-race, breakaway and tie-down calf-roping, steer undecorating, goat tying, team roping, bareback bronc riding, and bull riding. The most common is barrel-racing, which is fast, colorful, and financially rewarding. Still, it is often disparaged as a pseudo-competition. Florence Hughes Randolph, a former rodeo star of the 1920s, once said, "I don't consider these barrel racers of today real cowgirls."[111] Still, the Girls Rodeo Association names an annual World Champion in each of the seven standard events, while the International Rodeo Association names a World Champion Barrel Racer each year.[112]

Annie Oakley may have caught the public eye primarily with her performances in the Wild West arena, but because the ties between Wild West shows and rodeo were so intricately woven together, anything that athlete and performer Annie Oakley achieved had its impact on rodeo as well. As a case in point, Florence Reynolds, who with her father went into rodeo during the 1910s, regarded herself as a participant in the "change-over of the Wild West Show to the rodeo." According to Reynolds, she "watched the early day Wild West show change into today's rodeo."[113]

In addition, Oakley had provided a model and energetically worked on behalf of women in shooting sports, thus opening the way for thousands of other women who wanted to ride, hunt, shoot, and compete. By riding a horse and using a gun, Annie Oakley had encouraged others to do so. And by arguing for the benefits of such activities for women, Oakley had convinced generations of Americans that women should indeed engage in them.

Finally, Annie's ladylike behavior had acted as a subtle subversion, convincing thousands of people that women could perform and compete without losing their domestic virtues. Although cowgirls gradually became "tougher" than many Americans liked, Annie's demure image also held its ground. In fact, Annie's "ladyhood" probably underwrote the "Annie Get Your Gun" mentality.

Thus, although Cody and his confederates fabricated the idea of the cowgirl and Lucille Mulhall institutionalized it in rodeo, Annie created the first image of the cowgirl. In the minds of those who saw Annie Oakley ride, rope, and shoot sometime between her entrance into show business during the early 1880s and her death in 1926, or even read or heard about her, Annie *was* the first American cowgirl.

NOTES

1. See, for example, Louise Cheney, "Lucile [sic] Mulhall, Fabulous Cowgirl," *Real West* (March 1969): 13–15; Elizabeth Van Steenwyk, *Women in Sports: Rodeo* (New York: Harvey House, 1978), 9; Joyce Gibson Roach, *The Cowgirls* (Denton: University of North Texas Press, 1990), 79; and Willard H. Porter, *Who's Who in Rodeo* (Oklahoma City: Powder River Book Company, n.d.), 90–91. In *Cowgirls: Women of the American West* (Lincoln: University of Nebraska Press, 1991), 188, Teresa Jordan remarked that women in rodeo "really got their start in Wild West shows," but still maintained that Annie Oakley was not a cowgirl. Worse yet, in *Who's Who in Rodeo,* Porter not only claims that Mulhall "was the first female to be called a 'cowgirl,'" but even more erroneously that she was the "first female ever to get top billing in a Wild West Show." More recently, Mary Lou LeCompte, *Cowgirls of the Rodeo* (Urbana: University of Illinois Press, 1993), 36, claims that Gertrude Petran was the first to be called a cowgirl and Lucille Mulhall the first "famous cowgirl."

2. Oakley described prejudice against women performers in Annie Oakley, letter to "My dear Mr. Conning Tower Man," 20 January 1917, Annie Oakley Collection, Buffalo Bill Historical Center, Cody, Wyoming (hereafter AOC, BBHC).

3. George Waldo Brown, *The Tiger of Taos; or, Wild Kate, Dandy Rock's Angel* (New York: Beadle and Adams, 1879), and Joseph E. Badger, Jr., *The Barranca Wolf; or, The Beautiful Decoy, A Romance of the Texas Border* (New York: Beadle and Adams, 1883).

4. See, for example, the laudatory statements in Boston *The Rifle,* June, 1887; London *Society Times and Tribune,* 30 July 1887; Toronto, Canada *Forest and Farm,* 2 June 1888; *New York Herald,* 19 May 1889. For a detailed discussion of Annie Oakley's devotion to Victorian ladyhood, see Glenda Riley, *The Life and Legacy of Annie Oakley* (Norman: University of Oklahoma Press, 1994).

5. For an account of Oakley's early life, see Shirl Kasper, *Annie Oakley* (Norman: University of Oklahoma Press, 1992), 3–9, and Riley, *The Life and Legacy of Annie Oakley,* 3–26.

6. William E. Deahl, Jr., *A History of Buffalo Bill's Wild West Show, 1883–1913* (Ph.D. diss., Southern Illinois University, 1974), 10, and L. G. Moses, "Interpreting the Wild West, 1883–1914," in Margaret Connell Szasz, ed., *Between Indian and White Worlds: The Cultural Broker* (Norman: University of Oklahoma Press, 1994), 158–78.

7. Annie Oakley, Autobiography, c. 1926, copy in author's possession.

8. Joseph J. Arpad and Kenneth R. Lincoln, *Buffalo Bill's Wild West* (Palmer Lake, Colorado: Filter Press, 1971), 28; William E. Deahl, Jr., "Buffalo Bill's Wild West Show, 1885," *Annals of Wyoming* 47 (Fall 1975): 145; and Joseph G. Rosa and Robin May, *Buffalo Bill and His Wild West: A Pictorial Biography* (Lawrence: University Press of Kansas, 1989), 87.

9. Oakley, Autobiography.

10. Kasper, *Annie Oakley,* 41–2. For an analysis of Frank's role in Annie's career and image, see Tracy C. Davis, "Shotgun Wedlock: Annie Oakley's Power Politics in the Wild West," in Lawrence Senelick, ed., *Gender in Performance: The Presentation of Difference in the Performing Arts* (Hanover, NH: University Press of New England, 1992), 141–57, and Tracy C. Davis, "Annie Oakley and Her Ideal Husband of No Importance," in Janelle G. Reinelt and

Joseph R. Roach, eds., *Critical Theory and Performance* (Ann Arbor: University of Michigan Press, 1992), 299–312.

11. See, for example Carl Wimar's 1851 painting *The Abduction of Boone's Daughter by the Indians* in Robert V. Hine, *The American West* (Boston: Little, Brown, and Company, 1973), 191. Captivity narratives also presented women as victims, including Abbie Gardner-Sharp, *The Spirit Lake Massacre and the Captivity of Miss Abbie Gardner* (Des Moines: Iowa Printing Company, 1885), and Emmeline Fuller, *Left by the Indians: Story of My Life* (Mount Vernon, Iowa: Hawk-Eye Steam Printing, 1892). John Frost, *Pioneer Mothers of the West* (Boston: Lee and Shepard, 1875), iii–iv, 22, suggested that an imperiled western woman became a heroine not by fighting back, but by throwing "herself beneath the threatening tomahawk."

12. See, for example, such cowboy songs as "Fair Lady of the Plains" (about a capable ranch woman) and "Pecos River Queen" (about a woman cow-hand) in Margaret Larkin, *Singing Cowboys* (New York: Oak Publications, 1963), 148–50, and "The Dying Desperado" (about a woman wrangler), in John and Alan Lomax, *Cowboy Songs and Other Frontier Ballads* (New York: Macmillan, 1938), 241. A story that presented a strong women was Ned Taylor, "King of the Wild West's Nerve, or, Stella in the Saddle," *Rough Rider Weekly*, No. 123, August 25, 1906, 1–28, and a dime novel was Edward L. Wheeler, *Bob Woolf, The Border Ruffian, or, The Girl Dead-Shot* (New York: M.J. Ivers, 1884). See also the popular folk-tale of Sally Skulle (Juana Mestena), related in Dee Woods, "The Enigma of Juana Mestena," *Frontier Times* 40 (February/March 1966): 34–35, 52–53, and quotes from newspapers between 1877 to 1885 about ranch- and cattle-women in C. P. Westermeier, *Trailing the Cowboy* (Caldwell: Caxton Printers, 1950) 323–27.

13. See, for example, Mary Jane Gray, Letters, 1858–94, Kansas Historical Society; Alvin E. Dyer, ed., *Mrs. Nat Collins: The Cattle Queen of Montana* (Spokane: Dyer Printing Company, second edition variously dated from 1898 to 1914); Lottie Holmberg, interviewer, "Early Experiences of Miss Lucy Wells in Wyoming, 1936," Wyoming States Archives, Museum, and Historical Department, Laramie; Emily J. Shelton, "Lizzie Johnson: A Cattle Queen of Texas," *Southwestern Historical Quarterly* 50 (January 1947): 349–66; Ann Bassett Willis, " 'Queen Ann' of Brown's Park," *The Colorado Magazine* 24 (April 1952): 81–98; Stella Tanner Fowler, The Tanner Family, c. 1960, Montana Historical Society, Helena; Eve Ball, *Ma'am Jones of the Pecos* (Tucson: University of Arizona Press, 1969); Enid Bern, "The Enchanted Years on the Prairie," *North Dakota History* 40 (Fall 1973): 4–19; Sheryll Patterson-Black and Gene Patterson-Black, "Women Homesteaders on the Great Plains Frontier," *Frontiers* 2 (Spring 1976): 67–88; Evelyn King, *Women on the Cattle Trail and in the Roundup* (Bryan, Texas: Brazos Corral of the Westerners, 1983); Dorothy Kimball, "Alone on That Prairie: The Homestead Narrative of Nellie Rogney," *Montana, the Magazine of Western History* 33 (Autumn 1983): 52–62; and Paula M. Bauman, "Single Women Homesteaders in Wyoming, 1880–1930," *Annals of Wyoming* 58 (Spring 1986): 52–53. Also helpful are Nell Brown Propst, *Those Strenuous Dames of the Colorado Prairie* (Boulder, CO: Pruett Publishing Co., 1982), and Elizabeth Maret, *Women of the Range: Women of the Texas Beef Cattle Industry* (College Station: Texas A & M University Press, 1993).

14. Roach, *Cowgirls*, 81; Deahl, *A History of Buffalo Bill's Wild West*, 48; and 1886 Wild West Program, Western History Collection, Denver Public Library. For an account of

Cody's hiring of Lillian Smith, see Nellie Snyder Yost, *Buffalo Bill and His Family, Friends, Fame, Failures, and Fortunes* (Chicago: Swallow Press, 1979), 167–68.

15. Wayne Michael Sarf, *God Bless You, Buffalo Bill: A Layman's Guide to History and the Western Film* (East Brunswick, NJ: Associated University Presses, Inc., 1957), 237–39.

16. Quoted in Deahl, *A History of Buffalo Bill's Wild West*, 22.

17. Quoted in Henry Blackman Sell and Victor Weybright, *Buffalo Bill and the Wild West* (New York: Oxford University Press, 1955), 143.

18. Sarah Wood-Clark, *Beautiful Daring Western Girls: Women of the Wild West Shows* (Cody, WY: Buffalo Bill Historical Center, 1991) 4. See also Kathryn Derry, "Corsets and Broncs: The Wild West Show Cowgirl, 1890–1920," *Colorado History* (Summer 1992): 2–16.

19. Quoted in Rosa and May, *Buffalo Bill and His Wild West*, 116.

20. Deahl, *A History of Buffalo Bill's Wild West*, 74.

21. Wood-Clark, *Beautiful Western Daring Girls*, 4–5.

22. Annie Fern Swartwout, *Missie: An Historical Biography of Annie Oakley* (Blanchester, OH: Brown Pub. Co., 1947), 128.

23. London *Daily Telegraph*, 12 May 1887.

24. New York *Morning Journal*, 16 June 1894.

25. Women of other races and ethnic groups either had their own place in the Wild West shows or remained largely invisible. Native American women almost always appeared in limited roles; in the historical panoramas, they played torturers of white women or "squaws" accompanying their men. Between shows, they provided back-lot attractions for curious visitors.

26. Wood-Clark, *Beautiful Daring Western Girls* 6–7, 16–17. For more information on May Lillie, see Glenn Shirley, *Pawnee Bill* (Albuquerque: University of New Mexico Press, 1958).

27. Quoted in Wood-Clark, *Beautiful Daring Western Girls*, 6.

28. Roach,

29. Jean Meekin Hoard, Diary, 1911, held by Andrea Brown, Berlin, Wisconsin.

30. Frank's side-bets were revealed in *American Field*, November, 1888. For reports of Oakley's matches and records, see *The Country Gentleman*, 15 October 1887; *The American Field*, 28 April 1888; *Boston Herald*, 30 April 1888; *Pittsburgh Chronicle*, 26 September 1888; London *Land and Water*, 7 May 1897; *New York Journal*, 20 March 1900; *New York Press*, 12 December 1900; *New York Herald*, 12 January 1901; *Forest and Stream*, January 1902; *Field and Fancy*, c. 1902, Annie Oakley Scrapbooks, Buffalo Bill Historical Center, Cody, Wyoming (hereafter AOSB, BBHC); and Amon Carter Museum, *The Wild West* (Fort Worth: Amon Carter Museum, 1970) 22.

31. Oakley, Autobiography.

32. Sampson Morgan, letter to "Dear Miss Oakley," 11 October 1896, AOC, BBHC.

33. AOSB, BBHC.

34. Unidentified, undated items in AOSB, BBHC. Also New York *Sun*, 5 April 1900.

35. New York *West Chester Local News*, 5 January 1889; New York *Daily News*, 23 January 1889; and *Belgian News*, 5 June 1891.

36. Wild West Program, 1893, Western History Collection, Denver Public Library.

37. Oakley, Autobiography, and Glenda Riley, interview with Emily Patterson Black, 9 January 1993.

38. Oakley, Autobiography.

39. Hot Spring, Arkansas *Daily News,* 30 October 1896.

40. N. J. Hotchkiss, letter to "Dear Miss Oakley," 16 April 1900, AOC, BBHC.

41. Unidentified, undated items in AOSB, BBHC, and Oakley, Autobiography.

42. Glasgow, Scotland *Eastern Bells,* December 1891.

43. Annie Oakley, "Field Sports for Women," in *Shooting and Hunting,* undated, and "Ladies Should Use Fire Arms," undated, both in AOSB, BBHC.

44. London *Shooting Times* , 26 August 1893.

45. Gyp, "Ladies in the Field," *Shooting and Fishing,* c. 1894, AOSB, BBHC.

46. *New York Journal,* 10 January 1897.

47. *New York Journal,* 15 March 1897.

48. Annie Oakley, letter to "Hon. Wm. McKinley President," 5 April 1898, Annie Oakley Collection, Nutley Historical Society, Nutley, New Jersey.

49. "Famous Annie Oakley," 1900, AOSB, BBHC.

50. Washington (state), *The Times,* 25 April 1901.

51. Washington (state), *The Times* , 25 April 1901, and Edwyn Sandys, "The Game Field," undated clipping, AOSB, BBHC.

52. For the accident, see Kasper, *Annie Oakley,* 164–69.

53. Unidentified, undated series of photographs in AOSB, BBHC; *Newark Sunday News,* 10 July 1904; and *Newark Advertiser,* 16 February 1906.

54. *The Outer's Book* (formerly *The Northwestern Sportsman*), January 1907.

55. For the idea of a performance text in relation to Wild West shows in general, see Sarah J. Blackstone, *Buckskins, Bullets, and Business: A History of Buffalo Bill's Wild West* (New York: Greenwood Press, 1986), 105–30. Also useful is Beverly J. Stoeltje, "Custom and Ceremonies of Rodeo: From Custom to Ritual," unpublished paper read at the Conference of American Custom, American Folklife Center, Library of Congress, Washington, DC, n.d., in possession of the author.

56. Ohio *Marion Daily Mirror,* c. 1895, and *The St. Louis Republic,* c. 1896, AOSB; England *Liverpool Mercury,* 7 July 1891; New York *Evening Telegram,* 31 March 1898; and *Albany Express,* 21 May 1898. See also Kasper, *Annie Oakley,* 42–45.

57. James Cranbrook, "The Guns of Annie Oakley," *Guns Magazine* 2 (May 1956) 23–25, 42–44; London *Shooting,* 16 November 1887 and 14 December 1887. For comments on Oakley's ease in handling guns, see London *Daily Telegraph,* 10 June 1887; Birmingham, England *The Rod and Gun,* July 1891. For a fuller description of Annie Oakley's guns, see Riley, *The Life and Legacy of Annie Oakley* (Norman: University of Oklahoma Press, 1994), 68–70.

58. Oakley, Autobiography.

59. *New York Clipper,* 5 March 1887, and England *The Horticultural Times,* 10 October 1892.

60. Unidentified items, c. 1898, AOSB, BBHC.

61. Oregon, *Portland Sunday Times,* 17 June 1900.

62. Nottingham, England *Evening News,* 29 August 1891.

63. New York *The Sunday Mercury,* 15 March 1896.

64. Unidentified item, c. 1891, AOSB, BBHC, and Amon Carter Museum, *The Wild West,* 21.

65. Annie Oakley, *A Brief Sketch of Her Career and Notes on Shooting* (n.p., n.d.). The booklet was available for the price of a two-cent postage stamp sent to Oakley and Butler. It was excerpted in such journals as *Shooting and Fishing,* 1899.

66. That reviewers appreciated this trait is demonstrated in the London *Society Times and Tribune,* 16 July 1887; New York *Syracuse Post,* 6 July 1895; New Jersey *Newark Daily Advertiser,* 14 December 1897; and Tennessee *Knoxville Bulletin,* 1 May 1899.

67. Illustration of Annie riding side-saddle is found in *The Illustrated American* and the *New York Illustrated News,* both c. 1900, AOSB, BBHC; and in Isabelle Sayers, *The Rifle Queen-Annie Oakley* (Ostrander, Ohio: n.p., 1973) 13.

68. An account of Annie as an expert with a needle is found in Amy Leslie, unidentified clipping, 1904, AOSB, BBHC. Descriptions of Annie's tent and teas are found in the London *The Topical Times,* 22 October 1887; New York *Daily News,* 5 May 1893; New York *Daily News,* c. May, 1893, AOSB, BBHC; and Massachusetts *Portsmouth Times,* 8 June 1900.

69. Quoted in New Jersey *Newark Sunday News,* 11 May 1902. For a public letter written by Frank, see *The American Field,* July 1887. For the "Wandering American," see AOSB, BBHC.

70. *Daily State Gazette,* 6 October 1888, and unidentified clipping, c. 1888, AOSB, BBHC.

71. Oakley, Autobiography. See also Kasper, *Annie Oakley,* 51–57.

72. London *Daily Telegraph,* 10 June 1887.

73. *The New York Recorder,* c. September 1894, AOSB, BBHC.

74. For reviews see Bridgeton, New Jersey *Morning Star,* 22 December 1888, and New York *West Chester Local News,* 5 January 1889.

75. New York *Sunday World,* 11 November 1894; England *The Taunton Echo,* 2 January 1895; and Swansea, Wales *The Cambrian,* 25 January 1895. See also Kasper, *Annie Oakley,* 170–73.

76. Reviews can be found in *New York Herald,* 4 December 1894; Springfield, Illinois *Republican,* 28 May 1895; *South Wales Argus,* 16 January 1895; Gloucester, England *Chronicle,* 2 February 1895; and Nottingham, England *Evening News,* 5 February 1895. Oakley's stand at the Alhambra Theater is described in an unidentified, undated clipping, AOSB, BBHC.

77. *The New York Dramatic Mirror,* undated, and copies of publicity, 1903, AOSB, BBHC.

78. Rochester, New York *Evening Times,* 6 January 1903; Syracuse, New York *Evening Herald,* 9 January 1903; and Louisville, Kentucky *Courier Journal,* 22 February 1903.

79. Unidentified, undated item, c. December 1902, AOSB, BBHC.

80. Pennsylvania *Wilkes-Barre Record,* c. 27 November 1902, AOSB, BBHC.

81. For a thorough examination of Annie Oakley's western image, see Riley, *The Life and Legacy of Annie Oakley,* 145–75.

82. Roach, *Cowgirls,* 84–87.

83. Quoted in Wood-Clark, *Beautiful Daring Western Girls*, 8–9.

84. Wood-Clark, *Beautiful Daring Western Girls*, 10–12.

85. Ellsworth Collings and Alma Miller England, *The 101 Ranch* (Norman: University of Nebraska Press, 1937) 165–66.

86. Wood-Clark, *Beautiful Daring Western Girls*, 8, 10.

87. Amon Carter Museum, *The Wild West*, 89, 92.

88. Ibid., 93.

89. Ibid., 97, and Charles Eldrige Griffin, *Four Years in Europe with Buffalo Bill* (Albia, Iowa: State Publishing Com., 1908), 91.

90. Wood-Clark, *Beautiful Daring Western Girls*, 22.

91. See, for example, 1911 newspaper announcements of Annie Oakley's premier season with the Young Buffalo Show in AOSB, BBHC.

92. For Annie's years with the Young Buffalo Show, see Kasper, *Annie Oakley*, 190–96. Vera McGinnis, *Rodeo Road: My Life as a Pioneer Cowgirl* (New York: Hastings House, 1974), 15–20, and quoted in Jordan, *Cowgirls*, 198, 203–4. For Tad Lucas, see also Porter, *Who's Who in Rodeo*, 78–79.

93. An 1892 account puts the number at Oakley, "six other ladies," and "six Indian women." See London *The World*, 19 June 1892.

94. *New York Times*, 24 June 1888, and Wood-Clark, *Beautiful Daring Western Girls*, 16.

95. Jordan, *Cowgirls*, 189.

96. Roach, *The Cowgirls*, 84–88.

97. Roach, *The Cowgirls*, 89–93.

98. Sally Gray, "Florence Hughes Randolph," *Quarter Horse Journal* 23 (March 1971):50, and Porter, *Who's Who in Rodeo*, 102–3.

99. Dayton, Ohio *News*, 23 May 1926.

100. George Van Wagner, letter to "Dear Mrs. Butler," 4 May 1926, and Bee Biller, letter to "My Dear Miss Oakley," 1 May 1926, AOC, BBHC.

101. Isabelle S. Sayers, *Annie Oakley and Buffalo Bill's Wild West* (New York: Dover Publications, Inc., 1981), 87–88.

102. Ibid.

103. Herbert and Dorothy Fields, "Confessions of An Author's Team," undated, and assorted "Annie Get Your Gun" handbills, AOC, BBHC. See also Sayers, *Annie Oakley*, 87, 89.

104. "Sure as Shootin', It's Annie Oakley & Co.," undated clipping, AOSB, BBHC. See also Sayers, *Annie Oakley*, 87, 89 and Sandra Kay Schackel, "Women in Western Films: The Civilizer, the Saloon Singer, and Their Modern Sister," in Archie P. McDonald, ed., (Bloomington: Indiana University Press, 1987), 196–217.

105. "They Wronged Our Annie in Technicolor Fantasy," unidentified, undated, AOC, Nutley Historical Society. For a detailed account of Annie's and Frank's Nutley years, see Kasper, *Annie Oakley*, 128–39.

106. For a more detailed analysis of Annie Oakley's legend, see Riley, *The Life and Legacy of Annie Oakley*, 206–30.

107. Jordan, *Cowgirls*, 191.

108. Jordan, See also Kristine Fredriksson, *American Rodeo: From Buffalo Bill to Big Business* (College Station: Texas A & M University Press, 1985) 21–35.

109. Ibid.

110. Milt Riske, *Those Magnificent Cowgirls* (Cheyenne, WY: Frontier Printing, 1983), 85–86.

111. Quoted in Gray, "Florence Hughes Randolph," 52.

112. Van Steenwyck, *Women in Sports,* 13–18.

113. Quoted in Cleo Tom Terry and Osie Wilson, *The Rawhide Tree: The Story of Florence Reynolds in Rodeo* (Clarendon, TX: The Clarendon Press, 1957), 2, 47. See also Fredriksson, *American Rodeo,* 6–20.

CHAPTER TEN

WHEN FREDERICK JACKSON TURNER AND BUFFALO BILL CODY BOTH PLAYED CHICAGO IN 1893

RICHARD WHITE

Americans have never been a people with much use for history, but we do like anniversaries. Frederick Jackson Turner was in Chicago in 1893 as an historian presenting an academic paper on the occasion of the 400th anniversary of Columbus's arrival in the Western Hemisphere. The occasion for this essay is the anniversary of Turner's paper.

Although they often have educational pretensions, public anniversaries, unlike academic anniversaries, are primarily popular entertainments; and it is the combination of the popular and the educational that makes the figurative meeting of Buffalo Bill Cody and Turner at the Columbian Exposition in Chicago in 1893 so suggestive. Turner was in Chicago, of course, to give an academic talk on the frontier. Buffalo Bill and his Wild West were in Chicago to play twice a day, "every day, rain or shine" at "63rd St—Opposite the World's Fair" before a covered grandstand that could hold 18,000 people.[1] Turner was an educator, an academic, but he had great popular success which arose from his mastery of a popular iconography of the frontier. Buffalo Bill was a showman, but he never referred to his Wild West as a show. His program in 1893 bore the title Buffalo Bill's Wild West and Congress of Rough Riders of the World.[2] Cody had educational pretensions. In one of the innumerable endorsements reproduced in the program, Brick Pomeroy proclaimed the exhibition a "Wild West Reality . . . a correct representation of life on the plains . . . brought to the East for the inspection and education of the public."[3]

The convergence of Buffalo Bill and Turner on Chicago was a happy coincidence for academics like me, but the juxtaposition of Turner and Buffalo Bill is, as Richard Slotkin has fruitfully demonstrated in his *Gunfighter Nation*, a useful and revealing one.[4] I will juxtapose Turner and Buffalo Bill for somewhat different reasons than Slotkin, but, like him, I will take Buffalo Bill Cody as seriously as Frederick Jackson Turner because Cody produced a master narrative of the West as finished and culturally significant as Turner's own.

Turner and Buffalo Bill told separate stories; indeed, each contradicted the other in significant ways. Turner's history was a story of free land, the essentially peaceful occupation of a largely empty continent, and the creation of a unique American identity.[5] The Wild West told a story of violent conquest, of the wresting of the continent from the hands of the American Indian peoples who held it already. Buffalo Bill's story was a fiction, but it was a performance that claimed to represent a history, for, like Turner, Buffalo Bill worked with real historical events and real historical figures.

These different stories demanded different lead characters. For Turner the pioneer was the farmer; for Buffalo Bill the pioneer was the scout. Farmers were peaceful; their conquest was the wilderness. Indians were largely irrelevant to Turner's story, and he never bothered much with them. The scout, however, was the man distinguished by his "knowledge of Indians habits and language, familiar with the hunt, and trustworthy in the hour of extremest danger."[6] He was, as Richard Slotkin has emphasized, the "man who knew Indians" and who ultimately defeated them.[7] In Turner's telling the ax and the plow were the tools of civilization; for Buffalo Bill civilization's tools were the rifle and the bullet. The bullet, the wild West program declared, is "the pioneer of civilization."[8]

Yet, as different as these narratives were, each drew remarkably similar conclusions from their stories. Both declared the frontier over. Turner built his talk upon "the closing of a great historic movement."[9] Buffalo Bill's 1893 program opened with a conventional enough account of the "rapidly extending frontier" and the West as a scene of "wildness." But the opening paragraph of the program closes with significant parenthetical addition: "This last, while perfectly true when written (1883), is at present inapplicable, so fast does law and order progress and pervade the Great West."[10] The frontier, which according to Buffalo Bill, had opened on the Hudson, had now closed. Indeed, Buffalo Bill the Indian fighter and rancher had become Buffalo Bill the promoter of irrigated farming.

Both Turner and Buffalo Bill credited the pioneers with creating a new and distinctive nation, and both worried about what the end of the frontier signified. Buffalo Bill reminded his audience that generations were settling down to enjoy "the homes their fathers located and fenced for them."[11] But by implication the children of the pioneers had disdained, in his programs metaphor, to

Frederick Jackson Turner
(Photograph courtesy Henry E.
Huntington Library and Art Gallery,
San Marino, California.)

William "Buffalo Bill" Cody,
Symbol of the Wild West, 1893
(Photograph courtesy Buffalo Bill
Historical Center.)

crowd into cities to live like worms. But with the West won, with free land gone, urban wormdom seemed the inevitable destiny of most Americans.

The major elements of these two very different stories were not new in 1893. Take, for example, the close of the frontier. Predictions of the frontier's imminent demise had been current for a quarter of a century. In 1869 Albert Richardson was already predicting the end of an era in his popular *Beyond the Mississippi*.

> Twenty years ago, half our continent was an unknown land, and the Rocky Mountains were our Pillars of Hercules. Five years hence, the Orient will be our next door neighbor. We shall hold the world's granary, the world's treasury, the world's highway. But we shall have no West, no border, no Civilization, in line of battle, pressing back hostile savages, and conquering hostile nature.[12]

Theodore Roosevelt, wrong about so many things, was correct enough when he credited Turner with having "put into shape a good deal of thought that has been floating around rather loosely." For years now historians have found elements of the Turner thesis presaged in one form or another in the scholarship of the late nineteenth century. Forty years ago Henry Nash Smith took the process one step further by making the Turner thesis itself an expression of the nineteenth century pastoral myth of the garden.[13]

This contextualization of Turner, and indeed of Buffalo Bill, however, creates a mystery rather than solving one. For if these ideas and symbols were so prevalent, how did the particular versions offered by Turner and Buffalo Bill come to be so culturally dominant and persistent? Why did they overshadow, and indeed erase, their antecedents and competitors. No one, after all, reads Richardson, and Pawnee Bill—Buffalo Bill's sometime partner and sometimes competitor—is known only to antiquarians.[14]

The answer lies in two things. First, the very contradictions between Turner's story and Buffalo Bill's creates a clue. Turner and Buffalo Bill, in effect, divided up the existing narratives of American frontier mythology. Each erased part of the larger, and more confusing and tangled, cultural story in order to deliver up a clean, dramatic, and compelling narrative. Richardson, for example, offered a narrative of conquest that emphasized both hostile nature and hostile savages. Turner took as his theme the conquest of nature; he made savagery incidental. Buffalo Bill made the conquest of savages central; the conquest of nature was incidental. Yet both stories, it must be remembered, taught the same lessons. Secondly, it was the very ubiquity of the icons of the frontier that allowed both Turner and Buffalo Bill to deliver powerful messages with incredible economy and resonance. Precisely because they could mobilize familiar symbols, Buffalo Bill in a performance of several hours and Frederick Jackson Turner in a short essay could persuade and convince their audiences.

Both Buffalo Bill and Turner were geniuses in their use of the iconography of the frontier,—but not just with existing stories. The two men also used all kinds of symbolic representations—from log cabins to stage coaches—that were reproduced over and over in American life, then and now. Turner incorporated such icons into his talk. Buffalo Bill set out to represent them. And, indeed, he made himself into a walking icon, at once real and make-believe. As the program put it, "Young, sturdy, a remarkable specimen of many beauty, with the brain to conceive and the nerve to execute, Buffalo Bill par excellence is the exemplar of the strong and unique traits that characterize a true American frontiersman."[15] Turner and Buffalo Bill thrived on the modern talent for the mimetic—our ability to duplicate images and experiences.

Turner's "frontier thesis" soon became almost an incantation repeated in thousands of high school and college classrooms and textbooks: "The existence of an area of free land, its continuous recession, and the advance of American settlement westward explains American development." Turner asserted that American westering produced a series of successive frontiers from the Appalachians to the Pacific; the essence of the frontier thesis lay in his claim that in settling these frontiers migrants had created a distinctively American democratic outlook. Americans were practical, egalitarian, and democratic because the successive Wests of this country's formative years had provided the "empty" land on which equality and democracy could flourish as integral aspects of progress. Turner's farmers conquered a wilderness and extended what Thomas Jefferson had called an empire of liberty.[16]

Turner summoned the frontier from the dim academic backcountry, but in popular American culture the frontier was already central. Turner did not have to tell Americans about the frontier; he could play off of images they already knew. Ubiquitous representations of covered wagons and log cabins already contained latent narratives of expansion and progress. Americans had already long recognized the cultural utility of the frontier in their politics, folklore, music, literature, art, and speech for generations. All Turner had to do was to tell Americans about the *significance* of this familiar frontier.

Turner masterfully deployed the images of log cabins, wagon trains, and frontier farm making—and the stories that went with them. He made them elements in a sweeping explanation of the nation's past. To the familiar representations of people conquering a "wilderness" and remaking the land, Turner added another dimension. In the process of advancing the frontier, a diverse people of European origins had remade themselves into Americans. He extended the story of progress.[17]

Neither in a spoken paper nor in an academic article could Turner actually use images. Instead, he relied on an almost painterly prose which called to mind familiar images of migration, primitive beginnings, and ultimate progress. Americans already thought in terms of great achievements from primitive beginnings. Americans already thought of themselves as egalitarian and democratic. Americans had already symbolized such beliefs in images of log cabins and migration into a land of opportunity and had turned those images into icons. Turner used the icons.

Turner often placed himself and his audience not in the West but in popular representations of the West. Turner, for instance, instructed his audience to "stand at Cumberland gap and watch the procession of civilization marching single file—the Buffalo following the trail to the salt springs, the Indian, the fur trader and hunter, the cattleraiser, the pioneer farmer—and the frontier has passed by." He asked them to stand figuratively at the same place where George Caleb Bingham had placed the viewer in his "Daniel Boone Escorting Settlers through Cumberland Gap."[18] This standing at the gap, or on the height, or the border, and watching progress unfold was one of the central American icons of the frontier and progress. Turner's prose called to mind countless representations, from the famous and familiar Currier and Ives print, "Across the Continent: Westward the Course of Empire Takes Its Way," to such local variants as "Pictorial Map Showing the Route Travelled by Mormon Pioneers" (1890). All of them resonated with the Turnerian plot.

Let me take two other examples of the iconography upon which Turner relied: first, in his portrayal of a largely empty continent and, second, in his claim that in America progress involved a regenerative retreat back to the primitive and a recapitulation of ensuing states of civilization.[19] Iconographic representations of both ideas were ubiquitous in American life.

The portrayal of North America as largely empty and unknown was a cartographic convention by the nineteenth century, but this had not always been so. Earlier maps of the sixteenth and seventeenth centuries, for example, had portrayed a densely occupied continent teeming with people. Europeans knew little of the interior, but they assumed that it was fully occupied. But by the nineteenth century, all this had changed. In illustrated maps, as in contemporary prints, only a few scattered Indians appear. They are either retreating or quietly observing the coming of whites. The maps Americans saw in schools broadcast the same message even more forcefully. Emma Willard's widely used nineteenth-century school text vividly portrays the West as empty land. Small villages of French Canadians appear on the map, but Willard has completely erased Indians. This message of a largely empty continent peacefully occupied recurred in the popular literature of the West. Joaquin Miller's "Westward Ho," for example, celebrated a conquest without the guilt of "studied battle":

> O bearded, stalwart, westmost men,
> So tower-like, so Gothic built
> A kingdom won without the guilt
> Of studied battle, that hath been
> Your blood's inheritance . . .

Turner recognized conflict with the Indians, but it was merely part of a much larger contact with wilderness that necessitated the pioneers' initial regression and subsequent recapitulation of the stages of civilization. The "wilderness," Turner declared in Chicago, "masters the colonist . . . it puts him in the log cabin of the Cherokee and Iroquois . . ."[20] This association of pioneers with Indians through the log cabin is interesting, for by the 1890s the log cabin had long been the chief icon of the nineteenth-century frontier. Indeed, the log cabin was perhaps the central American icon. A cabin, built with simple tools and from local materials, proclaimed self-reliance and a connection with place. Usually isolated, it stressed the courage of the builder and the challenge that the surrounding wilderness represented. But, most of all and most interestingly, the cabin had come to represent progress.

The cabin was not intrinsically a representation of progress. Indeed, one of the earliest and most beautiful and haunting representations of the log cabin, the etching in the atlas accompany Collot's *Voyage dans L'Amerique Septentro-nale*, stressed only the isolation and the primitiveness of the structure. Similarly, at midcentury George Caleb Bingham's painting of a squatter's cabin had little progressive about it.[21] And later, in different contexts, sharecroppers' cabins or cabins in Appalachia represented backwardness and poverty rather than progress and prosperity. Only when coupled with the knowledge of the success that was to follow did the cabin proclaim great achievements from small beginnings. Presidential births in supposed log cabins took on meaning only in light of the subsequent presidency. Lincoln's cabin took on meaning with the knowledge of Lincoln's later achievements.[22] The achievements of modern America gave progressive meaning to frontier cabins. The cabin demanded such pairings to evoke its national historical narrative of progress achieved through self-reliance and energy.

The iconography of the cabin served in a quite real way as a groundwork for Turner. The cabin icon already associated the frontier with a retreat to the primitive followed by progress to great achievements. It had served as a symbol of personal and political progress in William Henry Harrison's Log Cabin campaign and in the Lincoln campaign. It was prominently featured in contemporary sheet music and local and popular histories.

But the cabin iconography probably most clearly prefigured Turner in the county histories and atlases that proliferated throughout the Midwest in the 1880s. A common feature in these books were illustrations of prosperous contemporary farms that included, either somewhere in the picture itself or as an inset, a log cabin. The movement from the cabin to the developed farm signified progress. Early maps of Chicago employed the same imagery. The Turner thesis was infinitely more sophisticated than either the county histories or popular histories, but each developed the same theme. These works had, in effect, prepared the way for Turner. His work would resonate with its readers, giving sophisticated form to what they already knew and accepted.

In 1893 Buffalo Bill told another story and employed a different set of icons. Perhaps the easiest way to see how his story differed from that of Turner is to look at the role Indians played in each. Indians were not so much absent from Turner as peripheral; they were not intrinsic to the meaning of his narrative. But Indians were everywhere in Buffalo Bill's Wild West. An Indian illustrated the advertisement in the *Chicago Tribune*. Illustrations of Indians were prominent throughout the program. A "horde of war-painted Arapahos, Cheyenne, and Sioux Indians" participated in the Wild West.[23]

The role of these Indians in the show was to attack. Many of the great set pieces of the Wild West—an attack on the "Prairie Emigrant Train Crossing the Plains," the "Capture of the Deadwood Mail Coach by the Indians," and, most famous of all, "The Battle of the Little Big Horn, Showing with Historical Accuracy the Scene of Custer's Last Charge"—featured Indian attacks.[24]

Buffalo Bill offered what to a modern historian seems an odd story of conquest, for it is an account of Indian aggression and white defense, of Indian killers and white victims, of, in effect, badly abused conquerors. These reenactments open a window onto a particularly interesting aspect of the American iconography of the frontier. To achieve Joaquin Miller's "kingdom won without the guilt of studied battle," Americans had to create an iconography that turned conquerors into victims. The great military icons of American westward expansion are not victories, they are defeats: the Alamo and the Battle of the Little Big Horn. We do not plan our conquests. We just retaliate against massacres.

Like Turner, Buffalo Bill found both the theme and the icons for this version of conquest readily available. The theme of white victimization was so common that Turner himself, in what amounted to an aside, similarly made conquerors into victims. He spoke of Indians as a "common danger" which kept alive "the power of resistance to aggression." He, as much as Buffalo Bill, presented this striking historical reversal of the actual situation as mere conventional wisdom.[25] What gave this reversal of roles its power was a popular iconography that surrounded Americans with images of valiant white victims overpowered by numerous savage assailants. In the version of the frontier Buffalo Bill developed, the continent was no longer empty; it teemed with murderous Indian enemies.

Buffalo Bill exploited an iconography that stretched back to Puritan captivity narratives and continued through the wars of the eighteenth and early nineteenth century. Nineteenth-century broadsides such as the "Massacre of Baldwin's Family by Savages" and "Murder of the whole family of Samuel Wells . . . by the Indians" kept this theme of white victimization central to American understanding of the Indian wars.

Buffalo Bill played no small part in making the defeat of Custer and the slaughter of most of his command both the culmination and the chief icon of this version of conquest. Where representation stopped and lived experience began were never very clear in Buffalo Bill's Wild West, and this gave the Wild West its power. Buffalo Bill created what now seems a postmodern West, in which performance and history were hopelessly intertwined. The story Buffalo Bill told gained credence from his claim (and the claim of many of the Indians who accompanied him) that he had lived part of it.

The show and lived historical reality constantly imitated each other. Sitting Bull, whom Americans credited with being the architect of Custer's defeat, had toured with the Wild West. Some of the Sioux who charged Custer at the Little Big Horn would later charge him nightly in the Wild West. And Indians who fought whites in the Wild West would return to the Dakotas to fight whites for real during the Ghost Dance troubles. Buffalo Bill would step off the stage during both the Custer campaign and during the Ghost Dance to serve as an army scout, each time incorporating aspects of his experience into the show.

The most dramatic and revealing example of this complicated mimesis is the Yellow Hand incident. Leaving the stage in Wilmington, Delaware, in June 1876, Buffalo Bill had joined the Fifth Cavalry as a scout. He was in the field when the Sioux defeated Custer. During a skirmish that July he had killed and scalped a Cheyenne named Yellow Hand.[26] The skirmish and Yellow Hand were being assimilated into Buffalo Bill's stage persona even as it happened.

Buffalo Bill had prepared for the anticipated engagement by dressing in his showman's outfit—"a Mexican vaquero outfit of black velvet slashed with scarlet and trimmed with silver buttons and lace"—which then could become in his performances the actual clothing in which he fought Yellow Hand.[27] Yellow Hand became the "first scalp for Custer." And the scalp, on display in theaters where Buffalo Bill performed in the "realistic Western Drama, . . . Life on the Border" became an actual prop in Buffalo Bill's performances that year.[28]

Joining Buffalo Bill in these pre–Wild West performances in 1877 was Captain Jack Crawford, the Poet Scout. Captain Jack went on to a long career of his own, but Custer and Buffalo Bill gave him his big break. Jack Crawford was an Omaha janitor who, traveling west to enlist with Custer (or so he said), got early news of the defeat and had the presence of mind to telegraph the story to the New York papers. He adopted the persona of a frontier scout who had carried the news from the battlefield and then appears to have been able to turn that fabricated experience as a scout into some real, but brief, army experience in the Southwest.

These combinations of experience and representation were quite malleable. In 1877 Buffalo Bill and Captain Jack, while performing together, combined their stories into a new one in which Buffalo Bill sent a dispatch to Captain Jack on Custer's death. This had supposedly been the occasion for Captain Jack to write a rather confused poem, "Custer's Death," which Buffalo Bill reproduced in the program for "Life on the Border." The poem demanded vengeance from "these demons" who killed Custer. The victimized Custer was to be avenged by volunteers whose identity (much like Captain Jack's own) wavered from stanza to stanza. Their efforts would not "leave a red."

As bewildering of the details of the anticipated slaughter of the Indians might be, the basic message was clear. The slaughter of the heroic Custer justified retaliatory massacre and revenge.[29] The inversion of aggressor and victim justified conquest, and it was played out over and over again.

Turner's "Significance of the Frontier" and Buffalo Bill's Wild West stand in complicated and revealing relation to each other. It is a point that we miss by trivializing Buffalo Bill and missing the common grounding of his story and that of Turner. To see Turner as serious and significant and Buffalo Bill as a charlatan and a curiosity, to see Turner as history and Buffalo Bill as entertainment, to see one as concerned with reality and the other with myth, misses their common reliance and promotion of the iconography of their time; it misses their ability to follow separate, but connected, strands of a single mythic cloth. And it misses, too, the ways in which, just as in Chicago in 1893, these seemingly contradictory stories only ultimately make historical sense when told simultaneously.

These are still essential stories because they are stories that define what being an American means. We still tell variants of both stories. And, indeed, for all the variant multicultural histories that the new western history introduces, these new histories still exist largely within the plotlines of these stories of conquest and stories of peaceful progress.

Indeed, the city of Chicago, where both Buffalo Bill Cody presented his Wild West and Frederick Jackson Turner delivered his paper in 1893, frequently represented itself in strikingly Turnerian terms of primitive beginnings, progress, and opportunity. Turner, in effect, wrote off of these icons; he made them part of a coherent and all-encompassing narrative and explanation of the American experience.

NOTES

1. See the advertisement in the *Chicago Tribune*, April 27, 1893.

2. *Buffalo Bill's Wild West and Congress of Rough Riders of the World* (Chicago: Blakely Printing Company, 1893), title page. The standard biography of Buffalo Bill is Don Russell, *The Lives and Legends of Buffalo Bill* (Norman: University of Oklahoma Press, 1960). Russell has also written the most comprehensive study of Wild West shows; see his *The Wild West or, A History of the Wild West Shows* (Fort Worth, TX: Amon Carter Museum of Western Art, 1970).

3. *Buffalo Bill's Wild West*, 9.

4. Richard Slotkin, *Gunfighter Nation: The Myth of the Frontier in Twentieth-Century America* (New York: Atheneum, 1992).

5. Frederick Jackson Turner, *The Significance of the Frontier in American History* (New York: Frederick Ungar, 1975). Turner did not entirely ignore Indians; he wrote, for example, that each frontier "was won by a series of Indian wars" (p. 33). He did, however, marginalize them: The *frontier*, defined as land populated by two people or more per square mile, did not, for example, include Indians (p. 29). Turner associated Indians with French traders not English farmers (pp. 36–37). Elements of Buffalo Bill's story were present in Turner's narrative—Indians were important for presenting "a common danger," necessitating rugged frontiersman who would "resist aggression" (p. 38)—but these elements were a minor part of Turner's story.

6. *Buffalo Bill's Wild West*, 4.

7. Slotkin, *Gunfighter Nation*.

8. *Buffalo Bill's Wild West*, 22.

9. Turner, *The Significance of the Frontier*, 27.

10. *Buffalo Bill's Wild West*, 4.

11. *Buffalo Bill's Wild West*, 10.

12. Albert Richardson, *Beyond the Mississippi* (Hartford: American Publishing Company, 1867), i. Proclamations of the centrality of the frontier were a staple of mid- and late-nineteenth-century writing: Justin Winsor, *Narrative and Critical History of America*, vol. 8

(New York: Houghton, Mifflin, and Company, 1888), Theodore Roosevelt, *The Winning of the West*, vol. 1 (New York: G.P. Putnam's Sons, 1889), Henry Howe, *Historical Collections of the Great West* (Cincinnati: H. Howe, 1856).

13. Henry Nash Smith, *Virgin Land: The American West as Symbol and Myth* (Cambridge, MA: Harvard University Press, 1970; orig. ed., 1950), 251.

14. For Pawnee Bill and other Wild West shows, see Russell, *The Wild West*, 32–33, 50–52, 75–76, 98–103, 129–33, and *passim*.

15. *Buffalo Bill's Wild West*, 7.

16. Turner, *The Significance of the Frontier*, 27–28, 51–52, 57. My emphasis here is on Turner's talk in Chicago in 1893. I have given a wider analysis of Turner's historical thinking elsewhere; see Richard White, "Frederick Jackson Turner," in John Wunder, ed., *Historians of the American Frontier: A Bio-Bibliographical Source Book* (Westport, Connecticut: Greenwood Press, 1988), 660–81.

17. Turner, *The Significance of the Frontier*, 44–45.

18. Bingham's painting, as Nancy Rash has emphasized, was notable for the way it featured pioneer families. She details its initial disappointing reception and its reproduction as a mass-produced print. Nancy Rash, *The Painting and Politics of George Caleb Bingham* (New Haven: Yale University Press, 1991), 60–65.

19. Turner, *The Significance of the Frontier*, 28–29.

20. Turner, "The Significance of the Frontier," 29.

21. For "The Squatters," see Rash, *Painting and Politics*, 58–60.

22. For a comparison of the log cabin mythology and actual social origins of presidents, see Edward Pessen, *The Log Cabin Myth: The Social Backgrounds of the Presidents* (New Haven: Yale University Press, 1984), 10–26.

23. *Chicago Tribune*, 27 April 1893, p. 2.

24. *Buffalo Bill's* Programme. See also Russel, *The Wild West*, 27, 46.

25. Turner, *The Significance of the Frontier*, 38.

26. For Yellow Hand, see Russell, *The Lives and Legends of Buffalo Bill*, 219–35, and Paul Andrew Hutton, ed., *Ten Days on the Plains* (Dallas: DeGolyer Library/SMU Press, 1985), 35–41.

27. Russell, *The Lives and Legends of Buffalo Bill*, 231.

28. Buffalo Bill (W. F. Cody) and Captain Jack (J. W. Crawford), "Life on the Border," Program, Oakland, CA, 13 June 1877, copy in Everett D. Graff Collection of Western Americana, 783, Newberry Library. For an account of the play in the East and the attack on the display of the scalp, see Russell, *The Lives and Legends of Buffalo Bill*, 254–55.

29. Captain Jack Crawford, "Custer's Death," in Buffalo Bill (W. F. Cody) and Captain Jack (J. W. Crawford), "Life on the Border," Program, Oakland, CA, 13 June 1877, copy in Everett D. Graff Collection of Western Americana, 783, Newberry Library. Also see Darlis A. Miller, *Captain Jack Crawford: Buckskin Poet, Scout, and Showman* (Albuquerque: University of New Mexico Press, 1993).

PART IV

THE HISTORIOGRAPHICAL WEST

Beryl Shinn Holding the Drake Plate as Herbert Eugene Bolton Looks On.
(Photograph courtesy Bancroft Library, University of California, Berkeley.)

CHAPTER ELEVEN

MORE SHADOWS ON THE BRASS

Herbert E. Bolton and the Fake Drake Plate

ALBERT L. HURTADO

If ever there was an historian who loved to write about heroic exploits, it was Herbert E. Bolton. For half a century, Bolton wrote about Spanish soldiers and missionaries, extolling their hardihood and supposed heroic virtues. Bolton's tendency to glorify frontiersmen was influenced by the ethnocentric world in which he lived, University of California politics, and the tastes of the generation of readers to whom he catered. While Bolton derived power and fame from his positive portrayal of California's Spanish and Catholic pioneers, he also had to be careful not to rile the state's elites, who were mostly white and Protestant. He and his students depended on these people for financial support, and so did the University of California. The University's presidents and the state's governors keenly understood this fact, and they were not above putting pressure on Bolton. Thus, Bolton occasionally raised up Anglo-American heroes to balance against his legion of Spanish missionaries and soldiers.[1]

This is an especially important consideration in the case of the brass plate that Bolton unwisely authenticated and erroneously attributed to Drake's 1579 trip to California. Bolton's papers, which are the basis for this essay, disclose some new information about the discovery and acquisition of the plate, its initial authentication, and Bolton's role in these matters. However, they do not reveal the perpetrator of the Drake plate hoax. Rather, Bolton's papers deepen the mystery that surrounds the plate and beg for further investigation of this disputatious episode. More importantly, the controversy over the plate reveals the cultural fault lines that marked California in the 1930s. The Drake plate forgery remains a murky episode in California history, but it demonstrates more concretely the world of race, ethnicity, religion, and institutional life that Bolton inhabited.

In 1937 Herbert E. Bolton was sixty-seven years old and nearing the end of a distinguished career at the University of California. In thirty-seven years he had trained hundreds of graduate students, written scores of books and articles, directed the Bancroft Library, headed the Department of History, and sat in the endowed Sather Chair for History. Italy and Spain had already knighted him, and in 1949 the Vatican would knight him, too, an honor that few Methodists enjoy. He was past-president of the American Historical Association, and enjoyed less notable tributes that are far too numerous to mention. Thus, Bolton was arguably one of the most honored historians of the century with nothing to prove and little to gain when he made the biggest mistake of his career. One February evening—for some reason, the exact date was not recorded—Beryl Shinn, a young department store employee, brought to Bolton a five-by-eight-inch brass plate with some crudely engraved writing. The previous summer Shinn had found the plate on a hill overlooking San Quentin Prison and San Francisco Bay. Ignorant of its identity and thinking that he might use it to repair his car, Shinn had kept the metal plate until he deciphered the word "Drake." Then, acting on the advice of some unnamed Berkeley student, Shinn took the plate to the famous university professor. Bolton surmised that the plate was the one that Francis Drake had left behind after a brief visit to California in 1579 and compared the text with the published accounts of Drake's voyage. The close agreement with one of the texts and the apparent antiquity of the artifact in his hand convinced him that it was the "real McCoy." Bolton contacted his friends in the California Historical Society, who raised the money to purchase the plate and then presented it to the University of California.[2] Soon thereafter Bolton publicly announced that the plate had been found. Then a cloud arose. William Caldeira, a chauffeur, told the newspapers that he had found the plate three years earlier near Drake's Bay on the Pacific Ocean, some twenty miles from the spot where Shinn said he found the plate. After keeping the plate for a few months, Caldeira discarded it near the site where Shinn had found it. Bolton quickly accepted the possibility that Caldeira was telling the truth. After all, in three hundred and fifty years the plate might have been moved many times. So Caldeira's claim did not much trouble Bolton, and others who believed in the plate used Caldeira to validate Drake's Bay as Drake's landing site.

The announcement of the discovery excited international interest, but not everyone was immediately persuaded that it was legitimate. Captain Reginald

Berti Haselden, curator of manuscripts at the Huntington Library, was skeptical and insisted that physical tests of the plate were needed. Henry Raup Wagner, the reigning authority on Drake, was also apprehensive. The suspicions of Haselden, Wagner, and others prompted the University and the California Historical Society to seek an outside expert, who conducted chemical and physical tests confirming that the brass was from Drake's time.[3] Not everyone was satisfied that the plate was genuine, but with a scientific report in hand, the proponents of the plate held the high ground. Criticism faded and the plate became a prized possession of the University that was proudly and solemnly displayed in the Bancroft Library.

The plate, however, later acquired a tarnish of a decidedly modern character. As the Drake quadrennial approached, new questions about its authenticity arose and the University of California ordered new tests, which showed that the plate was a fake.[4] It remains on display in the Bancroft, however, along with a brief typed report declaring it to be a fraud. The perpetrators of the hoax have never been identified, and a few diehards continue to believe that the plate is genuine.

In this brief version of a well-known tale, Bolton's role seems straightforward. He authenticated a document that later proved to be a forgery. Bolton had leaped all too quickly to the conclusion that the plate was genuine. But it should be added that he also urged independent tests of the plate that vindicated his textual analysis. Many other scholars—historians and scientists alike—supported Bolton's opinions, so he was not the only intelligent person to be taken in. A closer look, however, reveals that Bolton played a more complicated part in these matters.

Indeed, complications arose as soon as Bolton beheld the plate that Shinn brought to his office in the Bancroft Library. Seeing and touching the artifact convinced Bolton that Shinn had made an important historical find. Now Bolton had to acquire the plate, but how? There appears in Bolton's papers a carelessly scrawled note on scrap paper that sheds some light and casts some shadows on this question. It reads:

> In return for assistance given me by Prof Bolton in regard to the Plate found by me near San Rafael and on which Francis Drake took possession of the country in the name of England, I hereby agree to give Prof Bolton [the] oppor[t]unity to meet any price offered me for [the] plate less 10% (ten percent) after such opportun[it]y prof Bolton shall have no authority to prevent me from selling the plate to a third party. But in case of such sale Prof Bolton shall have 10% (ten per cent) of amount received by me.[5]

The note raises many questions. It is not signed or dated. The handwriting does not appear to be Bolton's. It is probably in Shinn's hand. The note is creased, as if folded for a pocket. Did Shinn bring it to Bolton with hopes of enlisting the famous professor's aid? Certainly, if Bolton confirmed the authenticity of the plate, it would increase in value. Did Bolton dictate the note, or suggest it to Shinn? Did he try to get Shinn's signature but fail? Did the note, in Shinn's own hand, make a signature superfluous? Did Bolton use the note merely as a device to give the California Historical Society the first chance to purchase the plate? And when Shinn left Bolton's office that night, did Bolton believe that he owned 10 percent of the plate? There are many questions, but two things are certain. First, Bolton kept the note. Moreover, he kept it in a folder with a copy of the bill of sale for the plate that Shinn subsequently executed.[6] So Bolton attached some sort of significance to the note, if only as a record of his involvement in what he believed was an important historical event. Second, the note casts doubt on Bolton's public assertion that Shinn's "chief interest in the plate was to have it preserved for the public, and he never asked nor would he discuss a price for it."[7] Perhaps Shinn did not put a specific price on the plate, but the note shows that Shinn recognized that the plate had substantial monetary value and that he might sell it. These were important considerations in his dealings with Bolton.

Thus, Bolton, convinced that the plate was genuine and perhaps with a pecuniary interest, enlisted the California Historical Society to purchase the plate for the University of California. Allen L. Chickering, an influential San Francisco lawyer who was also president of the California Historical Society, worked with Bolton to obtain the plate from Shinn. Deeply impressed, Chickering began to solicit donations from prominent Californians, citing Bolton's unqualified belief in the plate's authenticity. His letter to Templeton Crocker said simply, "There can be no doubt about its authenticity after you see it and learn the result of Dr. Bolton's studies and comparison of the plaque with the text of the accounts of the Drake voyages."[8]

On April 30, 1937, Chickering met Bolton and Shinn in the shadow of the campus campanile, piled in a car, and took the Richmond ferry to Point San Quentin.[9] They retraced Shinn's summer excursion and, after some difficulty, found the discovery site. Chickering kept a record of the trip that described the commanding view of the countryside and the Bay. Though bad weather obscured the scene at the time, he imagined that on a clear day one could see the "snowy Sierras." Real or imagined, the vista that he conjured inspired "the thought . . . that it might be the place where the plate had been set up, but this is another story. I am convinced that the young man is acting in good faith."

The trip to the site had left Chickering and Bolton more deeply convinced that the plate was Drake's and that it must be obtained from the young finder. On the ferry ride back to Richmond they ate lunch and the two men began to work on Shinn. Such an important historical relic ought to be on public exhibition, they argued, but arriving at a fair price would be a difficult matter. There was no telling what such an artifact was worth if a wealthy man wanted to get it for the Smithsonian or the British Museum. Chickering thought he could raise $2,500 as a "finder's reward" for Shinn. The buyers would assume the risk of the plate's genuineness and "any possible legal complications." Shinn said he was willing to "leave the matter" to Bolton and Chickering, but it is not clear from Chickering's account if Shinn meant the price, the assumption of risk, or both. They parted company, with Chickering saying that he "was not willing to let it go at $2500," but wanted to think the matter over. Again, it is not clear if Chickering meant that he might be able to raise more money, or that he hoped to get the plate at a lower price. If the latter was the case, Shinn would soon disappoint him.[10]

On the following Monday, March 1, Shinn appeared in Bolton's office, saying that he wanted to take the plate from Bolton to show to his uncle. A concerned Bolton called Chickering to alert him of this unwelcome turn of events. Then he gave the plate to Shinn, who promised to return it the next day, Tuesday. He did not. This was worrisome. Imagine the fears of Bolton and Chickering! Had the plate slipped from their grasp? Had he found another buyer? Would they ever see the plate again? On Wednesday Bolton telephoned Shinn, who said he would bring the plate to Bolton's office at eight that evening. Bolton got Chickering to come and they waited. Eight o'clock came, but Shinn did not. He made them wait until 8:45, when he showed up without the plate, but with a lot of problems. Chickering said that Shinn was "frightened to pieces because his uncle told him that he might be put in jail or prosecuted in connection with the thing, although exactly why I did not make out." Shinn threatened to ship the plate out of the state in order to get rid of it and the worries that it caused. Chickering soothed Shinn by explaining that the only reason anyone would have to bother him would be to get the plate. If Shinn sold the plate to them, Bolton and Chickering "would get the burden of dealing with" troublemakers. Besides, Chickering had talked about the matter with his associates, who agreed to pay Shinn $3,500, "taking the risks of genuineness and of any claims." The additional $1,000 and indemnification against claims of ownership and fraudulence quieted Shinn's fears, and he agreed to the deal immediately. Shinn had to retrieve the plate from his uncle. He left Bolton's office but returned without the plate, pleading that the house was locked. He would bring it the next morning, Thursday. Again the plate failed to appear. Finally, on Friday morning, Shinn exchanged the plate for $3,500.[11]

The documents that describe these negotiations can be read in two ways. In one view two wily and powerful older men are determined to have the plate and put enormous pressure on an innocent young man who is beyond his depth. In another view a shrewd negotiator sets the trap, presents the bait, gets his quarry to commit, withdraws the bait, drives up the price, limits his liability, and sells. Which view is most correct? Considering that the plate was a forgery, money was a plausible motive for the fraud. Perhaps it all happened just the way that Shinn said it did, but by art or by accident, he walked away from the plate with a nice sum of money.

The buyers wasted no time in conveying the plate to the University of California. On the same day that money changed hands, Bolton told Robert Gordon Sproul, president of the University of California, that he and Chickering had managed to get the plate with the assistance of Cal alumni as well as a member of the Board of Regents.[12] "Before any announcement is made," Bolton assured the president, "we shall make every investigation necessary to demonstrate the genuineness of the treasure and to meet any claims of ownership that might possibly arise."[13] Sproul, of course, was delighted, although his delight would turn to concern as questions about the plate emerged. In the meantime, Bolton had promised to "make every investigation necessary," but he had not said precisely what those investigations would entail. Indeed, it appears that Bolton did nothing but compare the text of the plate with the texts of the published accounts.

He had little time to go beyond that superficial level of investigation because the California Historical Society announced that Professor Bolton would give a luncheon address on April 6 called "Newer Light on Drake and the Location of His Anchorage in California." This was just thirty days after the purchase of the plate. The title of Bolton's talk was modest enough, but the brief description thrilled the imagination. "Dr. Bolton will make the most astounding revelation yet made respecting Drake and California. Members who miss this meeting will have cause to regret it."[14] Bolton would astonish his listeners at—where else—the Sir Francis Drake Hotel in San Francisco. By the time Bolton read his paper the title had become "Drake's Plate of Brass."[15] Evidently he was having second thoughts about what the plate had to say about Drake's anchorage. The draft of his essay shows that he interlineated words like "it seems" and "apparently." He substituted "surmised" for "decided," and "evidence" for "proof." He crossed out the concluding sentence predicting that a monument would be erected where Shinn had discovered the brass, and penciled in at the foot of the page, "*New Data* doesn't change anything." In making these changes, Bolton was not abandoning his commitment to the plate's authenticity—this he made abundantly clear in his presentation—however, he softened the certain tone of his original essay and backed away from the Point San Quentin discovery site.[16]

Why? Did Bolton have advance warning of the chauffeur Caldeira's claim that he had found the plate near Drake's Bay in 1934. Caldeira's employer was a member of the California Historical Society, and news of the previous discovery might have come to Bolton through him, for it was ten days before newspapers printed his chauffeur's claim.[17] But the warning was not in time to keep Bolton from embarrassing himself in print. The original version of the paper had gone to press as a special commemorative issue of the *Quarterly of the California Historical Society* and laid upon the tables at the Sir Francis Drake Hotel.[18] It was too late to turn back; Bolton pulled some punches and prepared the audience for the possibility that Drake might not have erected the plate above Point San Quentin. Two days after Bolton announced the plate's discovery and his conviction that it was Drake's, Chickering interviewed Caldeira. This was a full week before the story was printed in the newspapers. By then, Bolton and Chickering had satisfied themselves that Caldeira was truthful and that his account only made the plate's authenticity more convincing. If true, it certainly eliminated the possibility of fraud on Shinn's part—a point that Chickering was quick to point out to doubters.[19] In this case, as in all others, Bolton and Chickering converted negative evidence into positive proof for the plate's validity.

Nevertheless, doubters remained and they began to cause trouble. President Sproul, who had received this historical treasure on behalf of a grateful university, had occasion to travel to Southern California to UCLA, then called the "southern branch." He had dinner with a number of people from Pasadena who told him that "a reputable historical magazine" would soon carry a " 'blistering' attack on the genuineness of the Drake Plate," evidently referring to Haselden's soon to be published article.[20] Henry Raup Wagner of San Marino had given speeches "ridiculing" the plate because the spelling "is not Elizabethan and . . . the brass is not the kind that was being made in . . . Drake's time." Sproul sat next to the renowned astronomer Edwin Powell Hubble, who told him that there should be "a chemical analysis of the plate in order to be prepared for the onslaught." On purely historical matters, Hubble and Sproul believed that Bolton could "hold his own against any antagonist. . . . "[21]

Bolton was now in a tight spot. On his word bankers, lawyers, corporation presidents, distinguished alumni, the California Historical Society, and the University of California had committed their money and prestige to the plate. If the plate was proved a fake, more than a historian's reputation was at stake, as

President Sproul made plain to Professor Bolton. Accordingly, Bolton told the president that he had already taken steps to involve three Berkeley scientists in the question. Coincidentally, he had just shown the plate to Wagner, who reportedly took "a very fair-minded view" and complimented Bolton for the way he presented the matter at the California Historical Society luncheon. "Every new Fact noted or discovered regarding the Plate," Bolton told the president, "strengthens our belief in its genuineness."[22] Bolton's bluff assertions notwithstanding, months later the president confessed that he still "kept hearing from those who think that we are the victims of a hoax and am just a little nervous about the situation."[23]

In those days, when a university president became a little nervous, the faculty became anxious, and Bolton no doubt understood that he was expected to save the university from embarrassment. Perhaps to calm himself, President Sproul began to correspond with Captain Haselden at the Huntington Library.[24] Haselden continued to raise serious questions about the relic's authenticity and Sproul passed them along to Bolton, who defended the plate on every count. In Bolton's mind, the plate's very unusualness argued for its authenticity. Every error and oddity meant that it was genuine. As far as Bolton was concerned, only the problem of dating the metal remained to be addressed, and he was "earnestly trying" to find someone who knew how to do that. He concluded with this disingenuous statement: "The sponsors [of the plate] have never declared the plate to be genuine. They have expressed their belief in its authenticity, but always with an *if*."[25]

The "if," however, was often covered with Bolton's dense overburden of superlatives extolling the importance of the plate and its discovery, while minimizing or entirely ignoring evidence that called it into question. Bolton and Chickering began to use this approach even before the plate's discovery was officially announced when they were trying to raise money, and it clearly was evident in Bolton's California Historical Society address. On that occasion, Bolton noted the discrepancies about the plate in the two published accounts of Drake's voyage, Hakluyt's, and Parson Fletcher's in *The World Encompassed.* Drake himself had called Fletcher a liar, so his account seemed particularly questionable. Bolton declared that there was only one way to determine which account was correct, and that was to find the plate. Then, he said to the crowd, "Here it is! Recovered at last after a lapse of 357 years! Behold, Drake's plate— the plate of brasse! California's choicest archaeological treasure!"[26] Each sentence was punctuated with an exclamation mark. Bolton continued in more measured prose that "the plate, assuming its authenticity, completely vindicates Parson Fletcher."

Now here was a nice trick. He used the plate to validate the questionable account of Parson Fletcher instead of the other way around. Bolton used this slight of hand whenever called on to speak about the plate. In May, Bolton addressed the Ancient and Honorable Fraternal Organization, E Clampus Vitus, in Tuolumne, California. After explaining to the Clampers that the plate had to be found to resolve the differences between variant accounts, he said, "I did so," and then held aloft California's choicest archaeological treasure.[27] Bolton's occasional qualifiers got lost in thickets of grand pronouncements about his wonderful discovery.

But the scientific tests of the brass remained an unresolved and nettlesome problem. Allen Chickering was at first opposed to tests that would physically damage the plate, and was particularly wary after Berkeley scientists told him that there was no point in having it analyzed.[28] Chemical and physical tests were a high-risk venture. If tests did not show that the brass was from Drake's time, Haselden, Wagner, and other critics would have a field day. If it was old brass, the plate's authenticity still was not proven because a clever forger might have used old metal for his fake. Even so, Sproul thought that tests would help to put the university "in a much better position before the scholarly world," and Chickering came around to this view as well.[29] So, it was important to find a scientist who had experience with antique metals. Soon after the plate came to light, Bolton had consulted with Berkeley chemist Joel Hildebrand and two other university scientists. While these professors generally agreed that the plate was authentic, Chickering complained that they had not been cooperative. In October, Sproul officially asked Hildebrand and a philologist to aid Bolton. They, of course, "generously agreed," as the president put it. "Obviously," Sproul explained to Bolton, "neither of them will do much, because they do not desire, in the slightest degree, to take matters out of your hands."[30]

After accepting the president's courteous invitation to help, Hildebrand took a leading role in finding an appropriate scientist to work on the problem. Colin Fink of Columbia University was just such a scientist. Coincidentally, Fink had also been identified through a historical society member who was employed by a large brass company. So, early in 1938, Bolton shipped the brass to Columbia and waited for results.

Professor Fink had a few questions about the plate. First, even before he saw the plate, he was interested in its patina because he was certain that he could tell if the coating was very old or of recent derivation.[31] This was a problem, because the front of the plate appeared to be a burnished golden color. Chickering confessed that his son had asked the Wells Fargo Bank for advice about making reproductions of the plate, and bank employees had sent him and the plate to the Western Newspaper Union in San Francisco. The good guild members had cleaned the plate with kerosene. They were about to go at it with lye when Chickering Junior weakened and retrieved the plate.[32]

Once Fink had the plate, new questions arose. "Frankly," he wrote, "I know of no brass plate which we could set up on the Pacific Coast and expect to find in such good condition after 350 years." Fink also wondered why there was no corrosion in the hole that supposedly had held a sixpence. There should have been evidence of some electrolytic reaction between the silver and the brass, but there was none, and curiously a sixteenth-century sixpence still fit perfectly in the hole. Then Fink assured Bolton that he had raised these questions "to fortify ourselves against any attack that may be made now or in the future and so that we can have as a permanent record all the proof possible supporting the contention that the plate is genuine."[33] Bolton easily provided answers for Fink. The Indians did it. They might have taken the plate from its post and knocked the sixpence out of the hole. The plate was exposed when Caldeira and Shinn found it, but perhaps it had not always been so.[34]

While raising some questions about the plate, Fink also made clear that he believed it was his job to defend the genuineness of the plate, even before he had completed scientific tests. As Bolton told Chickering, "Professor Fink . . . has just about arrived at the place which we had reached several months ago."[35] Already Chickering had learned that Fink was "impressed with the sanctity of the plate. . . . "[36] So it seems that the plate itself convinced Doctor Fink of its antiquity and authenticity, just as it had first seduced Bolton. After Fink's work was completed, Chickering lunched with him in New York. Fink remained "deeply interested in the Drake plaque," Chickering explained. "He was so impressed with the importance of his job and the secrecy which he believed that it involved, that he did not even show it to his wife. In fact he showed it to no one except President Butler of Columbia, and to him only just before it was sent back." These revelations confirmed Chickering's "very high opinion of him as a man and a scholar."[37]

Several months passed before Fink completed the tests and filed his final report, but it was all that Bolton, Chickering, and Sproul could have hoped for. The report found that the brass was undoubtedly from Drake's time. His examination of the patina now showed that it accounted "for the good condition of the plate even after more than three centuries' exposure (whole or partial) on the shore of the Pacific."[38] Fink also suggested that the many irregular indentations on the plate were made by Indians "who were afraid of a mysterious or hostile power . . . and tried to destroy the plate by striking its surface with their tomahawks; they were not familiar with the toughness of metals."[39] By this time, Fink had found microscopic evidence of corrosion products, although he did not say that they resulted from a reaction between silver and brass.[40] Fink went far beyond confirming the antiquity of the brass material and wrote "that the brass examined by us is the genuine Drake Plate referred to in the book, *The World Encompassed by Sir Francis Drake*, published in 1628."[41] So Fink—like Bolton—found that the plate vindicated Parson Fletcher. And like Bolton, Fink was willing to use negative evidence to support the plate's authenticity. For example, the patina that the printer's union staff had so easily wiped away with a kerosene-soaked cloth became an invincible armor against the salt air. While maintaining the language and stance of objective scientific inquiry, the Fink report gave unqualified support not only to the plate's antiquity but also to it's documentary validity and authorship. Thus, Fink's historical conclusions extended far beyond his scientific evidence.

What does all of this mean? Did Bolton sell his lofty reputation for a mere $350? Was the accomplished lawyer Chickering really a dullard who could be easily fooled by any con man or college prankster? Was the distinguished scientist Fink a willing tool in the hands of Bolton and Chickering? And did the Drake plate involve a vast conspiracy of professors, lawyers, businessmen, and bankers that stretched from Berkeley to Columbia? Hardly. The motivations of these men were more subtle, and perhaps less conscious, than all that. Each was easily convinced of the plate's validity because they wanted to believe in it. For them, the plate was not just a metal document or a valuable antique. It was the holy grail—a venerable Anglo-American, Protestant, religious relic.

As such, the Drake plate figured in a struggle for California's cultural high ground, and afforded Bolton a unique opportunity to ingratiate himself with a California elite who identified with the state's non-Hispanic pioneers. For decades, Bolton had publicized the Spanish and Catholic founders of the Golden State—Serra, Crespi, Garces, Anza, and all the rest. He had emphasized the religious motives and imperfectly realized humanitarian goals of the Franciscan missions. His books gave scholarly recognition and respectability to California's venerable colonial roots, and academic weight to the romantic myth of Spanish California that evolved in the early twentieth century. English-speaking leaders were perfectly willing to make use of an alien past in order to advance California's image, but they were also eager to promote heroes of their own. In the 1920s the Native Sons of the Golden West—who provided fellowships for Bolton's graduate students—had told Bolton that more attention should be given to California's American period.[42] Bolton got the message and proposed for Native Sons' fellowships students who were working on topics closer to the hearts of non-Hispanic Californians, but his work remained rooted in the Spanish era.

Bolton's publications, appreciated though they were, fit uneasily with the sensibilities of Anglo-Americans and Protestants. Their heritage dated primarily to the Gold Rush; the Spanish and Catholic era was a colorful but unrelated preface to the bustle and drama of the argonauts. And Spanish beginnings, with their strong religious overtones, stood in stark contrast to the entrepreneurial beginnings of the dominant Protestant majority. Drake's plate offered a powerful counterweight in this cultural and historical balance because it testified to an ancient English claim to California and spoke to Protestant religious primacy as well. Bolton made this point explicit when he revealed the plate to the California Historical Society and explained the California Indians' fascination with Parson Fletcher's religious services and Drake's fervent prayers. "As an evangelist," Bolton said, "Father Serra himself could hardly have been more zealous than was Drake."[43] He also told his audience that Drake had looted and desecrated a Catholic Church in Guatulco on the Pacific coast of New Spain. When he gave a revised version of this lecture to the ancient and honorable fraternal organization, E Clampus Vitus, he included a Mexican folktale that recalled Drake's attempt to burn a large wooden crucifix that Saint Thomas was supposed to have erected before the time of Cortes. Though the English heretic piled burning fuel around the venerable cross, it would not ignite, and a chastened Drake sailed away. The good Catholics of Guatulco regarded the incident as a miracle. Drake may have plundered their poor town, but the Holy Faith prevailed over infidels in the end. Bolton called this talk, "The Cross of Saint Thomas and the Plate of Brass, or Parson Fletcher Vindicated."[44] Bolton was well aware of the spiritual significance of Drake's plate and the religious conflict that it symbolized.

Had Bolton forgotten about these sectarian matters, his correspondents would have reminded him. When Caldeira's story became public, one local fellow wrote to Bolton that the story was "rather fishy." He thought that "certain ones" desired that "the Jesuits . . . supplant Sir Francis Drake in the great honor" of discovering San Francisco Bay. "Make your name famous," the correspondent went on, "by words and writings that will not perish with time. The higher patriotic thots [sic] bring one to the hearts of mankind."[45] Evidently, patriotic thoughts were highest when they praised England's heroes over Spain's. A more subdued letter came from a member of the Mill Valley Episcopal Church. He wanted Bolton to confirm that Drake's divine services were the first Protestant services held in the New World, or at least on the Pacific Coast. What historical significance did Bolton attach to these divine services?[46] It was a good thing that Bolton had vindicated the questionable account of Parson Fletcher because it gave additional heft to the conviction that Protestant England had just as good a spiritual claim to California as Catholic Spain—and perhaps better.

Bolton's announcement of the discovery of the plate inspired a poet, who published in the San Francisco press the next day. Bolton kept a typescript of this poem that praised Drake and his accomplishments:

> Here for the Queen her courtier courted death
> Gambled warm life for England's deathless fame
> Signed, "Francis Drake," and from the golden page
> We take his message, and our heritage![47]

Bolton was able to understand this verse quite literally, as one of his letters to a Canadian woman reveals. She wanted him to give the plate to George VI, whom she regarded as the plate's rightful owner. Though Bolton was not willing to relinquish the plate, he assured her that he had only the most friendly feelings toward Canada and "Mother England," as he put it. "You will be able to understand my sentiments regarding this matter when I tell you that my ancestors were nearly all English, that my father grew to early manhood in Leeds, and that I am of the first American-born generation in my family."[48] The golden page was *his* heritage.

After three decades of fighting on the Spanish Catholic side in California's culture wars, Bolton could strike a blow for his people, his hero, and his religious roots. Bolton did not approach the plate as a detached scholar, but as the champion of English faith and cultural heritage. Finally, Methodist Bolton could speak up for Parson Fletcher and the evangelist Drake—heroes whose blood and beliefs he shared and whose exploits he saw reflected in the golden sheen of the plate of brass. In the case of the fake Drake plate, Bolton's promotion of a California hero clouded his critical sense. "Higher patriotic thots" may bring historians "to the hearts of mankind," as Bolton's correspondent put it, but they also can lead one into error.

Bolton was too personally and professionally entangled with the Drake plate to maintain the sense of scholarly detachment to which he paid lip service. Bolton's financial arrangements (if any) with Shinn, his professional association with the plate, the involvement of Bolton's wealthy and powerful friends, President Sproul's concerns for the University's reputation—all made it practically impossible for him to regard the plate with an unbiased eye.

In the Drake plate episode, Bolton failed to suspend his will to believe that the plate was an authentic document and failed to diligently weigh all of the evidence before reaching a conclusion—the dull routine of the historian's craft. However, Bolton inadvertently left us a valuable lesson about historians and their heroes, and how difficult a task it is to safely navigate the broken cultural terrain of the American West. Like it or not, historians inevitably are involved in the struggle for the cultural high ground because they mediate the vital dialog between past and present, between change and continuity. This was an especially difficult task for Bolton in California, where one person's hero was another's pirate, and a saint to one was a villain to another. Bolton thought the plate was a guide to the heroic highlands, but it led him astray. Whether Bolton ever realized his misstep remains an open question.

NOTES

1. The author wishes to thank Martin Ridge and Andrew Rolle for suggesting revisions for this essay. Albert L. Hurtado, "Herbert E. Bolton, Racism, and American History," *Pacific Historical Review* 62 (May 1993): 127–42; Albert L. Hurtado, "Parkmanizing the Spanish Borderlands: Bolton, Turner and the Historians' World," *Western Historical Quarterly* 26 (Summer 1995): 149–67; and Albert L. Hurtado, "Herbert E. Bolton and the Politics of California Hero Worship," Spain in the Americas Conference, The Huntington Library and Art Gallery, San Marino, California, 15–16 May 1992.

2. Herbert E. Bolton, "Francis Drake's Plate of Brass," *California Historical Society Quarterly* 16, no. 1, Part 2 (March 1937): 1–16; Douglas S. Watson, "Drake and California: The Finding of Evidence of His Visit and Its Implications," *California Historical Society Quarterly* 16, no. 1, Part 2 (March 1937): 19–24.

3. Colin G. Fink and E. P. Polushkin, *Drake's Plate of Brass Authenticated: The Report on the Plate of Brass* (San Francisco: California Historical Society, 1938).

4. Criticism of the plate had persisted even after the plate's antiquity was confirmed in 1938. See Joseph Ellison, "True of False?" *Saturday Evening Post*, April 4, 1943, 32, 35–36; Francis P. Farquhar and Walter A. Starr, "Drake in California," *California Historical Society Quarterly* 36 (1957): 21–34. In the 1970s Samuel Eliot Morison argued that the plate was a college prank, *The European Discovery of America: The Southern Voyages, A.D. 1492–1616* (New York: Oxford University Press, 1974), 677–80.

5. Undated note, Drake Correspondence, Box 42, Bolton Papers, C–B 840, Part II, Bancroft Library, University of California, Berkeley (hereafter Drake Correspondence, Box no., BP, Pt. II).

6. Bill of Sale, 3 March 1937, Drake Correspondence, Box 42, BP, Pt. II.

7. Bolton, "Drake's Plate of Brass," 2.

8. Chickering to Templeton Crocker, 23 February 1937, Drake Correspondence, Box 42, BP, Pt. II.

9. The next day Chickering, the careful lawyer, typed his recollection of the day, A. L. C., "Memorandum," 1 March 1937, Drake Correspondence, Box 42, BP, Pt. II.

10. A. L. C. [Allen L. Chickering], 3 March 1937, Drake Correspondence, Box 42, BP, Pt. II.

11. A. L. C. [Allen L. Chickering], 3 March 1937, Drake Correspondence, Box 42, BP, Pt. II.

12. Thirteen of the nineteen donors had graduated from the university. The regent was

Sydney Ehrman who also underwrote many of Bolton's publications. Chickering to Sproul, 12 April 1937, Drake Correspondence, Box 42, BP, Pt. II.

13. Bolton to Sproul, 5 March 1937, Drake Correspondence, Box 42, BP, Pt. II.

14. Announcement, California Historical Society Luncheon, 6 April 1937, Drake Correspondence, Box 42, BP, Pt. II.

15. "Drake's Plate of Brass," typescript, [April 1937], Drake Correspondence, Box 42, BP, Pt. II. The published version is Herbert E. Bolton, "Francis Drake's Plate of Brass," *California Historical Society Quarterly* 16, no.1 , Part 2 (March 1937): 1–16, also issued separately, Special Publication, No. 13, (San Francisco: California Historical Society, 1937).

16. "Drake's Plate of Brass," typescript, [April 1937], Drake Correspondence, Box 42, BP, Pt. II.

17. "Drake Plate Theory Upset by Oaklander," *Oakland Tribune*, 16 April 1937, 1, 2.

18. Herbert E. Bolton, "Francis Drake's Plate of Brass," Special Publication, No. 13, (San Francisco: California Historical Society, 1937).

19. Chickering to Sproul, 6 May 1937, Drake Correspondence, Box 42, BP, Pt. II.

20. R. B. Haselden, "Is the Drake Plate of Brass Genuine?" *California Historical Society Quarterly* 17 (1937): 271–74.

21. Sproul to Bolton, 3 May 1937, Drake Correspondence, Box 42, BP, Pt. II.

22. Bolton to Sproul, 6 May 1937, Drake Correspondence, Box 43, BP, Pt. II.

23. Sproul to Bolton, 29 October 1937, Drake Correspondence, Box 42, BP, Pt. II.

24. Sproul to Bolton, 21 October 1937, Drake Correspondence, Box 42, BP, Pt. II.

25. Bolton, "Comments on Captain Haselden's Letter of October 16, 1937," Drake Correspondence, Box 43, BP, Pt. II.

26. Bolton, "Drake's Plate of Brass," 11.

27. "The Cross of Saint Thomas and the Plate of Brass, or Parson Fletcher Vindicated," Drake Correspondence, Box 43, BP, Pt. II.

28. Chickering to Ralph L. Phelps, 30 April 1937, Drake Correspondence, Box 42, BP, Pt. II.

29. Sproul to Bolton, 29 October 1937, Drake Correspondence, Box 42, BP, Pt. II.

30. Sproul to Bolton, 29 October 1937, Drake Correspondence, Box 42, BP, Pt. II.

31. Fink to Hildebrand, [November 1937?], Drake Correspondence, Box 42, BP, Pt. II.

32. Allen L. Chickering to Hildebrand, 3 December 1937, Drake Correspondence, Box 42, BP, Pt. II.

33. Fink to Bolton, 21 March 1938, Drake Correspondence, Box 42, BP, Pt. II.

34. Bolton to Fink, 26 March 1937, Drake Correspondence, Box 43, BP, Pt. II.

35. Bolton to Chickering, 26 March 1938, Drake Correspondence, Box 43, BP, Pt. II.

36. Chickering to Bolton, 16 March 1938, Drake Correspondence, Box 42, BP, Pt. II.

37. Chickering to Bolton, 18 May 1939, Drake Correspondence, Box 42, BP, Pt. II.

38. Fink and Polushkin, *Drake's Plate of Brass Authenticated*, 14.

39. Fink and Polushkin, *Drake's Plate of Brass Authenticated*, 11.

40. Fink and Polushkin, *Drake's Plate of Brass Authenticated*, 18.

41. Fink and Polushkin, *Drake's Plate of Brass Authenticated*, 25.

42. Bolton to William J. Hayes, 3 May 1927, BP, Outgoing, Box 142.

43. Bolton, "Drake's Plate of Brass," 7.

44. "The Cross of Saint Thomas and the Plate of Brass, or Parson Fletcher Vindicated," Drake Correspondence, Box 43, BP, Pt. II.

45. Eli R. Deming to Bolton, 17 April 1937, Drake Correspondence, Box 42, BP, Pt. II.

46. William A. Hamilton to Bolton, 7 February 1939, Drake Correspondence, Box 42, BP, Pt. II.

47. "Signed 'Francis Drake,'" Drake Correspondence, Box 42, BP, Pt. II.

48. Bolton to R. G. Ellis, 8 June 1938, Drake Correspondence, Box 43, BP, Pt. II.

CHAPTER TWELVE

KEEPING THE FAITH

The Forgotten Generations of
Literary Turnerians, 1920–1960

HOWARD R. LAMAR

As we celebrate the hundredth anniversary of Frederick Jackson Turner's justly famous paper, "The Significance of the Frontier in American History," one of the questions that comes to mind is: why do we honor a hypothesis which has undergone such severe criticism—indeed repudiation—between the 1920s and the 1970s, and now a second rejection and ever harsher criticism by the so-called New Western historians during the 1980s and early 1990s?[1]

There are, of course, many explanations for the persistence of Turner and his frontier thesis. One is that he was the first to offer a coherent, logical, and at the same time, eloquent explanation of American exceptionalism—a convincingly causal rationale for the rise of a distinctive American national character, along with a historical account of the development of both our society and our democratic form of government. Moreover, the frontier thesis glorified the average American by casting him in the role of the westward-moving pioneer who conquered the land and built a nation. Somehow Turner managed to construct a democratic, classless, and therefore a non-Marxist version of the American experience.

A second major reason given for the popularity of the frontier hypothesis is that a national mythology had already grown up around such words as "frontier," "pioneer," and "individualism" as well as around such frontier figures as Daniel Boone, Lewis and Clark, Davy Crockett, Andrew Jackson, Kit Carson, and Abraham Lincoln. That same frontier mythic quality came to be associated with both official and unofficial explorers like John C. Frémont and mountain men like Jim Bridger and Jedediah Smith. These qualities were also attributed to empire builders such as Stephen F. Austin, John A. Sutter, and

Frederick Jackson Turner, Cambridge, Massachusetts, 1917
(Photograph courtesy State Historical Society of Wisconsin, Madison, WHi(x3)1354.)

Ray Allen Billington
(Photograph courtesy Henry E. Huntington Library and Art Gallery, San Marino, California.)

Martin Ridge
(Photograph courtesy Henry E. Huntington Library and Art Gallery, San Marino, California.)

Bernard DeVoto
(Photograph courtesy Mark DeVoto.)

Brigham Young. Later in the nineteenth century cowboys and ranchers, lawmen and outlaws, Indian leaders—whether heroes or villains—became the centerpiece of the frontier and western myths as both they and their promoters—Buffalo Bill Cody and a whole raft of journalists, memoirists, and novelists—relived the Wild West in action and in print. Working almost hand in hand with the promoters were powerful artists like Frederic Remington and Charlie Russell, whose paintings evoked an enduring nostalgia for a wonderful last but now lost West.[2]

However, even these factors do not quite explain why long into the twentieth century Americans took the idea so seriously that the nation's past was to be explained by the frontier experience. On the other hand, it is true that a whole generation of college and university history professors espoused some if not all of Turner's concepts for a half century after 1920. One thinks of Frederick Logan Paxson at the University of California, Berkeley, Vernon Parrington at the University of Washington, Walter Prescott Webb at the University of Texas, E. E. Dale at Oklahoma, Lewis Atherton at the University of Missouri, Paul Wallace Gates at Cornell, Ralph Henry Gabriel at Yale, and last, but far from least, that eloquent, dynamic scholar-teacher at Northwestern, Ray Allen Billington, to name only a few. And although he wrote about the Spanish borderlands rather than the Anglo-American frontier—Herbert Bolton at Berkeley, also embraced the frontier concept.

What does help explain the continuing popularity of Turner's ideas, however, is the presence of a generation of famous novelists, poets, folklorists and journalists, whose careers paralleled those of the academicians, and who also embraced Turner's ideas and incorporated them into their writings. In this essay, I would like to focus on four authors who kept the ideas and spirit of Frederick Jackson Turner alive and well between 1920 and 1960, and conclude with a mention of their spiritual and literary successors, who have been active right up to the present. They did so with such imagination and so effectively that they formed, as it were, a post-Turnerian school of their own. One was a novelist-historian, one a folklorist, and two were major American poets. It is my contention that although they voiced Turner's conceptions of America in their writings, they did not work so much in the shadow of the master as use his ideas for their own purposes.

Let me start with Bernard DeVoto whom many on the Harvard campus during the 1920s and '30s referred to as "the Wild Man" from the West. Born in Ogden, Utah, the son of a Mormon mother and a perpetual graduate student father, DeVoto attended the University of Utah before transferring to Harvard. He graduated from Harvard in 1920, having majored in English. Later he got a job teaching English at Northwestern. Fate intervened when his wife, who worked for a Chicago newspaper, brought home novels and books on the West for DeVoto to review.

As he did so, he began to see himself as a novelist, and, as James K. Folsom has noted, he eventually wrote no less than four western novels. The first, called *The Crooked Mile*, appeared in 1924. Folsom says the four "have not received the critical notice they deserve quite simply because DeVoto is often dismissed by literary critics as a 'historian.'"[3] And yet it is ironic that the *Reader's Encyclopedia of American Literature* lists him as teacher, editor, author, but not as a historian.[4]

As we all know, DeVoto was best known for his historical works— *The Year of Decision 1846* (1943), *Across the Wide Missouri* (1947), *The Course of Empire* (1952)—and for his editions of *The Journals of Lewis & Clark* (1953). But again the critics have dismissed him as a serious historian, claiming that these are "popularizations of history written by a literary dilettante."[5]

What is a common theme in everything DeVoto wrote, however, was his constant reiteration of "the significance of the West in the development of American culture."[6] But there is another common theme as well: he echoed and articulated the ideas of certain Harvard historians. Wallace Stegner wrote that while Paris was the home for some American literary exiles, Cambridge, Massachusetts, was that for DeVoto. And it is no wonder, for there he hobnobbed with Arthur Schlesinger, Sr. and Jr., with Frederick Merk, Garrett Mattingly, and John Kenneth Galbraith. He also liked Paul Buck and Samuel Eliot Morison and knew Archibald MacLeish. He was constantly in touch with Henry Steele Commager at Columbia University, and of course he saw his New York editor, Alfred Knopf, all the time. Stegner feels that the Americanists "who impinged on DeVoto's chosen field of the frontier and westward expansion, probably had more to do with the shaping of his mind and the formulation of his books than his close friend Garrett Mattingly did."[7]

At one point, when DeVoto decided to do a book on the Civil War, both Schlesinger Sr. and Merk dissuaded him, urging him to concentrate instead on the frontier and use his already voluminous collection of notes on that topic. Thus, as early as 1933 he was contemplating a three-volume history of the frontier and the westward movement.[8] DeVoto's western interests were strengthened when he befriended Wallace Stegner during the years the latter was in Cambridge. In his introduction to his insightful biography of DeVoto, *The Uneasy Chair*, Stegner explains that both were boys in Utah, westerners by birth and upbringing, "novelists by intention, teachers by necessity, and historians by the sheer compulsion of the region that shaped us."[9]

It is not my purpose here to rehash DeVoto's writings or the particulars of his lively career but to suggest (a) what the concept "frontier" meant to him, and

(b) the atmosphere that allowed him to write about it and to flourish as a popular historian in the 1930s, '40s, and '50s.

In 1920 DeVoto, age twenty-three, wrote his friend Melville Smith to say:

I burst with creative criticism of America—I have at last found a kind of national self-consciousness. . . . But I have begun to see American history with some unity, with some perspective, with some meaning. . . .

The nation, he cried, has emerged "from adolescence into young manhood," and that being the case, "we may at last do something for the better."[10]

Again as is well known, DeVoto felt there was something so grand about the story of the American past, about the conquest and occupation of a continent, that he was furious with literary critics who did not pay attention to or disparaged the American experience. Over the years he advised prospective graduate students to avoid literature and to take up history instead. As we shall see later, DeVoto, Constance Rourke, Archibald MacLeish, and Stephen Vincent Benét were all overwhelmed by a sense of both the sweep and importance of American history. Curiously, while that sweep was Turnerian, in the sense that it saw the frontier and West as key themes and democracy as triumphant, there is not much mention of Turner as guru or mind shaper by any of them; rather, it seems to have been their assumption that American history had its own unique glorious past and that we should be proud of the heritage.

Indeed, it seems likely that DeVoto was more influenced by Parkman than Turner—especially in his *The Course of Empire*. In a letter to Katherine Drinker Bowen, who was feeling depressed because she had been criticized for being a romantic historian, DeVoto declared that the study of Columbus, Cortez, LaSalle, Coronado, or John Ledyard had to be romantic.[11] During the time he was writing *The Course of Empire* he kept begging Garrett Mattingly to tell him what he was writing about—in short, how to make it grand history.[12] Later, DeVoto jokingly claimed that "Francis Parkman was plagiarizing me anticipatively eighty years ago."[13] And as late as 1951 he told his friend Frederick Merk that he was so sure the lure of the continent was a powerful theme in our history that he was forced to be a geographical determinist who believed natural formations like Cumberland Gap or South Pass determined history.[14]

DeVoto's first western hero was James Clyman, the mountain man, but once he had become curator of the Mark Twain Papers he made Twain the archsymbol of frontier Americans. Indeed, Wallace Stegner has called Twain DeVoto's surrogate father.[15] So strong was his devotion that his *Mark Twain's America* (1932) was written as a furious rebuttal to Van Wyck Brooks's book, *The Ordeal of Mark Twain* (1920), in which Brooks had argued that "greatness had eluded Twain because of the limitations of his Western environment."[16] Rather, DeVoto felt Twain's was the true voice of America and that it was his frontier experience that allowed him to develop that voice.

If there is a point to my remarks about Bernard DeVoto, it is that he had articulated his own vision of the frontier and the West from ingredients that reached far beyond but did not dispute Turner: his Utah boyhood, the experience of his Mormon mother, his desire to write American fiction, his discovery of American history in a circle of friends that included some of the leading historians and literary critics of the day, his awareness of Parkman's grand scheme of New World history, and his passionate belief in the richness and value of a distinctive American culture. In the latter conviction, he was aided and abetted, you might say, by another author whom he admired without reservation: Constance Rourke. About the time DeVoto was beginning to think of his grand trilogy, Constance Rourke (born in Cleveland, Ohio, and educated at Vassar and the Sorbonne) published *American Humor*, with the subtitle: *A Study of the National Character*.[17]

Rourke was a specialist in the field of American popular culture. She did her research, we are told, "by traveling about the country, talking to people, gathering legends and then repairing to the library for scholarly research.[18] Rourke proceeded with three assumptions: (a) that humor is a key to a national character; (b) that it arises in part out of one's local experiences—that is, it is regional and not necessarily inherited from Europe (In that sense, no one could have agreed more with Frederick Jackson Turner when he said our society did not come over on the Susan Constant but was born in the forest); and (c) that a study of the West and the frontier would give us our greatest clues to a distinctive American humor and an American character.

American Humor traces the evolution of American character types, one of which is the Yankee peddler, whom she saw as selling notions to Southerners, or "forever pushing into new regions," and eventually "walking all the way to Oregon at the heels of the settlers or on the march across the plains to the gold of California."[19] She finds that the Yankee image was popular because westerners thought Yankees bright enough to outwit the British, who were so condescending to us in our early national period.[20] Emerging along with the Yankee was the "gamecock of the Wilderness," of whom backwoodsmen like Davy Crockett or riverboatmen like Mike Fink were representative.[21] In the end, however, Rourke sees the Yankee and the backwoodsmen as having much in common: "a tie which had been fashioned out of a common mind out of which they sprang." She saw a third strain of humor in the Negro minstrelsy (remember Rourke is writing in the 1930s).[22] "The Negro minstrelsy joined with the Yankee and the backwoodsmen to make a comic trio, appearing in the same era, with the same timely intensity." Rourke sees each as a wanderer over the land. They symbolized freedom and resilience and therefore were appropriate emblems for a pioneer people.[23]

Rourke also felt that while the frontier had no true dramatic tradition, nevertheless it was "theatrical," and that a category she called "Strollers" brought life and color to the frontier.[24] Here again, as with the complexity of the minstrel stage, she sees the Strollers as addressing the role Indians played in the American experience. There were, in fact, many so-called Indian plays that dealt with "The Indian's pride, his grief, his lost inheritance, performed by the Strollers [and] his kinship with the boundless wilderness."

> About his figure the American seemed to wrap a desire to return to the primitive life of the wilderness. It was not for nothing that he [the frontiersman] had appropriated Indian methods of warfare, Indian costumes, Indian legends: this borrowing had left a wide imprint.[25]

Historic characters were so well known on the frontier, writes Rourke, that some theatrical groups satirized both Indians and whites, as John Brougham did in a satirical play about *Pocahontas* in which John Smith tells Powhatan:

> My very noble and approved good savage,
> That we came out here your lands to ravage
> Is most true: for this you see us banded.

Powhatan asks: "How do you mean to set about it?"
Smith responds: "Easy enough. We have full power to treat."
Powhatan then says: "If that's the case we'll take some whiskey neat."[26]
There is even a song in the play called "Grabaway While You May."

In another play, called *Columbus el Filibustero,* the expedition is seen as a gold-grabbing affair. Indeed, when Columbus gets back to Spain, Ferdinand knights him, saying:

> That in stealing gold you may not cease,
> Receive the Order of the Golden Fleece."[27]

On the whole, Constance Rourke preferred, as did Walt Whitman, to hear America singing rather than see the darker side of conquest and racism in American history, but here she voices the very themes Patricia Limerick has noted in her *Legacy of Conquest.* And, like DeVoto, Rourke saw Twain, and Whitman, as reflecting "the imprint of the West" in their writings.[28]

When Constance Rourke died at seventy-four, she was working on a three-volume history of *American Culture*. That might have been almost a social-history companion piece to DeVoto's volumes. All we have, however, are her essays, published as *The Roots of American Culture*, which, ironically, DeVoto's old antagonist, Van Wyck Brooks, edited, and in which he wrote, "her most striking discoveries were made in the West, in the old frontier region where it had been generally thought that nothing of the nature of art had ever existed."[29] DeVoto must have smiled when reading Brooks's words.

Constance Rourke was, you might say, squarely in the Turner camp in her belief that the frontier experience was the source of a unique American culture, but she was not in the Turner camp with regard to the nature of that culture. That is to say, she saw the arts, admittedly of a crude sort, flourishing on the frontier, whereas Turner always said the frontiersman was pragmatic, practical-minded, thus implying that he was non-cultured and non-aesthetic. Though Rourke was educated at Vassar and the Sorbonne, she was on the track of regional history, appreciated folk culture, and had some inkling of minority history. If Rourke believed in mobility as a form of process, she also believed in the frontier as a place with a distinctive society and culture. Moreover, she wrote when Americans were rediscovering Appalachian, African-American, and Hispanic-American folklore and arts and crafts, and writers like J. Frank Dobie were arguing that oral history and regional literature were to be taken seriously.

Among the circle of DeVoto's friends in Cambridge, though not close, so John Kenneth Galbraith tells me, was Archibald MacLeish, poet and Librarian of Congress. Born in Glencoe, Illinois, in 1892, he attended the Hotchkiss School in Connecticut and received his A.B. from Yale in 1915. He married at once, but then went off to serve in the U.S. Army in France. That brief stint in 1917 and 1918 saw him rise from the rank of private to captain. In 1919 he attained his LL.B. from The Harvard Law School and taught Constitutional and International Law at the University while qualifying for admission to the Massachusetts Bar as well.[30]

But MacLeish really wanted to be a poet and so, aided by fellowships, he and his wife and two children went off to France from 1923 to 1928, where he wrote poetry. MacLeish was one of the American literary exiles in Paris, and he knew Stephen Vincent Benét, Ernest Hemingway, and most of the others. But although he stayed five years he never considered himself one of the lost generation: rather, he saw himself as an American poet who needed to complete his education. After his return, to a farm in Conway, Massachusetts in 1928, he made a trip to Mexico, where on foot or by muleback he retraced the route of

Cortez from Vera Cruz to Mexico City. Out of that experience came his poem *Conquistador*, which is full of nostalgia about conquest and the West. In one of the lines, he has old Bernal Diaz del Castillo say: "And the West is gone now: the West is the open sky."[31]

In 1930 in his major series of poems called *New Found Land*, in a poem entitled "American Letter," MacLeish gave his own version of American history:[32]

> It is a strange thing—to be an American.
> Neither an old house it is with the air
> Tasting of hung herbs and the sun returning
> Year after year to the same door and the churn . . .

[and later]

> Neither a place it is nor a blood name.

[rather]

> America is West and the wind blowing.

Then he goes on to say:

> We dwell on the half earth, on the open curve of a continent.
> Sea is divided from sea by the day fall.
> The dawn
> Rides the low east with us many hours;
> First are the capes, then are the shorelands, now
> The blue Appalachians faint at the day rise;
> The willows shudder with light on the long Ohio
> The Lakes scatter the low sun: the prairies
> Slide out of dark: in the eddy of clean air
> The smoke goes up from the high plains of Wyoming
> The steep Sierras rise: the struck foam
> Flames at the wind's heel on the far Pacific.

In later stanzas of the poem it is clear that MacLeish sees America as a virgin land "where few bury before us"; and later: "This, this is our land, this is our people. This is neither a land nor a race. . . ."[33]

In short, MacLeish sees us inhabiting the New World and America by engaging in a form of westward expansion of a most Turnerian sort. And nowhere is there a mention of Native peoples. It is perhaps no surprise, therefore, that in 1932 he wrote *Conquistador*, a celebration of Cortez, which won the Pulitzer Prize in 1933, the same year Turner's last book won the Pulitzer Prize for History. In 1934 MacLeish wrote a piece called "Union Pacific," which later became a ballet.[34] However, in a poem called "Men" he describes the labor of a pioneer people, "buoyed by trust and faith and not harried by philosophical questions." Turner himself might have written the line. Indeed, throughout all his poems MacLeish speaks of pioneering and the West in reverential terms.[35]

Some years later MacLeish wrote a series of six poems entitled *Frescoes for Mr. Rockefeller's City*. One is called "Wild West," which calls up an image of Crazy Horse, "a lone rider, a thinker and a silent man." Here, MacLeish has at last discovered an Indian point of view by researching Crazy Horse's life. He writes: "These plains were his country and worth fighting for." However, Crazy Horse feels that the men who took his land "never looked at the land. It was only a matter of price to them." MacLeish concludes: "His heart would be big with the love he had for that country." At one point he has Crazy Horse say: "And all the game we had seen and the mares we had ridden. And how it went out from you wide and clean in the sunlight."[36]

In another poem MacLeish titled "Burying Ground by the Ties," he comments on the graves of those who helped build the Union Pacific. The irony is, he writes, that the real empire builders were "Negroes, Portuguese, Magyars, Polloks, Scotsmen, Englishmen, Chinese, Squarebacks or Australians."[37]

By the late 1930s, however, MacLeish had begun to write what you and I would call "environmental poems." In one, a line reads: "The stream beds stinking in the August sunlight: the pools sluggish with sewage: choked with tree trunks."[38] This is four years after his neighbor DeVoto had written the famous article called "*The West: A Plundered Province*," for *Harper's Monthly*.[39]

It does not seem too far-fetched to say that MacLeish's environmental poems and essays reflect the kind of panic Turner had experienced in 1890 when he realized that there was no more free land. In the 1930s MacLeish, too, felt that an older America had ended and that things would go from bad to worse. In the end, he took heart in the traditions of individualism and Jefferson and came to believe that in times of crisis leaders would rise to save the nation. He took heart during world War II, which he felt would prove America's superiority and restrengthen democratic ideals. It is clear that MacLeish equated West with individualism and freedom in a way Turner did.[40] To reiterate, one of America's most popular poets, who was twice a recipient of the Pulitzer Prize, had a Turnerian vision of American expansion, and of the role of pioneers in that process. And like DeVoto and others, he celebrated the image of a society in motion.

For the fourth important literary figure who celebrated America's frontier past, let us turn to Stephen Vincent Benét. Born in 1898, the third son of James Walker Benét, a Captain of Ordinance in the U.S. Army, Benét spent the youthful years of his life moving from arsenal to arsenal, for his father was frequently transferred. After schooling in a military academy in San Rafael, California, he went to Yale College, where he was on the *Yale Literary Magazine* and was already publishing poems while in his teens. He enlisted in the Army in 1918 but was honorably discharged because of bad eyesight. He graduated from Yale in 1919 with a B.A., but entered the graduate school for an M.A., during which time he took Henry Seidel Canby's writing course.[41] Benét's biographer suggests that in those years he was influenced by William Morris's later ideas and that his early poetry reflected the styles of Shelley and Keats.

In 1920–21 Benét went to Paris, got married, and published a novel two years before DeVoto published his first. Benét then went back to Paris where he wrote *John Brown's Body* (1928), which won the Pulitzer Prize for Poetry in 1929. While in Paris he befriended Archibald MacLeish, but unlike most of the expatriates, as his biographer, Parry Stroud, notes, "He found that separation merely deepened his love for his country."[42] By this time he was incredibly busy as a reviewer for the *Herald Tribune* and the *Saturday Review of Literature*, the latter of which DeVoto was editor for a time. Benét's short story, "The Devil and Daniel Webster," not only won the O. Henry Prize in 1936 for the best short story of the year, it became an operetta as well. Here again we see the poet using historical figures as his subject.[43] Unlike Constance Rourke, Benét argued that American culture is dual in nature in that it is both European and indigenous: "As native as the shape of Navajo quivers/And Native, too, as the sea-voyaged rose."[44]

Benét was always attracted by the poetry of Whitman, and especially his western or western-oriented poems. It is therefore not surprising that he chose as the title for his last epic poem the phrase "Western Star," which comes from Whitman's line: "O powerful western fallen star!"[45]

Western Star is a fragmentary work, published after Benét's untimely death in 1943 from a heart attack. He had intended it to be an American *Odyssey* and therefore a companion piece to *John Brown's Body*, which critics called his *Iliad*. Benét began taking notes for *Western Star* as early as 1928. Like *John Brown's Body, Western Star* grew out of Benét's fascination with American history. As Stroud has observed, Benét "conceived of our history as having two major and continuing phases: the preservation of national unity and the restless mobility of our people." In his prelude to *Western Star* Benét says, "Americans were always moving on."[46] One will recognize the latter as echoing both the what DeVoto called "the continental lure" and Rourke's belief that people in motion actually have a culture of their own.

His aim, like that of DeVoto in *The Course of Empire*, was very ambitious—that is, he wanted "to write a poetic history in ten books which would recount the westward push from its beginnings in England to the closing of the area of free land in America near the end of the nineteenth century"—as he expressed it, from Bristol, England, to Venice, California. Towards the beginning of *Western Star*, Benét writes: "There's ice to the north and Spain has the golden mines, but in between, there are wonders. Have you not seen, a fair fresh land—yea, an earthly paradise. There was a wild wind over England and it blew. There was a wild wind over England and it blew. There was a wind through the nation and it blew, strong, resistless, the wind of the Western star."[47]

Benét's chief problem, writes his biographer, Stroud, is that "he envisioned as that of portraying the changing panorama of frontier life from the perspective of the frontier, rather than from that of the East." Benét was so anxious to make his poem historically correct, "he rented a house within driving distance of the Yale library" where he spent "months reading historic and original documents."[48]

Benét was often frustrated by the historians. In a letter to his friend Paul Engle in 1937, he complained that historians had not used diaries and letters. "Why don't they let the people come through," he exclaimed.[49] Later he told Bernard Knollenberg, then librarian of Yale, that "if anybody in the world had written 'even a competent and connected history of the Western frontier from 1745 to 1815 I would feel better.' "[50] The irony was that Benét fully accepted the Turner thesis but could not find a text that expounded it. A year later he said: "I wish prominent historians wouldn't contradict each other as much as they do—how's a poor poet to know which is right?"[51]

The frontier theme is rife in *Western Star*. In the "Invocation" to the poem, Benét writes:

> This was frontier, and this,
> And this, your house, was frontier.

A major theme concerns the multitudes who colonized America and pushed its frontiers all the was to the Pacific. The frontier, he wrote, was the "shaper of American destiny. And though it is now gone, Something remains, obscure to understand, but living, and a genius of the land."[52]

Benét's biographer, Parry Stroud, feels that in these words, "Benét has seized upon a profound truth about America: that the search for her meaning and destiny must be endless."[53] Benét felt we could gain spiritual nourishment from our history. At the same time he was, like MacLeish, pessimistic about our greed and our fanaticism. And like MacLeish he told his story through individuals, something DeVoto and Rourke also did.

Even in his wartime propaganda, he never left the frontier concept. In his book *America* (1944), published after his death, there was yet another paean to the do-it-yourself pioneer.[54]

In *Western Star* Benét also stressed the mobility theme:

> Oh, paint your wagon with Pike's Peak or Bust!
> Pack up the fiddle, rosin up the bow,
> Vamoose, skidaddle, mosey, hit the grit!
> We're off for California
> We're off down the wild O-hi-o.
> And every girl on Natchez bluff
> Will cry as we go by-o[55]

In the poem are most of the words and phrases we would find in an older western history text.

In his time, Benét was incredibly popular. His *John Brown's Body* was performed as a dramatic reading all over the country. Everyone read him or knew of him. So, too, did they know MacLeish, as poet, Librarian of Congress, and as author of the play *J.B.* So, too, DeVoto, for his books and his *Harper's Monthly* column, "The Easy Chair," which he wrote for over twenty years. So, too, Constance Rourke's *American Humor*, and her biographies: *Davy Crockett* and *Audubon*. It is they who transmitted and modified Turnerian concepts and ideas down to succeeding generations. It is they who gave them a Parkmanesque grand sweep. It was they, and not just Turner alone, who portrayed a heroic American frontier past.

But just as revisionist historians would eventually do, they had also begun to see the darker side of America as well. DeVoto and MacLeish were both eloquent in their concerns about the environment. DeVoto, in particular, infuriated western ranchers and loggers by his reference to them as "hogs." MacLeish slowly and only briefly came to empathize with a Native American point of view in his *Crazy Horse* poem, but in 1963 when the Civil Rights movement began, he wrote a piece called "A View of Oxford, Mississippi" in which he finally admitted the presence of race hatred in the United States. By and large, however, they did not treat minorities, women, or social history. But if we are to criticize them for overplaying the frontier's role, let us at least give Turner some respite and do battle instead with this extraordinary galaxy of post-Turnerians, for it is they who most influenced the generally educated public regarding frontier concepts between 1920 and 1960. Being members of the literary establishment, they gave an establishment quality to the American frontier concept.

However, we should also remember that certain of their academic counterparts: Ralph Gabriel at Yale, Merle Curti at Wisconsin, J. Frank Dobie and Walter Prescott Webb at Texas, Vernon Parrington at Washington, and Kenneth Murdock and F. O. Matthiesson at Harvard, to name only a few, were busy defining what they believed was a distinctive American culture and civilization. Some of these same individuals helped found American Studies programs, which once again connected the frontier to national culture.[56] It is no accident that a Texan, Henry Nash Smith, a friend of Dobie, should go to Harvard to work with Frederick Merk and not only produce *Virgin Land*, a major landmark in the American Studies movement, but then move on to edit what DeVoto called the true voice of America: Mark Twain's works.[57]

In the decades since these literary figures and academic historians dominated the scene, a new generation of writers has continued to keep variations of the frontier concept alive. On the academic side, one thinks immediately of the dean of frontier historians, the late Ray Allen Billington, whose famous textbook, *Westward Expansion: A History of the American Frontier*, originally published in 1949, is now into its 5th edition.[58] Before his death in 1981 Billington published some twenty-six major books on Turner, his frontier hypothesis, and the West. In 1957 he also launched the *Histories of the American Frontier* series to which over a score of major contemporary historians of the West have contributed volumes.[59]

In his last book, *Land of Savagery/Land of Promise: The European Image of the Frontier* (1981), Billington analyzed the powerful images of America portrayed by scores of European writers and novelists from the seventeenth century onward.[60] In short, he demonstrated the thesis of this essay: namely that writers of fiction had played a key role in popularizing the American frontier far beyond what historians had done. And finally, after Billington had become senior research historian at the Huntington—a position Turner himself had once held, he advised at least two generations of younger and older scholars in the frontier and western fields.

Although hundreds of historians continue to teach western history in colleges and universities, in which field a critique of Turner is inevitable, none has been more active as both admirer yet critical analyst than Martin Ridge, Billington's successor at the Huntington. A distinguished biographer of Ignatius Donnelly, an outstanding editor of the *Journal of American History*, and long a professor of history at Indiana University before coming to the Huntington, Ridge has also encouraged young scholars to study the frontier and the American West, inspiring them by scholarly example as had Turner and Billington before him.[61]

Similarly, worthy successors to DeVoto, Rourke, MacLeish, and Benét abound. DeVoto's surrogate father, Mark Twain, continues to be seen as an arch-symbol of American culture. Rourke's probings into regional (frontier) culture have exploded into a massive discovery and study of Indian, African-American, and Hispanic-American societies and cultures. DeVoto's environmental concerns have now become the field of environmental studies as well as major issues of public policy debate. And although students draw inspiration more from the writings of John Muir, Henry David Thoreau, and Aldo Leopold than from DeVoto's, and seek the help of the social and biological sciences in their efforts to understand the environment, the historians take their lead from the sobering analyses of Roderick Nash, Stephen Pyne, William Robbins, William Cronon, and Donald Pisani. Both the scholars and a larger reading public have also been galvanized by the vivid language of Edward Abbey's *Desert Solitaire* (1968) and the eloquent writings of Donald Worster, Richard White, and Wallace Stegner.[62]

A large number of contemporary novelists also continue to use the West, and often a frontier setting, as major themes, as attested to by the remarkable reference work, *A Literary History of the American West* (1987).[63] Of the current generation of outstanding novelists, Larry McMurtry has been most successful in portraying both the depressing and the exhilarating sides of the western or frontier experience in his *Horseman Pass By* (1961), *The Last Picture Show* (1966), and *Lonesome Dove* (1985).[64]

Equally passionate in his love for the West and periodic despair over its future, is the best of them all, Wallace Stegner. Iowa born and raised partly on a hardscrabble farm in Montana, Stegner, like DeVoto, was educated in Utah and at Harvard. Stegner then taught at the University of Wisconsin before moving to Stanford University, where his creative writing program trained scores of future novelists and his own novels entranced millions of American readers. Whether it was in his historical works, such as his *Beyond the Hundredth Meridian: John Wesley Powell and the Second Opening of the West* (1954), or in his Pulitzer Prize–winning novel, *Angle of Repose* (1971), Stegner managed to puncture myths and record tragedy while at the same time seeing beauty and meaning even in a corrupted, environmentally threatened West. His eloquence and his probing ideas not only make the message of the western landscape seem profound but universal in its application to the problems of the nation and the world. In his way, Stegner is a literary Frederick Jackson Turner whose ideas and influences will stretch into the next century.[65]

By now it should seem obvious that Edward Abbey, Larry McMurtry, Wallace Stegner, and many others, each in his or her own different way, carry on the tradition of the earlier literary Turnerians. The ongoing popularity of McMurtry and Stegner suggests that both Old and New Wests continue to have a very special place in the American psyche.

This essay was written to honor Martin Ridge's long and distinguished career as a historian of the American West, and as an editor, but also to recognize his contributions as an admirer and yet critical interpreter of Frederick Jackson Turner and Ray Allen Billington. It ends with a plea that as we honor both him and our common predecessor, Frederick Jackson Turner, we also remember all the other historians and creative writers of great talent who took Turner's ideas and made them an ever more intrinsic part of a distinctive American culture. To praise or to blame Turner alone for what was good or bad, or right or wrong in the ideas he voiced is to miss the point. The fact is that he sparked the imagination of thousands of writers, who in turn gave millions a sense of understanding about America's past.

In the end, the poetic visionaries of the frontier may outwit us all, for as Archibald MacLeish wrote:

> Poets, deserted by the world before,
> Turn round into the actual air:
> Invent the age! Invent the metaphor![66]

NOTES

1. Frederick Jackson Turner, "The Significance of the Frontier in American History," American Historical Association, *Annual Report*, 1893 (Washington, 1894).

A historiography of the older criticisms of Turner may be found in Ray Allen Billington, *Westward Expansion: A History of the American Frontier* (New York: Macmillan Publishing Company, 1974), 667–71; a discussion of the hypothesis itself is in Billington, *America's Frontier Heritage* (New York: Holt, Rinehart, 1966; rev. ed., University of New Mexico Press, 1993). Recent criticisms of the frontier hypothesis are epitomized in Patricia Nelson Limerick, *The Legacy of Conquest: The Unbroken Past of The American West* (New York: W. W. Norton, 1987), and in Patricia Nelson Limerick, Clyde A Milner, II, and Charles E. Rankin, eds., *Trails: Toward A New Western History* (Lawrence: University Press of Kansas, 1991).

2. The "freezing" and perpetuation of the image is brilliantly treated by Brian W. Dippie in "The Moving Finger Writes: Western Art and the Dynamics of Change," in *Discovered*

Lands, Invented Pasts: Transforming Visions of the American West (New Haven: Yale University Press, 1992), 89–116.

3. James K. Folson, "Bernard DeVoto," *The Reader's Encyclopedia of the American West* (New York: Harper Collins, 1985), 301. Hereafter cited as *REAW*.

4. "Bernard DeVoto," in *The Reader's Encyclopedia of American Literature* (New York: Thomas Y. Crowell, 1962), 254–55.

5. Folsom, "DeVoto," *REAW*, 301.

6. Ibid., 301.

7. Wallace Stegner, *The Letters of Bernard DeVoto* (Garden City, NY: Doubleday and Company, Inc., 1975), 263. DeVoto's circle of friends reached far beyond Cambridge and included scores of western historians and novelists, among them A. B. Guthrie and Joseph Kinsey Howard.

8. Ibid., 265.

9. Wallace Stegner, *The Uneasy Chair: A Biography of Bernard DeVoto* (Garden City, NY: Doubleday and Company, Inc. 1973), ix.

10. DeVoto to Melville Smith, 22 October 1920, in *Letters*, vii.

11. To Catherine Drinker Bowen, "Dear Kitty" [n.d.], *Letters*, 285–86.

12. To Garrett Mattingly, 11 September 1949, *Letters*, 309–10.

13. To Garrett Mattingly, 28 October 1950, *Letters*, 314.

14. To Frederick Merk, 30 July 1951, *Letters*, 316–18.

15. Stegner comments, *Letters*, 57.

16. Folsom, "DeVoto," *REAW*, 301.

17. Constance Rourke, *American Humor: A Study of the National Character* (Garden City, NY: Harcourt, Brace and Company, 1931). For my reference I have used the later, 1953 edition (Garden City, NY: Doubleday and Company, 1953).

18. Ibid., 2.

19. Ibid., 16–17.

20. Ibid., 15–36.

21. Ibid., 37–69.

22. Ibid., 70–90.

23. Ibid., 86.

24. Ibid., 91–114.

25. Ibid., 98.

26. Ibid., 104–7.

27. Ibid., 108.

28. Ibid., 140.

29. Constance Rourke, *The Roots of American Culture, and Other Essays,* edited and with a Preface by Van Wyck Brooks (New York: Harcourt Brace and Company, 1942), ix.

30. Signi Lenea Falk, *Archibald MacLeish* (New York: Twayne Publishers, 1965), 6.

31. Ibid., 63.

32. "American Letter," in Archibald MacLeish, *New Found Land, Fourteen Poems* (Boston: Houghton Mifflin Company, 1930). The volume has no pagination.

33. "American Letter," fourth stanza.

34. Falk, *MacLeish*, 57–63, 69.

35. Ibid., 52.

36. Ibid., 65.

37. Ibid., 65.

38. Ibid., 96.

39. Bernard DeVoto, "The West: A Plundered Province," *Harper's Monthly Magazine* (June–November, 1934), 355–64. See also other devastating "Easy Chair" articles on the West.

40. Besides his poems, MacLeish's ideas about the West are expressed in various essays in his *A Time To Speak* (Boston: Houghton Mifflin Company, 1940), and *A Contemporary Journey* (Boston: Houghton Mifflin Company, 1968). See especially his essay, "Green River," in *A Time to Speak*, 176–84. Curiously, a more recent biography, Scott Donaldson, *Archibald MacLeish: An American Life* (Boston: Houghton Mifflin, 1992), completely ignores the frontier themes.

41. Parry Stroud, *Stephen Vincent Benét* (New York: Twayne Publishers, 1962), 17–18.

42. Ibid., 47.

43. Ibid., 19.

44. Ibid., 47.

45. Ibid., 144.

46. Ibid., 144, and Charles A. Fenton, *Stephen Vincent Benét: The Life and Letters of an American Man of Letters, 1898–1943* (New Haven, CT: Yale University Press, 1958), 344. Fenton also edited the *Selected Letters of Stephen Vincent Benét* (New Haven, CT: Yale University Press, 1960).

47. Stephen Vincent Benét, *Western Star* (New York: Farrar & Rinehart, 1943), 180–81.

48. Ibid., 144–45.

49. To Paul Engle, 16 September 1937, Fenton, *Selected Letters of Benét*, 302.

50. Bernhard Knollenburg, 24 December 1940, Ibid., 359.

51. To Carl Brandt, 11 August 1938, Ibid., 313.

52. Benét, *Western Star*, 10.

53. Stroud, *Benét*, 146.

54. Stephen Vincent Benét, *America* (New York: Farrar & Rinehart, Inc., 1944), 25. A typical passage on the frontier read as follows: "To the people of the frontier, colonial governors and assemblies were far away, and the rule of England still farther. Engaged in a life and death struggle with the wilderness, they had to govern themselves, for nobody else would do it for them. The King of England could not make your clearing. The Governor of Virginia could not plant your corn. You had to do these things yourself."

55. Benét, *Western Star*, 4.

56. See especially, Ralph Henry Gabriel, *The Course of American Democratic Thought* (New York: Greenwood Press, 1985), and Merle Curti, *The Growth of American Thought* (New York: Harper & Brothers, 1943). The Curti volume is dedicated to the memory of Frederick Jackson Turner.

57. Henry Nash Smith, *Virgin Land: The American West As Symbol and Myth* (Cambridge, MA.: Harvard University Press, 1950).

58. Billington, *Westward Expansion.*

59. Originally published by Holt, Rinehart and Winston, the Histories of the American Frontier Series is now published by the University of New Mexico Press.

60. Ray Allen Billington, *Land of Savagery/Land of Promise: The European Image of the American Frontier* (New York: W. W. Norton Company, 1981).

61. Besides his *Ignatius Donnelly: The Portrait of a Politician* (Chicago: University of Chicago Press, 1962), see his *Frederick Jackson Turner: Wisconsin's Historian of the Frontier* (Madison: State Historical Society of Wisconsin, 1986), as well as his introduction to *History, Frontier and Section: Three Essays by Frederick Jackson Turner* (Albuquerque: University of New Mexico Press, 1993).

Other prominent historians also continue to explore Turner and his contributions, among them Wilbur R. Jacobs. See especially his edited volume, *Frederick Jackson Turner's Legacy: Unpublished Writings in American History* (San Marino, CA: Huntington Library, 1965), and his *the Historical World of Frederick Jackson Turner*, with selections from his correspondence (New Haven: Yale University Press, 1968).

62. See Aldo Leopold, *A Sand County Almanac* (New York: Oxford University Press, 1949); Roderick Nash,, *Wilderness and the American Mind* (New Haven: Yale University Press, 1967; rev. ed., 1973); Stephen J. Pyne, *Fire In America: A Cultural History of Wildland and Rural Fire* (Princeton: Princeton University Press, 1982); William J. Cronon, *Changes in the Land: Indians, Colonists, and the Ecology of New England* (New York: Hill and Wang, 1983); William Robbins, *American Forestry: A History of National, State and Private Cooperation* (Lincoln: University of Nebraska Press, 1985); Donald Pisani, *To Reclaim a Divided West: Water, Law and Public Policy, 1848–1902* (Albuquerque: University of New Mexico Press, 1992).

Edward Abbey's *Desert Solitaire* (New York: MacGraw-Hill, 1968) should be read in connection with his other nature essays, two novels: *The Brave Cowboy: An Old Tale in a New Time* (New York: Dodd, Mead, 1956), and *The Monkey Wrench Gang* (Philadelphia: Lippencott, 1975), and his *Slumgullien Stew: An Edward Abbey Reader* (New York: E. P. Dalton, 1984).

Donald Worster's classic *Dust Bowl: The Southern Plains in the 1930s* (New York: Oxford University Press, 1979) and his *Rivers of Empire: Water, Aridity, and the Growth of the American West* (New York: Pantheon, 1985) should be supplemented by his *Under Western Skies: Nature and History in the American West* (New York: Oxford University Press, 1992).

Richard White, although a confirmed non-Turnerian, has nevertheless produced three brilliant books that deal with "frontiers" of a sort: *The Roots of Dependency: Subsistence, Environment and Social Change Among the Choctaws, Pawnees, and Navajos* (Lincoln: University of Nebraska Press, 1983) traces the devastating impact of whites and federal policy on Indian Americans; *The Middle Ground: Indians, Empires, and Republics in the Great Lakes Region, 1650–1815* (New York: Cambridge University Press, 1991) recounts the stage of relatively successful interaction between whites and Indian Americans in the Great Lakes area; "*It's Your Misfortune and None of My Own*": *A New History of the American West* (Norman: University of Oklahoma Press, 1991) is a superb, environmentally oriented narrative of the trans-Missouri West in which the power of federal policy is again analyzed.

Wallace Stegner's writings on the environment are to be found in scores of articles in dozens of journals and magazines, but also in his *Beyond the Hundredth Meridian: John Wesley Powell and the Second Opening of the West* (Boston: Houghton Mifflin, 1954), his *Wolf Willow: A History, a Story, and a Memory of the Last Plains Frontier* (New York: Viking, 1962), and his *Where the Bluebird Sings to the Lemonade Springs: Living and Writing in the West* (New York: Random House, 1992). But see also his *The American West as Living Space* (Ann Arbor: University of Michigan Press, 1987), and his introduction to *Wilderness at the Edge: A Citizen's Proposal to Protect Utah's Canyons and Deserts* (Salt Lake City: Utah Wilderness Coalition, 1990).

63. J. Golden Taylor and Thomas J. Lyon, eds., *Western Literature Association, A Literary History of the American West* (Fort Worth: Texas Christian University Press, 1987), is a remarkable compilation of the literary figures who have written about the frontier and the West.

64. Of these, *Horseman Pass By* (New York: Harper & Brothers, 1961), *The Last Picture Show* (New York: Dial Press, 1966); *Leaving Cheyenne* (New York: Harper & Row, 1963), and *Lonesome Dove* (New York: Simon and Schuster, 1985) are representative.

65. Stegner's recent death in an auto accident has triggered many evaluations of his fiction, historical works, and essays on the West. Discerning essays on his many accomplishments are printed in a special issue of *Montana: The Magazine of Western History*, 43 (Autumn 1993), 52–77, which was expanded in Charles E. Rankin, ed., *Wallace Stegner: Man and Writer* (Albuquerque: University of New Mexico Press, 1996).

66. Falk, *MacLeish*, 170.

CONTRIBUTORS

ALBERT L. HURTADO received his Ph.D. at the University of California, Santa Barbara and is currently the Director of Graduate Studies and Associate Professor of history at Arizona State University, Tempe. His publications include *Indian Survival on the California Frontier* (1988) and *Major Problems in American Indian History* (1994) as well as numerous articles. He is a past winner of the Ray Allen Billington Prize from the Organization of American Historians, the Bolton Prize from the Western History Association, the Paladin Award from the Montana Historical Society, and the Arizona State University Outstanding Mentor Award for his work with graduate students.

PAUL ANDREW HUTTON received his Ph.D. from Indiana University in 1981 and is Professor of History at the University of New Mexico and Executive Director of the Western History Association. He is the author of *Phil Sheridan and His Army* (1985), and the editor of *Ten Days on the Plains* (1985), *Soldiers West* (1987), and *The Custer Reader* (1992) as well as numerous essays. His work has won the OAH Billington Prize, the Western Writers Spur Award, the Evans Biography Award, the Paladin Award, and the Western Heritage Award from the National Cowboy Hall of Fame.

HOWARD R. LAMAR received his doctorate from Yale University in 1951. He has taught at Yale since 1949, serving as the W.R. Coe Professor of American History and the Sterling Professor of History. His many books include *Dakota Territory, 1861–1889* (1956) and *The Far Southwest, 1846–1912* (1966), while among his editing credits is the popular *Reader's Encyclopedia of the American West* (1977) which has been recently revised for Yale University Press and is entering its second edition. Lamar's teaching has guided generations of students, who have in turn made a significant impact upon the field of Western history. He served as President of the Western History Association in 1971–1972.

RICHARD LOWITT received his Ph.D. from Columbia in 1950 and has taught history at the University of Maryland, University of Rhode Island, Connecticut College, Florida State

University, University of Kentucky, and Iowa State University, before taking his current position as professor at the University of Oklahoma. He is perhaps best known for his three-volume biography of George Norris, (1963, 1971, 1978). He also authored *The New Deal and the West* (1984), and *Bronson M. Cutting: Progressive Politician* (1992), as well as many edited works and scholarly articles.

JAMES H. MADISON is Professor of History and chair of the Department of History, Indiana University, Bloomington. From 1976 to 1993 he served as editor of the *Indiana Magazine of History*. Among his publications are *The Indiana Way: A State History* (1986) and *Eli Lilly: A Life, 1885–1997* (1989). He has edited and contributed to two books, *Wendell Willkie: Hoosier Internationalist* (1992) and *Heartland: Comparative Histories of the Midwestern States*(1988). In 1994 Indiana University awarded him its Sylvia E. Bowmen Distinguished Teaching Award.

WALTER NUGENT earned his Ph.D. at the University of Chicago, and has taught history at Kansas State University (1961–1963), Indiana University (1963–1984), and at the University of Notre Dame as the Andrew V. Tackes Professor of History since 1984. He has held fellowships from the Newberry Library, the Guggenheim Foundation, and the National Endowment for the Humanities. His publications include several score essays, articles, and reviews, and eight books, among which are *The Tolerant Populists: Kansas Populism and Nativism* (1963), *Money and American Society 1865–1880* (1968), *From Centennial to World War 1876–1917* (1977), *Structures of American Social History* (1981), and *Crossings: The Great Transatlantic Migrations 1870–1914* (1992).

DONALD J. PISANI received his Ph.D. from the University of California, Davis. He is the Merrick Professor of History at the University of Oklahoma, and a specialist in the law and natural resources of the American West. His most recent book is *Water, Land, and Law in the West: The Limits of Public Policy, 1850–1920* (1996). Among his previous publications is *To Reclaim a Divided West: Water, Law, and Public Policy, 1848–1902*, which was published by the University of New Mexico Press in 1992.

CHARLES E. RANKIN received his Ph.D. from the University of New Mexico, and is Director of Publications for the Montana Historical Society, editor of *Montana: The Magazine of Western History*, and editor-in-chief of the Montana Historical Society Press. His most recent publications include two edited volumes, *Wallace Stegner: Man and Writer* (1996), and *Legacy: New Perspectives on the Battle of the Little Bighorn* (1996). He was co-editor of *Trails: Toward a New Western History* (1991) and is author of a variety of articles and essays related to the Civil War, journalism in the West, and western history.

GLENDA RILEY is the Alexander M. Bracken Professor of History at Ball State University. Since receiving her Ph.D. from the Ohio State University in 1967, she has held research fellowhips at the Newberry, Huntington, and Harry S Truman Libraries, and a Distinguished Fulbright at University College, Dublin, Ireland. Her books include

Frontier Women: The Iowa Experience (1981), *Women and Indians on the Frontier* (1984), *Inventing the American Woman* (1986), *The Female Frontier* (1988), *Divorce: An American Tradition* (1991), *A Place to Grow: Women in the American West* (1992), *The Life and Legacy of Annie Oakley* (1994), and *Building and Breaking Families in the American West* (1996). She served as President of the Western History Association in 1996–1997.

ROBERT C. RITCHIE received his Ph.D. from the University of California, Los Angeles. His specialty is early American history, but he also has a strong interest in Tudor-Stuart England. In 1969 he joined the History Department at the University of California, San Diego, where he went through the ranks to full Professor. He left UCSD in 1992 to become the W.M. Keck Foundation Director of Research at the Huntington. He has received a number of awards and fellowships from the Regents of the University of California, the Huntington, the National Endowment for the Humanities, the Danforth Foundation, and the American Council of Learned Societies. He was recently elected to membership in the Royal Historical Society and the American Antiquarian Society. Among his major publications are *The Duke's Province: A Study of Politics and Society in New York, 1664–1691* (1977), which was awarded the Manuscript Prize of the New York State Historical Association and *Captain Kidd and the War Against the Pirates* (1986).

JAMES P. RONDA is the H.G. Barnard Professor of Western American History at the University of Tulsa. He received a Ph.D. from the University of Nebraska, Lincoln, in 1969. He is the author of several books, including *Lewis and Clark Among the Indians* (1984) and *Astoria and Empire* (1990). He has written more than twenty articles for professional journals, and eight of his essays have been published as *Westering Captains: Essays on the Lewis and Clark Expedition* (1990).

MELODY WEBB received her Ph.D. from the University of New Mexico, where her dissertation, "Yukon Frontiers: The Westward Movement to the North Country," won the university's Popejoy Award before being revised and published as *The Last Frontier: A History of the Yukon Basin of Canada and Alaska* (1985). Her career with the National Park Service has included positions as Historian for the Southwest Region, Assistant Superintendent of Grand Teton National Park, and Superintendent of the Lyndon B. Johnson National Historical Park. She retired from the NPS in 1996.

RICHARD WHITE earned his Ph.D. from the University of Washington and is now the McClelland Professor of History at that university. Among his many publications are *The Roots of Dependency* (1983), *The Middle Ground* (1991), *"It's Your Misfortune and None of My Own": A History of the American West* (1991), and *The Organic Machine: The Remaking of the Columbia River* (1995). His many honors include the Alfred Beveridge and Western Heritage awards, as well as the Francis Parkman Prize. He has held a Guggenheim Fellowship, a Rockefeller Humanities Fellowship, a Fellowship from the McNickle Center for the History of the American Indian at the Newberry Library, and was the 1995 winner of a MacArthur Foundation grant. He was President of the Western History Association in 1995–1996.

INDEX

N.B.: Numbers in boldface indicate illustrations.

Abbey, Edward, 245
African Americans: Crockett almanacs, 160; steamer attendants, 17; western experience, 21–22
Agricultural Extension Service, 92. *See also* U.S. Department of Agriculture
Alamo, 144, 158, 208
A Literary History of the American West (1987), 245
Allen, Prairie Lillie, 189
America (1944), 243
American Humor: A Study of the National Character (1931), 236–38, 243
American Philosophical Society, 35
American Studies programs, 244
"Annie Get Your Gun" mentality, 189, 190. *See also* Oakley, Annie
Antiquities Act (1906), 128, 130
Apostle Islands park area, 127
Arizona, 17, 19
Asian Americans, 22
Aspinall, Wayne, 127–28, 129–30
Assateague Island National Seashore, 126
Assimilationist policy, 69
Atlases, 207, 208

Automobile: cross-country trips, 10–20; highway system, 96; industry, 49

Badger, Joseph, 170
Baker, Johnny, 176
Ballinger, Richard A., 110
Bancroft Library, 217
Barrel racing, 192
Battle of the Little Big Horn, 208, 209
Benét, Stephen Vincent, 241–44
Berry, Daniel M., 5, 7
Bigotry, 68, 160
Billington, Ray Allen, **232**: at Huntington Library, vii; final book, 24; Ridge works with, x; scholarly research, 244; Turner biography, 23
Bingham, George Caleb, 206, 207
Bison Moving Picture Company, 189
Black, Hugo, 118
Black, Irene Patterson, 176
Blancett, Bertha, 188 89
Bolton, Herbert Eugene, xv, **214**, 215–28; background, 216; frontier thesis, 233
Bonfils, F. G., 58
Borah, William, 114–15
Brandegee, Frank, 113–14, 117–18
Brooks, Van Wyck, 235–36, 238

Brougham, John, 237
Brown, George, 170
Buchanan, James, 163
Buffalo Bill Cody, xiv–xv, **203**; background, 170; bilked, 58; booklet selling, 184; Captain Jack, 210; at Columbian Exposition, 201–11; Congress of Rough Riders, 187; cowgirls, 169; Native Americans, 170, 208; white victimization, 208; women in show, 170, 171, 172, 188
Buffalo Bill/Pawnee Bill Film Company, 187–88
Buffalo Bill's Real Wild West, 187, 208, 209–10
Buffalo Bill's Wild West and Congress of Rough Riders of the World, 201
Bureaucracy: 19th century, 84, 86; features, 86–87; New Deal, 97–99; postwar opposition to, 93; rise and fall, 101. *See also* U.S. Forest Service
Burke, "Arizona" John, 172
Butler, Frank: as manager-agent, 171, 174, 179–80, 181, 183; gun collection, 175; marriage, 170; Sitting Bull, 183–84

Caldeira, William, 216, 221, 226
California: Angel Island, 22; Arroyo Seco, 5; Bolton's history, 215, 225, 227; elites, 215, 225; Hetch Hetchy bill support, 113; Hetch Hetchy Valley, 109–19; highway construction, 95; irrigation districts, 101–2, 111–12; Los Angeles, 8, 9; motor trips, 12, 14, 18, 20; Pasadena, 5–8, 44, 45; railroads promote, 8–10; San Diego, 8; San Francisco, 9, 109–19, 220; southern, 102; tourists from, 15–16; Tuolumne, 223; Tuolumne River, 110, 111; Turlock-Modesto region, 111–12; University of, 215; Yosemite cession, 114
California Historical Society, 216, 217, 218, 220, 221–22
California Railroad Commission, 118
Canada, 35

Canyonlands National Park, 124
Capitalism, 64, 84
Carmichael, William, 33
Cheyenne Autumn, 59
Chickering, Allen L., 218–19, 221, 222, 223–24
Chinese immigrants, 19, 22
Chrisman, Mildred Douglas, 189
Church, Denver S., 112
Civil War, 61
Clark, Clarence, 117
Clark-McNary Act (1924), 92–93, 97
Clark, W. Crawford, 176
Cleland, Robert Glass, vii
Clyman, James, 235
Colorado, 98
Columbia River, 35, 36–37
Columbus, Christopher, 27, 237
Congress of American Cowgirls, 187
Conjectural geography, 30
Conservation, xiii, 87, 121–31
Cooperative movement, 64
Cooper, James Fenimore, 141
Cowboys, 13, 171
Cowgirls, xiv, 171; acceptance, 188; Congress of American Cowgirls, 187; costumes, 186–87; image changes, 186–88, 192; Lillie, May, 172, 174; Meekin, Jane "Little Jean," 174; Lucille Mulhall, 169, 174, 186, 188; Oakley, Annie, 169–92; Oakley's persona, 186; on stage, 184–86; Lulu Bell Parr, 174; Annie Shaffer, 169, 174, 188; Lillian Smith, 171; term coined, 169, 172; Lillian Ward, 172, 174;
Crawford, Captain Jack, 210
Crazy Horse, 240, 243
Crockett almanacs, xiv, 141–64
Crockett, Comfort, 148–49
Crockett, Davy, 141–64, 236; death, 142, 144, 147
Cross-country motoring, 10–20
Currier and Ives, 206
Custer, George, 209–10

Deadwood Dick, or the Sunbeam of the Sierras, 184–85
Decentralization: Forest Service, 88–89; long view, 100; West and, 102
Delaware Water Gap National Recreation Area, 125
"Democratic collectivism," 97
Democratic Party, 117
DeVoto, Bernard, **232**, 233–36, 243, 245; Benét and, 241
Disney, Walt, 143
Dobie, J. Frank, 238
Drake plate forgery, xv, 215–28
Drake, Sir Francis, 222, 225, 226. *See also* Drake plate forgery
Duffy, George, 171
Dust Bowl, 4

Eakin, Joe, 177
E Clampus Vitus, 223, 226
Ecosystem management, 127, 131
Edison, Thomas Alva, 184
Eel River, 113
Eisenhower, Dwight D., 125
Electric power generation, 115, 116
Elites, xiii
Ellms, Charles, 141
Endangered Species Act, 127
Environmental issues, 121–31, 240, 243, 245
Exceptionalism, American: frontier experience, xi, 244; Turner and, xvi, 231

Family farm, 46, 48
Federal Highway Act, 11, 95
Federalism: concept, 85; dual, 100
Federal policy: after Civil War, 62; western tribes, 65–69
Federal power, xiii; grant-in-aid programs, 91; local communities, 84; origins, 85–86; postwar, 99; Progressive era, 86; state power versus, 99–100; Utah, 72; water, 83; western history, 83
Ferrel, Dell, 171

Fields, Dorothy, 190
Fields, Herbert, 190
Film. *See* Movies
Finerty, John, 58
Fink, Colin, 223–25
Fink, Mike, 144, 154, 236
Fire Island National Seashore, 123, 124
Fisher, Walter Lowrie, 110
Fitzgerald, F. Scott, 46
Five Civilized Tribes, 65, 66
Flagg, James Montgomery, 14–15
Fletcher, Parson, 222–23, 225
Florez, Manuel Antonio, 32–37
Forest Homestead Act (1906), 90
Forestry issues, 87, 89–90, 92–93; lumber, 93, 126
Forest Service. *See* U.S. Forest Service
Freeman-Custis Red River expedition, 39
Freeman, Leigh, 58
Freeman, Orville, 126–27
French, James S., 141, 143
Frontier: arts, 238; Buffalo Bill's story, 202; closes, 202–4; iconography, 205; narratives, 204; popular culture, 205; sequential, xii, 44, 205; values, 103
Frontier thesis. *See* Turner's frontier thesis
Fulton, Robert, 39
Fur trade, 37, 38

Gallatin, Albert, 37
Garfield, James R., 110
Gates of the Arctic national monument, 128–29
General Land Office, 87–88, 89, 101
Girls Rodeo Association, 192
Godbe, William S., 69
"Good roads" movement, 10
Graham, William, 174, 175
Grants-in-aid programs, 91–92, 94
Graves, Henry Solon, 88
Grazing, 89–90
Great Britain: Drake plate, 227; imperial rivers, 36–37; Oakley, 174, 176, 185

Great Depression, 97, 191
Great Society speech, 124
Gronna, Asle J., 113, 114
Gun as symbol, 180
Gun belt, 49, 50

Hackett, James, 142
Hakluyt, Richard, 29, 222
Harding, Ben, 144–45
Harrison, William Henry, 207
Hartzog, George, 124
Haselden, Reginald Berti, 216–17, 222
Hatfield, Mark, 22
Hayford, J.H., 58
Heavy industry, 46–47, 48–49
Held, Anna, 175
Heroes, 181, 231, 232
Hetch Hetchy Valley, xiii, 109–19; dam,
    118; description, 115–16
Hickel, Walter, 129
Hickok, Emma Lake, 172
Hickok, Wild Bill, 172
Highways, 10–20; construction, 93–96;
    New Deal, 94
Hildebrand, Joel, 223
Hill, Shelton, 21
Historians, ix-vi; exceptionalism, 244; Mid-
    west, 43–44; New West, 231; poets crit-
    icize, 242. See also Billington, Ray Allen;
    Bolton, Herbert Eugene; DeVoto, Ber-
    nard; Nelson, Patricia Limerick; New
    Western History; Parkman, Francis;
    Ridge, Martin; Smith, Henry Nash;
    Turner, Frederick Jackson; White,
    Richard; Worster, Donald
Historic sites, national, 125, 127
Historiography: Midwest, 43–46; New
    Western, ix, x, xi, xiii; state histories, 60;
    western journalism, 59–60
Hitchcock, Ethan Allen, 110
Howe, Ed, 58
Hubble, Edwin Powell, 221
Hudson River, 32

Humor, 141–64, 236–38
Hunting, 146, 176–77, 178
Huntington, Henry E., vii
Huntington Library, vii, xii–xiii, 18,
    244; Drake plate, 217; Turner invited,
    24
Hutton, Betty, 190
Hydro-electric power. See Electric power
    generation

Ickes, Harold, 118
Iconography, 205, 206–10, 211
Idaho, 21
Illinois, 160–61
Immigrants, 160
Indiana, 161
Indiana Colony, 5–8, 44, 45
Indiana Dunes, 123
Indian Territory, 65–69
Interstate compact, 102
Interstate highways, 10
Iowa, 15, 44
Irish Americans, 160
Irrigation districts, 111–12
"It's Your Misfortune and None of My Own":
    A History of the American West (1991), 83–
    84

Jackson, Andrew, 159
Japanese immigrants, 22–23
Jefferson, Thomas: Maury as tutor, 30–31;
    Michaux expedition, 35–36; Mississippi
    Question, 33–34; president, 36; Rivanna
    River, 27, 31; rivers, xii
Jews, 15
Jingoism, xiv, 155, 158–59
John Brown's Body (1928), 241, 243
Johnson, Lady Bird, 121, 125
Johnson, Lyndon Baines, xiii, 121–31, **122**
Johnson, Mrs. S. S., 179
Johnston, Mrs. S. S., 175
Journalists, western, 60, 75–76
Journal of American History, x, 43

Kansas: Arkansas City, 73; highways, 96; Lockley, 61, 64–65, 69, 73; slavery issue, 163
Keel, Howard, 190
Keim, De B. Randolph, 58
Kennedy, John F., 123
Kentucky, 33
Kent, William, 116, 118
Kern, John W., 117
Kiowa Indians, 66–69

Lacapede, Bernard, 38
Lake, Agnes, 172
Land and Water Conservation Bill, 123, 124
Land and Water Conservation Fund, 128, 131
Land of Savagery/Land of Promise: The European Image of the Frontier (1981), 24, 244
Lane, Harry, 117
Laperouse expedition, 35
Ledyard, John, 35
Lewis and Clark expedition, 37, 39
Lillie, May, 172, 174
Lincoln, Abraham, 207, 208
Lincoln Highway, 10, 12, 13, 14, 20
Lindsley, Mrs. M. F. "Wanda," 175
Lippitt, Henry, 118
Localism, 161
Lockley, Frederic E., **56**, 60–76; background, 60–61; career significance, 62–63; family, 61, 62, 63, 64–65, 69–70, 74; influence, xii
Log cabin icon, 207–8
Los Angeles, 7–8; Japanese relocation, 22–23
Lost generation, 238
Louisiana Purchase, 38

McCloud River, 113
McCormick, Langdon, 185
McCumber, Porter, 117
McDonald, Thomas, 95

Mackenzie, Alexander, 36–37
McLean, George P., 118
MacLeish, Archibald, 238–41, 243, 246
McMurtry, Larry, 245
Madison, James, 31–32
Manifest Destiny, 155
Mantle, Lee, 73
Maps, 206 7
Marble Canyon national monument, 129, 130
Mattingly, Garrett, 234, 235
Maury, James, 30–31
Meekin, Jane "Little Jean," 174
Merman, Ethel, 190
Mexico: California history, 225; Crockett almanacs, 155, 158–59; MacLeish poems, 238–39, 240; Mexico–U.S. War, 155, 158–59
Michaux, Andre, 35–36
Michigan, 160
Midwest, xii, 43–51; central elements, 46–47; creation, 46; highways, 95; history of west, 4; recent changes, 48–49, 50
Military icons, 208
Military industries, 49
Miller, Joaquin, 207, 208
Mississippi Question, 33–34
Mississippi River, 32–34
Missouri, 161
Missouri River, 34–36, 37, 38
Miss Rora, 185
Mokelumne River, 113
Montana, 13–14, 19, 21, 73, 98
Mormonism, 69–72
Movies, 59; *Annie Get Your Gun,* 190; *Annie Oakley,* 184, 189–90, 191–93; *Cheyenne Autumn,* 59; *The Grey Fox,* 59; *The Man Who Shot Liberty Valance,* 59; *Unforgiven,* 59
Mug histories, 60
Muir, John, 109, 111
Mulhall, Lucille, 169, 174, 186, 188, 192
Mythical West, xiii–xvi

Myth, western: Annie Oakley, 183–86; Crockett almanacs, 141–64; frontier heroes, 231, 232; traditional approaches, ix

National forests, 89, 90
National Highway Association, 93
National Historic Preservation Act, 127
Nationalism, 68, 155, 158–59, 161, 163
National monuments, 128–29
National Old Trails Road, 10
National park system, 121–31
National trails system, 128
National Wilderness Preservation System, 124
Native Americans: Bolton on, 226; Buffalo Bill, 202; in Crockett almanacs, 160; disappearance, 4; Drake plate, 224; empty continent idea, 206–7; federal policy, 65–69; frontier narratives, 204; Indian Territory, 65–69; Kiowa Indians, 66–69; log cabins, 207; MacLeish poems, 240, 243; Strollers portray, 237; Turner's frontier, 202; "West" concept for, 22; white women, 171; women, 170
Native Sons of the Golden West, 225
Natural resources, 84; forests, 87–91; management concept, 127; Progressive era, 86
Nature: Jefferson on, 33–34; nature lovers, 115
Navigability, 39
Nebraska, 98
Negro minstrelsy, 236–27
Nelson, Henry Loomis, 48
Nelson, Patricia Limerick, 237
New Conservation program, 125, 128
New Deal: agencies, 97; characterized, 97; Hetch Hetchy Dam, 118; highways, 94; western support, 98
New Federalism, 49
New Mexico, 12, 15, 17, 19, 98
Newspapers, local, 59
New Western history: federal power, xiii; frontier thesis, 231; Ridge defense of

Turner thesis, x, xi; traditional approaches and, ix
Nickelodeons, 184
Nixon, Harold, 17
Nixon, Richard M., 17, 49
Norris, George, 102, 114; Hetch Hetchy debate, 115–17
North America represented, 206–7
North Cascades National Park, 126–27, 128
North Dakota, 13, 98
Notes on the State of Virginia (1780), 34, 36
Novelists, 233–36, 244
Nye, Bill (Edgar Wilson), 57, 58

Oakley, Annie, xiv, 169–92, 173; background, 170; costumes, 182; death, 189; as entertainer, 179; gun collection, 175, 176, 180; heroism, 181; horses, 180–81; images, 169–70, 192; later years, 189; marriage, 170; movies and stage, 184–86; performance text, 180; as role model, 174–75, 177, 179; as shooter, 174–79
Ohio, Cleveland, 63–64
Oranges, 5, 6
Oregon, 98
Oregon River, 36
O'Shaughnessy, M. M., 118
Ozark Scenic Riverways, 123, 124

Pacific Gas and Electric Company, xiii, 116–17, 118, 119
Pacific passage, 29, 35
Panic of 1873, 5
Parkman, Francis, 235
Parr, Lulu Bell, 174
Pasadena (California), 5–8, 9, 44, 45; Drake plate, 221; Emily Post, 12–13
Paulding, James Kirke, 141, 143
Pawnee Bill, 174, 187, 204
Performance text, 180
Perkins, George C., 112–13
Phoenix, John (George Horatio Derby), 57
Pierson, De Vier, 129–30

Pinchot, Gifford, 87, 88, 89

Pioneer: character differs, 202; motif, 49, 50, 240, 242

Pittman, Key, 110

Platte River, 39

Pocahontas, 237

Poets, 238–44

Poindexter, Miles, 113, 117

Politics, frontier and, xii

Polygamy, 70

Popular culture, xiv–xv; Crockett almanacs, 141–64; frontier, 205; Rourke studies, 236–38

Post, Emily, 12–13

Potomac River, 31–32

Potomac Valley Park, 127

Powell, John Wesley, 101

Preservationist movement, 111, 113, 118–19; National Wilderness Preservation System, 124

Progressive era: bureaucracy, 86; forest service, 87–88

Progressive movement, 118–19

Progress, notion of: Buffalo Bill, 211; Lockley, 61, 66, 69; log cabin, 207; Turner, 206

Protestantism, 225–26

Public Lands Commission, 89

Quakers (Society of Friends), 65–68

Racism, 158, 160

Railroads: California promoted, 8–10; MacLeish poetry, 240; workers, 19, 21

Raker Act, 115, 118

"Rancheras," 172

Randolph, Florence Hughes, 189, 192

Rayburn, Sam, 93

Reagan, Ronald, 49

Real estate booms, 8

Reclamation Bureau, 90, 101

Redwood National Park, 124, 126, 127–28

Reed, James A., 109

Region: common questions, 50–51; journalism history, 60; Midwest versus West, 43–51; regional authorities, 102

Regional authorities, 102

Religion, Crockett almanacs, 148. *See also* Protestantism

Relocation, 22–23

Remington, Frederick, 233

Republican Party, 117–18

Reuther, Walter, 126

Reynolds, Florence, 192

Richardson, Albert, 204

Ridge, Martin, **ii,** vii–viii, **232;** background, x–xi; honored, ix–x, 244–45, 246

Rivers, xii, 27–40; Columbia River, 35, 36–37; Eel River, 113; Freeman-Custis Red River expedition, 39; Hudson River, 32; McCloud River, 113; Mississippi River, 32–34; Missouri River, 34–36, 37, 38; Mokelumne River, 113; Oregon River, 36; Ozark Riverways, 123; Platte River, 39; Potomac River, 31–32; Rivanna River, 27, 31; Tuolumne River, 110, 111; Wild and Scenic Rivers System, 128

Rivers of Empire: Water, Aridity & the Growth of the American West (1985), 83

Rockefeller, Laurance, 126, 127

Rodeos: barrel racing, 192; bronc riding, 191–92; relay races, 191; trick riding, 171, 172, 191; women's participation, 169, 191

Rogers, Will, 189

Roosevelt, Franklin, 130

Roosevelt, Theodore: conservation, 130; cowgirls, 169; Turner thesis, 204

Rough Riders, 187, 201

Rourke, Constance, 236–38, 243

Russell, Charlie, 233

Rust belt, 48–49

Rutherford, Otto, 21–22

Salsbury, Nate, 171, 188

San Francisco: earthquake, 111; Hetch Hetchy Valley, 109–19

San Gabriel Orchard Grove Association, 5

Santa Anna, Antonio López de, 158–59

Scott, Martin, 147

Scripps, Edward Willis, 64

Seavers, Vernon, 188

Sequoia National Park, 90

Settlement: Euro-American, 84; Great Plains, 4

Shaffer, Annie, 169, 174, 188

Sheppard, Morris, 117

Sherburne, J.H., 73

Shinn, Beryl, **214**, 216, 217–20, 221

Sierra Blue Lakes and Water Power Company, 116

Sierra Club, 109

Sitting Bull (Chief), 183–84, 209

Skocpol, Theda, 85

Slavery issue, 163

Sleeping Bear Dunes, 123

Smith, Henry Nash, 244

Smith, John, 29, 237

Smith-Lever Act (1914), 92

Smith, Lillian, 171

Smith, Marcus, 114

Smith, Richard Penn, 141

Sonoran Desert national monument, 129

Spain, 32–33, 35, 39

Spanish American War, 178

Special districts, 101–2

Sports: Annie Oakley, 175–79; costumes, 178; shooting, 175–79; women, 170

Spring Water Company, 111

Sproul, Robert Gordon, 220, 221–22, 223

Stanley, Henry Morton, 58

Stanwyck, Barbara, 189–90

State power, 99

States' rights issues, 93, 98

Stegner, Wallace, 234, 235, 245–46

Stereotypes, 62

Strollers, 237

Stroud, Parry, 241–43

Swartwout, Annie Fern, 172

Tall tale traditions, 145

Tammen, Harry H., 58

Taxation: Depression revenues, 97; grant-in-aid programs, 91; highway construction, 95; income tax, 91; revolution, 100

Tennessee, 33

Tennessee Valley Authority (TVA), 102

Texas, 158–59

Theater, 184–86; *Annie Get Your Gun,* 190

The Man Who Shot Liberty Valance, 59

Theodore Roosevelt Dam, 20

The Uneasy Chair (1973), 234

Thomas, Charles S., 112–13

Thompson, David, 36

Thompson, Minnie, 174

Thorpe, Thomas B., 147

Tiger Bill's Wild West, 187

Tompkins Real Wild West and Frontier Exhibition, 187

Travel accounts: colonial, 30; cross-country motoring, 10–20

Trick riders, 171, 172, 191

Trucking, 96

Turner and Fisher almanacs, 155, 158

Turner, Frederick Jackson, **203, 232**: at Columbian Exposition, xiv–xv, 201–11; California years, 23, 24; Constance Rourke influenced, 238; DeVoto influenced, 235; fiction celebrating, 233–46; legacy, xv–xvi; Midwest, 46; retirement, 23–24; Ridge research, viii; white victimization, 209; women, 171

Turner frontier thesis, 202, 205–8, 231; academic acceptance, 233; Benét and, 242; literary expressions, 231–46; MacLeish influenced, 240–41; Midwest, 44; poetry influenced, 240; post-Turnerians, 231–46; Ridge defends, x, xi

Twain, Mark (Samuel L. Clemens): books about, 235–36; DeVoto influenced, 245; *Dutch Nick Massacre,* 58; humorist, 57; provincial reporting, 58–59; Smith as editor, 244; western influence, 237

Udall, Stewart, **122**: as Johnson aide, 124; doubt expressed, 123; kudos for, 121; North Cascades National Park, 126–27; presidential proclamations, 128–30

University of California, 215, 216, 217, 221–22

U.S. Army, 84

U.S. Department of Agriculture (USDA), 90; Bureau of Public Roads, 94, 95; forest service, 89; grant-in-aid programs, 91, 92; highway construction, 93–95

U.S. Forest Service, 87–91

U.S. Geological Survey, 101

U.S. Highway 66, 10, 11

Utah, 69–72

Van Swearingen, Joseph, 147

Van de Water, Frederic, 15–16

Vaudeville, 185

Victorianism, 182–83

Vietnam War, 125, 126

Villany, 182

Virginia, water system, 31–32

Voting Rights Act, 125

Wagner, Henry Raup, 217, 221, 222

War with Mexico, 155, 158–59

Ward, Artemus (Charles Farrar Browne), 57

Ward, Lillian, 172, 174

Wars: Civil War, 61; with Mexico, 155, 158–59; Spanish American War, 178; Vietnam War, 125, 126; World War II, 22–23

Washington, 72

Washington, George, 32

Water: federal power, 83; Hetch Hetchy Valley, 109–19; Indiana colony, 45; interstate compact, 102; irrigation districts, 101–2, 111–12; waterway systems, 31–32

Watts riots, 125

Weeks Act (1911), 92–93

West: concept, xi, 3–4; Americanization of, 72; highway construction, 95–96; metropolitan, 4; motorists view, 11–20; urban, 4

Western Historical Quarterly, 43

Western History Association, founding, xi

The Western Girl, 186

Western Star (1943), 241–42, 243

Westward Expansion: A History of the American Frontier (1982), xi, 244

Whig Party, 163

Whirlwind, Sally Ann Thunder Ann, 151–55

White Horse (Chief), 68

White, Richard, 83–84, 86

White victimization theme, 209–10

White, William Allen, 58

Wild and Scenic Rivers System, 128

Wilderness Bill, 123, 124

Wilderness concept, 207

Willard, Emma, 206–7

Williams, Edward, 30

Women: Crockett almanacs, 142–43, 148–64; homesteaders, 171; images, 169–70; Native American, 170; Oakley, Annie, xiv, 169–92; rodeo participation, 191; self-defense, 179; shooting costumes, 178; sports, 175–79; trick riders, 172; western roles, 171

Working class, 63, 64

Works, John D., 111–12

World War II, Japanese relocation, 22–23

Worster, Donald, 83

Wyoming, 15, 19

Yankees, 160, 236

Yellow Hand incident, 209–10

Yellowstone National Park: cowboys, 13; crowding, 16; highways, 14

Yosemite National Park, 109, 110, 114

Young Buffalo Show, 188